JOHN A. RYCENGA is Assistant Professor of English at Marquette University. Dr. Rycenga also taught at Wayne State University and Northwestern University, where he received his Ph.D. He is a specialist in 18th and 19th Century English Literature and Linguistics.

JOSEPH SCHWARTZ is Associate Professor of English at Marquette University, where he is Chairman of the Department of English. He received his Ph.D. from the University of Wisconsin. Dr. Schwartz is a member of the National Council of Teachers of English.

PERSPECTIVES
ON
LANGUAGE

An Anthology

Edited by
JOHN A. RYCENGA
JOSEPH SCHWARTZ

Marquette University

THE RONALD PRESS COMPANY · NEW YORK

P
121
.R9

Library of Congress Catalog Card Number: 63-9249

PRINTED IN THE UNITED STATES OF AMERICA

PREFACE

The basic premise of this collection of essays is that language in and of itself is an important subject for study. The second, and equally important, premise is that one can learn about language by reading a variety of essays oriented to the best that modern scholars have thought and said about it.

Because the study of English is often atomized, it is effectively divorced from the broad and scholarly concerns that it is uniquely able to illuminate. In his study of language under the guise of composition, grammar, rhetoric, or poetics, the student is seldom made to think about the nature of language itself. He does not acquire attitudes toward language which could prove fruitful for him in his own approach to communication or expression in any form. The kind of overview provided by this anthology should furnish students with sophistication sufficient to enable them to approach language—in whatever area of study—with maturity and a sense of direction.

The organization of the volume is designed to give form to those areas of language which have been the habitual concern of scholars in the field. In Section I the student is directed to a consideration of the nature of language itself, beginning with a scientific definition and proceeding through what one might call the "magic" of language. Next, the student is asked to view the history of the English language, its origin and development, the influences which shaped it, its present character in America, and finally, its future. The third section deals with grammar and linguistics, formal approaches to language which seek to describe and classify the meaningful utterances of speech and writing. The problem of usage, the subject of Section IV, is next brought to the student's attention, because the notion of usage is essential to the revolution in grammar and to the properly scientific posture in observing the users of the language. And finally the student is asked to consider problems beyond linguistics—language in its relations—by studying some representative essays in which the investigation of language illuminates the things which it expresses.

JOHN A. RYCENGA
JOSEPH SCHWARTZ

Milwaukee, Wisconsin
January, 1963

CONTENTS

SECTION I
LANGUAGE: BY WAY OF DEFINITION

SECTION II
HISTORY: THE MATRIX OF LANGUAGE

SECTION III
GRAMMAR AND LINGUISTICS: THE STRUCTURE AND SYSTEM OF LANGUAGE

v

SECTION IV

USAGE: THE EMPLOYMENT OF LANGUAGE

SECTION V

METALINGUISTICS: LANGUAGE IN ITS RELATIONS

PERSPECTIVES
ON
LANGUAGE

SECTION I

LANGUAGE:
BY WAY OF DEFINITION

"Language arose not by dint of supreme logic controlling
it but in slow progression from 'zero' to the most highly
developed idiom, capable of rendering the minutest shades
of thought."

—N. H. Tur-Sinai

Basic to an understanding of language itself is the kind of knowledge that comes from a definition of it. Thus, this introductory section
on the nature of language calls to your attention four essays which are
fundamentally involved with definitions. In a forthright and economical manner, Edgar Sturtevant defines language in one packed
sentence: "A language is a system of arbitrary vocal symbols by which
members of a social group cooperate and interact." He explains with
clarity each term in this definition. Edward Sapir builds as it were on
Sturtevant's definition, but puts more emphasis on language as speech,
reminding the reader of the arbitrary nature of the systems of symbolism that are termed languages. Joshua Whatmough provides the most
extensive discussion by emphasizing the various ways in which language can be defined, depending upon the posture of the definer. He
also deals with the characteristics which make language what it is:
that it is conventional and that it has a pattern. Finally, he discusses
briefly but clearly the hierarchy of language, mentioning the fact that
various methods are used in the study and understanding of language.
This section concludes with an essay on the "mysticism" of language
by the eminent philologist, Otto Jespersen. One of the earlier great
scientific students of language, Jespersen's strong endorsement of the
magic and mystery of linguistic attitudes should be especially per-
suasive.

After reading these essays and taking a step beyond the physiological
view of Sapir, certain postulates become evident. Each one is fraught
with implications, permutations, and suggestions. Each must be studied and contemplated with respect and attention.

3

Language is human.
Language is a form of symbolism.
Language is systematic.
Language is verbal.
Language is a means of transmitting information.
Language is a form of social behavior.
Language is intellection.
Language is poetry.
Language is magic.

And when all of this has been said about language, there is still a great deal that is unsaid or perhaps that cannot be fully said. In no instance is this more evident than in the moving description in Helen Keller's autobiography when she records how "wordless sensation" became suddenly and dramatically the perception of names and objects in relation to the experience of the world. "The living word awakened in my soul," she wrote. Everything had a name and as a result every object "seemed to quiver with life" when she touched it. "The mystery of language was revealed to me." What that mystery is finally is the *experience* of language itself.

A DEFINITION OF LANGUAGE   *Edgar Sturtevant*

We shall have to examine the word *language* somewhat carefully, since it indicates the branch of science that we are going to study. For our immediate purpose we may set up the following definition, and then consider several of the terms employed in it:

A language is a system of arbitrary vocal symbols by which members of a social group coöperate and interact.

The word *system* marks a language off from mere sets of nonsense syllables like *ta-ra-ra-boom-de-ay* or *a-heigh-and-a-ho-and-a-heigh-nonny-no.* With the proper rhythm and intonation these or any other groups of syllables can carry a highly emotional message, but they do not form a part of the systematic structure of the English language. In contrast the sentence *the dog bites the man* is thoroughly systematic; we can transpose the words *dog* and *man* and still be understood by all English-speaking hearers, although the meaning of the sentence *the man bites the dog* is absurd. In spite of an entirely different mechanism the two Latin sentences: *canis hominem mordet* and *homō canem mordet,* stand in a similar relative position; it is only the system of the Latin language that compels us to take the second sentence in a sense that defies all experience.

The key word of the phrase *arbitrary vocal symbols* is the noun *symbols.* A symbol necessarily involves a dualism; there must be something that stands for or represents something else. This may be indicated by a diagram:

$$\frac{\text{the signifier }[1]}{\text{the signified}} \text{ or better } \frac{\text{form}}{\text{meaning}}$$

In the case before us the *form* is any meaningful segment of an utterance, and the *meaning* is the meaning of that segment. An *arbitrary*

From *An Introduction to Linguistic Science,* Yale University Press, New Haven, Conn., 1947.

[1] Cf. Ferdinand de Saussure, *Cours de linguistique générale,* Paris (1922). The horizontal line may be read, "combined with" or "simultaneous with."

5

symbol is one whose form has no necessary or natural connection with its meaning. English *dog* has roughly the same meaning as German *Hund*, French *chien*, Latin *canis*, and hundreds of other words in as many other languages. The only reason why *dog* carries this meaning is that the speakers of English use it with this meaning. The word *vocal* stands in the definition to exclude the human activities denoted by the phrases *gesture language, sign language, written language,* etc. All of these are important activities and proper subjects of investigation, and besides they have obvious connections with audible speech. The only reason for excluding them from our definition is convenience; they are found not to behave in the same way as audible language, and so they cannot conveniently be treated scientifically at the same time.

The final clause of the definition *by which the members of a social group coöperate and interact* designates the chief function of language in society. There are, of course, other means of coöperation between living beings, as witness the wolf pack, the swarm of bees, etc. Even men may coöperate not only by writing or by gesture but by actual physical compulsion or by a smile or by the raising of an eyebrow. All we mean to say is that among men language is by far the commonest and most important means of coöperation. Society as now constituted could not long continue without the use of language.[2] We must not forget, however, that language may also be used to interfere with the action of a group or to oppose one group to another; we cannot end our definition with the word *coöperate.*

A corollary of the final clause of the definition is that a language cannot function normally unless there are at least two speakers of it. When only one speaker remains, the language may be said to be dead.

LANGUAGE AS SPEECH   *Edward Sapir*

Language is a purely human and non-instinctive method of communicating ideas, emotions, and desires by means of a system of voluntarily produced symbols. These symbols are, in the first instance, auditory and they are produced by the so-called "organs of speech." There is no discernible instinctive basis in human speech as such, however much instinctive expressions and the natural environment

[2] Cf. Bloomfield, *Language,* p. 24.

From *Language: An Introduction to the Study of Speech,* by Edward Sapir, copyright, 1921, By Harcourt, Brace & World, Inc.; renewed, 1949, by Jean V. Sapir. Reprinted by permission of the publishers.

may serve as a stimulus for the development of certain elements of speech, however much instinctive tendencies, motor and other, may give a predetermined range or mold to linguistic expression. Such human or animal communication, if "communication" it may be called, as is brought about by involuntary, instinctive cries is not, in our sense, language at all.

I have just referred to the "organs of speech," and it would seem at first blush that this is tantamount to an admission that speech itself is an instinctive, biologically predetermined activity. We must not be misled by the mere term. There are, properly speaking, no organs of speech; there are only organs that are incidentally useful in the production of speech sounds. The lungs, the larynx, the palate, the nose, the tongue, the teeth, and the lips, are all so utilized, but they are no more to be thought of as primary organs of speech than are the fingers to be considered as essentially organs of piano-playing or the knees as organs of prayer. Speech is not a simple activity that is carried on by one or more organs biologically adapted to the purpose. It is an extremely complex and ever-shifting network of adjustments—in the brain, in the nervous system, and in the articulating and auditory organs—tending towards the desired end of communication. The lungs developed, roughly speaking, in connection with the necessary biological function known as breathing; the nose, as an organ of smell; the teeth, as organs useful in breaking up food before it was ready for digestion. If, then, these and other organs are being constantly utilized in speech, it is only because any organ, once existent and in so far as it is subject to voluntary control, can be utilized by man for secondary purposes. Physiologically, speech is an overlaid function, or, to be more precise, a group of overlaid functions. It gets what service it can out of organs and functions, nervous and muscular, that have come into being and are maintained for very different ends than its own.

It is true that physiological psychologists speak of the localization of speech in the brain. This can only mean that the sounds of speech are localized in the auditory tract of the brain, or in some circumscribed portion of it, precisely as other classes of sounds are localized; and that the motor processes involved in speech (such as the movements of the glottal cords in the larynx, the movements of the tongue required to pronounce the vowels, lip movements required to articulate certain consonants, and numerous others) are localized in the motor tract precisely as are all other impulses to special motor activities. In the same way control is lodged in the visual tract of the brain over all those processes of visual recognition involved in reading. Naturally the particular points or clusters of points of localization in the several tracts that refer to any element of language are connected in the brain by paths of association, so that the outward, or psycho-physical, aspect of language is of a vast network of associated localizations in the brain and lower nervous tracts, the auditory localizations being without doubt the most fundamental of all for speech. However, a speech-sound localized in the brain, even when associated with the particular movements of the "speech organs" that are required to produce it, is very far from being an element of language. It must be further associated with some element or group of elements of experience, say a visual image or a class of visual images or a feeling of relation, before it has even rudimentary linguistic significance. This "element" of experience is the content or "meaning" of the linguistic unit; the associated auditory, motor, and other cerebral processes that lie immediately back of the act of speaking and the act of hearing speech are merely a complicated symbol of or signal for these "meanings," of which more anon. We see therefore at once that language as such is not and cannot be definitely localized, for it consists of a peculiar symbolic relation—physiologically an arbitrary one—between all possible elements of consciousness on the one hand and certain selected elements localized in the auditory, motor, and other cerebral and nervous tracts on the other. If language can be said to be definitely "localized" in the brain, it is only in that general and rather useless sense in which all aspects of consciousness, all human interest and activity, may be said to be "in the brain." Hence, we have no recourse but to accept language as a fully formed functional system within man's psychic or "spiritual" constitution. We cannot define it as an entity in psycho-physical terms alone, however much the psycho-physical basis is essential to its functioning in the individual.

From the physiologist's or psychologist's point of view we may seem to be making an unwarrantable abstraction in desiring to handle the subject of speech without constant and explicit reference to that basis. However, such an abstraction is justifiable. We can profitably discuss the intention, the form, and the history of speech, precisely as we discuss the nature of any phase of human culture—say art or religion—as an institutional or cultural entity, leaving the organic and psychological mechanisms back of it as something to be taken for granted. Accordingly, it must be clearly understood that this introduction to the study of speech is not concerned with those aspects of physiology and of physiological psychology that underlie speech. Our study of language is not to be one of the genesis and operation of a concrete mechanism; it is, rather, to be an inquiry into the function and form of the arbitrary systems of symbolism that we term languages.

SCOPE AND METHOD   *Joshua Whatmough*

Nearly everybody talks, many can read and write, and some listen. Language is the most important meeting ground of the sciences and of letters. An age in which words play a greater role than any that has gone before calls for an examination and interpretation of linguistic processes—for language about language—to the end of better understanding and mastery of itself. Both the act of speaking or writing and the act of memory are events. But they are not random. They have, as we say, meaning; they are activities directed towards a goal, or goals, achieved if at all by their own mediation, so that understanding becomes a function of grammar. Modern computators demonstrate this peculiar feature of language in a peculiarly vivid way. But the verbal behavior of human beings has a self-starter and controls its own output —the stream of speech in which the successive words and sentences follow one another without premeditation. Moreover these remarkable feats are performed in such a way as to produce very extensive results with the help of materials of quite limited range. Thus it has been found that command of the 3000 most frequent words in a continuous sample of 100,000 running English words gives an understanding of 95 per cent of all the words, and that 2 per cent more can be acquired by derivation from these; but that a further 1 per cent increase can be attained only by the addition of 6000 additional words. Such statistical evidence raises a number of interesting problems.

How, for example, is meaning in different kinds of discourse related to the resources and structure of a language? And how is such a structure formed? We have modern 'information' theory of communication engineers, which is at least as much concerned with conformation as with 'information' (that is, with a measure of the restriction which habit, or structure, imposes on freedom of choice). But not all language is informative in the ordinary sense either. So much of language is emotive as to inspire distrust, even in much of that part of it which purports to be informative. Moreover, in languages with a great

From Joshua Whatmough, *Language: A Modern Synthesis*, St. Martin's Press, Inc., and Secker & Warburg.

literary tradition, far more than mere structure is of compelling interest. On the other hand, it has been maintained that even in languages devoid of such a literature, say of the Hopi or Shoshoni or Navaho, everything is really in the structure, in the form, of the language—that its way of saying things or mere grammar gives us the speaker's view of the universe, as contrasted with the totally different way in which scientific discourse says the same things, for example the causes of rain. Can this be true? Again scientific discourse transcends, from its own point of view, both a vernacular, devoid of the tradition of literature other than folk-tales orally transmitted, and also the literatures of the so-called 'great' languages. How far has scientific discourse its own peculiar structure, and why cannot it get on with ordinary discourse? What are the operative functional units to be isolated in the structure of a language? Or the operative units of meaning? Are these identical in one and the same language, or in more than one language, in all languages? Are there any items that are universal? Is there any language that comprehends, or seeks to comprehend, the world, and what then is its structure? Does the structure of the one correspond to the structure of the other, so that syntax is a model of the universe? Or must there always be a selection of units of meaning as well as of units of form? In Neanderthal society just how much was there to talk about? What, if any, are the limits to the variety of things to be talked about, and to human capacity to talk about them? Is knowledge itself coextensive with language? Or can anything be known that cannot be said? Does the emergence of an abundance of grammatical forms, as in early Indo-European languages, the age of inflection, represent a suddenly widened understanding, which was making unprecedented efforts to cope with previously guessed at, but very involved, relationships, which their modern representatives now face with simpler linguistic devices? And the almost complete absence of variety in grammatical forms, helped out by ample gesture to indicate even fairly simple relationships, as in the Aranta of Australia, does this represent a feral stage in which not much is found to talk about? May 'thought' be not merely sub-linguistic, but also non-linguistic, or both? What is the relationship between a language and a culture? Does language mold or reflect the culture, or do they react each constantly upon the other? What about those words, in Lewis Carroll or Edward Lear, which might have been structurally valid in English, but never occur elsewhere? Or the orders of words, in a poet like Hopkins or prose writer like Joyce, which are not structurally valid in English at all? These are some of the endless questions that present themselves.

This book is about language. Normally, all men and women, except idiots and, unless they are carefully trained, except deafmutes, join in this human babel before getting out of babyclothes; and there is nothing comes their way that they will not talk about. Language touches everything, human and inhuman, in heaven and on earth, and beneath the earth, language itself included. Language about language is called linguistics, a vast and highly technical subject, yet only a very small part of language. Since this book is about language, some attention must be given to linguistics. But the book is not solely or primarily about linguistics, but (to repeat) about language. Not everything, however, can be got into one book, and the subject matter of this one must be selected; even the aspects of the subject matter must be selected, and also what is to be said about each of them. The criterion of selection will be interest and importance, not technical detail or exhaustiveness.

What is language? It is customary to begin with definitions. But philosophically a definition comes at the end of an investigation. If we begin by defining language, that is because language has been investigated from more than one point of view already. We might indeed be clear first about the nature of a definition. To define is to set forth the proper or peculiar qualities of an object, the features that give it its character and quality. But to define is also to differentiate an object, to set forth the features that distinguish it from other objects with which it might be confused. Again a definition is not bound to be permanent, but may be changed. The ancients regarded vinegar as typical of acid substances, but vinegar is impure acetic acid; acetic acid (the acid of vinegar) in modern chemistry is $HC_2H_3O_2$, of which only one of the hydrogen (H) atoms has acid properties—an acid being a salt of hydrogen, in the language of chemistry a substance which gives a hydrogen ion in solution, or which neutralizes bases yielding water. In general, an acid is "a molecule with a positive field which is capable of neutralizing a basic molecule having a 'free' electron pair." In ordinary conversation, of course, the term 'acid' is not restricted by the scientific definition.

Now, to define language with precision is far less easy than to define acid or other chemical terms. This is because many scientific inquirers are interested in language, philosophers, psychologists, physicists, logicians, literary critics, neurologists, sociologists, as well as linguists, to name no others. There is also, just now, widespread interest in language and in meaning on the part of many intelligent men and women, no matter whether they regard an understanding of the nature and function of language as directly important for their daily work or not. No wonder, then, if many different definitions are made by different thinkers. But there need not be one, and only one, definition of language; and the different definitions advanced are not exclusive. They bring out different aspects of language, and supplement one another instead of excluding one another. Everything depends on the investigator's point of view and interest at the time that he makes his definition.

To many, language is the most important form of human communication, and this is the broadest way of regarding it. Certainly language is human, and human only. Insects, birds, and some mammals as well as man do communicate; but they do not talk. And language is normally, though not invariably, a form and a means of communication. Humans also use other means of communication, such as a red light, or a flag; but these are interpreted in language. 'Communication' means that an organism is affected by an external event and makes a reply to it. Clearly both the reply and the original event, in many cases itself also an utterance, are quite commonly what we understand by language: 'Is it raining?' (utterance) 'Not much' (response).

To others, language is first and foremost a form of symbolism. Here again we must stop to ask a question. What is a symbol? A symbol is a surrogate. We speak of mathematical symbols, for example x for any number, x^y for any number multiplied by itself any other number of times, i.e., x^y is the continued product of y x's, or x multiplied by itself $(y-1)$ times; Σ for any sum, and so on; or logical symbols, as a or b as variables in a statement or proposition, and then $\bar{a}$ to mean 'not a,' $a \vee b$ for 'a or b,' $\supset$ for implication as $a \supset b$ to mean 'a implies b,' and so forth. But all these surrogates have one feature in common. There is nothing in the nature of things that gives them the meanings stated; that is something *we* have given them, by agreement or convention, so that the symbol acquires a certain arbitrary character. This is something quite different from a *sign*. A sign has a direct relation to its object, like water dripping from the trees as a sign of rain; but the *word* rain (which obviously is not rain, or a sign of rain, for I can say it indoors, or for that matter I can say it repeatedly, even outdoors, without getting wet) is a symbol of 'rain' or 'raining,' as in our question *Is it raining? Not much!* or (to vary the event and therefore the response) *Not at all!*

Moreover, any consistent or coherent group of symbols, as in a language or dialect, is *systematic*. Like a family or society, it is not a merely accidental collection of stray individuals. The nature of symbols is such that to speak of an unsystematic symbolism is to fall into a contradiction in terms. Certainly linguistic symbols which are combined in such a way that the ties between them are unsystematic or are even bizarre—that is linguistic symbols unrelated to one another but merely juxtaposed—make nonsense; they cease to function as symbols. A haphazard jumble of symbols, say a pied text, is a mathematician's, or musician's, or a mere writer's or talker's, nightmare—but still a nightmare. An isolated symbol, on the other hand, remains just that to all eternity. The symbol for implication implies nothing by itself but implication in the abstract, and there it must rest; probability is probability in relation to something. All higher order abstractions are symbolic—'justice,' 'freedom,' 'goodness,' 'truth' and the like. Neither their content nor their form is directly or independently experienced, but only in relation to that which they symbolize; which is the reason why they are so much either distrusted or blindly worshipped, like the ideal of autonomy which destroyed the ancient Greek city-states.

But there remains one other factor even in this definition of language. Language is not only a systematic symbolism. Music is that, and also like language uses sound, and at times, as in singing, combines its own rhythm and melody with language. Language is a *verbal* systematic symbolism. That is to say, it makes use of verbal elements and structures, in brief, of what we commonly call words and of their arrangements. It will be better to postpone for a while any definition of words, or of what, in some languages such as Eskimo, behave pretty much as words do in others such as English. For the present it will be enough to take an example, say 'table.' There we have a symbol of a certain object; the symbol is also a word; that is, it is a verbal symbol. So, in like manner, *and* or *beer* or *have* or *embryo* or *drunk* or *man*. Now when we have occasion to use such a verbal symbol, we do so in a systematic way. Thus the verbal symbols 'table and embryo have drunk beer,' placed in that sequence are so unsystematic in arrangement as to symbolize nothing, unless possible dementia on the speaker's part; but 'the man has drunk beer,' by adhering to the system, retains the symbolic integrity of each symbol, and the arrangement enhances their symbolic values.

The same is true at each step; *table* is a symbol, *letab* is not. It is not even necessary to add that *elbat* or *letab* is not a symbol in English, implying that it is, or may be, in some other language. What we have said so far is true of languages, or of a language, as well as of language at large; for every case is a given case when you come to it, and this is true of languages as of everything else, from cabbages to kings. To raise the question of system or no-system of a symbol outside its own systematic symbolism is idle. How deep-seated this principle is may be seen by taking the following groups of Latin words:

saxum 'stone' but sexum (acc. sing.) 'sex,' and sex 'six'
lacus 'lake' but locus 'place'
līquens 'clear' but līquens 'fluid,' lŏquens 'speaking,' and līquans
    'liquefying.'

Lucretius, like all the ancient atomists, was aware of all this, and fond of it as an illustration of his theories: ignis is 'fire,' which may be had from lignum 'firewood' by disturbing or subtracting from or adding to the constituent particles of the words as well as of the substances! The principle may be illustrated from the system of any language whatever. It is astonishing how few of the primary units, that is the speech-sounds, will serve, and how little strain is put upon them, or upon the user, by quite severe demands for efficiency in their use. Even a child, or even a very dull adult, can easily make this powerful instrument serve all his needs.

But there are other ways of looking at language. One other way of putting what has just been said about the systematic character of linguistic symbolism is to say that language is a form of order, a pattern, a code. That is to say, at any given status of its history, a language is found to show a statistical regularity which may be put in terms of formulae that are concerned with classical probability of frequency of occurrence of the constituent elements, and of permitted combinations of them within the pattern of a particular language. Objectively, therefore, a language may be described as a body of physically discrete events in which relations of similarity occur in a statistically definable pattern. The sequence of events is governed by probabilities of occurrence; i.e. proceeds by probability, ranging from 0 to 1, in a series of mass phenomena showing repetitive events. The successive steps in the process are dependent also upon preceding steps. Finally, a sufficiently large sample of the sequence is representative of the whole, precisely because the events are repetitive. For example, in modern written English the occurrence of the symbol q guarantees that the symbol which follows it will be u; the symbol th in English may be followed by a, e, i, o, u, r, w, y but not by l (unless in borrowed words) or x or any of the other English alphabetic symbols. Thx would be a zero probability in genuinely English words; tha and the rest will always be less than 1. Even th- (as in then) is not followed by r, but only *th-* (as in *thin*); likewise English *shr-* occurs, but not *shl-*, or *pw-*: if you hear *pwivate* 'private' from a few speakers [w] is a variant, phonematically speaking, of [r]. The probability that *th* will be followed by *e* is considerably higher than that it will be followed by *u*. This is a very simple illustrative example.

In modern English, if a permissible sequence of symbols that makes a word, for example the series *f u r i o u s*, is followed by anything at all, then those following symbols are already prescribed and limited; in this case they must be *l y* or *n e s s* (not normally *e r* or *e s t*) and nothing else, for example not *th* (like *wide* : *width*). In other words, the symbols *l y* or *n e s s*, in this particular sequence, are determined by what went before.

But in all this, there is one feature of language that must never be lost sight of. *Language is first and foremost a means of transmitting information,* and its study a branch of the study of symbols and of the signs and objects that they symbolize. Language is made up of messages purposively produced in such a way as to be decoded word-by-word in the easiest, i.e. most economical, possible fashion. The length and arrangement of linguistic structures such as words, the nature and relation of speech-sounds (phonemes) one to another, the length and relation of constituent clauses in a sentence or period, all these have evolved in such a way as to promote an economical, but powerful, means of communication.

Language is also a form of social behavior. If all normal humans talk, and only humans, they also talk to one another. At the moment I am talking to my reader, as much as if I were 'on the air'; there is a greater time-lag in a printed book, as in a recording, than there is in face-to-face talk, the telephone, or direct, unrehearsed radio. A letter is written not to its writer, but to his family or friends or business acquaintances, to his tailor or grocer, to the tax-collector, and so forth. If I make notes for my own subsequent use, then I am practically two different persons, in different places or at different times, one here and now, the other somewhere else in the future. Some forms of language, shall we say those partially tabooed (but often infuriating or laughable) varieties of language, profanity and obscenity, have been made the objects of psychological study. Perhaps it is a mistake to treat them solely as matters of individual psychology. When language, or verbal behavior, is taken up by the psychologist, it is or should be as a matter of social as well as of individual conduct. Linguistic phenomena are conditioned by the social group, by circumstances which are socially determined—both the linguistic patterns of the community, and extra-linguistic group habits, e.g. customs such as taboo or courtesy or the like.

To say that language may be studied as a form of behavior by no means admits that the school of psychology known as behaviorist is unreservedly supported by linguistics or by all linguists, or that a behaviorist interpretation of linguistic phenomena is the correct and only one. The serious objection to behaviorism is that it fails to take adequate account of intelligence. Intelligence consists in the power to make a new departure instead of repeating the old habit, to take a new step. A high degree of intelligence is always abnormal, and it occurs in the individual. How can behaviorists explain any initial success which they may themselves experience by their own professed theory that initial success is to be explained only in terms of chance and habit? A behaviorist who sets himself the purpose of proving that purpose does not exist is in the impossible position of starting himself into flight by tugging on his own bootstraps; he seems not to have noticed that the more frequently something has been tried, the less likely it is to recur if it has been unsuccessful, so that an intelligent result calls for deviation from normal habit. This is true also of language. Even on the mathematical view, a striking utterance is found, on inspection, to disturb commonplace encoding and decoding processes, as in T. S. Eliot's "The yellow fog" (not 'dog') "that rubs its back upon the window-panes."

A notion of language that was common, at least by implication, in the nineteenth century, is held by nobody today, though many of the old ways of expression are constantly met with. We speak of mother languages, sister languages, dead and living languages. These expressions clearly suggest the view of language as an organism. But a moment's reflection must always have shown that the expressions are figurative only. Languages do not intermarry and produce offspring; to talk of a 'family' of languages means that a number of mutually unintelligible languages all represent divergent forms that can be shown historically to go back to a common original, that they possess a common stock of words, forms, sentence-structure, and speech-sounds, all greatly modified in the course of time, the relationships of which one to another can be accounted for only on the assumption that they represent a previous single, more-or-less homogeneous, speech. Provided that this fact is clearly understood, there is little harm in talking about this or that 'family' of languages.

But the whole matter was often put in the terms of a family-tree relationship. This idea was fostered in part by the evolutionary theories associated with the name of Darwin which were very much in the air in the middle of the nineteenth century. It was also encouraged by the work of a prominent philologist of the time, August Schleicher, who happened also to be a botanist, and was tempted to apply not only his scientific attitude of mind to his theorizing about language, which was all to the good, but also the current ideas of genetic relationships among plants or animals, which was misleading. Yet language certainly is an activity of living organisms, and through them shows remarkable power of adaptation to a changing environment.

But if language is not itself an organism, neither is it a mechanism. Many modern linguists are confirmed believers in a mechanist theory of language which shuns all mental interpretations and all mentalist terms. The theory of course claims to be objective. But it is difficult to admit the validity of the claim. For then we are asked to accept language about language about language about language ... (and so on to infinity), and all of it starting from the hypothesis that language is nothing more than a matter of mechanical stimulus and response. If the theory were correct it would refute itself; for it would, on its own showing, be reduced to being a response or series of responses made by a certain linguist or linguists to certain stimuli, chiefly verbal. Such responses might tell us something about the linguist or linguists concerned and even about his or their use of language, but hardly anything about language as such. It is impossible to explain x by x; an unknown cannot be interpreted by itself. The mechanist theory aims at strictly scientific method, and therefore pretends to use only direct observation of communicating individuals; but in practice it leans heavily on indirect observation through records of all kinds. It tends also to restrict itself to observing and discussing the effects of language on the behavior of the individual, notwithstanding the fact that verbal behavior is essentially social. It is difficult to see how a mechanical theory of communication can ever escape the charge of solipsism: the mechanist always overlooks the fact that he himself, an organism like any other, is doing the observation, so that his much-vaunted objectivity is false.

As for the quaint notion that language arose from primitive facial gestures, and therefore does not differ fundamentally from other muscular behavior, not only does the idea rest on nothing stronger than conjecture; it naively assumes the validity of an absurdly simple solution to an extremely complicated problem. A truly philosophical account of language must comprehend, for example, poetic as well as scientific discourse, the power of human intellect as well as the chit-chat of everyday conversation.

But it will not do to fly to the opposite extreme and regard language as pure intellection. In scientific discourse, in logic, a large part of the total utterance serves intellectual operations, in mathematics close to 100 per cent (a definite article, demonstrative pronoun, the substantive verb, short phrases or sentences, and the like here and there in a page of mathematics perhaps are supererogatory); in poetry and creative writing generally, in aesthetic discourse too, a high percentage may still be said to be concerned with intellect. But in ordinary conversation as much as 90 to 95 per cent of what we say is neutral, and the meaning is carried largely by the overtones of the remainder—say such words as 'friend,' or 'enemy,' that arouse the emotions. Even here there is still a crude correspondence between the structure of the utterance and the structure of experience. But in some commercial and political propaganda any such correspondence may be not seriously attempted at all. There is often a pretense at making the statements informative, but it is a pretense unworthy of human intellect. It is, however, precisely the intervention of the individual cerebral (or mental) event between stimulus and response that effectively rescues language from being an automatic mechanist affair, even when it proceeds from the mouth of a dictator.

Finally, it has been suggested that language is a relation, or (better) a means of establishing and sustaining relations between members of a community, large or small—a village or hamlet, or on a world-wide scale. This is another, and in a way a more concrete, statement of what is meant by saying that language is a form of social behavior. Think of a human being as a point on a plane; and of what he says as projected like a double cone with the point on the plane, the cones produced above and below the plane and the axes variable; suppose also a number of such points, each corresponding to a human being, close together or more widely separated, as the case may be, on the plane. The cones will intersect. And the farther each cone is projected into space, the greater the volume of intersection. Even cones widely separated, people who are, if you like, 'poles apart,' may be brought into contact by the speading influence of what they say, especially if they use modern techniques of communication, including the light-swift radio. The members of a family, however, clan, village, city, or nation —the latter usually, if not always, having a single language—are bound together not less by language than by law and government; and, under modern conditions, more than by religion and some other institutions such as education or 'amusement.'

But no matter in which of these different ways we look at language, we shall always find that all languages have certain characteristics which make language what it is. For example, there is the high degree of convention that characterizes linguistic symbolism—its features are conventional rather than arbitrary, for they are evolutionary. Then again, every language has its pattern, to which it adheres consistently. Diverse as are the aspects of language, and even more varied as are actual language-patterns, and the national languages that are utterly incomprehensible, without learning, to their several groups of speakers, still there are universals, fundamental and intrinsic to language, that appear in every particular language that has been examined.

Very early in life each normal human being becomes aware of his own existence, conscious of self and environment, and may continue so as long as he lives. Language is indeed part of this environment, and though we believe it to be a derivation from the background of human nature and experience, it has become relatively independent of the immediate environment. We may conveniently separate, therefore, from all other events (and their relations) those events which constitute that which is said about them.

The domain of this second kind of events, namely linguistic, is limitless; for clearly not only does it run the gamut from everyday conversational discourse to philosophy and mathematics, but there may be constructed a hierarchy of language in which we have language about language about language and so on—like a set of Chinese boxes. We distinguish, therefore, between (a) language at large and (b) language that is concerned with the interpretation of language and with logic; further we distinguish (c) language that is concerned with the description, history, and comparison of languages (linguistics); and (d) language which reports on sciences preliminary or auxiliary to the study of language (e.g. acoustics or phonetics) in the sense of linguistics proper (description, history, and comparison).

Any field of knowledge which is being actively cultivated may be expected to produce new crops, and in the field of linguistics spectacular results have been won in recent decades. In the eighties of the last century leading linguists insisted on strict historical method in tracing the relationship between, for example, Hindi *punch* 'five' (hence applied to a drink compounded of five ingredients) and English *five* and French *cinq*, all of which are the modern representatives of one and the same original word, which can be shown (by the same methods) to be connected with the English *fist* and *finger*, so that *five* has to do with counting on your fingers (and thumbs) or toes, five to each hand or foot. The theory which embodied the method was that historical changes or substitutions of sounds are absolutely regular and must be stated in terms which adhere strictly to this principle. This was definitely a new departure, and the leading spirits behind it were called 'new grammarians.' At that time there were hardly any other concepts behind the study of general linguistics.

Now we have new methods again, logical, psychological, physical, structural, statistical and mathematical, which are giving a tremendous impulse to the study and understanding of language.

MYSTICISM OF LANGUAGE   Otto Jespersen

We shall never thoroughly understand the nature of language, if we take as our starting point the sober attitude of the scientifically-trained man of today, who regards the words he uses as means for communicating, or maybe further developing, thought. To children and savages a word is something very different. To them, there is something magical or mystical in a name. It is something that has power over things and is bound up with them in a far more intimate manner than we are wont to imagine. This view may begin very early in the child's life. The child that notices that it does not get anything if it does not ask for it nicely, but that its parents at once fulfill its wishes when it says 'water, please,' rejoices in the magical power he has come to possess by the utterance of these syllables. As Sully expresses it: 'children regard names as objective realities mysteriously bound up with the things, and, in a manner, necessary to them. A nameless object is, for a child, something incomplete—almost uncanny',[1] and 'the childish tendency to "reify" the name, that is, to regard it as part of the real thing itself, instead of something extraneous and arbitrarily attached to it'.[2]

We meet similar conceptions among the savage tribes of very different parts of the globe.[3] Knud Rasmussen several times describes the Greenlanders' view of the Name as something self-existent: 'They divide a person into a soul, a body, and a name.... The name is a

From *Mankind, Nation and Individual from a Linguistic Point of View*, Instituttet for Sammenlignende Kulturforskning, Oslo, 1925.

[1] *Nineteenth Century* Nov. 1891 p. 739.
[2] *The Human Mind*, 1892, p. 312.
[3] The magical power of the Name is treated psychologically in C. K. Ogden and I. A. Richards' *The Meaning of Meaning* (London 1923).

soul, with which a certain stock of vital power and dexterity is bound up. A person who is named after a dead man, inherits his qualities, and the dead man is not at rest, his life's-soul cannot pass to the land of the dead, until a child has been named after him. Connected with this view is the fear of mentioning a dead man's name, before a child has received it, lest the man should thus lose some part of its virtue. After the death of the body, the name takes up its abode in a pregnant woman, and keeps her inwardly pure during her pregnancy; then it is born with the child'.[4]

Connected with such superstitious conceptions are the customs found under varying forms in many other parts of the world for perpetuating a man's name. Some of the facts were brought to light by Gustav Storm, who succeeded in drawing from them some interesting conclusions in regard to Scandinavian history in the Middle Ages. A collection of other material is to be found, e.g. in Feilberg's Jutland Dictionary under the word 'navn' [name], where many references are given. The main principle in old times was that a child was called after that relative, recently dead, whose soul and power and luck it was desired that the child should inherit, on the supposition that these things would come to the child with the name. Long after this conception had passed, it lived on in customs connected with the naming of children. So in many places there was a disinclination to give a child its father's name, unless the latter had died before the child's birth, in which case the child took his name almost as a matter of course. So, children were named much more frequently after dead grandparents than after living ones. Many other peculiar points with regard to the naming of children find a simple explanation, when the ideas of a primitive race on the nature and vital significance of the name are taken into account.

Many primitive peoples are afraid of mentioning their name to strangers: it is a part of their being, and they do not wish others to get power over them by knowing their names (Niceforo GA p. 208 f.). The Sakalava's in Madagascar are not allowed to communicate to strangers either their own name or the name of their village, for fear the strangers should make a mischievous use of it. (Walen).

In some Australian tribes everyone has two names:—a general name, and a special name only known to members of his totem-group (Spencer and Gillen). The Araukans carefully conceal their personal-name from strangers: in their presence they are called by their family-name. Near

---

[4] *Nye mennesker*, pp. 121, 130: *Grønland*, p. 124.

Tver's Lake in Victoria the natives mention no one by his name, but call him brother or cousin, or use designations like the left-handed one, the little fool (Lefébure).

In South Italy a man who is suspected of being a 'jettatore', having the 'evil eye', is never spoken of by name, but only as 'he who cannot be named' or 'Mr. . . . ., let us not name him'. It is thought that the mere naming of the 'jettatore' brings ill-luck, just as much as seeing or touching him. (Niceforo GA 210.)

In popular belief as reflected in fairy-tales, songs, and traditional legends, we find again and again the idea that knowledge of the name of a person or thing gives one power over the person or the thing. One example must suffice. When St. Lawrence was building the cathedral at Lund, he received supernatural assistance from a goblin ('trold') who by way of reward was to have the saint's two eyes unless the latter could name his name. When the church was nearly finished, Lawrence heard a woman on a little hill outside the town hush her weeping children with the promise that their father Finn was soon coming with gifts for them. Lawrence could therefore hurl the name at the goblin, who on the instant lost his power and was turned to stone.[5]

A similar magical power, according to popular belief, lies in various formulas, which, if spoken or merely written, are powerful enough to keep anything evil away, to cure sickness, bring good to him who knows them and applies them, and cause harm to his enemy. Such formulas are found in all countries: they often contain words or fragments of words which are not intelligible. Here I will only bring evidence from Greenland where, according to Knud Rasmussen,[6] one finds charms with old untranslateable, apparently meaningless, words which old men have dreamt. 'They are handed on from generation to generation. Everyone regards them as of great value, but he is not allowed to impart them till he feels the approach of death'.

It is also well-known what great magical importance has been attached in many places to words or letters, scratched or written in different ways on different objects, to give the writer power over persons or things. The runes were originally not so much means of communications as charms. One of the most important passages for the understanding of the subject is the stanzas woven into the songs about Sigurd in the Edda, in which it is said:

---

[5] Connected with this is the great mystical importance assigned in various poems of the Edda (e. g. Vafþrúþnismál, and especially Alvismál) to knowledge of names, especially of the names of gods and things connected with the gods.
[6] Grønland, p. 123.

Winning-runes learn, if thou longest to win,
And the runes on thy sword-hilt write;
Some on the furrow, and some on the flat,
And twice thou shall call on Tyr.

Ale runes learn, that with lies the wife
Of another betray not thy trust;
On the horn thou shalt write, and the backs of thy hands,
And Need (N) shalt mark on thy nails.

Birth-runes learn, if help thou wilt lend,
The babe from the mother to bring.

And thus it goes on with sea-runes, medicinal runes, and runes of wisdom.

Speech-runes learn, that none may seek
To answer harm with hate . . . .

Thought-runes learn, if all shall think
Thou are keenest minded of men.[7]

But about charms and similar magical expedients in other countries, others are far more competent to speak than I.

A consequence of the primitive view of the close mystical connexion between name and thing is the importance often attached to a man's changing his name when he becomes a ruling sovereign. His power and authority is now different from what it was before, he has become a different man, and this is expressed by his taking a new name,[8] often with a solemn ceremonial. Again, not unfrequently, a young man changes his name, when with solemn religious ceremonies he is formally received into the body of grown-up men which often takes place only after hard probation accompanied by downright torture.

In many countries it is not persons merely who change their name, towns do so also. And this change of name is not a mere shifting of a label: it is supposed to be of great symbolical importance to the life of the nation. It betokened a new epoch in the national life of the Japanese when their capital gave up its ancient name *Yeddo*, and took the new name *Tokyo*, meaning 'the eastern residence'. And elsewhere on the earth's surface capitals change their name and deep importance is attached to the change. St. Petersburgh became Petrograd, and has now become Leningrad: Christiania has become Oslo.

[7] *Sigrdrifomál* 6 ff., transl. by H. A. Bellows, New York 1923.
[8] For the effect of this custom on the general vocabulary, see below.

In the Anemerina tribes of Madagascar the King changes his name on his coronation-day; for instance, Rabodo became Ranavalona I, Rakoto called himself Radama II. But at the same time all names of things or beings, which resemble the King's new name, disappear from the ordinary vocabulary. When Queen Rasoherina came to the throne, the word *soherina* (silkworm) was forbidden, and replaced by *zana dandy*, which means, 'silk's child'. If the prince takes the name *Andria-mambra*, the word *mambra* (crocodile) in the ordinary language must be replaced by *voay:* if he calls himself *Ramboa*, the word *amboa* (dog) must vanish, and people must say *fandroaka* (the hunter) or *famovo* (the barker).[9] Similar customs are found in many other parts of the world.

According to W. Thalbitzer,[10] 'The principal cause of the difference between East and West Greenlandic is the religious taboo-custom that made it compulsory to alter a word whenever a person died who bore the same word as a name; for the name of the deceased must never be spoken unless before his death his name had been given to a person still alive, and even then it was better not to mention the name. The new word was formed by derivation from another stem with a similar meaning, or that meant something that could be used as a metaphoric paraphrasing of the word tabooed. When the two men *Umiaq* and *Inik* died, their names, that were common words for "women's boat" and "human being", were tabooed, and replaced with *Aawtarit* and *Taaq*, the former a paraphrase of "women's boat", meaning "a means of moving by boat from the winter residence to the summer place", the latter meaning literally 'a shadow' ... In other cases obsolete words, or words of the sacred language of the priests (angakkut) seem to have been made use of'.

In the same work, p. 159, he is speaking of native Greenland poets who are famous in their life time, but 'the death of the poet or artist casts the fatal shade of taboo over his name, which it is forbidden to mention, and therefore everlasting fame does not fall to the lot of the classical product of any Eskimo poet'.

The Todas of Southern India have very similar conceptions and customs. The late Dr. W. H. R. Rivers writes [11] : 'If two men have the same name, and one of the two should die, the other man would change his name, since the taboo on the name of the dead would prevent people from uttering the name of the living ... two men named

9 Sibree; Niceforo GA p. 240; Frazer, *Golden Bough*, III, p. 378.
10 *The Ammassalik Eskimo* in *Meddel. fra Grønland* XL 1923, p. 115.
11 *The Todas* p. 625 f.

Matowan ... one died, and the other changed his name to *Imokhvan*.
... This change of name may also be effected even when there is only
a similarity between the two names ... when *Oners* ... died, *Einers*
changed his name to *Tokulvan* ... When a man is ill, change of name
is sometimes recommended by the diviner, but this is not often done ...
A man may not utter the names of his mother's brother, his grandfather
and grandmother, his wife's mother, and of the man from whom he has
received his wife, who is usually the wife's father. The names of the
above are tabooed in life, while after death the restrictions are still
wider, and it is forbidden to utter the name of any dead elder relative,
while the names of the dead are in any case only said reluctantly ...
The Todas dislike uttering their own names, and a Toda, when asked
for his name, would often request another man to give it'. On the other
hand there is no taboo-prohibition among the Todas against uttering
'the names of the objects which correspond to the names of the dead,
or to parts of their names'.

The common prohibition of uttering the dead man's name is due according to Niceforo GA p. 245) to the belief that the dead man is
included in the class of untouchable (holy or unclean) beings which
must not be touched without observing the very strictest precautions:
the dead man's name and the dead man himself making up only one
single being.

Often again people dare not mention the names of various gods,
devils, or good and evil spirits, as by doing so they may bring upon
themselves the wrath of the invisible powers. The best known case
is *Jehovah (Jahveh)*, whom the Jews dared not name and so substituted
Adonai, 'the lord'. But a corresponding prohibition and fear is found
in many places. We have indeed something of it in our European
forms of oath, as when we Danes instead of swearing by *'guds død og
pine'* ('God's death and passion') are content to say *død og pine*. So
in English the word God is either shortened as in the obsolete
oath *drot, drat* from *God rot*, or transformed to *gosh, Gad, cock, bob,
Great Scott, gog, gough, gum, golly, gummy, dad (bedad, adad)*, not to
speak of *goodness*, and similar harmless substitutes. In German, to
take an example, they have *Pott* for *Gott (Potts slapperment* for *Gottes
sakrament)*, in French *bleu* in *morbleu* from *mort Dieu*, etc. People
are shy again about naming the devil (*djævelen, fanden*, in Danish) and
to avoid the proper name say *den onde*, 'the evil one', or the like.

(Both the above Danish names for devil are originally noa-names:
diabolos, properly, the calumniator, the enemy, and *fanden*, either a

transformation of *fjenden*, the enemy, or more probably, the 'tempter', from the verb which we have in Old English, *fandian*, to prove, tempt.)

The ancient Romans believed that their city had a special god, whose name however was so holy that it was a capital offence to disclose it, and it was even forbidden, as Plutarch tells us, to inquire into the god's sex. The city itself had also a secret holy name, the mention of which involved the punishment of death. As an illustration drawn from quite modern times I may quote what Vambéry [12] relates of his Jewish-orthodox home in Hungary, where to avoid mention of the Christian cross, *(kreuz)*, they had to call the coin *kreuzer* a *schmeitzer*.

Similar ideas of the nature of a name and of the mystical power of a word are at the bottom of a multitude of superstitions the whole world over. Many of these are as much alive as ever among the peasantry, though many have been driven out in civilized countries during the last few centuries, or perhaps, actually, only within the last few decades. A mass of illustrations of name-superstitions and word-taboo drawn from many countries and languages is collected in Kr. Nyrop's very able work *Navnets magt* and in the third volume of Sir J. G. Frazer's *Golden Bough.*

It is now coming to be generally recognized by linguistic investigators that such name-taboos have had a great influence on the evolution of vocabulary. So in many places the proper name for the 'bear' has been lost. In Lapland people are so much afraid of its killing the cattle that they do not call it by its usual name *guouzhja*, but say *moedda-aigja*, which means 'grandpapa with the skin coat' (Leem, Nyrop, p. 30): other names also are given. In Siberia the Yakuts call the bear Our lord, famous old man, good father, and so on. This helps us to understand how the old Aryan name for the bear, which we know from the Gk. *arktos*, Sk. *rksah*, Zend *aršo*, Lat. *ursus*, Erse *art*, etc., has entirely disappeared in a number of related languages, and has been replaced by different circumlocutions: Slavonic *medvědi*, Russian *medvěd*, which originally means 'honey-eater', Lithuanian *lokys*, which probably means 'the sweet-toothed', and the Danish *bjørn*, Germ. *bär*, Engl. *bear*, which means 'the brown'.

Finally, we have the special 'women's language', found in many different parts of the world. Often it merely includes a number of expressions specially used by women (or by women and children). But often it also embraces special grammatical forms or customary pronunciations; but all these peculiarities are largely or entirely dependent

---

[12] *Story of My Struggles*, p. 29.

on old beliefs, according to which certain words and expressions are taboo for certain persons and must therefore be replaced by other words, by noa-words.[13]

It has often been remarked how tenaciously savage races cling to everything that is traditional: how, for example, they fashion and employ their tools without deviating a hair's breadth from the manner in which their ancestors did so before them. This conservatism has rightly been recognized [14] as resulting from an active faith in the things' possessing mystical properties, the potency of which depended on the objects' forms, so that by making the least change in them one would lose one's power over them. Mysterious dangers were threatened if anything was changed. For similar reasons primitive races cling with equal tenacity to their inherited language. Of course mutations of language to a great degree elude human observation, and it therefore happens that without the natives detecting it, their language does alter little by little with the daily use made of it and with its transmission to new generations. But, so far as they can, they see to it strictly that nothing shall be changed, (apart from the case where a belief in the mystical power of the name actually demands the adoption of new words) and the most scrupulous watch is kept that there should be no change in the holy forms of religious worship and ceremonial hymns. It is owing to this careful watch over the old traditional sounds of words that the old Vedic hymns of the Indians have been orally preserved with such great fidelity that we are acquainted with their forms and pronunciation to the minutest detail. According to Sylvain Lévy, the old Vedic language was to such an extent an exclusively religious language, that it was not till the arrival of conquerors from without who were strange to Indian tradition that people dared to employ Sanskrit in profane literature.

While, then, in discussing the fear of mystical effects from the use of one word instead of another, we spoke, from our civilized standpoint, of *superstition,* here, where we are speaking of keeping unchanged what one's ancestors have handed down to one, we will rather regard this as an outcome of a commendable religious feeling, closely allied to the warm feeling with which each one of us conceives his own native language as a holy national inheritance.

[13] See my *Language,* Chap. XVI.
[14] See Lévy-Bruhl FM, p. 35.

SECTION II

HISTORY:
THE MATRIX OF LANGUAGE

"It is impossible to have a complete understanding of any
individual language without knowledge of its history."

—Louis H. Gray

Our interest in language is usually a matter of the present tense.
We ask questions about language forms and language usage; we inquire only casually about language changes. We may remember that
our grandfather called his suspenders "braces," and we chuckle at his
"old-fashioned" language. Or we may wonder at the genuine power
and relevancy possible for a literature written in the "archaic" English
of Chaucer or Shakespeare. But our curiosity remains "mere" curiosity;
we seldom elevate this curiosity toward significance by bringing together in any purposeful way our interest in language and our awareness of history. And yet the study of the history of a language is of
prime, inescapable importance. Since language is in a constant state
of flux and change, we shall remain hopelessly naive if we base our
appreciation and use of language on only the transient, limited sampling
we use and observe. If we would acquire genuine linguistic sophistication, we need to know what kinds of changes and permutations our
language has undergone over a wide range of time, and in response to
a wide range of influences.

An interest in the historical side of language may at first seem to
be an exercise solely for the learnedly curious or pedantic. A knowledge of the laws of sound change, for example, appears strictly technical, and hardly liberating. Likewise, the ability to recite semantic
changes undergone by a venerable word is certainly impressive but
seemingly impractical. But within just such apparently lifeless material
is concealed the drama of a whole civilization. For the record of a
people's language is the record of that people. Consider, for a moment,
the simple generalization of the sentence you have just read. Does it
not signify, clearly and compellingly, that the development of the

29

English character has in part been influenced by the language of such writers as Chaucer, Shakespeare, Spenser, Donne, Dryden, Pope, Wordsworth, Tennyson, and Eliot? And does it not signify also that we cannot truly know or understand a nation unless we know the history of its language in addition to, say, the history of its political, social, and religious institutions? The point is not worth belaboring; it needs only to be raised. Once the relevance of a language's history is grasped, the student's responsibility is clear enough. One more example may be useful in dramatizing the point. Even the close student of American culture will find valuable, novel enlightenment as he reads, for instance, in a book such as Albert Marckwardt's *American English* the ways in which American English can be shown to "reflect the American tradition and the American character." Mark Twain will mean something new and different to him, as will the very educative processes he has been exposed to in a grammar school whose language curriculum was the product of nineteenth century linguistic philosophy. In a word, he comes to know himself, linguistically, in terms of the culture which has produced him.

The essays in this section have been arranged to give the reader a useful sense of the development of his language. From the engagingly accurate overview of the history of English presented by Paul Roberts in the opening essay, the student moves to a focus, in the essay by Greenough and Kittredge, upon the most decisive specific influences that have operated upon the English language. The remaining essays introduce the problem of the history of the English language in America, the present status of American as over against British English, and finally the possible post-history of English.

SOMETHING ABOUT ENGLISH   Paul Roberts

No understanding of the English language can be very satisfactory without a notion of the history of the language. But we shall have to make do with just a notion. The history of English is long and complicated, and we can only hit the high spots.

The history of our language begins a little after A.D. 600. Everything before that is pre-history, which means that we can guess at it but can't prove much. For a thousand years or so before the birth of Christ our linguistic ancestors were savages wandering through the forests of northern Europe. Their language was a part of the Germanic branch of the Indo-European family.

At the time of the Roman Empire—say, from the beginning of the Christian Era to around A.D. 400—the speakers of what was to become English were scattered along the northern coast of Europe. They spoke a dialect of Low German. More exactly, they spoke several different dialects, since they were several different tribes. The names given to the tribes who got to England are *Angles, Saxons,* and *Jutes.* For convenience, we can refer to them all as Anglo-Saxons.

Their first contact with civilization was a rather thin acquaintance with the Roman Empire on whose borders they lived. Probably some of the Anglo-Saxons wandered into the Empire occasionally, and certainly Roman merchants and traders traveled among the tribes. At any rate, this period saw the first of our many borrowings from Latin. Such words as *kettle, wine, cheese, butter, cheap, plum, gem, bishop, church* were borrowed at this time. They show something of the relationship of the Anglo-Saxons with the Romans. The Anglo-Saxons were learning, getting their first taste of civilization.

They still had a long way to go, however, and their first step was to help smash the civilization they were learning from. In the fourth century the Roman power weakened badly. While the Goths were pounding away at the Romans in the Mediterranean countries, their relatives, the Anglo-Saxons, began to attack Britain.

From Paul Roberts, *Understanding English,* Harper & Brothers, New York, 1958.

The Romans had been the ruling power in Britain since A.D. 43. They had subjugated the Celts whom they found living there and had succeeded in setting up a Roman administration. The Roman influence did not extend to the outlying parts of the British Isles. In Scotland, Wales, and Ireland the Celts remained free and wild, and they made periodic forays against the Romans in England. Among other defense measures, the Romans built the famous Roman Wall to ward off the tribes in the north.

Even in England the Roman power was thin. Latin did not become the language of the country as it did in Gaul and Spain. The mass of people continued to speak Celtic, with Latin and the Roman civilization it contained in use as a top dressing.

In the fourth century, troubles multiplied for the Romans in Britain. Not only did the untamed tribes of Scotland and Wales grow more and more restive, but the Anglo-Saxons began to make pirate raids on the eastern coast. Furthermore, there was growing difficulty everywhere in the Empire, and the legions in Britain were siphoned off to fight elsewhere. Finally, in A.D. 410, the last Roman ruler in England, bent on becoming emperor, left the islands and took the last of the legions with him. The Celts were left in possession of Britain but almost defenseless against the impending Anglo-Saxon attack.

Not much is surely known about the arrival of the Anglo-Saxons in England. According to the best early source, the eighth-century historian Bede, the Jutes came in 449 in response to a plea from the Celtic king, Vortigern, who wanted their help against the Picts attacking from the north. The Jutes subdued the Picts but then quarreled and fought with Vortigern, and, with reinforcements from the Continent, settled permanently in Kent. Somewhat later the Angles established themselves in eastern England and the Saxons in the south and west. Bede's account is plausible enough, and these were probably the main lines of the invasion.

We do know, however, that the Angles, Saxons, and Jutes were a long time securing themselves in England. Fighting went on for as long as a hundred years before the Celts in England were all killed, driven into Wales, or reduced to slavery. This is the period of King Arthur, who was not entirely mythological. He was a Romanized Celt, a general, though probably not a king. He had some success against the Anglo-Saxons, but it was only temporary. By 550 or so the Anglo-Saxons were firmly established. English was in England.

All this is pre-history, so far as the language is concerned. We have no record of the English language until after 600, when the Anglo-

Saxons were converted to Christianity and learned the Latin alphabet. The conversion began, to be precise, in the year 597 and was accomplished within thirty or forty years. The conversion was a great advance for the Anglo-Saxons, not only because of the spiritual benefits but because it reëstablished contact with what remained of Roman civilization. This civilization didn't amount to much in the year 600, but it was certainly superior to anything in England up to that time.

It is customary to divide the history of the English language into three periods: Old English, Middle English, and Modern English. Old English runs from the earliest records—i.e., seventh century—to about 1100; Middle English from 1100 to 1450 or 1500; Modern English from 1500 to the present day. Sometimes Modern English is further divided into Early Modern, 1500–1700, and Late Modern, 1700 to the present.

When England came into history, it was divided into several more or less autonomous kingdoms, some of which at times exercised a certain amount of control over the others. In the century after the conversion the most advanced kingdom was Northumbria, the area between the Humber River and the Scottish border. By A.D. 700 the Northumbrians had developed a respectable civilization, the finest in Europe. It is sometimes called the Northumbrian Renaissance, and it was the first of the several renaissances through which Europe struggled upward out of the ruins of the Roman Empire. It was in this period that the best of the Old English literature was written, including the epic poem *Beowulf*.

In the eighth century, Northumbrian power declined, and the center of influence moved southward to Mercia, the kingdom of the Midlands. A century later the center shifted again, and Wessex, the country of the West Saxons, became the leading power. The most famous king of the West Saxons was Alfred the Great, who reigned in the second half of the ninth century, dying in 901. He was famous not only as a military man and administrator but also as a champion of learning. He founded and supported schools and translated or caused to be translated many books from Latin into English. At this time also much of the Northumbrian literature of two centuries earlier was copied in West Saxon. Indeed, the great bulk of Old English writing which has come down to us is in the West Saxon dialect of 900 or later.

In the military sphere, Alfred's great accomplishment was his successful opposition to the viking invasions. In the ninth and tenth centuries, the Norsemen emerged in their ships from their homelands in Denmark and the Scandinavian peninsula. They traveled far and attacked and plundered at will and almost with impunity. They ravaged Italy and Greece, settled in France, Russia, and Ireland, colonized Iceland and Greenland, and discovered America several centuries before Columbus. Nor did they overlook England.

After many years of hit-and-run raids, the Norsemen landed an army on the east coast of England in the year 866. There was nothing much to oppose them except the Wessex power led by Alfred. The long struggle ended in 877 with a treaty by which a line was drawn roughly from the northwest of England to the southeast. On the eastern side of the line Norse rule was to prevail. This was called the Danelaw. The western side was to be governed by Wessex.

The linguistic result of all this was a considerable injection of Norse into the English language. Norse was at this time not so different from English as Norwegian or Danish is now. Probably speakers of English could understand, more or less, the language of the newcomers who had moved into eastern England. At any rate, there was considerable interchange and word borrowing. Examples of Norse words in the English language are *sky, give, law, egg, outlaw, leg, ugly, scant, sly, crawl, scowl, take, thrust.* There are hundreds more. We have even borrowed some pronouns from Norse—*they, their,* and *them.* These words were borrowed first by the eastern and northern dialects and then in the course of hundreds of years made their way into English generally.

It is supposed also—indeed, it must be true—that the Norsemen influenced the sound structure and the grammar of English. But this is hard to demonstrate in detail.

We may now have an example of Old English. The favorite illustration is the Lord's Prayer, since it needs no translation. This has come to us in several different versions. Here is one:

> Fæder ure þu ðe eart on heofonum si þin nama gehalgod. Tobecume þin rice. Gewurðe þin willa on eorðan swa swa on heofonum. Urne gedæghwamlican hlaf syle us to dæg. And forgyf us ure gyltas swa swa we forgyfaþ urum gyltendum. And ne gelæd þu us on costnunge ac alys us of yfele. Soðlice.

Some of the differences between this and Modern English are merely differences in orthography. For instance, the sign æ is what Old English writers used for a vowel sound like that in modern *hat* or *and.* The *th* sounds or modern *thin* or *then* are represented in Old English by *þ* or *ð*. But of course there are many differences in sound too. *Ure* is the ancestor of modern *our*, but the first vowel was like that in *too* or *ooze*. *Hlaf* is modern *loaf;* we have dropped the *h* sound and changed the vowel, which in *hlaf* was pronounced something like the vowel in *father*. Old English had some sounds which we do not have. The sound represented by *y* does not occur in Modern English. If you pronounce the vowel in *bit* with your lips rounded, you may approach it.

In grammar, Old English was much more highly inflected than Modern English is. That is, there were more case endings for nouns, more person and number endings for verbs, a more complicated pronoun system, various endings for adjectives, and so on. Old English nouns had four cases—nominative, genitive, dative, accusative. Adjectives had five—all these and an instrumental case besides. Present-day English has only two cases for nouns—common case and possessive case. Adjectives now have no case system at all. On the other hand, we now use a more rigid word order and more structure words (prepositions, auxiliaries, and the like) to express relationships than Old English did.

Some of this grammar we can see in the Lord's Prayer. *Heofonum*, for instance, is a dative plural; the nominative singular was *heofon*. *Urne* is an accusative singular; the nominative is *ure*. In *urum gyltendum* both words are dative plural. *Forgyfaþ* is the third person plural form of the verb. Word order is different: "urne gedæghwamlican hlaf syle us" in place of "Give us our daily bread." And so on.

In vocabulary Old English is quite different from Modern English. Most of the Old English words are what we may call native English: that is, words which have not been borrowed from other languages but which have been a part of English ever since English was a part of Indo-European. Old English did certainly contain borrowed words. We have seen that many borrowings were coming in from Norse. Rather large numbers had been borrowed from Latin, too. Some of these were taken while the Anglo-Saxons were still on the Continent (*cheese, butter, bishop, kettle,* etc.); a larger number came into English after the Conversion (*angel, candle, priest, martyr, radish, oyster, purple, school, spend,* etc.). But the great majority of Old English words were native English.

Now, on the contrary, the majority of words in English are borrowed, taken mostly from Latin and French. Of the words in *The American College Dictionary* only about 14 percent are native. Most of these, to be sure, are common, high-frequency words—*the, of, I, and, because, man, mother, road,* etc.; of the thousand most common words in Eng-

lish, some 62 percent are native English. Even so, the modern vocabulary is very much Latinized and Frenchified. The Old English
vocabulary was not.

Sometime between the years 1000 and 1200 various important
changes took place in the structure of English, and Old English became
Middle English. The political event which facilitated these changes
was the Norman Conquest. The Normans, as the name shows, came
originally from Scandinavia. In the early tenth century they established themselves in northern France, adopted the French language,
and developed a vigorous kingdom and a very passable civilization.
In the year 1066, led by Duke William, they crossed the Channel and
made themselves masters of England. For the next several hundred
years, England was ruled by kings whose first language was French.

One might wonder why, after the Norman Conquest, French did not
become the national language, replacing English entirely. The reason
is that the Conquest was not a national migration, as the earlier Anglo-
Saxon invasion had been. Great numbers of Normans came to England, but they came as rulers and landlords. French became the language of the court, the language of the nobility, the language of polite
society, the language of literature. But it did not replace English as the
language of the people. There must always have been hundreds of
towns and villages in which French was never heard except when
visitors of high station passed through.

But English, though it survived as the national language, was profoundly changed after the Norman Conquest. Some of the changes—
in sound structure and grammar—would no doubt have taken place
whether there had been a Conquest or not. Even before 1066 the case
system of English nouns and adjectives was becoming simplified; people came to rely more on word order and prepositions than on inflectional endings to communicate their meanings. The process was
speeded up by sound changes which caused many of the endings to
sound alike. But no doubt the Conquest facilitated the change. German, which didn't experience a Norman Conquest, is today rather
highly inflected compared to its cousin English.

But it is in vocabulary that the effects of the Conquest are most obvious. French ceased, after a hundred years or so, to be the native
language of very many people in England, but it continued—and continues still—to be a zealously cultivated second language, the mirror of
elegance and civilization. When one spoke English, one introduced not
only French ideas and French things but also their French names. This

was not only easy but socially useful. To pepper one's conversation with French expressions was to show that one was well-bred, elegant, *au courant*. The last sentence shows that the process is not yet dead. By using *au courant* instead of, say, *abreast of things*, the writer indicates that he is no dull clod who knows only English but an elegant person aware of how things are done in *le haut monde*.

Thus French words came into English, all sorts of them. There were words to do with government: *parliament, majesty, treaty, alliance, tax, government;* church words: *parson, sermon, baptism, incense, crucifix, religion;* words for foods: *veal, beef, mutton, bacon, jelly, peach, lemon, cream, biscuit;* colors: *blue, scarlet, vermilion;* household words: *curtain, chair, lamp, towel, blanket, parlor;* play words: *dance, chess, music, leisure, conversation;* literary words: *story, romance, poet, literary;* learned words: *study, logic, grammar, noun, surgeon, anatomy, stomach;* just ordinary words of all sorts: *nice, second, very, age, bucket, gentle, final, fault, flower, cry, count, sure, move, surprise, plain.*

All these and thousands more poured into the English vocabulary between 1100 and 1500, until at the end of that time many people must have had more French words than English at their command. This is not to say that English became French. English remained English in sound structure and in grammar, though these also felt the ripples of French influence. The very heart of the vocabulary, too, remained English. Most of the high-frequency words—the pronouns, the prepositions, the conjunctions, the auxiliaries, as well as a great many ordinary nouns and verbs and adjectives—were not replaced by borrowings.

Middle English, then, was still a Germanic language, but it differed from Old English in many ways. The sound system and the grammar changed a good deal. Speakers made less use of case systems and other inflectional devices and relied more on word order and structure words to express their meanings. This is often said to be a simplification, but it isn't really. Languages don't become simpler; they merely exchange one kind of complexity for another. Modern English is not a simple language, as any foreign speaker who tries to learn it will hasten to tell you.

For us Middle English is simpler than Old English just because it is closer to Modern English. It takes three or four months at least to learn to read Old English prose and more than that for poetry. But a week of good study should put one in touch with the Middle English poet Chaucer. Indeed, you may be able to make some sense of Chaucer straight off, though you would need instruction in pronuncia-

tion to make it sound like poetry. Here is a famous passage from the
General Prologue to the Canterbury Tales, fourteenth century:

> Ther was also a nonne, a Prioresse,
> That of hir smyling was ful symple and coy,
> Hir gretteste ooth was but by Seinte Loy,
> And she was cleped Madame Eglentyne.
> Ful wel she song the service dyvyne,
> Entuned in hir nose ful semely.
> And Frenshe she spak ful faire and fetisly,
> After the scole of Stratford-atte-Bowe,
> For Frenshe of Parys was to hir unknowe.

Sometime between 1400 and 1600 English underwent a couple of
sound changes which made the language of Shakespeare quite different
from that of Chaucer. Incidentally, these changes contributed much
to the chaos in which English spelling now finds itself.

One change was the elimination of a vowel sound in certain unstressed positions at the end of words. For instance, the words *name,
stone, wine, dance* were pronounced as two syllables by Chaucer but as
just one by Shakespeare. The *e* in these words became, as we say,
"silent." But it wasn't silent for Chaucer; it represented a vowel sound.
So also the words *laughed, seemed, stored* would have been pronounced
by Chaucer as two-syllable words. The change was an important one
because it affected thousands of words and gave a different aspect to
the whole language.

The other change is what is called the Great Vowel Shift. This was
a systematic shifting of half a dozen vowels and diphthongs in stressed
syllables. For instance, the word *name* had in Middle English a
vowel something like that in the modern word *father; wine* had the
vowel of modern *mean; he* was pronounced something like modern *hey;
mouse* sounded like *moose; moon* had the vowel of *moan.* Again the
shift was thoroughgoing and affected all the words in which these
vowel sounds occurred. Since we still keep the Middle English system
of spelling these words, the differences between Modern English and
Middle English are often more real than apparent.

The vowel shift has meant also that we have come to use an entirely
different set of symbols for representing vowel sounds than is used by
writers of such languages as French, Italian, or Spanish, in which no
such vowel shift occurred. If you come across a strange word—say,
bine—in an English book, you will pronounce it according to the English system, with the vowel of *wine* or *dine.* But if you read *bine* in a

French, Italian, or Spanish book, you will pronounce it with the vowel of *mean* or *seen*.

These two changes, then, produced the basic differences between Middle English and Modern English. But there were several other developments that had an effect upon the language. One was the invention of printing, an invention introduced into England by William Caxton in the year 1475. Where before books had been rare and costly, they suddenly became cheap and common. More and more people learned to read and write. This was the first of many advances in communication which have worked to unify languages and to arrest the development of dialect differences, though of course printing affects writing principally rather than speech. Among other things it hastened the standardization of spelling.

The period of Early Modern English—that is, the sixteenth and seventeenth centuries—was also the period of the English Renaissance, when people developed, on the one hand, a keen interest in the past and, on the other, a more daring and imaginative view of the future. New ideas multiplied, and new ideas meant new language. Englishmen had grown accustomed to borrowing words from French as a result of the Norman Conquest; now they borrowed from Latin and Greek. As we have seen, English had been raiding Latin from Old English times and before, but now the floodgates really opened, and thousands of words from the classical languages poured in. *Pedestrian, bonus, anatomy, contradict, climax, dictionary, benefit, multiply, exist, paragraph, initiate, scene, inspire* are random examples. Probably the average educated American today has more words from French in his vocabulary than from native English sources, and more from Latin than from French.

The greatest writer of the Early Modern English period is of course Shakespeare, and the best-known book is the King James Version of the Bible, published in 1611. The Bible (if not Shakespeare) has made many features of Early Modern English perfectly familiar to many people down to present times, even though we do not use these features in present-day speech and writing. For instance, the old pronouns *thou* and *thee* have dropped out of use now, together with their verb forms, but they are still familiar to us in prayer and in Biblical quotation: "Whither thou goest, I will go." Such forms as *hath* and *doth* have been replaced by *has* and *does;* "Goes he hence tonight?" would now be "Is he going away tonight?"; Shakespeare's "Fie on't, sirrah" would be "Nuts to that, Mac." Still, all these expressions linger with us because of the power of the works in which they occur.

It is not always realized, however, that considerable sound changes have taken place between Early Modern English and the English of the present day. Shakespearian actors putting on a play speak the words, properly enough, in their modern pronunciation. But it is very doubtful that this pronunciation would be understood at all by Shakespeare. In Shakespeare's time, the word *reason* was pronounced like modern *raisin; face* had the sound of modern *glass;* the *l* in *would, should, palm* was pronounced. In these points and a great many others the English language has moved a long way from what it was in 1600.

The history of English since 1700 is filled with many movements and countermovements, of which we can notice only a couple. One of these is the vigorous attempt made in the eighteenth century, and the rather half-hearted attempts made since, to regulate and control the English language. Many people of the eighteenth century, not understanding very well the forces which govern language, proposed to polish and prune and restrict English, which they felt was proliferating too wildly. There was much talk of an academy which would rule on what people could and could not say and write. The academy never came into being, but the eighteenth century did succeed in establishing certain attitudes which, though they haven't had much effect on the development of the language itself, have certainly changed the native speaker's feeling about the language.

In part a product of the wish to fix and establish the language was the development of the dictionary. The first English dictionary was published in 1603; it was a list of 2500 words briefly defined. Many others were published with gradual improvements until Samuel Johnson published his *English Dictionary* in 1755. This, steadily revised, dominated the field in England for nearly a hundred years. Meanwhile in America, Noah Webster published his dictionary in 1828, and before long dictionary publishing was a big business in this country. The last century has seen the publication of one great dictionary: the twelve-volume *Oxford English Dictionary,* compiled in the course of seventy-five years through the labors of many scholars. We have also, of course, numerous commercial dictionaries which are as good as the public wants them to be if not, indeed, rather better.

Another product of the eighteenth century was the invention of "English grammar." As English came to replace Latin as the language of scholarship it was felt that one should also be able to control and dissect it, parse and analyze it, as one could Latin. What happened in practice was that the grammatical description that applied to Latin was removed and superimposed on English. This was silly, because English is an entirely different kind of language, with its own forms and signals and ways of producing meaning. Nevertheless, English grammars on the Latin model were worked out and taught in the schools. In many schools they are still being taught. This activity is not often popular with school children, but it is sometimes an interesting and instructive exercise in logic. The principal harm in it is that it has tended to keep people from being interested in English and has obscured the real features of English structure.

But probably the most important force on the development of English in the modern period has been the tremendous expansion of English-speaking peoples. In 1500 English was a minor language, spoken by a few people on a small island. Now it is perhaps the greatest language of the world, spoken natively by over a quarter of a billion people and as a second language by many millions more. When we speak of English now, we must specify whether we mean American English, British English, Australian English, Indian English, or what, since the differences are considerable. The American cannot go to England or the Englishman to America confident that he will always understand and be understood. The Alabaman in Iowa or the Iowan in Alabama shows himself a foreigner every time he speaks. It is only because communication has become fast and easy that English in this period of its expansion has not broken into a dozen mutually unintelligible languages.

THE LATIN IN ENGLISH
James Greenough and G. L. Kittredge

English began to borrow words from the Latin before there was any English. *Street* (L. *strata* [*via*], 'a paved road'), *wall* (L. *vallum*), *chalk* (L. *calx, calcis,* 'lime'), and a few other terms entered the West Germanic dialects before the Anglo-Saxon Conquest of Britain. A few others were learned by the invaders from the Britons, who had been Roman colonists for three or four hundred years. Among these were *port* (L. *portus*) and *-chester, -caster* (L. *castra,* 'camp'), as seen in the name of the County of *Chester,* and in *Silchester, Lancaster,* etc. The conversion of the invaders to Christianity immediately brought in a number of religious and ecclesiastical words, like *pope, bishop, monk,* *nun.* From this time to the present, the borrowing of Latin words has gone on incessantly. We have seen that this is true of the technical dialects of divinity, philosophy, law, and natural science. But the influence of Latin is not confined to the technical vocabulary. It is felt in almost every sentence that we utter. It pervades the whole system of English speech.

The relations between French and Latin on the one hand, and English and French on the other, make the influence of Latin on English extremely complex. In outline, however, the subject may be easily grasped.

One fact of cardinal importance should be kept constantly in mind. In the eighth century, when Anglo-Saxon was developing a written literature, every educated Englishman spoke and wrote Latin as easily as he spoke and wrote his mother tongue. Indeed, the ability to use Latin freely was, until a comparatively recent period, the chief distinguishing mark of an educated man. Hence in all the earlier periods of our language, anybody who was learned enough to borrow a Latin word at all, was sufficiently familiar with that language to borrow the word in conversation as well as from the written page. This significant fact is often lost sight of.

Before the Norman Conquest, then, a good many Latin words had been introduced into English, either orally or with the pen. Many of these disappeared when the literary West Saxon went to pieces, but a few have survived and are still in use.

After the Conquest, as we have seen, French words began to come into our language,—first from Norman French, and afterwards, in much larger numbers, from the Central dialect, the 'French of Paris' which Chaucer's Prioress had never learned. The Norman-French words which became English were mostly 'popular' from the outset. They include such simple terms as *peace, tower, castle, grief, prison, court, countess,* and the like, which are indistinguishable in the minds of all English-speaking persons from the commonest words of native origin. Later, from 1300 on, there took place a wholesale importation of words from Central French, and to this the large proportion of French words in our language is chiefly due. This importation was made by Englishmen to whom French was almost a second mother tongue, and was therefore effected, to a considerable extent, through oral rather than written borrowing. Yet many French words came in through literary channels as well. Now, all literary Englishmen in the fourteenth and fifteenth centuries knew a good deal of Latin. Gower, for instance, wrote three long poems,—one in English, one in French, and one in

Latin,—and handled the three languages with equal facility. Thus the same persons who were borrowing from French were at the same time borrowing from Latin, and, since French itself is only Latin in a corrupt form, it is often impossible to determine from which of the two languages a particular word was directly taken. The mere fact that the *form* of the English word is rather French than Latin does not settle the question. For the form which a Latin word assumed when it became English was frequently determined by the habits of the French language. Thus our word *figure* is ultimately derived from the Latin *figura*, of which the French *figure* is a clipped form. It is probable that we took the word directly from the French. Yet this is not certain. For any English writer who had wished to introduce the Latin *figura* into the vernacular would at once have modified the word after the French fashion. Thus, whether *figure* came from Latin directly or from French, it would inevitably have taken the same form in English: namely, *figure*. *Texture*, for example, is known to have come directly from the Latin *textura;* yet it has been remade, after the French model, as set by *figure* and other words already in the language, so that, so far as appears from its form, it might perfectly well have come from the French *texture*. So *flexure*, from the Latin *flexura*, has a similar form, as if it came from a French word *flexure*, though, in fact, no such word as *flexure* exists in the French language. How strong was this tendency to follow the French fashion in adapting words from the Latin may be seen in Chaucer's forms for proper names. The Old French form for *Cato* was *Catoun*, and this is regularly used by Chaucer and his contemporaries. So Chaucer writes *Achilles* and *Achille, Pandarus* and *Pandare*, indifferently. Indeed, when a word existed in both Latin and French, it must often have been impossible for the borrower himself to tell from which language he was taking it.

This state of things continued through the fourteenth and fifteenth centuries. A huge number of words came in from both Latin and French, and we are frequently at a loss to distinguish between them. In doubtful cases, however, the distinction is of almost no importance, since, even if the word passed through the French, it is none the less Latin, and was felt as quite as much Latin as French, whatever its immediate source may have been.

In many cases, however, it is easy to distinguish a word borrowed from the French. Thus we see at a glance that *deceive* does not come directly from the Latin *decipere*, but from its French form *décevoir*. So of *voyage* from Fr. *voyage* (L. *viaticum*), *poison* from Fr. *poison* (L. *potionem*), *venge* from Fr. *venger* (L. *vindicare*), *point* from Fr. *point*

(L. *punctum*). In these examples, and many others, the French form
has wandered so far from the Latin that doubt is impossible. This
points to an important observation. French is, in the main, the vulgar
Latin of the Gallic provincials in the shape in which centuries of decay
have left it, just as Spanish is the Latin of the provincials of Spain, and
Italian the remainder Latin of the Tuscans. By the ninth century this
Gallic Latin had become so different from its prototype as to constitute
a distinct language. There were, then, two kinds of Latin in Gaul at
this time, the rustic and debased dialect, which we may, with a slight
anticipation, call 'French,' and the educated Latin of the schools. Both
had a continuous tradition from Roman times; but the former came
from a vernacular and untutored tradition, the latter from the learned
tradition of the church and the schools, identical with the scholar's
dialect throughout the Western World. From the ninth to the twelfth
century the vernacular changed rapidly. Recognized as a genuine
language, not a mere *patois*, it received literary cultivation, which has
ever since continued, until French has become the 'polite language' of
Europe. With this cultivation, a multitude of words were borrowed
from the classic Latin by educated men, exactly as was the case with
English, and these 'learned' words are close to the Latin, whereas the
'popular' words that come from the rustic tradition usually bear a much
less distinct resemblance to the Latin. Thus *sevrer* (our *sever*) and
séparer both represent the Latin *separare*, but *sevrer* is the 'popular' or
continuous vernacular form, and *séparer* a 'learned' or literary borrowing. Again, *sûreté* (older *seürté*) and *sécurité* both come from L. *secu-
ritatem*, but *sûreté* is 'popular' and *sécurité* is 'learned.' We could
never hesitate to derive our *surety* from the French *sûreté*. *Security*,
however, might come either from *sécurité*, or, as is more likely in this
instance, directly from the Latin, the form which it takes being influenced by *surety* and other similar words which we have taken from the
French.

These considerations not only serve to illustrate the difference between learned and popular words (to which we have already given some
attention), but they suggest the complexity of the influences which
Latin, both as a learned and as a popular tongue, has had upon the
language which we speak, or, in other words, the continuity and complexity of the civilization which the English language expresses to the
student of philology.[1]

---

[1] We may remark, in passing, that nearly all the English words that are from
Norman French are from popular forms, whereas the later borrowings include
many learned terms.

If we pass on to the sixteenth century, we find the relation of French and Latin to our vocabulary quite different from that in the fourteenth and early fifteenth. The time of wholesale borrowing from the French has passed, but Latin borrowing is more active than ever. It is, however, distinctly *learned* borrowing. The Revival of Learning has sent men directly to the classics. Theological and philosophical studies are also pursued with vigor, and this means an immersal in Latin. Latin is still the scholar's language, but to speak French has become a mere accomplishment (as it is to-day) and the men who are adding words to our vocabulary no longer feel that French and Latin are equally near to them. These are 'learned times,' and a multitude of words are taken directly from the Latin, with no thought of their French relations. The fashion of reforming such words after the French model is still in force, for it has become a law of our speech, but we no longer hesitate to which language to refer an ambiguous form: we refer it to Latin without hesitation. In fact, the best test in all these doubtful cases is the age of the word in English. If it came in after 1500, the chances are overwhelmingly in favor of its having come directly from the Latin unless it bears an unmistakably French imprint. This learned borrowing from Latin went on vigorously till very recently, and is still common, as we have seen, in the technical vocabulary of the sciences. It brought in a multitude of useful words, and tended especially to enrich our language in its means of expressing shades of thought and securing variety of expression in general. But it was carried to pedantic lengths, and in the eighteenth and nineteenth centuries there was a revolt against it, which has restored the equilibrium between the several main components of the English language. The borrowings from French since 1500 have been scanty compared with those that preceded and with the borrowings from Latin. Yet a good many words have come in from that language,—especially military terms and society phrases. The latter have manifested themselves particularly in the times from the Restoration to the present day, during which French has been the language of diplomacy and polite society, as well as a general medium of communication for travellers of all nationalities.

In addition to the great stock of Latin words that have entered our language through the French, or under its influence, we have a huge mass of words and phrases taken directly from the Latin without change. Few persons realize the extent of this element in our vocabulary, and fewer still its significance.

A number of examples will bring out instantly some of the main points: *superior, minimum, vim, bonus, stimulus, animal, folio, item, nostrum, recipe, veto, vacuum, inertia, innuendo, dictum, alibi, errata, interim, memorandum, affidavit, via* (in 'via New York'). Here we have a score of words taken bodily from the Latin without change. Yet they are undoubtedly English and in common use. One of them (*vim*) is so very 'popular' as to be almost slangy. Their diversity of form is also remarkable. They represent almost every turn and twist of Latin inflection. We find the first, second, and third declensions of nouns, all three genders, and both numbers. Three cases appear (nominative, accusative, and ablative), a verb, two perfect participles, a gerundive, a gerund in *o*. There are masculine and neuter adjectives, the comparative and superlative degrees, a possessive pronoun, three adverbs, the present and perfect indicative, and an imperative. In short, a boy who can explain all the Latin forms involved in this short list of thoroughly English words need fear no examination in Latin accidence.

This great diversity of form is highly significant. It suggests that we owe many words of this class, not to deliberate borrowing of a learned or literary character, but to the haphazard linguistic processes of conversation and daily life. Nor should we be surprised at this. Latin, as we have observed already, was a second vernacular to educated men for many centuries. Not only was it the language of the learned professions, but it long served as a means of communication among all but the positively illiterate. To learn to read was to learn to read Latin. Grammar was Latin grammar. Roger Ascham remarks in a matter-of-fact way that it would, of course, have been easier for him to write his Toxophilus in Latin than in English. Legal documents, even of the most ordinary kind, were indited in that language. So were records of every sort, not only those of the state, but the journals of guilds and trade-companies. All important accounts were also in Latin. Queen Elizabeth talked Latin with foreign ambassadors; Cromwell had Milton for his Latin secretary.

All this means that to a large fraction of the community Latin terms were, and always have been, actually the only familiar terms for certain ideas and certain things. This is still true in a measure, as with lawyers, for instance, and physicians; but it becomes more and more significant as we trace our history back to mediæval times. It was as natural for all persons who had occasion to mention such things, to use the Latin words for them when they were talking English as when they were talking Latin. Even to-day, when the doctors talk little Latin, and write it no more than they can help, it is far easier for them to speak of the *sequelae* of a disease than its 'consequences,' and it would be mere affectation if they avoided such terms as *prophylaxis* and *diagnosis*, or tried to translate them into English. We have seen how easily learned words pass into the ordinary vocabulary and become popular. A man does not use vernacular words merely because they are vernacular, but because they are the words that he hears; and few Englishmen of any period have been so out of contact with the Church or the courts, with medicine or the arts, as not to be influenced by the language of those who are professionally identified with such pursuits. The habit, once established, propagated itself, as habits do, and became one of the regular tendencies of our language. The borrowings in question, then, are of all dates, remote and recent.

A moment's consideration of some of our examples will enforce what has just been said. *Recipe* is an imperative directing the apothecary to 'take' such and such drugs and compound them; it is the physician's formula in beginning a prescription, and has come to be the name of the document itself. *Nostrum* means 'our own' (or 'my own'), that is, 'a proprietary remedy,' unknown to the profession in general,—hence, a 'quack medicine.' *Innuendo* is the gerund of *innuo*, 'to suggest,' used as a present participle to mean 'suggesting' or 'signifying'; it has passed from the language of legal documents into its familiar use in ordinary speech. *Folio* is the ablative of *folium*, and means, literally, 'on such and such a *leaf*' (in a written document); it is thus the common term in referring to a particular page, and, being constantly heard in the ablative, has become English in that case-form. *Memorandum* (often abbreviated to *mem.*) is the gerundive of *memoro*, 'remember,' and means '(that which) must be borne in mind.' *Item*, 'also,' is an old accountant's term. It was formerly prefixed to all the items in a bill or inventory except the first,[2] but gradually it lost its specific sense of 'also' and came to be used with them all; hence its meaning as an English word. *Bonus* is a recent addition to our vocabulary, and shows the persistence of the influences that we are studying. Perhaps it comes from the stock exchange. It means 'a good thing,' something 'to the good,'—and ought, strictly speaking, to be the neuter *bonum*. Its recent or jocose origin is indicated by this error in gender. Compare *premium*, which (being an older word in English) shows a correct form.

The genuinely vernacular nature of these words is emphasized when we pass to whole phrases, which have been taken into our language with the greatest freedom. No one when he says *ex parte*, or *post mortem*, or *bona fide*, is conscious of talking a foreign language; for these phrases and scores of others have become a part of the vernacular by inheritance and constant use, and although their home is Latin,

2 Which was *imprimis*, 'first.'

they are as much English as if they had been translated, as they often are. No one can say that *dividers* is any more English than *divisor* The only difference is that *divisor* is orginally a technical term, Latin in form, which the progress of education has made known to every schoolboy, while *dividers* has been made over by means of an English termination and then specialized into a technicality. It is even doubtful which word is more vernacular to-day.

Subpoena has become an English noun and is used as a verb as well. It is merely the law term *sub poena,* 'under penalty.' Still more vernacular is the verb to *nonplus.* It is originally a term of scholastic disputation. A man was 'at a non plus' when he had 'no more' to say.

Sometimes such phrases are translated, but often the translation is more artificial—less English, indeed—than the Latin itself. An '*ex cathedra* opinion' is a perfectly natural phrase for one delivered authoritatively, but we should attach no such meaning to the English 'from the chair,' except by thinking of the Latin. 'In the article of death' is a mere slavish rendering of *in articulo mortis.* In itself, it means nothing, for *article* has no such sense in our language, but we understand the phrase by association with the Latin original. Similarly, *sine die* is occasionally made into pigeon-English as 'without day.' So with the French *mariage de convenance,* 'an arranged marriage.' We sometimes translate it by 'marriage of convenience,' which has no sense in English except as it has acquired one by virtue of the French. 'Cela va sans dire' has given us 'That goes without saying,' though '*goes*' does not mean 'is valid,' 'holds,' nor does *saying* mean 'statement.' The English phrase is not very well established, but it is always understood, for our language is so tolerant of foreign phrases that anything will pass muster that suggests one.

'Generally speaking' is an idiom that gives the strict grammarian some trouble. For it is constantly used in apparent violation of the rule that the participle must have a noun to agree with: as, '*Generally speaking,* bank notes are as good as gold.' But all difficulty vanishes when we observe that the phrase is merely the Late Latin *generaliter loquendo,* for nobody expects the gerund to agree with a noun.[3]

Inclusive, in such phrases as 'pages thirty to thirty-three *inclusive,*' is a curious instance of a Latin word made English. It is really the

---

[3] *Considering, regarding,* and the like, are related to this use, but are commonly disposed of by calling them 'prepositions.' Similarly the 'preposition' *notwithstanding* is a mere translation of the Latin ablative absolute (*non obstante*). Cf. Bishop Andrewes (in 1620): "For either of these *non obstante,* nay notwithstanding both these, she had the happiness to see His Angels." Ninety-six Sermons, ed. 1841, III, 5.

Latin adverb *inclusive,* 'inclusively,' and was felt as Latin in the six-teenth century (so also *exclusive*). [4] Probably it was first anglicized by a blunder, as we hear people pronounce *fide* as one syllable in *bona fide*. The possibility of the error, however, is strong evidence of the 'popularity' of such Latin phrases.

A remarkable bit of testimony consists in the habitual use of Latin abbreviations in English writing, and in the fact that these almost always suggest not the Latin words for which they stand, but the English equivalent. *£, s., d.* mean to everybody 'pounds,' 'shillings,' and 'pence'—not *librae, solidi,* and *denarii*. Falstaff's tavern-bill showed *ob. (obolus)* among its entries, but Prince Hal read it 'half-penny.' *Pp. (paginae)* means 'pages,' and *LL.B. (Legum Baccalaureus)* 'bachelor of laws,' to most of us, though the doubling of the letter to indicate a plural is not an English, but a Latin habit, and though *laws* is not a legitimate translation of *leges* in the sense of 'two kinds of law'—civil and canon. So *i.e. (id est)* is read 'that is,' e.g.' *(exempli gratia),* 'for example.' Now and then a foreigner in writing uses *f.e.* or *f.i.,* but we find it hard to guess that he means 'for example' or 'for instance,' though the Latin *e.g.* occasions us no difficulty. *Viz.* is a curious example. It is *videlicet* ('you may know,' 'to wit'), the *z* being not a *z* at all, but an old sign of abbreviation resembling that letter in shape. We seldom say *videlicet* nowadays, preferring 'namely' or 'to wit' (a translation of *scilicet,* for *scire licet*), and even *viz* is sometimes heard.

Again we constantly use the Roman numerals without thinking of the Latin words for which they stand, or remembering that accounts were kept in Latin down to a pretty recent date. Most striking of all is the sign &, which, though merely a short way of writing *et,* is always called 'and,' and used to be annexed to the English alphabet under that designation. *Ampersand,* the name for the sign, is a corruption of '*and* per se *and.*' *&c.* and *etc.,* then, both stand for *et cetera;* yet we commonly read the former 'and so forth,' and reserve the Latin phrase for the latter.

It would require a special treatise to exhaust the subject of Latin words in English. Enough has been said to explain their presence and to indicate the main channels through which they entered the language. Few persons realize the extent of our indebtedness. Computations have often been made, but they have usually been based on the English vocabulary as a whole or on the vocabulary of a particular author. If the former course is adopted, the question rises 'What is the whole

[4] See Andrewes, Ninety-six Sermons, ed. 1841, I, 27.

English vocabulary?' for every large dictionary contains a multitude of obsolete and technical terms that have no place in such a problem. If the works of a single author are taken as a basis, there are equally great objections to the method, though of a different kind. A better method is to see what proportion of the Latin vocabulary has passed into English. With this in view, we have counted the words beginning with *A* in Harper's Latin Dictionary (Andrews-Freund, revised by Lewis), excluding proper names, doublets, parts of verbs, and adverbs in *-e* and *-ter*. Of the three thousand words there catalogued, one hundred and fifty-four (or about one in twenty) have been adopted bodily into our language in some Latin form, and a little over five hundred have some English representative taken, or supposed to be taken, through the French. Thus we have in the English vocabulary about one in four or five of all the words found in the Latin lexicon under *A*. There is no reason to suppose that this proportion would not hold good approximately for the whole alphabet. No doubt some words have been included in this computation that should have been omitted, but others have just as certainly been overlooked, and no account has been made of Low and Middle Latin. Roughly speaking, then, we are safe in asserting that our language has appropriated a full quarter of the Latin vocabulary, besides what it has gained by transferring Latin meanings to native words. Our indebtedness to Greek is chiefly in the way of learned or scientific terms which have been borrowed in very recent times.

The extent of the French and Latin influence upon the English vocabulary makes our borrowings from other languages seem insignificant. The Celtic tongues have contributed very little, not because the Celts were exterminated, but partly because of the great dissimilarity between Celtic and Anglo-Saxon, partly because those Britons with whom the invaders had most intercourse had been Romanized to a considerable degree. *Bannock, bard, bog, brock* ('badger'), *brogue, down* ('hill'), *dun* ('dark-colored'), *glen, lad, loch, shamrock,* and *slogan* are specimens of the Celtic contingent in our language; but of these examples only *brock, dun,* and *down* go back to the Anglo-Saxon period.[5]

The Scandinavian influence is more important. It began as early as the ninth century, and was felt particularly in those northern and eastern districts in which there were Danish (or Norwegian) settle-

---

[5] *Basket* and *cradle* are often cited as Celtic words, but there is no evidence for such a derivation. *Crock* is doubtful. *Mop* may be from the French. *Bodkin, mattock,* and *slough* are of uncertain origin.

ments. Many Scandinavian words did not survive the Middle English period, except dialectically. Most of our Old Norse contingent came into English in oral intercourse, but a few terms have been borrowed in recent times by literary men (as, *skald, edda, viking, valkyrie, Norn*). Among the old borrowings are *aloft* (O.N. *ā lopte*, 'up in the air,' from O.N. *loptr*, for *loftr*, cognate with A.S. *lyft*, Ger. *Luft*), *call, cast, sky, take, wrong*.

The influence of Italian and Spanish upon our literature has been very great, but upon our vocabulary these languages have had no appreciable effect. The reason is plain. Before the time when such an influence could have been exerted, our language was already fully formed, and had adopted from French or Latin nearly all those terms which it might conceivably have borrowed from related Romance languages. Art and music have brought in a number of Italian terms, however; and Spanish has contributed *flotilla, grandee, junta, pronunciamento, renegade, siesta*, and a few others. A good many Spanish forms that were current in the sixteenth and seventeenth centuries have become obsolete.

Of the Semitic tongues, Hebrew and Arabic have made small contributions to our vocabulary. The Hebrew words are mostly biblical: as,—*cherub, seraph, shekel, hallelujah, mannah, Messiah*. Several of the Arabic words are connected with mathematics or chemistry,—sciences much cultivated by learned Arabs of the Middle Ages. Thus we have *algebra* (from the Arabic article *al*, 'the,' and *jebr*, 'reduction' [by equations]); *alkali* (from *al* and *qali*, 'ashes of the soda plant'); *alembic* (*anbīq*, from Gr. ἄμβιξ, *ámbix*, 'cup,' 'cap of a still'); *elixir* (from *al-iksīr*, 'the philosopher's stone,' from Greek ξηρός, *xērós*, 'dry,' since it was thought that this mysterious substance might be discovered in the form of a powder); *cipher* (from *çifr*, 'zero,' literally 'empty'). Other Arabic derivatives are *sofa, salaam* (literally 'peace'), *sherbet, admiral*. In *admiral* (formerly *amiral*), the final syllable is again the Arabic article, the word being a fragment of the phrase *amīr-al-bahr*, 'commander of the sea.'

The enterprising spirit of the English people and their fondness for travel and colonization, as well as the great development of their commerce, have brought in miscellaneous words from every quarter of the earth. No language is so hospitable as our own to these newcomers, perhaps because no other language already contains so many foreign elements. None of these borrowings, however, have affected the structure of our speech, since they have been for the most part simply the adoption of names for particular things. Thus we have *binnacle* and *dodo,* from Portuguese; *boor, brackish, hustle, isinglass, kink, knapsack, landscape, loiter, marline, slender, stove, yacht,* from Dutch or Low German; *bazaar* and *caravan,* from Persian; *polka,* from Polish; *hussar,* from Hungarian; *hominy, moccasin, tomahawk, squaw, wigwam,* from North American Indian; *tea, nankeen,* from Chinese; *taboo,* from Polynesian; *boomerang, kangaroo,* from native Australian, and so on. Such words enrich and diversify our vocabulary without essentially changing its character.

SOME CHARACTERISTICS OF AMERICAN ENGLISH AND THEIR BACKGROUNDS   *Thomas Pyles*

Our early settlers were not for the most part illiterate peasants speaking local dialects, but Englishmen of the upper-lower and lower-middle classes, with the prejudices and intolerances, linguistic as well as religious and economic, which are frequently attendant upon those stations in life. Though there were some dialect speakers among them, the greater part spoke the common speech of the regions to which they were native. This had been greatly influenced by the literary standard which had arisen in London and had come to be accepted in most parts of England, at least as a standard written language, by the latter part of the fifteenth century. But in their pronunciation and in their vocabularies they retained characteristics of the regions and even of the localities whence they sprang, for common speech is inevitably based upon folk speech.

About two-thirds of the earliest settlers around Massachusetts Bay hailed from the southeastern counties of England—many from East Anglia, which was the principal center of Puritanism in England. With them came families from Yorkshire, Lancashire, and even farther north, with more than a sprinkling of West Countrymen. It is not of course suggested that these folk from the north and the west of England were immediately upon their arrival on these shores to adapt their regional usage to that of southeastern England, but it is certain that a basically southeastern English type of speech was to prevail in Massachusetts.

From the small settlements around Massachusetts Bay, colonists spread throughout New England and into the Middle Atlantic states.

From *Words and Ways of American English,* by Thomas Pyles. Copyright 1952 by Random House, Inc. Reprinted by permission.

Eastern New Jersey was early dominated by them, and, after the Revolution, a large number of settlers migrated westward from Connecticut into New York, where the Dutch had never actually been very numerous, and into northern Pennsylvania, the Western Reserve on Lake Erie, and ultimately the Great Lakes area. New Englanders not many generations removed from transplanted Old Englanders carried westward with them their customs, their beliefs, their language and their place names. Hundreds of places throughout the Middle West were settled by families from western New England—mostly farming people, for eastern New England had in the meantime become largely mercantile and industrial. In the course of their migrations, these folk from western New England—using a development of an early type of Massachusetts Bay speech—mingled with the predominantly Scotch-Irish folk from Pennsylvania, from Kentucky, and from West Virginia who were in the great westward tide which followed the opening up of the Old Northwest Territory.

The middle colonies, with the exception of the southern sections of Maryland and Delaware, were settled by people whose speech was native to the north and, to some extent, the west of England. Pennsylvania was originally planned as a refuge for Quakers, some of whom also settled on the Delaware in western New Jersey. Since their sect had arisen in the north of England and found most of its early converts there and in the west, a large proportion of Penn's colonists probably came from these regions. The Society of Friends had not in the late seventeenth century acquired the intellectual and social prestige that it has in our own day. The speech of Penn's protégés, who were for the most part simple folk who had never been near a university and had had no contact with high life, obviously had a good many characteristics peculiar to the north and west of England, with pious overtones from the King James Bible.

Maryland was settled originally by English Roman Catholics, but all Trinitarian Christians were made to feel welcome in the colony. As a result of this enlightened policy—enlightened for those days, at any rate—it was soon swarming with Protestants. The northern and northwestern sections were later settled from Pennsylvania, and these sections are linguistically, and to a large extent culturally, quite distinct from the earlier settlement areas of the state.

The Scotch-Irish who, beginning about 1720, settled the back country were mostly descendants of lowland Scotsmen who had only a few generations earlier settled the northeastern part of Ireland. They were Calvinists, not to be confused with the Catholic Irish who emigrated

to this country in the following century. The fortunes of these Scotsmen in their Ulster home had been consistently bad; they had been the
victims of flint-hearted landlords, drought, sheep rot, and epidemics of
smallpox. The New World must have seemed a haven of hope to
them, as also to the Germans who were arriving at about the same
time, Protestant pietists from the Palatinate who had suffered religious,
political, and economic persecution in their homeland.

These Germans, whose influence on our language has been principally confined to the sphere of vocabulary—and even here it has
been small—settled in the valleys of the Lehigh and the Susquehanna.
In a few of the communities of this region "Pennsylvania Dutch" (for
what might more accurately be called Pennsylvania German) may still
be heard. Benjamin Franklin computed that the Germans comprised
a third of the population of Pennsylvania in about 1750. Many of
these, and most of their descendants, were to acquire the northern
English speech of their Scotch-Irish neighbors.

Linguistic geography has made clear the direct relationship of dialect areas to settlement areas, as well as to trade areas and culture
areas. In his *Word Geography of the Eastern United States* Professor
Kurath has demonstrated the existence of a speech area, the Midland,
separating the North from the South—an area which on the coast
stretches only from the southern half of New Jersey to midway through
Delaware. Its boundaries, which are those of the Pennsylvania settlement area, expand considerably as one travels inland: the northern
boundary, bisecting New Jersey, swings to the northwest and runs
along the northern part of Pennsylvania; the southern boundary, bisecting Delaware, goes through northern Maryland and turns south-
westward to run along the crest of the Blue Ridge in Virginia. This
concept of a Midland speech area separating North from South fits the
historical facts better than the older concept of American English as
comprising New England (sometimes called Eastern), Southern, and a
so-called General American.

Many of the Scotch-Irish and some Palatinate Germans as well
pushed into the hinterlands of the South Atlantic states in the half-
century preceding the Revolution. The speech of the upper Potomac
and the Shenandoah valleys, of West Virginia, and of the western
Carolinas consequently has many features in common with that of the
upper Ohio Valley, the Susquehanna Valley, and the Delaware Valley
—all together constituting the Midland, though it is quite possible that,
after further examination and evaluation of the data, what is now designated the South Midland (the southern Appalachians and the Blue

Ridge south of the James River) may have to be regarded as a subarea of the South.

Throughout this whole vast Midland area the *r* sound is retained in *farm, board, beard, door, father,* and the like, as in northern British English, though it has been considerably weakened. In the leveling-out process which apparently occurred as a result of the frequent intermingling of different elements in our population, the trilled *r*'s of the Scotch-Irish seem in a few generations to have toned down to the sound presently heard in the Midland and its western and southwestern extensions as well as in its northwestern settlement area. It may well be that the present Midland *r* in such words is at the same stage as the *r* which must previously have existed in eastern New England and the coastal South and which was subsequently lost, probably under British influence. In any case, it is only a slightly less obvious means of differentiation from present-day eastern New England and tidewater Southern speech than the trilled *r* would be.

The Midland is also set off from other regions by its use of certain words, usually having to do with the house and farm and invariably simple and homely. It is, in fact, more sharply differentiated from the North in this respect than in pronunciation; for instance, Northern *pail* and *faucet* are in the Midland *bucket* and *spicket (spigot)* respectively (as also in the South). *Skillet* is primarily a regional word of the Midland, though it has spread elsewhere; in the North and a large part of the coastal South the utensil is usually called a *spider,* though the trade term *frying pan* may be heard in towns and cities all over the country. Midland cows are called by shouting *sook* or *sookie;* in the North the call is *boss, co-boss, come boss, co,* or *coaf;* in the South it is *co-wench, co-inch,* or *co-ee.* The construction *I want in* (or *out* or *off)* is, according to the records of the *Linguistic Atlas of the United States and Canada,* in frequent use in the Midland area, though avoided by educated speakers. This construction is not a Pennsylvania Germanism, as has been supposed, though its agreement with the German idiom may have aided somewhat in its preservation in German settlement areas; it occurs in older English and was presumably transmitted to this country in the northern English speech of the Scotch-Irish, who subsequently carried it with them in their western migrations.

To turn now to the settlement history of the South, the Virginia settlers were a motley group of royalists, roisterers, blackguards, indentured servants, Commonwealth soldiers, Puritans, and, painful as it is to contemplate, a good many transported criminals. Defoe's Moll Flanders, "twelve year a whore, five times a wife (whereof once to her

own brother), twelve year a thief, eight year a transported felon in
Virginia," is a fictitious character, but she probably did not altogether
lack real-life counterparts in the colony. Although people from all the
counties south of Yorkshire were well represented among them, more
than half of the colonists were from the southern part of England,
with London quite well represented. As in the Massachusetts Bay
colony, a type of speech basically southeastern English was to prevail
here.

The dissemination of the speech of the South Atlantic settlements
was similar to that of New England. Although there had been a good
many Puritans among its earliest settlers, the coastal South suffered
less from the Calvinistic *mythos* than had New England. Perhaps the
softer climate helped to mitigate the Puritan harshness; perhaps the
more productive soil; perhaps the arrival of large numbers of Cavalier
immigrants fleeing the military dictatorship of Cromwell. In any case,
by the early years of the eighteenth century the plantation system had
come into being in the Southern coastal areas, and with it an attitude
towards living unlike anything ever known before or since in this
country. Even when allowances are made for romancing, it remains
the most charming form of life that our country has ever known.
Nevertheless, the tidewater Southerners did some colonizing. Obviously, not all could be fortunate enough to live the gracious life
of the plantations. Shortly after the middle of the eighteenth century
a large number of emigrants from Virginia and the Carolinas joined
Oglethorpe's colonists in Georgia. In the early years of the nineteenth
century sons of planters from Virginia and the Carolinas carried their
Southern speech to the cotton lands of the Gulf States.

In the lands beyond the Appalachians to the south, other migrations
were taking place. Virginians, Marylanders, Pennsylvanians, and
North Carolinians settled in large numbers in Kentucky. Scotch-Irish
from the southern mountain country joined the French in Louisiana;
some of them pushed westward from the Appalachians to the Ozarks;
some got as far west as eastern Texas.

The Atlantic coastal area, extending from Maine to Georgia and
occupied at the time of the first Federal Census in 1790 by ninety-five
percent of our total population of about four million, thus formed the
mold from which have come all types of American speech. Its speech-
ways were, as we have seen, to be carried westward to the lands
beyond the Alleghenies and the Appalachians, and there transplanted.
New varieties of English which were blendings of the usages of western
New England, the large Pennsylvania settlement area, and the coastal

South, were to be developed in the course of that great westward migration which plays so important a part in American history.

Although there is evidence that the speech of the north and west of England was sufficiently noticeable to be used as a shibboleth in the colonial period, features of it have made their way into American English, and it has undoubtedly modified American speech considerably. But it should be constantly borne in mind that many, if not most, of the settlers from the north and the west of England did not speak local dialects, but rather regional variants of the London Standard, retaining unconsciously no doubt certain phonological features and word usages characteristic of their native regions. Many indentured servants were, incidentally, men of sufficient education to be employed as schoolmasters. Perhaps some among the great number of Scottish and Irish teachers who "have had no inconsiderable influence in the Middle States, upon our pronunciation and language," according to John Pickering in the *American Quarterly Review* for September, 1828, had been or were indentured.

Specific evidence is of course lacking as to the number of speakers of local dialects among our earliest settlers. There probably were not very many of them, despite the existence of a good many dialect words in unsophisticated American speech. In its grammatical forms and even in its pronunciation, the educated speech we use today resembles an older form of the English Standard to such an extent that we must conclude that those who did speak peasant dialects were persons of little prestige in the New World and consequently that their speech had little influence upon the development of American English other than to contribute a number of dialectal expressions to its vocabulary.

Patterns for the linguistically ambitious were furnished by the usage of the cities which sprang up along the coast and at the heads of navigation on rivers—notably Boston, New York, Philadelphia, Richmond, and Charleston. These cities, which are of great significance in the development of American English, were not only important centers of trade, but also seats of culture and fashion. By the rest of the country they were regarded much as London is regarded by the rest of England. From their bustling ports ships plied to England bearing the produce of the colonies and bringing back new goods and new settlers. Though immigration from England slackened somewhat after the middle of the seventeenth century, it never ceased altogether during the entire colonial period. It is likely that many of the later immigrants were people of a higher social and cultural level than the earlier settlers and that they brought with them the latest fashions in speech as in clothes.

In refinement and éclat, the cities set the tone for the back country. Language is an important part of the cultural and social equipment of a people, and these centers of wealth and high life became the mold of fashion linguistically as well as otherwise for their hinterlands. Consequently, the more or less localized expressions of the inland were in large part to give way to the usage of the cities. This must in turn have been much affected by the changing usage of England, as indicated by the fact that American English reflects so many of the changes which took place in British English during our colonial period —changes such as the shifting of the *ay* sound in words like *sea, peak, leap,* and the like, to the *ee* sound which they have in standard British and American English at present. Similarly, words with *oi, oy,* such as *boil, join, poison, hoist, boy* have had an identical development in British and American English. In the seventeenth and early eighteenth centuries these words were pronounced approximately as *bile, jine, pizen, hist* (riming with *iced*), and *bye*—pronunciations which survive in the speech of folk who live far from the centers of linguistic fashion. Toward the end of the eighteenth century this pronunciation gave way to that now usual in England and America alike. Except for the usage of simple people living in isolated regions, who have lacked any contact with British English since long before the sound shift took place, American English has here again chosen the same variant as British English.

On the other hand, changes which occurred in standard British English during the eighteenth century, such as the loss of preconsonantal and final *r* and the shift from "flat" to "broad" *a* in certain words, are not reflected in American English away from the Atlantic coast. Except for eastern New England and the coastal South, which seem to have followed the British practice, the *r* sound is regularly retained in American English. The British treatment of *a*, sometimes written *au*, before certain consonants and consonant combinations, as in *after, staff, ask, grasp, grass, path, past, command, aunt, dance,* and *half,* has likewise had no effect upon the natural speech of Americans outside eastern New England, eastern Virginia, and the Charleston area. All these words had the flat *a* in standard British English until the latter part of the eighteenth century, the broad *a* beloved of Anglophile Americans being up to that time considered low.

Evidence of this sort leads Professor Eilert Ekwall to conclude in his *American and British Pronunciation* (Upsala, 1946), that "educated

American pronunciation on the whole remains at the stage which British pronunciation had reached about the time of the Revolution, while modern British pronunciation has left that stage far behind." It is an attractive theory. Certainly there can be no doubt that for many details it holds true. There is ample evidence that American English preserves a good many pronunciations which were current in standard British English in the latter years of the eighteenth century. Although Ekwall is concerned only with pronunciation, his theory finds some support in vocabulary, for our use of many words can also be said to be about the same as British usage at the time of the Revolution.

Even though we are not able to determine its extent with perfect accuracy, we cannot doubt the existence of this influence from the mother country, an influence which continued throughout the colonial period. Nor can there be any reasonable doubt that it must be reckoned among the factors which have brought about the present homogeneity of American English.

There were also at work, in New England at least, such uniformizing agencies as the compulsory schools, with their spellers by Dilworth, Fenning, and later the famous blue-backed spelling book of Noah Webster and the Grammar of Lindley Murray, and the churches, with their interminable but literate sermons. The Yankee farmers and artisans whose usage Webster frequently preferred to that of what he smugly referred to as "the gay and fashionable world" were for the most part able to read, though certainly not much given to *belles lettres*. There can be no doubt that the comparatively high degree of literacy which prevailed among them has been an important factor in the development of American English.

In the Southern seaports speech was modeled to a large extent upon that of London, for ties with the mother country were even stronger in the South than in New England. The same was true of the speech of the planters. In the countryside, although a successful small farmer might and sometimes did rise into the plantation caste, the plantation system frequently had the effect of forcing those who were not at the top of the social and economic scale into what amounted to cultural isolation. As a consequence of this isolation, local differences in the speech of marginal farmers and poor whites had little chance of blending into a broader regional usage; hence the great diversity of local usages in the South. Such usages are preserved to this day in the speech of the descendants of those who did not acquire the cultured regional speech of the planter class: some of them are thriving business and professional men, prosperous farmers, and holders of public office; many others are simple folk still, whose social contacts have been almost exclusively with others of the same kidney—in the crossroads store and the nearest clapboarded evangelical tabernacle, with an occasional trip to the county seat.

In the Midland, social differences were hardly noticeable. From the very beginning Philadelphians had a culture of their own, not dependent upon London. Away from Philadelphia, the Scotch-Irish and the Palatinate Germans who had settled the back country of the Midland were also not much interested in the fashions, linguistic or otherwise, of London. The Scotch-Irish with a certain amount of justice blamed most of their woes on England, which they certainly had no reason to love. As for the Germans, there was absolutely no reason why they should have had any regard for the London Standard, even if they knew of it. In this great Midland area, less class-conscious and hence more democratic than either eastern New England or the tidewater South, there were no distinctly marked social dialects. Instead, there was the common speech of a sturdy middle class which, on the educated level, was to evolve into a new type of speech, different in many of its details from that of both the North and the South.

The comparative lack of class dialects in the United States is certainly to be attributed to the theoretical and to some extent actual classlessness of American society. American English has no such marked class variants as distinguish the speech of Mayfair from that of Limehouse. This is not to say that all types of speech are socially acceptable or even that all types which are socially acceptable have equal prestige values. In the single state of South Carolina the absence of preconsonantal and final *r* is indicative of higher social position than its presence, because *r*-lessness is characteristic of the speech of the plantation caste who occupied the tidewater region of that state, particularly those living in the Charleston area. It is true, however, despite the prestige sometimes associated with the speech of Boston and the tidewater South, that we have no single standard stemming from the usage of a particular section, nothing at all comparable to the Southern English Standard, a form of speech which is to some extent geographical but nowadays to a considerably larger extent social. In actual fact the Midwesterner is likely to be as proud of his *r*'s as the Bostonian is of his *r*-lessness. A Southwesterner whose oil wells have "come in" may send his daughter to a finishing school in Virginia and complain that he is not getting his money's worth if she fails to acquire what is popularly thought of as a "Southern accent."

So long as she can manage to insert an occasional *you-all* and *sho'* *'nough* into her conversation, she may with impunity fall down on her *r*'s from time to time, for the fact would hardly be noticed. As an embellishment of Western and Southwestern American womanhood, a "Southern accent," or something vaguely resembling one, is all well and good. But the chances are all that the old man will send his sons to the state university where they will not be subjected to linguistic influences other than those current in the educated speech of the region.

To say that American speech is uniform is thus not the same as saying that the speech of any one section of the country is precisely the same as that of any other section; such a claim could not be made even for individuals of the same cultural background in the same section of the country. Indeed, the distinctive speech areas of the original English settlements extending along the Atlantic seaboard from Maine to Georgia—a relatively small section of our present nation, but extremely significant from a linguistic point of view as the matrix whence sprang all types of American English—are a refutation of any such notion.

Nevertheless, practically all who have written knowingly upon the subject have noted that American English is characterized by a high degree of uniformity. It is well to remember, however, that the conception of uniformity in speech must be to a large extent relative; that is, much depends upon who is doing the observing. He who looks for differences will surely find them, and very interesting and significant differences they are. The danger lies in not seeing the woods for the trees—in losing sight of the larger unity of American English by becoming absorbed in a mass of details. The linguistically unsophisticated, for instance, are prone to be so intolerant of deviations from their own usage as to exaggerate the frequency of their occurrence.

It cannot be denied, of course, that a person with even one good ear is able to identify the speech of the tidewater Southerner, the eastern New Englander, and the New Yorker, and to distinguish these types of speech from that of the Middle West. Furthermore, on a more or less unsophisticated level, the usage of words pertaining largely to the farm and the home—words such as the synonymous *andirons, hand irons, fire dogs, dogs,* and *dog irons,* all used in the eastern United States—varies from region to region. Even on a sophisticated level there is some variation in word usage. For instance, what in other parts of the country is called a *sidewalk* was and may still be called in my native section of Maryland a *pavement,* and what is elsewhere called a *pavement* was in our usage the *street* if in town and the *road* if in the country. Whether the road was paved or not, it would never have been called a *pavement*; pavements were in towns and cities and were for the use of pedestrians only. Consequently, I step from the pavement to the street; speakers from other sections step from the sidewalk to the pavement. No serious problem has thus far resulted from the ambiguity.

The study of the historical, sociological, and geographical distribution and background of such differences is fascinating and rewarding. It should not, however, obscure the picture of an essentially homogeneous American English, which no one cognizant of the far more prominent and significant regional and dialectal differences in French, in Spanish, in Italian, in German, and even in British English could ever fail to recognize. Such matters as the different treatment of postvocalic *r* in Boston and Omaha, while they are of major significance to the student of American English, have never really been significant so far as intelligibility is concerned, and no serious misunderstanding is likely to arise even when the context fails to make immediately clear that when a man from Maine speaks of *curd cheese* he means what is elsewhere designated variously as *sour-milk cheese, Dutch cheese, pot cheese, smearcase, clabber cheese,* and *cottage cheese,* revealing as the study of such differentiae may be. The fact that the last-named term, the trade name, is understood by all who have been to school and are thus able to read advertisements is a further instance of the uniformizing tendency.

Nevertheless, regional and even local usages are still with us, on various cultural levels ranging from educated or cultivated speech, where they are rarest, through common speech to the folk speech heard in more or less isolated localities. In a civilization such as ours, however, the local usages of folk speech give way rapidly, as in the past they gave way slowly but steadily, to regional common speech— the speech of the independent farmer, the skilled craftsman, the shopkeeper, the man in the street, spiritual descendants all of Noah Webster's American yeoman. This regional common speech in its turn is influenced and may be in a generation superseded by educated or cultivated speech, to some extent regional also but tending to be national. A very simple illustration is provided by the tendency of a word like *waiter,* the Southern folk term for an attendant at a wedding, to be supplanted, as consolidated schools, the radio, and the automobile continue to increase rural sophistication, by the regional *groomsman.* This regional word, current in parts of the South in both common and cultivated speech, may in its turn be supplanted by the national terms *usher* and *best man.*

Local and regional variations are most noticeable on the Atlantic seaboard because of the comparative isolation of communities from each other in colonial times. Nevertheless, there can be little doubt that from a geographical point of view American English is characterized by an even greater degree of uniformity at present than it had in 1781, when Dr. Witherspoon remarked upon this quality, which he attributed to the fact that "being...unsettled, and moving frequently from place to place, they [Americans] are not so liable to local peculiarities either in accent or phraseology." To this day, one of the characteristics which foreign observers note about us is the fact that we do not "stay put." On the contrary, we like to be "on the go"; a not inconsiderable part of our population is on wheels the year around, in cars and trailers.

In addition, such mass entertainment as is provided in our present age of enlightenment by the motion pictures, the radio, and television has been on the whole a uniformizing influence. "Artists" in all these media have striven to achieve a type of American speech unmarked by local, regional, or class peculiarities. The stress which radio lays upon "diction"—the network announcers are popularly believed to be highly trained specialists in speech—must certainly have had some effect upon American English. It is as yet impossible to define this influence, but it is a fact that specific pronunciations of the more highly paid announcers are frequently cited as authoritative by those who listen to them. In time the announcer may come to usurp some of the authority of the schoolmarm and her textbooks. His criteria of excellence are, however, essentially the same as those of the schools, which have by and large been a most potent standardizing influence.

BRITISH AND AMERICAN ENGLISH   *Simeon Potter*

The language taken by John Smith to Virginia in 1607 and by the Pilgrim Fathers to Massachusetts in 1620 was the English of Shakespeare and Milton. During the following century and a half most of the colonists who reached the shores of New England were British, but the Dutch founded New Amsterdam and held it until it was seized by the British in 1664 and re-named after the King's brother, the Duke of

From *Our Language,* Penguin Books Ltd., Harmondsworth, Middlesex, England, 1950.

York. When, in 1790, the thirteen colonies on the Atlantic seaboard ratified the Federal Constitution, they comprised four million English-speaking people, most of whom still dwelt to the east of the Appalachian Mountains. From the linguistic point of view this was the first and decisive stage in the history of United States English, which, by universal consent but less accurately, we call American English for short.

During the period from 1790 to the outbreak of the Civil War in 1860, new States were created west of the Appalachians and the Alleghanies and fresh immigrants arrived in large numbers from Ireland and Germany. The Irish potato famine of 1845 drove one and a half million Irishmen to seek a home in the New World and the European revolution of 1848 caused as many Germans to settle in Pennsylvania and the Middle West.

The third period, from the end of the Civil War in 1865 to the present day, was marked ethnographically by the arrival of Scandinavians, Slavs and Italians. During the closing decades of the nineteenth century one million Scandinavians, or one fifth of the total population of Norway and Sweden, crossed the Atlantic Ocean and settled, for the most part, in Minnesota and in the Upper Mississippi Valley. They were followed by millions of Czechs, Slovaks, Poles, Yugoslavs, and Italians, whose numbers were still further augmented by refugees in flight from the dire political persecutions which degraded Europe in the first half of the twentieth century. As the great American Republic took shape with the attachment of French and Spanish populations, with the addition of native Indian tribes in the Middle West, and with the absorption of Chinese and Japanese who landed on the Pacific Coast, so the cosmopolitan character of the United States became more accentuated. Further, the African Negroes have come to number over ten millions. Never, however, has the language of Washington and Lincoln been in jeopardy. At no time has there threatened any real danger that English might not be capable of completely assimilating the immigrant tongues or that the children of the French in Louisiana, the Germans in Pennsylvania, the Scandinavians in Minnesota, or the Slavs and Italians in Michigan might not all be able to understand, speak, read, and write English in the third and fourth generations.

The literary language, indeed, has seldom diverged perceptibly from that of the homeland. Washington Irving, Edgar Allen Poe and Nathaniel Hawthorne spared no pains in their day to write impeccable standard English. Henry James, Logan Pearsall Smith and Thomas Stearns Eliot were born in America but found an intellectual home in Europe. Edmund Wilson, Elmer Edgar Stoll, George Sherburn, Doug-

las Bush, and other eminent American critics write not unlike their
British models, George Saintsbury, Andrew Cecil Bradley, Oliver Elton,
and Sir Herbert Grierson. English literature is now cosmopolitan and
worldwide: no sea or ocean bounds can be set to its domain. Hence-
forth English literature must include all excellent and memorable writing in the English language, regardless of political and geographical
boundaries.

In spelling, vocabulary, and pronunciation, and in the syntax of the
lower levels of speech, divergences remain. The distinctive features
of American spelling are mainly a legacy bequeathed by that energetic
little pale-faced man Noah Webster (1758–1843), whose *American
Spelling Book* appeared in 1783 and whose *American Dictionary of the
English Language,* the ancestor of all later Webster Dictionaries, was
published in 1828. Webster would have liked to effect more drastic
reforms in spelling, but he was restrained by necessity. 'Common
sense and convenience', he averred, 'would lead me to write *public,
favor, nabor, hed, proov, flem, hiz, giv, det, ruf,* and *wel* instead of
publick, favour, neighbour, head, prove, phlegm, his, give, debt, rough,*
and *well.'* The practical man of business, however, prevailed over the
theoretical reformer. Webster sought a market for his new book on
both sides of the Atlantic and he was advised to modify his drastic
changes considerably. Today the second unabridged edition (1934) of
Webster's *New International Dictionary* is the official spelling guide of
the Government Printing Office and the accepted authority in all American courts. It sanctions such spellings as *-or* for *-our* in *favor, honor,
humor, labor, odor,* and *valor* for English *favour, honour, humour,
labour, odour,* and *valour; -er* for *-re* in *caliber, center, fiber, meter,* and
theater for English *calibre, centre, fibre, metre,* and *theatre;* one consonant for two in *traveler, traveling, traveled, jewelry,* and *wagon* for
English *traveller, travelling, travelled, jewellery,* and *waggon; -s-* for
-c- in the substantives *defense, offense,* and *practise* for English *defence,
offence,* and *practice;* various simplifications such as *ax, catalog, check,
forever, jail, mask, medieval, program, story, tho, thoro, thru,* and *today*
for English *axe, catalogue, cheque, for ever, gaol, masque, mediaeval,
programme, storey* (of a building), *though, thorough, through,* and
to-day. On the analogy, as he thought, of *affection, collection,* and
direction, Noah Webster clung to *connection* and *reflection* and these
spellings are still favoured in America instead of the preferable forms
connexion and *reflexion.* In general, however, the modified spellings
of Webster's Dictionary are sound and sensible. Hundreds of American spellings have won acceptance in England, not only *public* for

publick, jail for *gaol, cider* for *cyder, asphalt* for *asphalte,* and the like, but also the *-or* spellings for all agent substantives—*author, censor, conqueror, donor, juror, tailor, tutor,* and *visitor*—all, in fact, except *paviour* and *saviour.* The schoolchildren of England are no longer penalized for spelling in the American way and in recent years certain American publishers have deliberately restored a more old-fashioned English spelling.

On arriving in the United States for the first time the Englishman is made unduly aware of differences in vocabulary because these differences happen to loom exceptionally large in the language of travel and transport. Let us assume, by way of illustration, that he decides to continue his journey by rail, that is, by *railroad.* He does not register his luggage but he *checks* his *baggage,* which is then placed, not in the luggage van, but in the *baggage car;* perhaps he must first rescue it from the left-luggage office, which, he discovers, is called the *checkroom.* A goods train is referred to as a *freight train* and a brake-van becomes a *caboose.* He looks for the inquiry office in order to corroborate details and he finds that it is called the *information bureau;* or he may decide to consult a *bulletin-board,* in England a notice-board, or a *schedule,* in England a time-table, on his own account. He is surprised to learn that a season ticket is a *commutation ticket* and that a season-ticket holder is a plain *commuter.* The driver of his train is the *engineer* and the guard is the *conductor.* He hears someone refer to a *switch,* which turns out to be a *point,* and he soon discovers that a *grade crossing* is merely a level crossing. When he reaches his destination he finds an *automobile* waiting for him at the *railroad depot.* He cannot help noticing that the windscreen is called the *windshield,* the bonnet the *hood,* and that petrol is alluded to as *gasoline* or plain *gas.* That explains why the filling station is named the *gas station* and why *accelerating* is described as *stepping on the gas.* On his way through the town he passes trams or *street cars* with their trolley-poles or *contact rods.* He observes cyclists, *cyclers* or *wheelmen,* riding near the pavement or *sidewalk.* One of them has just stopped to mend a puncture or *fix a flat.* Not far away a lorry or *truck* is in difficulties and the breakdown gang or *wrecking crew* is getting to work. Having alighted at his hotel, he finds that it has no personal lift or *elevator* to take him up to his room on the *fifth floor* (which, luckily for him, turns out to be only what he calls the fourth), but that a service lift or *dumbwaiter* may be used for luggage or *baggage.*

At no point is the intelligent traveller inconvenienced by these hitherto unfamiliar, but easily assimilable, expressions. The more

15901

~ living and ever-changing idioms of
.nt about colloquial and slang idioms
.at journal *Dialect Notes*, which began
..90; and from numerous articles appearing
..nich was founded as a monthly in 1925, and
which now continues to thrive as a quarterly publication of the Columbia University Press. Much, too, may be learnt from the large fourth
edition (1936) of Henry Louis Mencken's *The American Language* and
its two copious *Supplements* of 1945 and 1948. From *A Dictionary
of American English on Historical Principles* (1938–44), by Sir William
Craigie and James R. Hulbert, much may be learnt about the 'more
serious and solid elements of American English' and about those
'speech-ways' which mirror the American life of the past. Here, naturally, information may be gleaned about those many trees, shrubs, animals, birds, and reptiles which are rare or unknown in Europe. The
countless new arts and techniques of a highly developed civilization
figure prominently in its pages, but slang and dialect are restricted to
expressions of early date or of special prominence. Twentieth-century
neologisms do not appear in it at all, for the editors set the year 1900
as their arbitrary time-limit. Since that date many thousands of new
words have become current American and have made their way up
from slang to the more respectable levels of colloquial speech. 'Today',
wrote the Baltimore journalist H. L. Mencken in 1945 (*The American
Language Supplement One*, p. 323), 'it is no longer necessary for an
American writer to apologize for writing American. He is not only
forgiven if he seeks to set forth his notions in the plainest and least
pedantic manner possible; he is also sure of escaping blame (save, of
course, by an Old Guard of English reviewers) if he makes liberal dips
into the vocabulary of everyday, including its most plausible neologisms. Indeed, he seems a bit stiff and academic if he doesn't make
some attempt, however unhappy, to add to the stock of such neologisms
himself. How many are launched in this great Republic every year I
do not know, but the number must be formidable. . . . So many novelties
swarm in that it is quite impossible for the dictionaries to keep up with
them; indeed, a large number come and go without the lexicographers
so much as hearing of them. At least four-fifths of those which get any
sort of toe-hold in the language originate in the United States, and
most of the four-fifths remain here. We Americans live in an age and
society given over to enormous and perhaps even excessive word-mak-
ing—the most riotous seen in the world since the break-up of Latin.
It is an extremely wasteful process, for with so many newcomers to

choose from it is inevitable that large numbers of pungent and useful words and phrases must be discarded and in the end forgotten by all save linguistic paleontologists. But we must not complain about that, for all the great processes of nature are wasteful, and it is by no means assured that the fittest always survive'. Such neologisms are clipped words like *lube* for *lubricating oil* and *co-ed* for *co-educational;* back-formations like *to televise* (1931) from *television* and *to propagand* (1939) from *propaganda;* blends like *cablegram* from *cable* and *telegram, Aframerican* from *African* and *American, radiotrician* from *radio* and *electrician, sportcast* from *sport* and *broadcast,* and *sneet* from *snow* and *sleet;* artificial or made-up formations like *carborundum, cellophane,* and *pianola;* and acronyms or telescoped names like *nabisco* from *National Biscuit Company* or *socony* from *Standard Oil Company.* Hundreds of new expressions have also arisen by a revival and extension of grammatical conversion or the free interchange of function among parts of speech. When we *park* our cars we are using the substantive *park* as a verb in a particular sense. Shakespeare, it is true, used *to park* as a verb in the sense 'to confine or enclose as in a park' in I *Henry the Sixth,* IV. ii. 45: 'How are we park'd and bounded in a pale!' But *to park* in the sense 'to place compactly in a park' was a new conversion made by the British Army in 1812 at the time of the Napoleonic Wars. Nearly one hundred years later, in 1910, it was adopted by British chauffeurs and by American automobilists into their vocabulary. Since then *to park* has come to mean 'to leave or keep other things and persons in a suitable place until required' and Americans park not only their automobiles but also their children, their dogs, and their chewing-gum (P. G. Wodehouse, *The Inimitable Jeeves*). *Stream-line* was first recorded in 1873 in the highly technical language of hydrodynamics. Later, in 1907, it was applied in aerodynamics to the shape given to cars and aircraft offering the minimum resistance to the air. Later still, in 1913, it was converted into the verb *to streamline,* which has recently become a vogue-word in America and has been extended to mean any attempt whatever at simplification. That 'nasty newcomer' *to panic* was used by Thomas Hood in 1827, but apparently by no other writer until it was re-invented in the United States in 1910. To-day Americans no longer hesitate to *loan* (as well as to *lend*), to *audition* (grant a hearing or audition to), to *accession* (new library-books), to *remainder* (unsold and unsalable books), to *service* (a car or an automobile), to *blueprint* (to make any plan of any thing), to *contact* (to get into touch with), to *deadhead* (to admit as a 'deadhead' without payment), to *highlight* (to bring out the brightest parts or chief features

in what we English prefer to call a brains-trust). A bargain
buy, articles of food are *eats*, and technical skill is the *know-how*.

We refer quite naturally in everyday English to 'children and
grown-ups' without realizing, perhaps, what an interesting linguistic
form the word *grown-ups* is. It is the second or past participle of the
intransitive durative verb *grow* (the past participle of which, because
durative, has present signification) + the adverb *up;* compounded,
converted into a substantive, and given the plural inflexion -*s*. This
precise form is not old. It is first recorded in a letter penned by Jane
Austen in 1813, although *grown-up* had been used as an epithet adjective in the seventeenth century. When we speak of giving our friends
a good *send-off* we are employing an expression first used in this sense
of 'a good-will demonstration' by Mark Twain in 1872. Hitherto this
verb-adverb substantive had referred to the sending off or starting of
contestants in a race. Many other substantives of this type have since
found favour in America. A place of concealment is a *hide-out*, a drop
in social esteem a *come-down*, a re-organization of staff a *shake-up*,
and a free lunch a *hand-out*. Any arrangement or establishment is a
set-up, a meeting of any kind is a *get-together*, and an escape is a *get-
away*. Any action which brings matters to an issue or forces men to
disclose their plans is a *show-down* as, at card-games, the players suddenly lay cards on the table. The Americans have a liking, too, for
picturesque and vivid verb-phrases, both old and new: *to cut a shine,
go the whole hog, shell out, go for, go in for, rope in, go him one better,
go it blind, face the music, go it alone, stand from under, do the square
thing, knock the spots off, spread it on thick, shinny on one's own side,
get away with it,* and *paint the town red.* Journalists, gossip-columnists,
makers of film and radio scripts, song writers and advertising agents are
busy coining new turns of speech day by day. Some of these are
literally ephemeral. They do not 'catch on'; they have their day and
they are forgotten. Others live on and eventually, perhaps, they are
tacitly adopted by the whole English-speaking world.

Suffixes may be resuscitated and multiplied by analogy. In conformity with *mathematician* and *electrician* the old *undertaker*, itself
shortened from *funeral undertaker*, becomes *mortician* (1923), not to
mention *beautician*. *Cafeteria* in Spanish is a 'coffee-house': in American English it is extended to mean a 'help-yourself restaurant' and
thence proceed *caketeria, fruiteria, groceteria, smoketeria,* and a host

of others, some accepted, others transitory, if not merely facetious. On
the basis of *sanatorium*, other institutions are named *healthatorium*,
restatorium, and *shavatorium*. Thomas Carlyle and others sought to
revive the suffix *-dom*, corresponding to German *-tum*, in the nineteenth
century and among their creations that survived were *boredom*, *official-
dom*, and *serfdom*. Hundreds of new *-dom* compounds—*filmdom*, *star-
dom*, *crosswordpuzzledom*, *dictatordom*, *gangsterdom*, and *slumdom*—
are now fashionable in America. The ancient agent suffixes, Greek *-ist*
and Germanic *-ster*, have likewise come to life again in *vacationist*
(holiday-maker, 1888), *manicurist* (1889), *behaviorist* (coined by John
B. Watson in 1913), *receptionist* (1923), *blurbist* (concoctor of blurbs or
slip-cover encomiums, 1925), and *editorialist* (1944); *ringster* (1879),
gangster (1896), *roadster* (1910), and *speedster* (1918).

Among the more outstanding features of American pronunciation
a few may here be noted. In words like *for, door, farm,* and *lord* the *r*
is still sounded as a fricative, whereas in English it is silent except in expressions like *far away* and *the door opens* where a linking *r* is naturally
inserted. In most dialects of Southern England the rolled or trilled *r*
sound was weakened in pronunciation in the seventeenth century and
lost in the eighteenth. Americans pronounce words like *dance, fast,
grass, half,* and *path* with a low front *a* sound [æ] as in *cat*, which is
still heard in the northern counties of England and which persisted in
the southern counties until the end of the eighteenth century. Americans pronounce words like *dock, fog, hot,* and *rod* with a low back *a*
sound [ɑ] like the vowel sound in *car* and *father* shortened. They pronounce words like *dew, duke, new,* and *steward* with the [juː] sound
reduced to [uː] so that *dew* and *duke* sound like *do* and *dook*. Just as
in Spanish, Portuguese and Provençal, the Latin and Italian *armata*,
past participle feminine, 'armed (force)', has become *armada*, so in
present-day American *-t-* is often voiced, so that *beating* sounds very
much like *beading*, *matter* like *madder*, and *metal* like *medal*. The
plosion, however, is softer and less aspirated than in English.

Further, it may be noted that both word-stress and sentence-stress
are weaker in American than in British English and intonation is more
level. Consequently American speech is more monotonous, but at the
same time it is generally more distinct. It is, as Mencken puts it, 'predominantly *staccato* and *marcato*', whereas British English, like Russian, 'tends toward *glissando*'. Unstressed syllables are pronounced
with more measured detachment and therefore with greater clarity.
There is less variety of tone and the customary tempo is slower. Many
speakers have fallen into a habit which they have unconsciously in-

herited from seventeenth-century East Anglian Puritans. They allow the soft palate or velum to droop while speaking, and as a result part of the breath stream passes through the nose giving a certain nasalized quality or 'nasal twang' to vowel sounds which may vary considerably in degree from individual to individual.

Compare the way in which a New Yorker says *extraordinary, supernumerary, temporary,* and *unexceptionable* with the pronunciation of a Londoner. The American invariably gives to the unstressed syllables in these words greater 'prominence' (to use the technical term in phonetics) and, consequently, greater audibility. In words like *dormitory, monastery, necessary,* and *secretary* he habitually places a not unpleasing secondary stress upon the penult or last syllable but one. Some words he stresses differently from us. He stresses *aristocrat, detail, eczema, frontier, harass, primarily,* and *subaltern* on the second syllable whereas we stress then on the first. Conversely, he stresses *address, alloy, ally, corollary, defect, idea, inquiry, opponent, quinine, recess, recourse, redress, research, resource,* and *romance* on the first syllable, whereas we English stress them on the second. Other words, like *advertisement* and *financier,* are stressed on the second syllable in London but on the third syllable in New York.

Now these observations apply not only to the speech of New York City but also to the so-called General American dialect as a whole, which includes the Middle Atlantic States, that is, New Jersey, Pennsylvania and the whole of New York State west of the Hudson River, as well as all the Middle and Western States. General American thus comprises two-thirds of the whole population and four-fifths of the land surface of the United States reaching from the Atlantic Ocean in the east to the Pacific Ocean in the west. The other two dialects, New England and Southern, are important and significant, but they are much more limited. The dialect of New England is spoken in Maine, New Hampshire, Vermont, Massachusetts, Rhode Island, Connecticut and the strip of New York State lying to the east of the Hudson River. It is nearer British English in many respects. For example, the rounded vowel is retained in *dock,* the long low back *a* is heard in *dance* and the *r* is dropped in *far* and *farm.* At the same time, it is less homogeneous than General American. Even within its narrower confines the New England dialect has far more social and regional variations. The Southern dialect includes the States of Maryland, Virginia, North and South Carolina, Georgia, Florida, Kentucky, Tennessee, Alabama, Mississippi, Arkansas, and Louisiana, as well as a great part of Missouri, Oklahoma, and Texas. In other words, it is spoken in all the States, except Delaware and West Virginia, lying south of Pennsylvania and the Ohio River and east of a line running from St. Louis to the middle waters of the Colorado River and thence down that river to its mouth in the Gulf of Mexico. Many people in these parts speak with a drawl. They speak with slow enunciation and they frequently drag out and diphthongize stressed vowels, saying [jeɪs], or even [jeɪjəs], for *yes*, and [klæɪs], or even [klæjəs], for *class*.

In spite of countless smaller variations in pronunciation, vocabulary, and idiom, the three American dialects do not greatly differ from one another. For two centuries and more American families have been constantly on the move: speech communities have seldom been isolated for more than one generation. It would be no exaggeration to say that greater differences in pronunciation are discernible among the speech-forms of Northern England between Trent and Tweed than among the dialects of the whole of North America.

It is now customary for American and British scholars and scientists to co-operate in the writing of composite books addressed to the whole English-speaking world and the councils of learned societies have taken steps to standardize technical nomenclature. Other potent forces are now at work bringing the two main streams of English more closely together. Future historians of our language, with their longer perspective in looking back, may well record that it was during the century and a quarter from 1800 to 1925 that British and American English showed the greatest divergence and that, after 1925, unifying factors—the ubiquity of radio and the interchange of films, novels, journals, and plays—all worked in one and the same direction to make that divergence narrower and narrower. Films and newspapers bring the latest American slang to England, so that even a trained observer may no longer differentiate with certainty between native and imported neologisms. Such a highly expressive phrase as *It's up to us* sounds so very American. We take it for granted that it *is* American. But who could be really certain about its provenance without looking a little more closely into the matter, without consulting Mencken, Horwill and *American Speech* on the one hand, and Partridge and the Supplement to *The Oxford English Dictionary* on the other? In 1942 the United States War Department furnished men and women serving in Europe with *A Short Guide to Great Britain* which included a long list of American and English variants. It was a painstaking, if over-elaborate, publication: its aim—to obviate every conceivable occasion of misapprehension —was entirely meritorious. This aim was shared by H. W. Horwill in his two careful studies which had appeared a few years previously and which have already acquired historical value: A *Dictionary of Modern American Usage* (1935) and *An Anglo-American Interpreter* (1939). In his Preface to the last-mentioned book the author quotes the statement of a 'distinguished journalist' that 'an American, if taken suddenly ill while on a visit to London, might die in the street through being unable to make himself understood. . . . He would naturally ask for the nearest drugstore, and no one would know what he meant.' Everyone would now know the meaning of this and hundreds of other expressions marked American in Horwill's *Interpreter* and in the War Department's *Short Guide*. Indeed, they may now be heard from the lips of English children every day. The most fashionable American locution of the hour may be heard all over England within the space of a few weeks and then, perhaps, heard no more.

WORLD ENGLISH?
Stuart Robertson and Frederic Cassidy

If the English language in the past century or so has entered a new phase of growth to suit it to the rapidly developing democratic-industrial society of today, a phase in which it necessarily breaks free of the eighteenth century's static ideals, and gradually becomes adapted to the needs of a more dynamic age, we must realize that it does not throw over all tradition or historical continuity—indeed, with language that would be suicidal. The chief patterns of the language, in its modern stage, remain firm: what proves good in past usage, and what proves good of new acquisition, continues. Just as the stylists of the Restoration laid aside the Latinized brocade, splendid as it was, of Sir Thomas Browne, and put on the plain English broadcloth of Defoe and Dryden, so the writer of today weaves a new fabric of his own, experimenting in many types. The prose of today (if any generalization can be made about so various a thing) is less formal, more rapid and practical; it travels light, throwing off the weight of convention, decoration, or structural complexity. At its worst this makes it seem harried, mean, flaccid, or flat; but at its best it can be pungent, sinewy, clear, and direct. Mass-produced it is like any other such product—less finely wrought, but achieving an art of its own, reaching a larger number of minds, and supporting a larger number of artisans than has been

Stuart Robertson & Frederic Cassidy, *The Development of Modern English*, 2d ed. 1954. Prentice-Hall, Inc., Englewood Cliffs, N.J. Reprinted by permission.

possible in former ages. Mass-production, in its early stages, scorns
art—but once established, it returns to art. This explains why it can
be said with some measure of truth that more people are using the
language better today than ever before. It is also true, no doubt, that
there is a larger audience for cheap, inartistic, stupid, and vulgar uses
of language than ever before. The Elizabethan broadsides and chap-
books have their innumerable, and equally ephemeral, modern counterparts. If language is mechanized, like everything else it is dehu-
manized and dies; but the forces of renewal are perpetually at work,
and whatever is really vital survives. The English language is changing and will change still, but it is in no serious danger of decay.

Meantime, as we have remarked before, one of the most important
considerations for the future of the language is that English, in the
past three centuries, has spread all over the world. Its use as an international language is constantly increasing. That some general medium of expression is really to be desired we have the experience of
history to testify. In the Middle Ages, Latin occupied this position,
and in modern times French has approximated it, especially as the
language of international diplomatic relations. Is English, possibly,
in line for the succession? Before examining the claims of English as
a world auxiliary language, however, we must first consider whether a
natural language or an artificial one—such as Esperanto—holds out the
best hope of effective use and general acceptance.

The ideal of an artificial speech, scientifically constructed so as to
combine the merits of some of the leading naturally developed languages and at the same time embody none of their defects, is by no
means a new thing. Some of the projected artificial languages do not,
it is true, fulfil the first of these conditions; that is, they are based not
on one or more existing languages, but are purely *a priori* schemes.
None of these, however, is seriously advocated at present; it is quite
generally recognized that a universal language must be founded on
one or more of the vernaculars of the world. To go into the many
variations of the project [1]—such as Volapük, Ido, "Latino sine flexione,"
Novial—would take us too far afield. A few words must nevertheless
be said about Esperanto, the claimant favored by the majority of the
advocates of a universal language.

Esperanto has Latin, as the most nearly international and neutral of
elements, as the chief basis of its vocabulary; its grammar is exceedingly simple and its spelling is phonetic. That it has won a real,

---

[1] Cf. particularly L. Couturat and L. Leau, *Histoire de la langue universelle,*
Paris (Hachette), 1903, and Jespersen, *An International Language.*

though necessarily limited, measure of successful adoption, is indicated by the support given it after the first World War by the League of Nations, the International Telegraphic Union (1925), and the Union Internationale de Radiophonie (1927).[2] The second World War, of course, set the movement back considerably, and the United Nations has been less hospitable to Esperanto than was the League: it has five official languages—English and French as "working languages" and in addition Chinese, Russian, and Spanish. The Esperantists have resumed activity, however, as witness their thirty-fifth annual conference, which met in Paris in 1950, with 2500 delegates from 34 countries. Nevertheless, they can lay claim to only one and a half million people who use Esperanto daily, which is less than the number who speak even a minor natural language, and is utterly dwarfed by the daily users of any major one. No more than five thousand daily users are claimed for the United States—yet a dozen natural foreign languages are spoken by more people than that in the United States. Thus even the most successful of the artificial languages, after more than sixty years of existence, has achieved very little actual acceptance, and not even the acceptance of all who favor an artificial auxiliary language.

Furthermore, the arguments that have been urged against Esperanto in the past [3] are still valid. The uniformity claimed for it all over the world is partly vitiated by its different pronunciation in various countries. And while its grammatical system is simple by European standards, it is still very difficult for speakers of non-European languages. A recent Esperantist publication [4] makes much of the international misunderstandings that have resulted through mistranslation from one natural language to another (French, English, Russian). The implication is that the use of Esperanto would remove all such difficulties. But of course this is quite without foundation, since the various languages would themselves have to be translated into Esperanto words, and the possibilities for misunderstanding would be just as great.

If, then, the project of an artificially constructed universal language has so far met with only a very limited measure of success, what claims may be advanced for English as an international language? It seems

[2] *Encyclopaedia Britannica*, article *s.v.* "Universal language" (14th ed., Vol. 22, p. 861).

[3] Those, for example, of Krapp, *Modern English*, New York (Scribner), 1909, pp. 40–43.

[4] Compiled by G. A. and D. T. Connor, W. Solzbacher, and J. B. S-T. Kao, *Esperanto, The World Interlanguage*, New York (Beechhurst), 1948. See especially pp. 4–5.

more and more certain that if any living speech attains this position, it will be English.[5] In our own day, English has come to rival French in the field of diplomacy, and since the second World War, has virtually replaced French as the "second" language—the language most useful for the traveler—all over Europe.[6] In other parts of the world, its prestige and usefulness are still more commanding. Though India gained independence in 1950 and might have been expected to set up one of its native languages as a national standard, the rivalry existing among them, combined with the fact that English was already known everywhere among educated people, has led to the retention of English. As someone has said, the Indians, in coming together to throw off the British yoke, found it necessary to communicate with each other in the language of the British.

Beach-la-Mar or Sandalwood-English, spoken and understood all over the Western Pacific, and Pidgin-English, known in China and to some extent in Japan and in California, are the most conspicuous examples of corrupt forms of English that have been evolved from the contact with exotic tongues [7] and spread over large areas. It is said, incidentally, that the American share in these trade languages is becoming larger than the British.[8] But it is not, of course, merely in such corrupt jargons that Modern English has gained a world-wide ascendancy; in its more standard British and American forms, it is, especially since the first World War, more and more dominating the civilized, and a large part of the uncivilized, world.

This leadership among the languages of the world has been achieved well within the Modern English period. In the Renaissance, and prob-

---

[5] A middle position between those who support the claims of an artificial language like Esperanto and those who support the claims of English is taken by those who advocate the artificially simplified form of English known as "Basic English." See C. K. Ogden, *Basic English*, London (Kegan Paul), 1930, and *The System of Basic English*, New York (Harcourt, Brace), 1934. For some discussion see Chad Walsh, "The Verb System of Basic English," *American Speech*, Vol. XVII, No. 3 (Oct. 1942), pp. 137–143, and the reply in the following issue by I. A. Richards.

[6] It is now the first foreign language taught in the schools in France, Holland, Norway, and other countries.

[7] For a description of these and similar jargons, see the section "Pidgin and Congeners" in Jespersen's *Language* (pp. 216–236). *Pidgin,* as Jespersen explains, is derived from the Chinese distortion of *business.*

[8] Cf. Mencken, *op. cit.,* p. 597. He also quotes (p. 598) a striking testimony to the use of English as a world language in the account of an English traveler who observed Chinese mandarins speaking English not only in conversation with German ship's officers and Japanese travelers but even with one another. Since they came from various provinces of China, they found English a more convenient medium than their less standardized native tongues.

ably as late as the period of the Restoration, the speakers of English were fewer than the speakers of at least four other European languages —German, French, Spanish, and Italian. Even in the eighteenth century, English was still, for a time, outdistanced in numbers of speakers by four other European languages, since, if Italian had been left behind, a new rival, Russian, had asserted itself. In the nineteenth century, however, English came rapidly to the front, largely as a result of the swift increase in the population of the United States and of the British colonies. Probably by the middle of the century it had outdistanced its competitors. Estimates, in millions of speakers, made at several times since then, are as follows: [9]

	English	German	Russian	French	Spanish
1868	60	52	45	45	40
1890	111	75+	75	51+	42+
1900	116(123)	75(80)	70(85)	45(52)	44(58)
1912	150	90	106	47	52
1921	170	87½	120½	45	65
1936	191	85	90	—	100
1952	225	—	180	—	110

The figures, necessarily only approximations, have at least the merit of coming from a number of different sources and representing various points of view. Their testimony to the recent and rapid increase in the number of those speaking English is perhaps for this very reason the more impressive. It is evident, of course, that they do not tell the whole story as to the languages of the world; but China's 450 millions speak dialects that are mutually unintelligible [10] and that, besides, scarcely spread beyond her borders; and a similar situation holds for those who speak cognate varieties of Indic—the Indo-European languages of India—perhaps 325 millions. Clearly, any rivalry for the position of a world language must come from the tongues of Europe; and the figures that have been quoted are a striking evidence of the way in which English has outdistanced its European competitors. In numbers of native speakers, English is rivalled only by North Chi-

[9] The following sources have been used: for 1868 and 1900, the figures quoted by Mencken, *op. cit.*, 3rd ed., pp. 383–384; for 1936, his 4th ed., pp. 592–593; for 1900 (minimum and maximum) and 1912, those quoted by Jespersen, *Growth and Structure*, p. 252; for 1921 the estimate of L. Tesnier in Meillet, *Langues*, as quoted by Bloomfield, *Language*, p. 44; for 1952, Werner, *op cit.*, p. 16.

[10] Though one of them, North Chinese, in all probability has more native speakers than even English, and another, Cantonese, is not very far behind.

nese; in numbers of native *and foreign* speakers, it is quite unrivalled by any language in the world. The fact that English has gained the ascendancy is not to be disputed. There may be difference of opinion, however, as to *why* it has done so.

The reason for the spread of English is probably quite unconnected with the language as such, or with any intrinsic virtues over other languages which it may be thought to have: England's rise as a world power, beginning in the days of Elizabeth, is accompanied, step by step, by the ascendancy of English as a world language. The political union of England and Scotland under James I in 1603, followed by the formation of the United Kingdom of Great Britain and Ireland, helped to make it certain that English would be used, and in a form substantially the same, throughout the islands and in the newly founded Colonies. In the New World, the fall of New Amsterdam in 1664 and that of Quebec in 1759 assured the triumph of English over two important rivals, Dutch and French; and the expansion of the United States brought it about that Spanish, the only remaining competitor of English on the North American continent, was reduced to a decidedly subordinate position. In the latter half of the eighteenth century and throughout the nineteenth century, the English language was established in every corner of the earth through conquest, colonization, and the commercial ascendancy of the English-speaking peoples. It may even be conjectured, as Krapp suggests,[11] that the tenacity with which the British and the Americans hold to their own language and their own ways has been a real factor in spreading the English language; for if the English-speaking people would not learn a foreign language, it is evident that foreigners, to trade with them, had to learn English. The contrast has been observed, for example, in the far greater readiness of the Germans, as compared both with the English and with the Americans, to learn the Spanish language and adapt themselves to Latin ways, when engaged in commerce with South America. Doubtless, the more complacent Anglo-Saxon attitude is bad for trade, when better linguists, like the Germans, are competitors; but, just as evidently, it has proved in the past to be an appreciable factor in the world-wide use of English.

Having, by the middle-nineteenth century, won first place among the languages of the world, English has been favored by more recent developments so that its primacy is less and less questioned. Inventions that make communication between nations easier have inevi-

[11] *Modern English,* p. 39.

tably lent themselves to the spread of English. So we may regard the telephone, the telegraph, the radio, the movies, and no doubt, once its range is increased, television. Here too, it may be said, it is often the American brand of English that is spread abroad, frequently to the chagrin of the British. The second World War, particularly, took great numbers of Americans into places where they had never been before; and airplane travel takes tourists, businessmen, and many others in increasing numbers almost everywhere. The fact that since the close of the war only Americans have been in the economic position to travel much beyond their national borders has made English even more the language that goes abroad.

But what of the intrinsic merits of English? Is it on the whole well- or ill-fitted for the role of auxiliary world speech? Has it not spread, in part, because it is a better language than its competitors? This is a dangerous question! In the first place, linguists nowadays are agreed that there is no real evidence to prove any one language better than any other *as a language*. That is, though languages compared will certainly be found to differ in structure and resource, the "advantages" of one sort in any language will generally be offset by its "disadvantages" of another sort. The structure of "primitive" languages is no less complex, and no different in potentiality, than that of "cultivated" languages. To make value-judgments about them, therefore, is not a matter for the linguist. But the greatest danger in such questions comes from the fact that our emotions are so deeply and secretly involved with our native language that it is almost impossible to be objective. The best medicine, in such a case, is to read Edward Sapir's excellent tenth chapter of *Language*, "Language, Race, and Culture."

Once alert to the dangers of subjectivity, however, we may note with some interest what has been said about the values of English by competent observers. One foreign scholar who has studied English and other languages intensively, and who can more dispassionately assess merits and shortcomings, Otto Jespersen, has written, "The English language is a methodical, energetic, businesslike, and sober language"; [12] and again (with particular reference to its increasing use as a world language),[13] "It must be a source of gratification to mankind that the tongue spoken by two of the greatest powers of the world is so noble, so rich, so pliant, so expressive and so interesting. . . ." In still another place, he states his view of English as compared with other languages in these terms: ". . . it seems to me

[12] *Growth and Structure,* p. 17.
[13] *Ibid.,* p. 252.

positively and expressly *masculine*, it is the language of a grown-up man and has very little childish or feminine about it." [14]

The foregoing terms represent, with entire adequacy, the usual favorable view of Modern English. It is most frequently praised for its businesslike simplicity—in sound-system, in grammar, and in at least the more frequently used core of its vocabulary. This simplicity, it is commonly thought, makes it easy for a foreigner to learn, and hence makes it particularly adaptable for use as a world tongue. To modify this judgment, however, we have such an admission as the following, from the pen of an enthusiastic defender of this very quality of simplicity: "The foreigner essaying it, indeed, finds his chief difficulty, not in mastering its forms, but in grasping its lack of forms." [15] More subtly, and from a different angle, the apparent simplicity of English has been declared to be a delusion and a snare:

> The fact that a beginner in English has not many paradigms to learn gives him a feeling of absence of difficulty, but he soon learns to his cost that this is only a feeling. . . . The simplicity of English in its formal aspect is . . . really a pseudo-simplicity or a masked complexity. . . . He [the foreigner] may well feel that the apparent simplicity of English is purchased at the price of a bewildering obscurity.[16]

Granting that there is some truth in these strictures and that the superficial impression of simplicity that English gives is somewhat ambiguous, one may still feel that its forms, its words, and its sounds compare favorably, in the ease with which at least approximate mastery of them can be attained, with those of other languages. Its vocabulary has the enormous advantage of being compounded almost equally of Germanic and Romanic elements, so that a good part of it is already familiar to the speakers of many other European languages. Its morphology is so inconsiderable that the language has been called "the grammarless tongue"—which is, of course, inaccurate, since what it lacks in morphological complexity is fully counterbalanced by syntactical complexity; yet the phrase does emphasize its simplicity in one respect. In inflections and word order, as we have seen, the

[14] *Ibid.*, p. 2.

[15] Mencken, *op. cit.*, 3rd ed., p. 387.

[16] Edward Sapir, "Wanted: A World Language," *American Mercury*, Vol. XXII, No. 86 (February 1931), pp. 202–209. Reprinted by permission of author and publisher. These excerpts cannot do justice to the keenness of the writer's analysis of the deficiencies of English as an international language. Sapir presents this point of view also in his contribution to *International Communication*, a symposium by H. N. Shenton, Sapir, and Jespersen, London (Paul, Trench, Trubner), 1931.

modern speech has greatly simplified and regularized the practices of Old English. (On the other hand, it has acquired a complex array of phrase-groupings, using function-words, which are no less difficult than the inflections of Old English.)

The greatest stumbling-block in the way of the foreigner who would acquire English is, as will be granted on all sides, the spelling —"that pesudo-historical and anti-educational abomination." [17] On the subject of English as a world speech it is perhaps worth recalling that long ago the great German linguist Jacob Grimm congratulated other Europeans that the English had not yet discovered that only one thing prevented the universality of English from being completely apparent: its "whimsical, antiquated orthography." Today, with the English language perceptibly nearer the indicated goal, the same handicap remains. If it could be removed, or at least reduced, that might bring English still nearer to acceptability as a world language. Even with this handicap, English can perhaps qualify on its merits—insofar as these can be judged. But it is worth remarking that the point will be decided in the future, however it goes, not on linguistic grounds, but on grounds of the continued rise in world influence—or the fall—of those whose language is now English.

[17] Jespersen, *Growth and Structure,* p. 250.

SECTION III

GRAMMAR AND LINGUISTICS:
THE STRUCTURE AND SYSTEM
OF LANGUAGE

> "Grammar is the construction placed by mind on the unorganized materials of speech."
>
> —William J. Entwistle

> "Respect for tradition . . . does not forbid us to live and work in the twentieth century."
>
> —James Sledd

For many users of this book, the terms "grammar" and "linguistics" suggest areas of learning that are perhaps forbidding or unknown. For that reason, and because grammar and linguistics are at the heart of any serious, objective study of language, a somewhat detailed introduction is appropriate. Since grammar can claim historical priority, we shall first discuss its meaning, and then move on to a description of the meanings which may be usefully and legitimately attached to the term "linguistics."

The term "grammar" carries with it a strong suggestion of the recondite; hence, it demands—more, perhaps, than does any other term associated with language—special scrutiny and consideration. By anatomizing the term, by isolating and inspecting its implications both linguistic and social, "grammar" can become a clear, useful, and practical concept.

We can begin by noting that the term "grammar" is sometimes used simply to designate the essential elements or principles of any complex phenomenon. In this sense the term has been used in such books as Karl Pearson's *The Grammar of Science*, Kenneth Burke's *A Grammar of Motives,* and John Henry Newman's *A Grammar of Assent.* Linguistically, "grammar" alludes specifically to the discernible pattern, structure, or method of any language. The sum total of the devices such as inflections and word order that make a language operative, that provide the system by which we put words into meaningful relationship with one another in sentences and paragraphs, is justly and appropriately called the "grammar" of that language. Used in this way grammar is a clear, scientific concept. But it is obvious that this meaning of the term is not the one that has inspired distrust on the part of generations of otherwise tractable students. To find the root of this distrust we must turn to the history of grammar.

The history of speculation about grammar does not take us very far back in time. As Charlton Laird remarks in his brief but valuable *Thinking About Language:* "Barbarians are not notably curious about grammar," which is another way of saying that it was relatively late in the development of English culture before men began to be curious about either the structure or the system of their language. This earliest curiosity—beginning with the sixteenth and seventeenth centuries —began at a time when English was not considered a particularly distinguished language. Its history before the Renaissance had been interwoven with the prestigious use of other languages, especially French and Latin. When men began to think of English as a possibly appropriate language in its own right, they discovered, as Albert Baugh ironically phrases it in his *History of the English Language,* "that English had no grammar." Since scholars brought a classical training to their study of English, they often attempted to accommodate English grammar to a Latin grammatical pattern—a process impossible of satisfactory result since the "grammars" of the two languages were constructed on different sets of grammatical devices: in Latin meaning is usually dependent upon form or inflection, while in English meaning depends primarily upon the positions of words in the sentence. Some of our earliest grammars, based upon the false linguistic premise just described, gave a confused description of the system of English—a description that has led inevitably to English grammar's reputation for awesome difficulty since the grammarians had recourse to elaborate stratagems to force these early descriptions into consistency.

It would be a mistake to assert, however, that the meanings attached to the term "grammar" are exhausted with either the scientific or the Latinate. The same eighteenth century grammarians who erred so magnificently in respect to grammar had other important (and equally mistaken) notions about language. For reasons ultimately theological, literary, and philosophical which are not relevant here, they felt that English was in danger of "corruption" even greater than it had heretofore suffered. Hence, a prime goal was the "fixing" or stabilization of the language in terms of some prescribed standard of usage. Even the normally clear-headed and realistic Dr. Johnson, for example, felt it was his duty, as chief lexicographer of his age, to "correct or proscribe" the "improprieties and absurdities" of the language. As a result of such efforts, the term "grammar" was extended to include not only a description of the pattern of English structure but also a listing of "rules" which would result in the elimination of "undesirable" or "barbaric" locutions in English. These rules were based either on tradition or logic. Dr. Johnson, for example, selected the English of the Elizabethan period as his standard and urged his readers to adjust their language accordingly. On the other hand, scholars sometimes reasoned in accordance with Latin grammar as combined with school-logic. This sort of reasoning is responsible for such "rules" as those prohibiting the split infinitive and the double negative.

Our "anatomizing" reveals, then, three meanings that have been attached to "grammar." (1) Grammar may refer to the objectively observed and described pattern or structure of a language. (2) Grammar may refer to the "traditional" description—largely mistaken—of English transmitted to us by Latin-oriented grammarians of the seventeenth and eighteenth centuries. (3) Grammar may refer to a body of rules for the "correct" or "best" use of the language—rules based upon canons of "appropriate" usage.

Central to our discussion of grammar has been the notion that the study of grammar has its roots in a series of rather complex historical and cultural events. Linguistics, on the other hand, does not have a comparable historical dimension. As Leonard Bloomfield observed in his massively important *Language: "Linguistics,* the study of language, is only in its beginnings. The knowledge it has gained has not yet become part of our traditional education." This disjunction between grammar and linguistics is an important one; if we keep firmly in mind that "grammar" comes to us out of a welter of social, cultural, and historical developments, we have taken the first step toward the understanding of what "linguistics" is. For "linguistics" comes to us claiming to be modern, to be objective, to be accurate—in a word, it claims to be scientific. To properly assess this claim we must now consider the material upon which linguists work, and the kind of evidence linguistic labor is able to produce.

Early in his seminal book already referred to, Bloomfield writes: "The most difficult step in the study of language is the first step. Again and again, scholarship has approached the study of language

without actually entering upon it." Though this generalization may
seem puzzling, even cryptic, Bloomfield means by it to indicate that
before the scientific study of language can begin, the linguist must be
certain that he is studying material amenable to the axioms of scientific method. In the case of language, this material cannot be the
written record. The written record, first of all, is a fragmentary record. It exists only in part, and it exists, furthermore, as a specialized
and disciplined variant of the record of speech. If we look for pattern or whole-ness in such other attributes of language behavior as
gesture, physiology, psychology, we are involving ourselves with problems that transcend the simply linguistic, problems that involve inevitably and unmistakably ethical and intellectual dimensions that
are by definition non-scientific, although certainly not non-rational.
When we confine ourselves, however, to the study of speech, we gain
exemption from the value-judgments which are so obvious and desirable a part of the other areas of language behavior mentioned.
Speech can be shown to exist as pattern; observations, carefully controlled, will lead us to an objective, scientific description of the ways
in which a language functions. The task of the linguist, then, is first
of all deciphering this system of speech in order to give us the essential, relatively fixed, structural basis of the language.

What sort of data is derived from the study of speech patterns?
A linguist would say that the study of sounds reveals a range of possibilities, which are usually termed *phonemes.* Phonemes may conveniently be defined as the smallest independent, agreed-upon sound
features of a language. The number of phonemes in a language is
likely to be small; there are forty-six in English. They are the basic
material out of which further and more complex linguistic structures
are built. With just such an analogy in mind, Henry L. Gleason, Jr.,
in his lucid textbook on descriptive linguistics, compares the phonemes of a language to the elements of chemistry which are the building blocks of all substance.

Having observed the system of sounds that are available to the
user of any language, a linguist looks to the combinations of sounds
into larger units. While sounds may be combined into sequences of
all sorts, those sequences which "make sense" are our concern here.
As sound structures take on relevance to a number of individuals
within a speech-community, they have become transformed into significant symbols. These symbols, in their most basic denomination,
the linguist calls *morphemes.* Perhaps a brief example may be helpful. A morpheme is the smallest unit which carries a discernible

meaning of its own. Thus, in the sentence you are now reading, we see that the -*ing* of "reading" is a morpheme, as is the word "in," the longer word "sentence," and the word-part -*morph*. As words, constructed out of permissible sequences of sound and the necessary morphemic constituents are themselves brought together into sentences, we have entered the area of *syntax*. While syntax is an area not so apparently amenable to scientific description as was the area of sound, some linguists are now turning to syntax as a possible basis for the description of language—a basis that might seriously challenge the position of the "structural linguists" who are currently fashionable. Professor Gleason's essay entitled "Transformations" is a good explanation of the work of this new "transformational" or "generative" group, as are the works cited in the bibliography by Noam Chomsky and Robert Lees.

Although linguists disagree about the degree to which their science can be, or has been utilized pedagogically or practically, they certainly agree that language study on all levels must eventually adopt the accurate description that will be the result of scientific linguistics. The more tolerant among them will see the need for prudent application of the new principles, and will recognize that older approaches should not be summarily and flippantly anathematized. As James Sledd put it in his recent "Plea for Pluralism": "We do not want just one book or one syllabus—we want many books and many syllabi, taking a variety of positions." It is in harmony with the spirit of Professor Sledd's remark that the essays in this section have been assembled, and this introduction has been written. Both the essays and the introduction are designed to introduce the student to a wide variety of positions, ranging from the sensible description of grammars by Robert Pooley through the structural approach espoused by Charles Fries to the newer transformational model discussed by Professor Gleason.

THE ORIGIN OF GRAMMAR

Margaret Bryant and Janet Aiken

In any language the structure of grammar tends to grow simpler with the passage of time. It may reasonably be conjectured that we look back at what may be compared to one side of a hill or mountain of complication, and that there must be another side, hidden from our eyes, which includes the stages of grammatical development which occurred while the systems were acquiring complication. Obviously speech cannot have burst complete into being; and it may be profitable to include in our study some conjectures concerning the primary stages of grammar.

Earlier theorists, more naïve than we, were sure there was such a thing as a first word, and they even theorized concerning what part of speech that first word must have been. Was the noun first? Did primitive man learn to point to a tree, a mammoth, a flint, and give to each that particular grunt which was the great-great-grandfather of our word? Now and again one sees references to nouns as "the oldest words," or "the earliest forms of language." How much credence may we place in such phrases?

Similar superlatives are applied to the verb, and it is easy to recognize the usefulness of the verb to primitive man in giving commands, transmitting messages, and generally showing action. Is the verb, then, the oldest word? The term itself, deriving from *verbum,* which means *word,* seems to indicate it.

Few if any linguists have favored the adjective as the earliest sort of word, and yet it may be that it does not lack all claim to that distinction. One can visualize a primitive message bearer gasping out the primitive equivalent of "sick," or "dead." A primitive mother might easily say *Sh-h-h,* or its equivalent, meaning *quiet,* to her baby. And if the tender emotions brought words to man as they brought the mating calls to birds, there must have been very early equivalents for *beautiful* or *dear.*

From *Psychology of English,* Frederick Ungar Publishing Co., Inc., New York, 1940.

The interjection was designated by many nineteenth-century linguists as the earliest word. When hurt, even animals emit distinctive cries corresponding semantically to the human *Ow*. Indeed, an entire explanation or theory of language origins has been built on the notion that interjections were the heralds of speech. These independent utterances of no particular grammatical type are still viewed by many as the oldest words.

But today linguists refuse to dwell long on the relative claims to priority of the various parts of speech. The controversy is shelved as not worth fighting over. In the nature of things, it is held, we cannot know what word was first said by man; there is neither television nor telaudition to the past. It is a waste of time to give thought to a matter which must remain in the sphere of what has been called "lunar politics." For is not the genesis of human speech as insoluble a puzzle as that old game of squaring the circle?

It may be possible at least to throw some light upon this question by holding to a psychological view of it and by pointing out as a necessary preliminary to its consideration that language was and is a natural by-product of voice, occurring inevitably and independently as soon as mental development has attained a certain degree or standard.

In the older theories of the origin of language it was a well-nigh universal error to attempt to account for the origin of sound, or of meaningful sound. Since language was thought of as having been created out of nothing, theories were built up to explain what required no explanation. It is entirely true that the old theories of speech origin are vulnerable, but this is because they are all based on a false assumption—the assumption that sounds, even communications, are peculiar to human language.

Everything human has grown out of something earlier, and language is no exception. It grew out of the multiplicity of primitive cries and calls such as are made today by monkeys, birds, cats, dogs, and many other animals. It is entirely probable that this development occurred at the same time or at different times independently in various parts of the earth: it may even be that it has occurred within very recent times. Prehistoric man found himself at the dawn of human language with an animal language already fully developed. From this point on, his speech progress is to be explained by principles of psychology rather than of history or science.

But just what is the difference between animal language and human language? At what point does a significant cry such as the animals make become a human word or sentence? All of us have had experience with the "language" of animals, and we know that it implies a certain degree of reasoning power on the part of the animal using it. What is it then that differentiates such language from human speech?

The key to the solution may be found in the idea of context. Birds, cats, dogs, and monkeys—all the animals capable of emitting significant cries—make these cries in context, that is, in the particular situation which naturally gives rise to them. When a dog growls defiance it is because he means it. His playful growl is a different "sentence," reserved for a different occasion. He cannot talk about growling, cannot tell his master the story of a situation where growling was called for—cannot lift growling out of its context in his mind.

This is not, of course, to imply that dogs lack memory. Given a repetition of the occasion for growls, or even a part repetition of it, the growl may result. But this is still a growl in context. Canine noises out of context, such as the "speaking" which is rewarded by a bit of food, are the result of human training.

In the same way a hen may give a danger signal to her chicks if she sees or fancies approaching danger. It is incredible that such a signal could be given out of context or that on the roost at night the hen should talk over the various perils of the day. In a way it shows a greater honesty on the part of hens, and of the animal world generally, this inability to tell anything but the actual fact about danger. It distinguishes man as the only animal capable of lying; for that is how speaking out of context may at times be regarded.

Human speech alone enables the speaker to talk about his experiences without actually living them, to discuss hunger when well fed and rest when fatigued. And it was at the precise moment when cries came to be used out of context that they became, not cries, but human speech. The word *meow* (as contrasted to the feline cry *meow)* is a word, just because it is not a response to a physical or mental stimulus, but an idea capable of use under any circumstances. The difference between word and cry is not one of genesis, of meaning, or of usefulness; it is a difference of motive, of outlook, of circumstance.

Thus language in the human sense is seen to be conditioned on memory and imagination, the ability to make a topic of conversation out of what one says. The origin of language is subjective rather than objective and denotes a psychological change in the use of meaningful cries. And it is important to remember that at the moment when this subjective change occurred primitive man found himself already supplied with a limited "wordhoard," or stock of cries, which by their new use became language.

Slowly at first, and then perhaps more rapidly, this new use of cries stimulated an increase in the number and complexity of language elements. Speech was found to be a toy as well as a tool, a delightful game as well as a protection and a weapon. This multiplying of speech-cries, of course, served still further to differentiate them from animal cries, which as everyone knows are sharply limited in number, the animal's "vocabulary" seldom or never including more than a dozen items. It is the manner in which speech-cries developed which constitutes the history of primitive grammar.

Consider once again the warning cluck of the hen to her chicks. It may be interpreted variously as a noun, *danger,* as a verb, *beware,* as an adjective, *unsafe,* as an interjection, *scat,* as a preposition, *off.* We cannot read into it a part-of-speech classification; in fact, it is no one part of speech as opposed to any other.

Is it not apparent that this significant cry of the hen has no more to do with English syntax and word-analysis than with Chinese? Completely formulated, perhaps what the hen is saying is, "Danger is approaching, my children, and you had better make yourselves as scarce as you can, as soon as possible." All those twenty words are implicit in the single note. The squawk of the hen is obviously the great-great-grandmother of the sentence, not of the word. In itself it is precisely what we call a nonsentence in modern English.

But here again we encounter the fallacy almost universal among linguists, the fallacy of the sentence. A sentence is, or it is not, a group of words complete with subject and predicate, expressing a thought. If it is, then language is not made up exclusively of sentences, since the nonsentence, a complete thought lacking formal subject and predicate, is extremely common in speech, and to a less degree in writing. It is the nonsentence rather than the sentence which is the primitive unit of grammar, and it is the nonsentence rather than the word which explains the character of the earliest language.

What we may call "pre-language" consisted of meaningful cries used exclusively in context to express emotions, messages, commands, and other necessities of communication. Eventually such cries came to be used apart from the particular situation which might evoke them. People began to "talk over" their experiences, as well as to experience them; and with this "talking over" language and grammar were simultaneously born. The nonsentence is nearer to this primitive type of communication just because it is a conglomerate similar to and less analyzable grammatically than the sentence. Gradually, over long ages of human progress, the word emerged, through the breaking up into parts of this primitive nonsentence. As the word appeared, the parts of nonsentences became free as separate units suitable for recombining, and such recombinations paved the way for the gradual development of the formally complete sentence containing subject and predicate.

These primitive "pre-sentences" came to be broken up, and in the *Ursprache* which ancestored our own English they came regularly or normally to follow the subject-verb pattern. In Chinese, Eskimo, and many other languages, while they broke into parts, they never adopted the sentence pattern. Besides subject and predicate, the Indo-European languages developed more minute subdivisions, which attained great complexity in such languages as Greek and German; in English many such subdivisions have been sloughed off as unnecessary and trammeling.

Thus the progress of language is from significant cries to the pre-sentence or complete communication in unanalyzable form; from this to the word as a separable part of the communication unit; and from this differently in various language families to their distinctive syntactical elements and patterns. It is mirrored in our word *word*, which may apply to a message of any extent and is often used (for example, in the Bible) to mean communication. The first words were words only in this large sense. They were sentence words such as the animals now use, but used by primitive man imaginatively, lyingly, out of their proper occasion and context.

But in pointing out the subjective character of the beginning of grammar and its dependence upon the nonsentence, we are only setting off on the long march from primitiveness to complexity, around the corner, and back toward simplicity. Our next task must be to trace the later development of grammar so that we may understand why it looks as it does today.

We may notice, then, that the primitive cries out of which grammar was to develop were entirely independent of one another, as much so as are today the various items in the cat's "vocabulary."

The earliest grammar of all would have consisted merely of an inventory (if primitive man ever bothered to make one) of sound complexes, each as different from the other as a whistle from a sob. No synthesis was possible because there were no elements common to all the nonsentence cries which made up this earliest vocabulary.

Even today it is noticeable that nonsentences are far less analyzable grammatically than are sentences, and this may be one of the reasons why they are almost entirely disregarded in books of grammar. It is the nonsentence which retains most clearly the character of primitive speech, just as the so-called irregular verb is older than the regular verb. And it is certain that long before there existed anything which could be called a verb, man had his little stock or hoard of nonsentences, each one grammatically a law to itself.

Grammar began to develop as more nonsentences began to be added to this initial stock. These new items were, no doubt, often as distinct from all the rest as these had been from one another. But as time progressed, and more items were added to the language stock, it became impracticable to find new sound combinations, even if it was desirable. Synthesis began to come into being.

No doubt primitive ears were not sensitive to such small differentiations in sound as exist, for example, between the words *fern* and *farm,* and the aim in adding new speech-cries was undoubtedly clarity, intelligibility, and differentiation from anything already in the inventory. Perhaps a modern analogy to the progression of primitive utterances may be found in the choice of names for new telephone exchanges. Such names must be very distinctly different from the old, as Susquehanna and Butterfield and Endicott differ from Worth and John and Main. New nonsentences must be easily distinguishable to primitive ears from the old ones, and this necessitated a wide range of speech sounds and clear differentiation of sound combinations.[1]

New speech-cries might be made up out of nothing, but if modern word making is any criterion, it does not seem likely that this occurred often, since it almost never happens in modern speech that a new word is made up out of whole cloth. It seems probable that

[1] In Aiken, *Why English Sounds Change,* it is shown how the range of speech sounds has narrowed even within historic times. It can scarcely be doubted that primitive speech, like animal language, was drawn from a wider vocal area than is civilized speech.

even at the very start existing speech-cries were modified or combined in the making of new cries. No doubt much innovation took place as well, but it must have been very early that nonsentence combinations were developed. If, for example, there was a grunt accompanied perhaps by a pointing to indicate what we call *he,* then this grunt might from early times have been combined with other sounds indicating *danger* or *love* or *discomfort.*

Many speech-cries no doubt were originated which never came to general use; but out of babbling, whining, cooing, growling, grunting, and so forth, there must have emerged the regular combinations which we may call syntactical.

With this combining of speech-cries we have the beginning of grammar; previous additions to the stock of speech-cries were in the nature of vocabulary. Such combining had later to be differentiated into inflexions and syntax, but the latter term better describes this primitive juxtaposing of nonsentence cries. Many speech-cries were no doubt combined in whole or in part to express new ideas or idea-combinations, and it is these new speech patterns which we may call syntactical.

No doubt much grammar was originated by children, and much from play, as well as from the sterner preoccupations of life. The fascination of language juggling must have early felt, and one new combining led rapidly to another, so that the linguistic stock expanded at a comparatively quick rate because of the pleasures of out-of-context use.

It is important to emphasize that inflexions were in all probability a later development than syntax. As many writers on the subject have pointed out, the pronouns still show themselves clearly embedded in verbal and other affixes in such languages as Latin and Hebrew, and Hebrew also shows prepositional and conjunctional affixes, which may well point to the manner in which case may have originated in the Indo-European group of tongues. Inflexion is a younger process than syntax and one which we may reasonably suppose grew out of it.

If this is the fact, then the earliest inflexion, like the earliest speech-cry itself, was an independent communication. It was not an inflexion in the modern sense, that is, a sound or syllable added to a certain "part of speech" with complete or fair regularity. It was merely a tag or modification in a single word, somewhat of the nature of a compounding, but susceptible of extension to other words after the fashion of an inflexion.

On this basis it is easy to understand how inflexions should have grown up so luxuriantly in the early stages of grammar. Every word was a potential inflexion. It had only to prove itself useful in combination with numerous words, not necessarily all of a single kind, and it was likely to become more and more closely embedded in these words, until finally it lost its separate existence.

Modern English illustrates the process (which of course is recurrent and not confined to primitive languages) in the adverbial termination *ly*, used in *readily, easily, frankly, silently,* and hosts of other English words. Even so recently as the Anglo-Saxon period this *ly* was *lice*, meaning *like*. The compounded adverb is still found, particularly in Irish dialect: *He walked soft-like.* In most uses the word has become a suffix of a semi-inflexional character.

It was inevitable, likewise, that inflexions should be partial rather than complete in their applicability, since several different words might be used for a given idea, such as *many* or *past*, and such words might compound readily with only a few other terms. There is nothing peculiar in the fact that we find primitive languages with a plethora of declensions, conjugations, and other such categories. Even in Modern English, which has dropped most of its inflexional forms, we still have two ways (*more* and *er, most* and *est)* of forming the comparative and the superlative; and plurals are formed in several different ways.

Synthesis is a power relatively lacking in early stages of mental and social development. In many departments of grammar in many languages synthesis has failed to appear, even down to present times. Anyone could construct an English more synthesized than the one we speak. It is entirely consistent with what we know of the mentality of man in the various stages of his development to conclude that he would at first see grammatical relationships one by one rather than in categories. It was only very slowly and gradually that such grammatical categories could have developed, if indeed they ever developed at all.

In the beginning of grammar every word must have formed a category by itself, and it may be that in the Chinese language we have an example of a speech which never abandoned this primitive heterogeneity. Scholars are divided on the question whether Chinese ever went through an inflexional or a syntactical stage, but it is evident that so far as its grammar goes the language is today in a state similar to that which must have obtained in primitive speech.

In Chinese, as is well known, every word consists of a single syllable, and there are no such things as inflexions. Inflexional relationships are indicated, if at all, by separate words. There are no parts of speech; words shift around freely from function to function just as they are increasingly doing in the English language. Intelligibility is attained by sentence order and context. A distinction is made between "full" and "empty" words, the latter being what are known as "structural" words, such as prepositions, conjunctions, articles, and so forth. This absence of inflexions by no means hinders the Chinese from expressing complicated meanings with complete clarity, and it is entirely possible that the inflexionless state of Chinese has existed since the origin of that language.

In the western dialects, as well as in many eastern tongues, categories of person, gender, case, tense, mood, and the rest appeared. In the manner just described these categories multiplied themselves; but no sooner had great diversity appeared than certain categories began to merge and simplify.

To recur to the figure of a mountain used at the beginning of this chapter, we had in the early stages of grammar a steeply ascending curve of grammatical complication. The peak came at the point where the tendency to simplify overtook the tendency to multiply complications, and language began to descend to the state well represented by Modern English, where grammatical complications of form are tending to disappear.

Thus grammar in the shape of inflexions tends to be simple only at the birth and at the complete maturity of a language. In the field of syntax, on the other hand, grammar develops by juxtaposition of elements into a more or less fixed word order, out of which, in the Indo-European and Semitic languages, the sentence as we know it has developed.

The chief syntactical necessity in any language is to achieve a word pattern or group of patterns which will convey meanings with clarity. In Chinese nothing like the English sentence has developed, and the order of sentence elements is extremely fluid. In the Semitic- and Indo-European-language families we have roughly parallel developments into a fixed word order to which the term *sentence* may be applied.[2]

It is worth noting that all these developments into and out of grammatical forms are impelled by a variety of forces, most of them

---

[2] This order differs in the Hebrew in that it is ordinarily verb-subject-complement, instead of subject-verb-complement as in English.

having little or nothing to do with logic. We can understand these forces as they apply to Modern English, and we may conjecture that they were similar at earlier stages of linguistic experience. In this fashion can grammatical origins be analyzed.

WHERE OUR GRAMMAR CAME FROM   *Karl Dykema*

The title of this paper is too brief to be quite accurate. Perhaps with the following subtitle it does not promise too much: A partial account of the origin and development of the attitudes which commonly pass for grammatical in Western culture and particularly in English-speaking societies.

The etymology of *grammar* shows rather sharp changes in meaning: It starts with Greek *gramma, letter* (of the alphabet), itself a development from *graphein, draw* or *write*. The plural *grammata* develops in meaning through *letters* to *alphabet* to the *rudiments of writing*, to *the rudiments of learning*. The adjective form *grammatike* with *techne* meant the art of knowing one's letters. From this form comes the Latin *grammaticus*. The medieval vernacular forms with *r* are something of a mystery, appearing first in Old Provençal as *gramaira* and developing in English with a variety of spellings, often with only one *m* and ending in *er*. One of the more amusing forms is that with the first *r* dissimilated to *l*, *glamour*.

In present usage at least four senses can be distinguished which have an application to language: (1) The complete structural pattern of a language learned unconsciously by the child as he acquires his native tongue; (2) an attempt to describe objectively and systematically this fundamental structure, usually called descriptive grammar; (3) a partial description of the language based on puristic or pedagogical objectives, usually called prescriptive grammar, (4) a conviction held by a good many people that somewhere there is an authoritative book called a grammar, the conscientious memorization of which will eliminate all difficulties from their use of language. This I call grammar as remedy. It is mainly with the last two of these notions of grammar that I shall concern myself, prescriptive grammar and grammar as remedy, and how the earlier conceptions of grammar were metamorphosed into them.

From *College English*, April, 1961. Reprinted with the permission of The National Council of Teachers of English, and of the author.

As the etymology of the word suggests, Western grammar begins with the ancient Greeks. As early as Plato we find in the *Sophist* the statement that a word describing action is a verb (rhema), one which performs the action is a noun (onoma). Aristotle adds conjunctions (syndesmoi), recognizes that sentences have predicates, and is aware of three genders and of inflection (*Rhetoric*, etc.). The Stoics attempted to separate linguistic study from philosophy and made important contributions to the discipline. In their writings we find terms which are approximately equivalent to *noun, verb, conjunction, article, number, gender, case, voice, mood,* and *tense.*[1] But the direct source of most of our widely used grammatical terms is Dionysius Thrax's little *Techne Grammatike,* which Gilbert Murray recollects his great-uncle still using at the Merchants Taylors' School in the nineteenth century to learn Greek from.[2]

A few quotations from this little work will illustrate how close many of our school grammars still are to their source of more than 2000 years ago:

> A sentence is a combination of words, either in prose or verse, making complete sense. . . . Of discourse there are eight parts: noun, verb, participle, article, pronoun, preposition, adverb, and conjunction. . . . A noun is a part of discourse having cases, indicating a body (as 'stone') or a thing (as 'education'), and is used in a common and a peculiar way (i.e., is common or proper). . . . A verb is a word without case, admitting tenses, persons, and numbers, and indicating action and passion (i.e., being-acted-upon). . . . A pronoun is a word indicative of definite persons and used in place of a noun. . . . The adverb is an uninflected part of discourse, used of a verb or subjoined to a verb. . . . The conjunction is a word conjoining or connecting thought in some order and filling a gap in the expression.[3]

The few examples I have given emphasize analysis by meaning, because that is the aspect of classical grammar which our traditional grammar has dwelt upon. But the definitions of noun and verb, it should be observed, begin with formal distinctions—case and tense— and throughout the work there is clearly an awareness of the importance of structure in the functioning of the language. The contribution of the Greeks to linguistics was a great one, as Gilbert Murray and

[1] R. H. Robins, *Ancient and Medieval Grammatical Theory in Europe* (London, 1951), pp. 20–35.

[2] Gilbert Murray, *Greek Studies* (Oxford, 1946), p. 181.

[3] "The Grammar of Dionysius Thrax," translated . . . by Thos. Davidson, *Journal of Speculative Philosophy,* VIII (1874), 326–339.

others have pointed out. But for twenty centuries their work was carried on by slavish and unimaginative imitators incapable of developing the work of their predecessors. Especially in the less highly inflected languages like English and French it did not occur to them that the inflectional devices of Latin and Greek must have some counterpart in the structure of the modern language.

Though today there are a few scholars in universities who assert that they pursue grammar for its own sake as an academic discipline, most people conceive of grammar only as a utilitarian thing, as a means of learning to use a language correctly. This notion was certainly completely absent from the thinking of Plato, Aristotle, and the Stoics, and probably from that of Dionysius Thrax. Grammar began as a philosophical inquiry into the nature of language. Now, for most people, it is merely a dogmatic means of achieving correctness. It is this transformation that I am mainly concerned with.

How the transformation took place is not easy to document. Perhaps the most plausible explanation lies in the familiar desire of younger teachers to regurgitate undigested fragments of what they have swallowed in the course of their higher education. All too often a high school teacher just out of college will use his college lecture notes as the foundation of his high school teaching, or a teacher of undergraduates tries to give them exactly what he got in his graduate seminar.

Then there is the fundamental difference between the prevailing purposes of elementary and advanced instruction. Primary education is severely utilitarian; and though it can hardly be denied that, especially in our society, graduate instruction is often infected by utilitarianism, the speculative approach does persist, and inquiry for its own sake plays a major role. The curriculum at all levels of education is and has been determined partly by tradition, partly by immediate utilitarian objectives, partly by a desire to perpetuate the best elements of the cultural heritage. The application of these criteria is of ascending difficulty. Easiest is to accept without question the practice of one's predecessors; not much harder is to accept a limited practical goal and provide instruction intended to achieve it. Most difficult is to select critically what is most valuable in the cultural heritage, and the Romans weren't up to it.

Because of Greek prestige in the ancient world, less developed cultures borrowed extensively from that of Greece. The influence of Greek art, philosophy, and literature on Rome is familiar, but Greek grammar was quite as influential and became the model not only for grammars of Latin but of Syriac, Armenian, Hebrew, and possibly Arabic as well.

It could not be a good model. The structure of every language is peculiar to itself—though there are, of course, similarities between members of the same linguistic family—and the best description of it derives from a careful examination of the language itself, not from an attempt to fit it into the pattern of another. To be sure, both Greek and Latin are rich in inflections and the Latin of Varro was not much further away from the parent Indo-European than was the Greek of Dionysius Thrax; so the deformation imposed by the model was less distorting than when the same procedure was followed many centuries later and attempts were made to strait-jacket the modern vernaculars of Europe within the model of Latin grammar. For example, Greek had a definite article, Latin had none, though in Varro's *De Lingua Latina*, the term *articuli* is applied to the demonstrative *is* and *hic* (VIII, 45, 51). Latin has more cases but a different tense system and no dual. English has only two inflected active tenses against six for Latin, but many more periphrastic verbal constructions than had Latin.

The attention given to grammar by the ancients seems to have been considerable. Susemihl in his *History of Greek Literature in the Alexandrian Period* discusses over fifty grammarians. One of them, Aristophanes of Byzantium (ca. 257–ca. 180 B.C.), was librarian to Ptolomy Epiphanius, who imprisoned him to prevent the king of Pergamum from hiring him away.

Among the Romans, grammarians were also in demand. The slave Lutatius Daphnis, a grammarian, was bought for 700,000 sesterces, perhaps $35,000, which puts him about in the class of a lesser baseball player. Caesar put this Lutatius Daphnis in charge of the public libraries, though it was not until much later, according to Suetonius, that a regular salary of 100,000 sesterces was paid from the privy purse for Latin and Greek teachers of rhetoric (Suetonius, *Lives of the Caesars*, VIII, xviii). Caesar himself took part in one of the persisting grammatical quarrels of the time, that of the analogists and the anomalists, by producing a work called *De Analogia*, known to us only in fragments. Though he favored the analogists, who demanded complete inflectional consistency, it is significant that he wanted no radical departures from usage.[4] Suetonius also states that Claudius "invented three new letters and added them to the [Latin] alphabet, maintaining that they were greatly needed; he published a book on their theory

---

[4] Jean Collart, *Varron, Grammairien Latin* (Paris, 1954), pp. 10, 19, 146; Robins, p. 58.

when he was still in private life, and when he became emperor had no difficulty in bringing about their general use" (Suetonius, *Lives of the Caesars*, V, xli). Theodore Roosevelt was less successful when he tried to impose a few spelling reforms on the Government Printing Office; Congress refused to permit the changes.

Though Caesar favored the analogists, he was unwilling to depart from established usage. His position was that of many of his cultivated contemporaries, as it has been of many cultivated people ever since. The appeal of analogy is the appeal of logic, a creation of the Greeks and a tool that has been used with interesting and surprising effects in most areas of Western thought ever since. The foundation of Aristotelian logic is the syllogism. As the analogists applied the syllogism to language it worked like this: The form of the personal pronoun determines the form of the verb of which the pronoun is the subject. The form *you* is plural; therefore the form of the verb *be* which follows it must be plural; hence *you were*, not *you was*. So we have in cultivated English today only *you were*. But the cultivated dare not apply this syllogism to the intensive or reflexive, where the eighteenth-century practice of agreement with the notional number of the pronoun still persists. The eighteenth century had both *you was there yourself* and *you were there yourselves;* while we have *you were there yourselves* when the notional number of *you* is plural, but *you were there yourself* when it is singular.

Language has its own logic, which it is the function of the descriptive grammarian to discover if he can. Whatever it may be, it is not Aristotelian logic. But for two millennia our attitudes toward language have been colored by the assumption that the system of a language can be analyzed and prescribed by an intellectual tool that is inapplicable.

Conformity to a standard, or correctness if you like, is, of course, socially of the greatest importance. There is a long record of the penalties imposed on those who deviate from the standard, the earliest I know of being the account given in *Judges* (12, 4-6) of the forty and two thousand Ephraimites who were slain by the Gileadites because they pronounced *shibboleth sibboleth*. Later examples are less gory. Aristophanes in the *Lysistrata* (lines 81–206) ridicules the dialect of the Spartan women, though they are the allies of the Athenian women in their campaign of sexual frustration. Stephen Runciman in his *Byzantine Civilization* says "the Patriarch Nicetas in the Eleventh Century was laughed at for his Slavonic accent, and the statesman Margarites treated with disrespect in the Thirteenth because he spoke with a rough rustic voice." [5] And Chaucer's nun spoke the provincial French of the Benedictine nunnery of Stratford-Bow, the French of Paris—standard French—being to her unknown.

Conformity to the standard is what matters. But how is the standard to be determined? Quintilian, whom Professor T. W. Baldwin calls "The Supreme Authority" in his *Shakespeare's Small Latine and Lesse Greeke*, provides a most illuminating basis for discussion. In the *Institutes* Quintilian tells us that:

> Language is based on reason, antiquity, authority and usage. Reason finds its chief support in analogy and sometimes in etymology. As for antiquity, it is commended to us by the possession of a certain majesty, I might almost say sanctity. Authority as a rule we derive from orators and historians. For poets, owing to the necessities of metre, are allowed a certain licence. . . . The judgment of a supreme orator is placed on the same level as reason, and even error brings no disgrace, if it results from treading in the footsteps of such distinguished guides. Usage however is the surest pilot in speaking, and we should treat language as currency minted with the public stamp. But in all cases we have need of a critical judgment. . . . (I.vi.1–3)

This is fuller than Horace's neater statement: "Use is the judge, and law, and rule of speech" (*De Arte Poetica*, 72: *Quem* [*usus*] *penes arbitrium est et ius et norma loquendi.*) and shows more clearly why we have troubles. Usage "is the surest pilot" but "we have need of a critical judgment."

Quintilian has more to say on the matter:

> Usage remains to be discussed. For it would be almost laughable to prefer the language of the past to that of the present day, and what is ancient speech but ancient usage of speaking? But even here the critical faculty is necessary, and we must make up our minds what we mean by usage. If it be defined merely as the practice of the majority, we shall have a very dangerous rule affecting not merely style but life as well, a far more serious matter. For where is so much good to be found that what is right should please the majority? The practices of depilation, of dressing the hair in tiers, or of drinking to excess at the baths, although they may have thrust their way into society, cannot claim the support of usage, since there is something to blame in all of them (although we have usage on our side when we bathe or have our hair cut or take our meals together). So too in speech we must not accept as a rule of language words and phrases that have become a vicious habit

[5] Stephen Runciman, *Byzantine Civilization* (Meridian Books, New York, 1956), pp. 173, 176.

with a number of persons. To say nothing of the language of the uneducated, so we are all of us well aware that whole theatres and the
entire crowd of spectators will often commit *barbarisms* in the cries
which they utter as one man. I will therefore define usage in speech
as the agreed practice of educated men, just as where our way of life is
concerned I should define it as the agreed practice of all good men.
(I.vi. 43–45)

But Quintilian makes it quite apparent from the many examples he
cites that educated men are not entirely agreed on their practice, and
that they lean heavily on the authority of Greek usage:

> More recent scholars have instituted the practice of giving Greek nouns
> their Greek declension, although this is not always possible. Personally
> I prefer to follow the Latin method, so far as grace of diction will per-
> mit. For I should not like to say *Calypsonem* on the analogy of *Iuno-
> nem,* although Gaius Caesar in deference to antiquity does adopt this
> way of declining it. Current practice has however prevailed over his
> authority. In other words which can be declined in either way with-
> out impropriety, those who prefer it can employ the Greek form: they
> will not be speaking Latin, but will not on the other hand deserve cen-
> sure. (I.v. 63–64)

A thorough knowledge of Greek, learned from slave-tutors, had long
been common among educated Romans, but it was Varro who trans-
ferred the entire body of Greek grammatical scholarship to Latin in
his *De Lingua Latina,* written between 47 and 45 B.C. Though of the
original 25 books of that work only V through X survive relatively
intact, we have a fairly good account of what was in the rest because
Varro is the source which all later Latin grammarians follow, and they
have apparently borrowed from him most faithfully.

Greek grammar, is, then, a development of Greek philosophy, an attempt to treat systematically an important aspect of human behavior.
It is a late development which in Alexandrian culture is given a practical application through its use in the editing, elucidation, and interpretation of texts, especially that of Homer; and in the correction
of solecisms. Since there was little of the speculative in the Romans,
Varro's encyclopedic treatment of Latin language and literature was
the ultimate source of a host of school texts.

What has been presented so far is a partial account of the development of philology, though this ancient term has been an ambiguous
one for almost as long as it has existed—naturally enough, since it
derives from the Greek roots usually translated as *love* and *word.*
Some people love words as the means of argument, others because they

are the foundation of literature, others still for their forms and relations in discourse. All these senses have been designated by the word since it first appeared in Greek, and in nineteenth-century France and Germany it normally included literary history, textual and literary criticism, and linguistics. (We might well revive the word; it would provide a single term by which we could describe ourselves along with chemists, historians, and the rest; we are philologists.)

The ancients called the various aspects of this study by a variety of names: *philologos, grammatikos, grammatistes, kritikos* in Greek; *philologus, grammaticus, litterator, criticus* in Latin. They were evidently no more certain of exactly what the terms signified than we are today with similar terms. Suetonius writes:

> The term *grammaticus* became prevalent through Greek influence, but at first such men were called *litterati*. Cornelius Nepos, too, in a little book in which he explains the difference between *litteratus* and *eruditus* says that the former is commonly applied to those who can speak or write on any subject accurately, cleverly and with authority; but that it should strictly be used of interpreters of the poets, whom the Greeks call *grammatici*. That these were also called *litteratores* is shown by Messala Corvinus in one of his letters, in which he says: "I am not concerned with Furius Bibaculus, nor with Ticidas either, or with the *litterator* Cato." For he unquestionably refers to Valerius Cato, who was famous both as a poet and as a grammarian. Some however make a distinction between *litteratus* and *litterator,* as the Greeks do between *grammaticus* and *grammatista,* using the former of a master of his subject, the latter of one moderately proficient. Orbilius too supports this view by examples, saying: "In the days of our forefathers, when anyone's slaves were offered for sale, it was not usual except in special cases to advertise any one of them as *litteratus* but rather as *litterator,* implying that he had a smattering of letters, but was not a finished scholar."
>
> The grammarians of early days taught rhetoric as well, and we have treatises from many men on both subjects. It was this custom, I think, which led those of later times also, although the two professions had now become distinct, nevertheless either to retain or to introduce certain kinds of exercises suited to the training of orators, such as problems, paraphrases, addresses, character sketches and similar things; doubtless that they might not turn over their pupils to the rhetoricians wholly ignorant and unprepared. But I observe that such instruction is now given up, because of the lack of application and the youth of some of the pupils; for I do not believe that it is because the subjects are underrated. I remember that at any rate when I was a young man, one of these teachers, Princeps by name, used to declaim and engage in dis-

cussion on alternate days; and that sometimes he would give instruction in the morning, and in the afternoon remove his desk and declaim. I used to hear, too, that within the memory of our forefathers some passed directly from the grammar school to the Forum and took their place among the most eminent advocates. *(On Grammarians,* iv)

Another writer who provides evidence on the Roman attitudes towards language is Aulus Gellius in his *Attic Nights.* Gellius represents the aristocrat's conviction that what he himself does must be right coupled with the conservative attitude that older practice is to be preferred:

> Valerius Probus was once asked, as I learned from one of his friends, whether one ought to say *has urbis* or *has urbes* and *hanc turrem* or *hanc turrim.* "If," he replied, "you are either composing verse or writing prose and have to use those words, pay no attention to the musty, fusty rules of the grammarians, but consult your own ear as to what is to be said in any given place. What it favours will surely be the best." Then the one who had asked the question said: "What do you mean by 'consult my ear'?" and he told me that Probus answered: "Just as Vergil did his, when in different passages he has used *urbis* and *urbes,* following the taste and judgment of his ear. For in the first *Georgic,* which," said he, "I have read in a copy corrected by the poet's own hand, he wrote *urbis* with an *i. . . .*
>
> But turn and change it so as to read *urbes,* and somehow you will make it duller and heavier. On the other hand, in the third *Aeneid* he wrote *urbes* with an *e: . . .*
>
> Change this too so as to read *urbis* and the word will be too slender and colourless, so great indeed is the different effect of combination in the harmony of neighbouring sounds. . . . .
>
> These words have, I think, a more agreeable lightness than if you should use the form in *e* in both places." But the one who had asked the question, a boorish fellow surely and with untrained ear, said: "I don't just understand why you say that one form is better and more correct in one place and the other in the other." Then Probus, now somewhat impatient, retorted: "Don't trouble then to inquire whether you ought to say *urbis* or *urbes.* For since you are the kind of man that I see you are and err without detriment to yourself, you will lose nothing whichever you say." (XIII, xxi, 3-8)

And his attitude towards grammarians is expressed quite as explicitly in this passage:

> Within my memory Aelius Melissus held the highest rank among the grammarians of his day at Rome; but in literary criticism he showed

greater boastfulness and sophistry than real merit. Besides many other
works which he wrote, he made a book which at the time when it was
issued seemed to be one of remarkable learning. The title of the book
was designed to be especially attractive to readers, for it was called *On
Correctness in Speech*. Who, then would suppose that he could speak
correctly or with propriety unless he had learned those rules of Melissus?
From that book I take these words: *"Matrona,* 'a matron,' is a woman
who has given birth once; she who has done so more than once is called
mater familias, 'mother of a family'; just so a sow which has had one
litter is called *porcetra;* one which has had more, *scrofa."* But to decide
whether Melissus thought out this distinction between *matrona* and
mater familias and that it was his own conjecture, or whether he read
what someone else had written, surely requires soothsayers. For with
regard to *porcetra* he has, it is true, the authority of Pomponius in the
Atellan farce which bears that very title; but that "matron" was applied
only to a woman who had given birth once, and "mother of the family"
only to one who had done so more than once, can be proved by the
authority of no ancient writer.... (XVIII, vi. 1-7)

By the Middle Ages the aristocrats were unlikely to have had much
education, and the classical heritage was perpetuated by the grammarians, whose dogmatic victory was complete. Donatus (fl. 400) and
Priscian (fl. 500) are the dominating figures. The name of the first,
shortened to Donat or Donet, became synonymous with 'grammar' or
'lesson' in Old French and Middle English, and the grammar of the
second survives in over a thousand manuscripts.[6] He also has the
distinction of being consigned to Hell by Dante (*Inferno*, 15:110).

As an example of Priscian, here is the beginning of an analysis of
the *Aeneid*—this is not from his big grammar, which was in eighteen
books, but from a smaller one, *Partitiones Duodecim Versuum Aeneidos
Principalium:*

Scan the verse. *Arma vi/rumque ca/no Tro/iae qui/primus ab/oris.*
How many caesuras does it have? Two. What are they? Semiquinaria
(penthemimeral) and semiseptenaria (hephthemimeral). How? The
semiquinaria is *arma virumque cano* and the semiseptenaria is *arma
virumque cano Troiae.* How many figures are there? Ten. For what
reason? Because it consists of three dactyls and two spondees. How
many parts of speech has this verse? Nine. How many nouns? Six:
arma, virum, Troiae, qui, primus, oris. How many verbs? One: *cano.*
How many prepositions? One: *ab.* How many conjunctions? One,

---

[6] John Edwin Sandys, *A History of Classical Scholarship* (Cambridge, 1920),
vol. 1, p. 230, note; p. 274.

que. Discuss each word; *arma,* what part of speech is it? Noun. Of what sort? Appellative (or common). What is its species? General. Its gender? Neuter. Why neuter? Because all nouns which end in *a* in the plural are unquestionably of neuter gender. Why is the singular not used? Because this noun signifies many and various things. . . .[7]

And this is not the end of the catechism on the opening line of Virgil. Evidently this sort of drill was to accompany the study of the poem from beginning to end, if the end was ever reached.

Increasingly in the Middle Ages the written heritage of Greece and Rome was accepted unquestioningly because literate men did not have a cultural background which would permit them to ask pertinent questions. We learn, for example, that one of the best sources for the text of Diogenes Laertius is a manuscript of about 1200 written by a scribe "who obviously knew no Greek."[8] To be sure, there were sometimes conflicts between the Christian heritage and the classical, usually resolved in favor of the Christian. In a medieval manuscript is this comment: "Concerning the words *scala* (step), and *scopa* (broom), we do not follow Donatus and the others who claim they are plural because we know that the Holy Ghost has ruled that they are singular." And it was comforting when the traditions of classical grammar could be given divine corroboration. For example: "The verb has three persons. This I hold to be divinely inspired, for our belief in the Trinity is thereby manifested in words." Or this: "Some maintain that there are more, some that there are fewer parts of speech. But the world-encircling church has only eight offices [Presumably Ostiariat, Lektorat, Exorzistat, Akolythat, Subdiakonat, Diakonat, Presbyterat, Episkopat]. I am convinced this this is through divine inspiration. Since it is through Latin that those who are chosen come most quickly to a knowledge of the Trinity and under its guidance find their way along the royal road into their heavenly home, it was necessary that the Latin language should be created with eight parts of speech."[9]

On the other hand, St. Boniface's (675-754) "sense of grammatical accuracy was so deeply shocked when he heard an ignorant priest administering the rite of baptism *in nomine Patria et Filia et Spiritus sancti*

[7] Heinrich Keil, *Grammatici Latini* (Leipzig, 1859), vol. 3, p. 459.

[8] Diogenes Laertius, *Lives of Eminent Philosophers,* with an English translation by R. D. Hicks (Loeb Classical Library) (Cambridge & London, 1925), vol. 1, p. xxxv. (The quotations from Suetonius, Varro, Quintilian, and Aulus Gellius are from the translations in the Loeb Classical Library editions.)

[9] J. J. Baebler, *Beiträge zu einer Geschichte ler lateinischen Grammatik im Mittelalter,* (Halle a. S., 1885), p.. 22/Hans Arens, *Sprachwissenschaft, der Gang ihrer Entwicklung von der Antike bis zur Gegenwart* (Munich, 1955), pp. 30, 31.

[that is, with complete disregard of the required case endings] that he almost doubted the validity of the rite." [10]

Up to about the twelfth century Donatus and Priscian, whose grammars were based ultimately on classical Latin, were followed unquestioningly except where there seemed to be a conflict with sacred texts. The Vulgate and various theological writings were in a later Latin which might disagree with classical grammar, as in the more frequent use of the personal pronouns.[11]

But in the twelfth century the reintroduction of Greek philosophy had a tremendous impact on medieval thought, as is best illustrated by the Aristotelianism of Aquinas. And St. Thomas, as might be expected, deals with philological matters in the *Summa Theologica,* and again as might be expected through the syllogism:

> It seems that in Holy Writ a word cannot have several senses, historical or literal, allegorical, tropological or moral, and anagogical. For many different senses in one text produce confusion and deception and destroy all force of argument. Hence no argument, but only fallacies, can be deduced from a multiplicity of propositions. But Holy Writ ought to be able to state the truth without any fallacy. Therefore in it there cannot be several senses to a word. (First Part, Question One, Article 10, Objection 1)

A more explicitly grammatical example is this one from the thirteenth century:

> For a complete sentence, two things are necessary, namely a subject and a predicate. The subject is that which is being discussed; it is what determines the person of the verb. The predicate is that which is expressed by the subject. Nouns were invented to provide subjects.... Verbs were invented to provide predicates.

This concept of grammar being something created is found in another thirteenth-century writer:

> Was he who invented grammar a grammarian? No, because the creation of grammar cannot be based on teaching since that would presuppose its existence. Grammar was invented. For the invention of grammar must precede grammar. So it was not the grammarian but the philosopher who created grammar, for the philosopher studies the nature of things and recognizes their essential qualities.[12]

[10] Sandys, p. 469.
[11] Baebler, p. 22.
[12] Arens, pp. 32, 34.

The authority of the grammarian was occasionally challenged. In a seventeenth-century German satirical treatment of schoolmasters is this account of a fifteenth-century episode:

> The Emperor Sigismund came to the Council of Constance and said: "Videte patres, ut eradicetis schismam Hussitarium." There sat an old Bohemian pedant in the Council who was convinced that with this box on the ear to Priscian the Emperor had sinned against the Catholic Church as gravely as had John Hus and Hieronymus of Prague. So he said [in Latin]: Most Serene Highness, *schisma* is neuter gender." The emperor said [in German]: "How do you know that?" The old Bohemian pedant answered [now in German]: "Alexander Gallus says so." The emperor said: "Who is Alexander Gallus?" The Bohemian pedant answered: "He is a monk." "Yes," said Sigismund, "I am the Roman emperor, and my word is worth at least that of a monk." (Joh. Balthaser Schupp, *Der Teutsche Schulmeister*, 1663) [13]

It now remains to consider the transfer of these attitudes to the modern vernacular languages. But first a brief review of the three preceding stages. The first is the unique situation in Greece, which differed from that of any of the succeeding cultures in two significant ways: It was essentially a monolingual society, and at least during the period of its greatest intellectual and artistic achievement it knew nothing of formal grammar. Rome differed in both essentials. The cultivated Roman was educated in Greek, and formal grammar was a part of his Latin education, though this does not mean that he learned Greek through formal grammar. In the Middle Ages the two-language requirement for the educated, which was characteristic of Rome, was continued, but with an important difference. Whereas for the Roman, Latin was a respectable language with a respectable literature, for the educated man of the Middle Ages his native vernacular was not respectable and at least at first had no important literature. Also he learned the language of scholarship and literature in a way quite different from that used by the Roman. He learned it with the aid of formal grammar.

Of these three stages, the third, the medieval, is much the longest; in formal education and scholarship it lasts well into the eighteenth century and therefore has a duration of well over a thousand years. Of course during the last two or three hundred of those years a great change had come over Europe, due partly to an intimate reacquaintance with the heritage of Greece and Rome. But in the field of philology

[13] Baebler, p. 118.

this meant largely a return to the attitudes of the ancients. It also meant the transference of the whole philological approach—ancient and medieval—to the modern vernacular languages.

The history of vernacular grammars and of English grammars in particular comes next in this development, but there is no space for it here.

One consequence of this transfer must be illustrated: The ambivalence it has given us toward language. Here are some examples. Trollope in his *Autobiography* writes:

> The ordinary talk of ordinary people is carried on in short sharp expressive sentences, which very frequently are never completed,—the language of which even among educated pople is often incorrect. The novel-writer in constructing his dialogue must so steer between absolute accuracy of language—which would give to his conversation an air of pedantry, and the slovenly inaccuracy of ordinary talkers, which if closely followed would offend by an appearance of grimace—as to produce upon the ear of his readers a sense of reality. If he be quite real he will seem to attempt to be funny. If he be quite correct he will seem to be unreal.[14]

The nineteenth-century German philologist Wilhelm Scherer, discussing the great dramatist Heinrich Kleist, remarks that "he did distinguished work in all forms. There dwells in his language an individual magic, though he has an uncertain control of German grammar."[15] And in a recent review in the *TLS* is this sentence: "He [Leonard Clark] died after completing the first draft of his book, *Yucatan Adventure*, which would have gained some grammar, while losing some of the punch of its author's virile enthusiasm, if it had been more carefully revised."[16]

In a detective story, Rex Stout has Archie Goodwin make this comment after one of the principal characters has said, "Yes. . . . We shall see.":

> But what really settled it was her saying, "We shall see." He [Nero Wolfe] will always stretch a point, within reason, for people who use words as he thinks they should be used.[17]

[14] Anthony Trollope, *An Autobiography* (World's Classics, Oxford, 1953), p. 206.
[15] Wilhelm Scherer, *Geschichte der deutschen Literatur* (Knaur, Berlin, n. d.), p. 752.
[16] *Times Literary Supplement,* March 20, 1959, p. 156.
[17] Rex Stout, "Murder Is No Joke," *And Four to Go, A Nero Wolfe Foursome* (Viking, New York, 1958), p. 155.

But in another story Wolfe is made to say, "If it's her again ..." [18]

And Mark Twain, who took Cooper severely to task for his "ungrammatical" English did what was perhaps his best work, in *Huckleberry Finn*, by using a narrative device which relieved him of all responsiblity for conforming to standard usage.

One of the most eloquent and emphatic in condemnation of the Latin grammatical tradition was Macaulay but, as you might guess, he is much too long to quote here.[19]

I conclude by returning to the four senses of the term grammar outlined at the beginning. Contemporary philologists who specialize in linguistics have, it seems to me, attempted to strip away the accretions of two thousand years and are turning to a rigorously descriptive approach, the seeds of which are to be found in the Greeks. Other philologists have other interests, such as literary history, literary criticism, and of course, the problem of getting freshmen to write better. As an inescapable burden of their academic heritage, they have to bear the weight of the ancient and medieval grammatical tradition, which survives in the other two senses, prescriptive grammar and grammar as remedy. What I have tried to do is to give some account of how that tradition developed, how it was transmitted, and why much of it is essentially irrelevant to the problems the philologist faces today.

REVOLUTION IN GRAMMAR   W. Nelson Francis

I

A long overdue revolution is at present taking place in the study of English grammar—a revolution as sweeping in its consequences as the Darwinian revolution in biology. It is the result of the application to English of methods of descriptive analysis originally developed for use with languages of primitive people. To anyone at all interested in language, it is challenging; to those concerned with the teaching of English (including parents), it presents the necessity of radically revising both the substance and the methods of their teaching.

[18] Rex Stout, "Too Many Women," *All Aces, A Nero Wolfe Omnibus* (Viking, New York, 1958), p. 237.

[19] T. B. Macaulay, "The London University", Edinburgh Review, February, 1826, in *Critical, Historical and Miscellaneous Essays and Poems* (Porter and Coats, Philadelphia, n. d.), vol. 3, pp. 631-634.

From W. Nelson Francis, "Revolution in Grammar," *Quarterly Journal of Speech*, October, 1954.

A curious paradox exists in regard to grammar. On the one hand it is felt to be the dullest and driest of academic subjects, fit only for those in whose veins the red blood of life has long since turned to ink. On the other, it is a subject upon which people who would scorn to be professional grammarians hold very dogmatic opinions, which they will defend with considerable emotion. Much of this prejudice stems from the usual sources of prejudice—ignorance and confusion. Even highly educated people seldom have a clear idea of what grammarians do, and there is an unfortunate confusion about the meaning of the term "grammar" itself.

Hence it would be well to begin with definition. What do people mean when they use the word "grammar"? Actually the word is used to refer to three different things, and much of the emotional thinking about matters grammatical arises from confusion among these different meanings.

The first thing we mean by "grammar" is "the set of formal patterns in which the words of a language are arranged in order to convey larger meanings." It is not necessary that we be able to discuss these patterns self-consciously in order to be able to use them. In fact, all speakers of a language above the age of five or six know how to use its complex forms of organization with considerable skill; in this sense of the word—call it "Grammar 1"—they are thoroughly familiar with its grammar.

The second meaning of "grammar"—call it "Grammar 2"—is "the branch of linguistic science which is concerned with the description, analysis, and formulization of formal language patterns." Just as gravity was in full operation before Newton's apple fell, so grammar in the first sense was in full operation before anyone formulated the first rule that began the history of grammar as a study.

The third sense in which people use the word "grammar" is "linguistic etiquette." This we may call "Grammar 3." The word in this sense is often coupled with a derogatory adjective: we say that the expression "he ain't here" is "bad grammar." What we mean is that such an expression is bad linguistic manners in certain circles. From the point of view of "Grammar 1" is it faultless; it conforms just as completely to the structural patterns of English as does "he isn't here." The trouble with it is like the trouble with Prince Hal in Shakespeare's play—it is "bad," not in itself, but in the company it keeps.

As has already been suggested, much confusion arises from mixing these meanings. One hears a good deal of criticism of teachers of English couched in such terms as "they don't teach grammar any more." Criticism of this sort is based on the wholly unproved assumption that teaching Grammar 2 will increase the student's proficiency in Grammar 1 or improve his manners in Grammar 3. Actually, the form of Grammar 2 which is usually taught is a very inaccurate and misleading analysis of the facts of Grammar 1; and it therefore is of highly questionable value in improving a person's ability to handle the structural patterns of his language. It is hardly reasonable to expect that teaching a person some inaccurate grammatical analysis will either improve the effectiveness of his assertions or teach him what expressions are acceptable to use in a given social context.

These, then, are the three meanings of "grammar": Grammar 1, a form of behavior; Grammar 2, a field of study, a science; and Grammar 3, a branch of etiquette.

II

Grammarians have arrived at some basic principles of their science, three of which are fundamental to this discussion. The first is that a language constitutes a set of behavior patterns common to the members of a given community. It is a part of what the anthropologists call the culture of the community. Actually it has complex and intimate relationships with other phases of culture such as myth and ritual. But for purposes of study it may be dealt with as a separate set of phenomena that can be objectively described and analyzed like any other universe of facts. Specifically, its phenomena can be observed, recorded, classified, and compared; and general laws of their behavior can be made by the same inductive process that is used to produce the "laws" of physics, chemistry, and the other sciences.

A second important principle of linguistic science is that each language or dialect has its own unique system of behavior patterns. Part of this system may show similarities to parts of the systems of other languages, particularly if those languages are genetically related. But different languages solve the problems of expression and communication in different ways, just as the problems of movement through water are solved in different ways by lobsters, fish, seals, and penguins. A couple of corollaries of this principle are important. The first is that there is no such thing as "universal grammar," or at least if there is, it is so general and abstract as to be of little use. The second corollary is that the grammar of each language must be made up on the basis of a study of that particular language—a study that is free from preconceived notions of what a language should contain and how it should operate. The marine biologist does not criticize the octopus for using jet-propulsion to get him through the water instead of the method of a self-respecting fish. Neither does the linguistic scientist express alarm or distress when he finds a language that seems to get along quite well without any words that correspond to what in English we call verbs.

A third principle on which linguistic science is based is that the analysis and description of a given language must conform to the requirements laid down for any satisfactory scientific theory. These are (1) simplicity, (2) consistency, (3) completeness, and (4) usefulness for predicting the behavior of phenomena not brought under immediate observation when the theory was formed. Linguistic scientists who have recently turned their attention to English have found that, judged by these criteria, the traditional grammar of English is unsatisfactory. It falls down badly on the first two requirements, being unduly complex and glaringly inconsistent within itself. It can be made to work, just as the Ptolemaic earth-centered astronomy can be, but at the cost of great elaboration and complication. The new grammar, like the Copernican sun-centered astronomy, solves the same problems with greater elegance, which is the scientist's word for the simplicity, compactness, and tidiness that characterize a satisfactory theory.

III

A brief look at the history of the traditional grammar of English will make apparent the reasons for its inadequacy. The study of English grammar is actually an outgrowth of the linguistic interest of the Renaissance. It was during the later Middle Ages and early Renaissance that the various vernacular languages of Europe came into their own. They began to be used for many kinds of writing which had previously always been done in Latin. As the vernaculars, in the hands of great writers like Dante and Chaucer, came of age as members of the linguistic family, a concomitant interest in their grammars arose. The earliest important English grammar was written by Shakespeare's contemporary, Ben Jonson.

It is important to observe that not only Ben Jonson himself but also those who followed him in the study of English grammar were men deeply learned in Latin and sometimes in Greek. For all their interest in English, they were conditioned from earliest school days to conceive of the classical languages as superior to the vernaculars. We still sometimes call the elementary school the "grammar school"; historically the term means the school where Latin grammar was taught. By the time the Renaissance or eighteenth-century scholar took his university degree, he was accustomed to use Latin as the normal means of communication with his fellow scholars. Dr. Samuel Johnson, for instance, who had only three years at the university and did not take a degree, wrote poetry in both Latin and Greek. Hence it was natural for these men to take Latin grammar as the norm, and to analyze English in terms of Latin. The grammarians of the seventeenth and eighteenth centuries who formulated the traditional grammar of English looked for the devices and distinctions of Latin grammar in English, and where they did not actually find them they imagined or created them. Of course, since English is a member of the Indo-European family of languages to which Latin and Greek also belong, it did have many grammatical elements in common with them. But many of these had been obscured or wholly lost as a result of the extensive changes that had taken place in English—changes that the early grammarians inevitably conceived of as degeneration. They felt that it was their function to resist further change, if not to repair the damage already done. So preoccupied were they with the grammar of Latin as the ideal that they overlooked in large part the exceedingly complex and delicate system tht English had substituted for the Indo-European grammar it had abandoned. Instead they stretched unhappy English on the Procrustean bed of Latin. It is no wonder that we commonly hear people say, "I didn't really understand grammar until I began to study Latin." This is eloquent testimony to the fact that the grammar "rules" of our present-day textbooks are largely an inheritance from the Latin-based grammar of the eighteenth century.

Meanwhile the extension of linguistic study beyond the Indo-European and Semitic families began to reveal that there are many different ways in which linguistic phenomena are organized—in other words, many different kinds of grammar. The tone-languages of the Orient and of North America, and the complex agglutinative languages of Africa, among others, forced grammarians to abandon the idea of a universal or ideal grammar and to direct their attention more closely to the individual systems employed by the multifarious languages of mankind. With the growth and refinement of the scientific method and its application to the field of anthropology, language came under more rigorous scientific scrutiny. As with anthropology in general, linguistic science at first concerned itself with the primitive. Finally, again following the lead of anthropology, linguistics began to apply its techniques to the old familiar tongues, among them English. Accelerated by the practical need during World War II of teaching languages, including English, to large numbers in short time, research into the nature of English grammar has moved rapidly in the last fifteen years. The definitive grammar of English is yet to be written, but the results so far achieved are spectacular. It is now as unrealistic to teach "traditional" grammar of English as it is to teach "traditional" (i.e. pre-Darwinian) biology or "traditional" (i.e. four-element) chemistry. Yet nearly all certified teachers of English on all levels are doing so. Here is a cultural lag of major proportions.

IV

Before we can proceed to a sketch of what the new grammar of English looks like, we must take account of a few more of the premises of linguistic science. They must be understood and accepted by anyone who wishes to understand the new grammar.

First, the spoken language is primary at least for the original study of a language. In many of the primitive languages,[1] of course, where writing is unknown, the spoken language is the *only* form. This is in many ways an advantage to the linguist, because the written language may use conventions that obscure its basic structure. The reason for the primary importance of the spoken language is that language originates as speech, and most of the changes and innovations that occur in the history of a given language begin in the spoken tongue.

Secondly, we must take account of the concept of dialect. I suppose most laymen would define a dialect as "a corrupt form of a language spoken in a given region by people who don't know any better." This introduces moral judgments which are repulsive to the linguistic scholar. Let us approach the definition of a dialect from the more objective end, through the notion of a speech community. A speech community is merely a group of people who are in pretty constant intercommunication. There are various types of speech communities: local ones, like "the people who live in Tidewater Virginia"; class ones, like "the white-collar class"; occupational ones, like "doctors, nurses, and other people who work in hospitals"; social ones, like "clubwomen." In a sense, each of these has its own dialect. Each family may be said to have its own dialect; in fact, in so far as each of us has his own vocabulary and particular quirks of speech, each individual has his own

---

[1] "Primitive languages" here is really an abbreviated statement for "languages used by peoples of relatively primitive culture"; it is not to be taken as implying anything simple or rudimentary about the languages themselves. Many languages included under the term, such as native languages of Africa and Mexico, exhibit grammatical complexities unknown to more "civilized" languages.

dialect. Also, of course, in so far as he is a member of many speech communities, each individual is more or less master of many dialects and shifts easily and almost unconsciously from one to another as he shifts from one social environment to another.

In the light of this concept of dialects, a language can be defined as a group of dialects which have enough of their sound-system, vocabulary, and grammar (Grammar 1, that is) in common to permit their speakers to be mutually intelligible in the ordinary affairs of life. It usually happens that one of the many dialects that make up a language comes to have more prestige than the others; in modern times it has usually been the dialect of the middle-class residents of the capital, like Parisian French and London English, which is so distinguished. This comes to be thought of as the standard dialect; in fact, its speakers become snobbish and succeed in establishing the belief that it is not a dialect at all, but the only proper form of the language. This causes the speakers of other dialects to become self-conscious and ashamed of their speech, or else aggressive and jingoistic about it—either of which is an acknowledgment of their feelings of inferiority. Thus one of the duties of the educational system comes to be that of teaching the standard dialect to all so as to relieve them of feelings of inferiority, and thus relieve society of linguistic neurotics. This is where Grammar 3, linguistic etiquette, comes into the picture.

A third premise arising from the two just discussed is that the difference between the way educated people talk and the way they write is a dialectal difference. The spread between these two dialects may be very narrow, as in present-day America, or very wide, as in Norway, where people often speak local Norwegian dialects but write in the Dano-Norwegian *Riksmaal*. The extreme is the use by writers of an entirely different language, or at least an ancient and no longer spoken form of the language—like Sanskrit in northern India or Latin in western Europe during the Middle Ages. A corollary of this premise is that anyone setting out to write a grammar must know and make clear whether he is dealing with the spoken or the written dialect. Virtually all current English grammars deal with the written language only; evidence for this is that their rules for the plurals of nouns, for instance, are really spelling rules, which say nothing about pronunciation.

This is not the place to go into any sort of detail about the methods of analysis the linguistic scientist uses. Suffice it to say that he begins by breaking up the flow of speech into minimum sound-units, or phones, which he then groups into families called phonemes, the minimum significant sound-units. Most languages have from twenty to sixty of

these. American English has forty-one: nine vowels, twenty-four consonants, four degrees of stress, and four levels of pitch. These
phonemes group themselves into minimum meaningful units, called
morphemes. These fall into two groups: free morphemes, those that
can enter freely into many combinations with other free morphemes
to make phrases and sentences; and bound morphemes, which are
always found tied in a close and often indissoluble relationship with
other bound or free morphemes. An example of a free morpheme is
"dog"; an example of a bound morpheme is "un-" or "ex-." The linguist
usually avoids talking about "words" because the term is very inexact.
Is "instead of," for instance, to be considered one, two, or three words?
This is purely a matter of opinion; but it is a matter of fact that it is
made up of three morphemes.

In any case, our analysis has now brought the linguist to the point
where he has some notion of the word-stock (he would call it the
"lexicon") of his language. He must then go into the question of how
the morphemes are grouped into meaningful utterances, which is the
field of grammar proper. At this point in the analysis of English, as of
many other languages, it becomes apparent that there are three bases
upon which classification and analysis may be built: form, function,
and meaning. For illustration let us take the word "boys" in the utterance "the boys are here." From the point of view of form, "boys" is a
noun with the plural ending "s" (pronounced like "z"), preceded by the
noun-determiner "the," and tied by concord to the verb "are," which
it precedes. From the point of view of function, "boys" is the subject of
the verb "are" and of the sentence. From the point of view of meaning,
"boys" points out or names more than one of the male young of the
human species, about whom an assertion is being made.

Of these three bases of classification, the one most amenable to objective description and analysis of a rigorously scientific sort is form.
In fact, many conclusions about form can be drawn by a person unable
to understand or speak the language. Next comes function. But except
as it is revealed by form, function is dependent on knowing the meaning. In a telegraphic sentence like "ship sails today" [2] no one can say
whether "ship" is the subject of "sails" or an imperative verb with "sales"
as its object until he knows what the sentence means. Most shaky of all
bases for grammatical analysis is meaning. Attempts have been made
to reduce the phenomena of meaning to objective description, but so far
they have not succeeded very well. Meaning is such a subjective

[2] This example is taken from C. C. Fries, *The Structure of English* (New York,
1952), p. 62. This important book will be discussed below.

quality that it is usually omitted entirely from scientific description. The botanist can describe the forms of plants and the functions of their various parts, but he refuses to concern himself with their meaning. It is left to the poet to find symbolic meaning in roses, violets, and lilies.

At this point it is interesting to note that the traditional grammar of English bases some of its key concepts and definitions on this very subjective and shaky foundation of meaning. A recent English grammar defines a sentence as "a group of words which expresses a complete thought through the use of a verb, called its predicate, and a subject, consisting of a noun or pronoun about which the verb has something to say." [3] But what is a complete thought? Actually we do not identify sentences this way at all. If someone says, "I don't know what to do," dropping his voice at the end, and pauses, the hearer will know that it is quite safe for him to make a comment without running the risk of interrupting an unfinished sentence. But if the speaker says the same words and maintains a level pitch at the end, the polite listener will wait for him to finish his sentence. The words are the same, the meaning is the same; the only difference is a slight one in the pitch of the final syllable—a purely formal distinction, which signals that the first utterance is complete, a sentence, while the second is incomplete. In writing we would translate these signals into punctuation: a period or exclamation point at the end of the first, a comma or dash at the end of the second. It is the form of the utterance, not the completeness of the thought, that tells us whether it is a whole sentence or only part of one.

Another favorite definition of the traditional grammar, also based on meaning, is that of noun" as "the name of a person, place, or thing"; or, as the grammar just quoted has it, "the name of anybody or anything, with or without life, and with or without substance or form." [4] Yet we identify nouns, not by asking if they name something, but by their positions in expressions and by the formal marks they carry. In the sentence, "The slithy toves did gyre and gimble in the wabe," any speaker of English knows that "toves" and "wabe" are nouns, though he cannot tell what they name, if indeed they name anything. How does he know? Actually because they have certain formal marks, like their position in relation to "the" as well as the whole arrangement of the sentence. We know from our practical knowledge of English grammar (Grammar 1), which we have had since before we went to school, that if we were to put meaningful words into this sentence, we would have to

[3] Ralph B. Allen, *English Grammar* (New York, 1950), p. 187.
[4] *Ibid.*, p. 1.

put nouns in place of "toves" and "wabe," giving something like "The slithy snakes did gyre and gimble in the wood." The pattern of the sentence simply will not allow us to say "The slithy arounds did gyre and gimble in the wooden."

One trouble with the traditional grammar, then, is that it relies heavily on the most subjective element in language, meaning. Another is that it shifts the ground of its classification and produces the elementary logical error of cross-division. A zoologist who divided animals into invertebrates, mammals, and beasts of burden would not get very far before running into trouble. Yet the traditional grammar is guilty of the same error when it defines three parts of speech on the basis of meaning (noun, verb, and interjection), four more on the basis of function (adjective, adverb, pronoun, conjunction), and one partly on function and partly on form (preposition). The result is that in such an expression as "a dog's life" there can be endless futile argument about whether "dog's" is a noun or an adjective. It is, of course, a noun from the point of view of form and an adjective from the point of view of function, and hence falls into both classes, just as a horse is both a mammal and a beast of burden. No wonder students are bewildered in their attempts to master the traditional grammar. Their natural clearness of mind tells them that it is a crazy patchwork violating the elementary principles of logical thought.

V

If the traditional grammar is so bad, what does the new grammar offer in its place?

It offers a description, analysis, and set of definitions and formulas—rules, if you will—based firmly and consistently on the easiest, or at least the most objective, aspect of language, form. Experts can quibble over whether "dog's" in "a dog's life" is a noun or an adjective, but anyone can see that it is spelled with " 's " and hear that it ends with a "z" sound; likewise anyone can tell that it comes in the middle between "a" and "life." Furthermore he can tell that something important has happened if the expression is changed to "the dog's alive," "the live dogs," or "the dogs lived," even if he doesn't know what the words mean and has never heard of such functions as modifier, subject, or attributive genitive. He cannot, of course, get very far into his analysis without either a knowledge of the language or access to someone with such knowledge. He will also need a minimum technical vocabulary describing grammatical functions. Just so the anatomist is better off for knowing physiology. But the grammarian, like the anatomist, must beware of allowing his preconceived notions to lead him into the error of interpreting before he describes—an error which often results in his finding only what he is looking for.

When the grammarian looks at English objectively, he finds that it conveys its meanings by two broad devices: the denotations and connotations of words separately considered, which the linguist calls "lexical meaning," and the significance of word-forms, word-groups, and arrangements apart from the lexical meanings of the words, which the linguist calls "structural meaning." The first of these is the domain of the lexicographer and the semanticist and hence is not our present concern. The second, the structural meaning, is the business of the structural linguist, or grammarian. The importance of this second kind of meaning must be emphasized because it is often overlooked. The man in the street tends to think of the meaning of a sentence as being the aggregate of the dictionary meanings of the words that make it up; hence the widespread fallacy of literal translation—the feeling that if you take a French sentence and a French-English dictionary and write down the English equivalent of each French word you will come out with an intelligible English sentence. How ludicrous the results can be, anyone knows who is familiar with Mark Twain's retranslation from the French of his jumping frog story. One sentence reads, "Eh bien! I no saw not that that frog has nothing of better than each frog." Upon which Mark's comment is, "if that isn't grammar gone to seed, then I count myself no judge." [5]

The second point brought out by a formal analysis of English is that it uses four principal devices of form to signal structural meanings:

1. Word order—the sequence in which words and word-groups are arranged.

2. Function-words—words devoid of lexical meaning which indicate relationships among the meaningful words with which they appear.

3. Inflections—alterations in the forms of words themselves to signal changes in meaning and relationship.

4. Formal contrasts—contrasts in the forms of words signaling greater differences in function and meaning. These could also be considered inflections, but it is more convenient for both the lexicographer and the grammarian to consider them separately.

[5] Mark Twain, "The Jumping Frog; the Original Story in English; the Retranslation Clawed Back from the French, into a Civilized Language Once More, by Patient and Unremunerated Toil," *1601 . . . and Sketches Old and New* (n.p., 1933), p. 50.

Usually several of these are present in any utterance, but they can be separately illustrated by means of contrasting expressions involving minimum variation—the kind of controlled experiment used in the scientific laboratory.

To illustrate the structural meaning of word order, let us compare the two sentences "man bites dog" and "dog bites man."—The words are identical in lexical meaning and in form; the only difference is in sequence. It is interesting to note that Latin expresses the difference between these two by changes in the form of the words, without necessarily altering the order: "homo canem mordet" or "hominem canis mordet." Latin grammar is worse than useless in understanding this point of English grammar.

Next, compare the sentences "the dog is the friend of man" and "any dog is a friend of that man." Here the words having lexical meaning are "dog," "is," "friend," and "man," which appear in the same form and the same order in both sentences. The formal differences between them are in the substitution of "any" and "a" for "the," and in the insertion of "that." These little words are function-words; they make quite a difference in the meanings of the two sentences, though it is virtually impossible to say what they mean in isolation.

Third, compare the sentences "the dog loves the man" and "the dogs loved the men." Here the words are the same, in the same order, with the same function-words in the same positions. But the forms of the three words having lexical meanings have been changed: "dog" to "dogs," "loves" to "loved," and "man" to "men." These changes are inflections. English has very few of them as compared with Greek, Latin, Russian, or even German. But it still uses them; about one word in four in an ordinary English sentence is inflected.

Fourth, consider the difference between "the dog's friend arrived" and "the dog's friendly arrival." Here the difference lies in the change of "friend" to "friendly," a formal alteration signaling a change of function from subject to modifier, and the change of "arrived" to "arrival," signaling a change of function from predicate to head-word in a noun-modifier group. These changes are of the same formal nature as inflections, but because they produce words of different lexical meaning, classifiable as different parts of speech, it is better to call them formal contrasts than inflections. In other words, it is logically quite defensible to consider "love," "loving," and "loved" as the same word in differing aspects and to consider "friend," "friendly," "friendliness," "friendship," and "befriend" as different words related by formal and semantic similarities. But this is only a matter of convenience of analysis, which permits a more accurate description of English structure. In another language we might find that this kind of distinction is unnecessary but that some other distinction, unnecessary in English, is required. The categories of grammatical description are not sacrosanct; they are as much a part of man's organization of his observations as they are of the nature of things.

If we are considering the spoken variety of English, we must add a fifth device for indicating structural meaning—the various musical and rhythmic patterns which the linguist classifies under juncture, stress, and intonation. Consider the following pair of sentences:

> Alfred, the alligator is sick.
> Alfred the alligator is sick.

These are identical in the four respects discussed above—word order, function-words, inflections, and word-form. Yet they have markedly different meanings, as would be revealed by the intonation if they were spoken aloud. These differences in intonation are to a certain extent indicated in the written language by punctuation—that is, in fact, the primary function of punctuation.

VI

The examples so far given were chosen to illustrate in isolation the various kinds of structural devices in English grammar. Much more commonly the structural meaning of a given sentence is indicated by a combination of two or more of these devices: a sort of margin of safety which permits some of the devices to be missed or done away with without obscuring the structural meaning of the sentence, as indeed anyone knows who has ever written a telegram or a newspaper headline. On the other hand, sentences which do not have enough of these formal devices are inevitably ambiguous. Take the example already given, Fries's "ship sails today." This is ambiguous because there is nothing to indicate which of the first two words is performing a noun function and which a verb function. If we mark the noun by putting the noun-determining function-word "the" in front of it, the ambiguity disappears; we have either "the ship sails today" or "ship the sails today." The ambiguity could just as well be resolved by using other devices: consider "ship sailed today," "ship to sail today," "ship sail today," "shipping sails today," "shipment of sails today," and so on. It is simply a question of having enough formal devices in the sentence to indicate its structural meaning clearly.

How powerful the structural meanings of English are is illustrated by so-called "nonsense." In English, nonsense as a literary form often consists of utterances that have a clear structural meaning but use words that either have no lexical meanings, or whose lexical meanings are inconsistent one with another. This will become apparent if we subject a rather famous bit of English nonsense to formal grammatical analysis:

> All mimsy were the borogroves
> And the mome raths outgrabe.

This passage consists of ten words, five of them words that should have lexical meaning but don't, one standard verb, and four function-words. In so far as it is possible to indicate its abstract structure, it would be this:

> All ....y were the ....s
> And the ......s ....

Although this is a relatively simple formal organization, it signals some rather complicated meanings. The first thing we observe is that the first line presents a conflict: word order seems to signal one thing, and inflections and function-words something else. Specifically, "mimsy" is in the position normally occupied by the subject, but we know that it is not the subject and that "borogroves" is. We know this because there is an inflectional tie between the form "were" and the "s" ending of "borogroves," because there is the noun-determiner "the" before it, and because the alternative candidate for subject "mimsy," lacks both of these. It is true that "mimsy" does have the function-word "all" before it, which may indicate a noun; but when it does, the noun is either plural (in which case "mimsy" would most likely end in "s"), or else the noun is what grammarians call a mass-word (like "sugar," "coal," "snow"), in which case the verb would have to be "was," not "were." All these formal considerations are sufficient to counteract the effect of word order and show that the sentence is of the type that may be represented thus:

> All gloomy were the Democrats.

Actually there is one other possibility. If "mimsy" belongs to the small group of nouns which don't use "s" to make the plural, and if "borogroves" has been so implied (but not specifically mentioned) in

the context as to justify its appearing with the determiner "the," the
sentence would then belong to the following type:

> (In the campaign for funds) all alumni were the canvassers.
> (In the drought last summer) all cattle were the sufferers.

But the odds are so much against this that most of us would be prepared to fight for our belief that "borogroves" are things that can be
named, and that at the time referred to they were in a complete state of
"mimsyness."

Moving on to the second line, "and the mome raths outgrabe," the
first thing we note is that the "And" signals another parallel assertion to
follow. We are thus prepared to recognize from the noun-determiner
"the," the plural inflection "s," and the particular positions of "mome"
and "outgrabe," as well as the continuing influence of the "were" of the
preceding line, that we are dealing with a sentence of this pattern:

> And the lone rats agreed.

The influence of the "were" is particularly important here; it guides
us in selecting among several interpretations of the sentence. Specifically, it requires us to identify "outgrabe" as a verb in the past tense,
and thus a "strong" or "irregular" verb, since it lacks the characteristic
past-tense ending "d" or "ed." We do this in spite of the fact that there
is another strong candidate for the position of verb: that is, "raths,"
which bears a regular verb inflection and could be tied with "mome" as
its subject in the normal noun-verb relationship. In such a case we
should have to recognize "outgrabe" as either an adverb of the kind
not marked by the form-contrast "ly," an adjective, or the past participle of a strong verb. The sentence would then belong to one of the
following types:

> And the moon shines above.
> And the man stays aloof.
> And the fool seems outdone.

But we reject all of these—probably they don't even occur to us—
because they all have verbs in the present tense, whereas the "were" of
the first line combines with the "And" at the beginning of the second to
set the whole in the past.

We might recognize one further possibility for the structural meaning of this second line, particularly in the verse context, since we are

used to certain patterns in verse that do not often appear in speech of prose. The "were" of the first line could be understood as doing double duty, its ghost or echo appearing between "raths" and "out-grabe." Then we would have something like this:

> All gloomy were the Democrats
> And the home folks outraged.

But again the odds are pretty heavy against this. I for one am so sure that "outgrabe" is the past tense of a strong verb that I can give its present. In my dialect, at least, it is "outgribe."

The reader may not realize it, but in the last four paragraphs I have been discussing grammar from a purely formal point of view. I have not once called a word a noun because it names something (that is, I have not once resorted to meaning), nor have I called any word an adjective because it modifies a noun (that is, resorted to function). In-stead I have been working in the opposite direction, from form toward function and meaning. I have used only criteria which are objectively observable, and I have assumed only a working knowledge of certain structural patterns and devices known to all speakers of English over the age of six. I did use some technical terms like "noun," "verb," and "tense," but only to save time; I could have got along without them.

If one clears his mind of the inconsistencies of the traditional gram-mar (not so easy a process as it might be), he can proceed with a sim-ilarly rigorous formal analysis of a sufficient number of representative utterances in English and come out with a descriptive grammar. This is just what Professor Fries did in gathering and studying the material for the analysis he presents in the remarkable book to which I have al-ready referred, *The Structure of English*. What he actually did was to put a tape recorder into action and record about fifty hours of tele-phone conversation among the good citizens of Ann Arbor, Michigan. When this material was transcribed, it constituted about a quarter of a million words of perfectly natural speech by educated middle-class Americans. The details of his conclusions cannot be presented here, but they are sufficiently different from the usual grammar to be revolu-tionary. For instance, he recognizes only four parts of speech among the words with lexical meaning, roughly corresponding to what the traditional grammar calls substantives, verbs, adjectives and adverbs, though to avoid preconceived notions from the traditional grammar Fries calls them Class 1, Class 2, Class 3, and Class 4 words. To these he adds a relatively small group of function-words, 154 in his materials, which he divides into fifteen groups. These must be memorized by anyone learning the language; they are not subject to the same kind of general rules that govern the four parts of speech. Undoubtedly his conclusions will be developed and modified by himself and by other linguistic scholars, but for the present his book remains the most complete treatment extant of English grammar from the point of view of linguistic science.

VII

Two vital questions are raised by this revolution in grammar. The first is, "What is the value of this new system?" In the minds of many who ask it, the implication of this question is, "We have been getting along all these years with traditional grammar, so it can't be so very bad. Why should we go through the painful process of unlearning and relearning grammar just because linguistic scientists have concocted some new theories?"

The first answer to this question is the bravest and most honest. It is that the superseding of vague and sloppy thinking by clear and precise thinking is an exciting experience in and for itself. To acquire insight into the workings of a language, and to recognize the infinitely delicate system of relationship, balance, and interplay that constitutes its grammar, is to become closely acquainted with one of man's most miraculous creations, not unworthy to be set beside the equally beautiful organization of the physical universe. And to find that its most complex effects are produced by the multi-layered organization of relatively simple materials is to bring our thinking about language into accord with modern thought in other fields, which is more and more coming to emphasize the importance of organization—the fact that an organized whole is truly greater than the sum of all its parts.

There are other answers, more practical if less philosophically valid. It is too early to tell, but it seems probable that a realistic, scientific grammar should vastly facilitate the teaching of English, especially as a foreign language. Already results are showing here; it has been found that if intonation contours and other structural patterns are taught quite early, the student has a confidence that allows him to attempt to speak the language much sooner than he otherwise would.

The new grammar can also be of use in improving the native speaker's proficiency in handling the structural devices of his own language. In other words, Grammar 2, if it is accurate and consistent, *can* be of use in improving skill in Grammar 1. An illustration is that famous bugaboo, the dangling participle. Consider a specific instance of it, which once appeared on a college freshman's theme, to the mingled delight and despair of the instructor:

> Having eaten our lunch, the steamboat departed.

What is the trouble with this sentence? Clearly there must be something wrong with it, because it makes people laugh, although it was not the intent of the writer to make them laugh. In other words, it produces a completely wrong response, resulting in total breakdown of communication. It is, in fact, "bad grammar" in a much more serious way than are mere dialectal divergences like "he ain't here" or "he never seen none," which produce social reactions but communicate effectively. In the light of the new grammar, the trouble with our dangling participle is that the form, instead of leading to the meaning, is in conflict with it. Into the position which, in this pattern, is reserved for the word naming the eater of the lunch, the writer has inserted the word "steamboat." The resulting tug-of-war between form and meaning is only momentary; meaning quickly wins out, simply because our common sense tells us that steamboats don't eat lunches. But if the pull of the lexical meaning is not given a good deal of help from common sense, the form will conquer the meaning, or the two will remain in ambiguous equilibrium—as, for instance, in "Having eaten our lunch, the passengers boarded the steamboat." Writers will find it easier to avoid such troubles if they know about the forms of English and are taught to use the form to convey the meaning, instead of setting up tensions between form and meaning. This, of course, is what English teachers are already trying to do. The new grammar should be a better weapon in their arsenal than the traditional grammar since it is based on a clear understanding of the realities.

The second and more difficult question is, "How can the change from one grammar to the other be effected?" Here we face obstacles of a formidable nature. When we remember the controversies attending on revolutionary changes in biology and astronomy, we realize what a tenacious hold the race can maintain on anything it has once learned, and the resistance it can offer to new ideas. And remember that neither astronomy nor biology was taught in elementary schools. They were, in fact, rather specialized subjects in advanced education. How then change grammar, which is taught to everybody, from the fifth grade up through college? The vested interest represented by thousands upon thousands of English and Speech teachers who have learned the traditional grammar and taught it for many years is a conservative force comparable to those which keep us still using the chaotic system of English spelling and the unwieldy measuring system of inches and feet, pounds and ounces, quarts, bushels, and acres. Moreover, this army is constantly receiving new recruits. It is possible in my state to become certified to teach English in high school if one has had eighteen credit hours of college English—let us say two semesters of freshman composition (almost all of which is taught by people unfamiliar with the new grammar), two semesters of a survey course in English literature, one semester of Shakespeare, and one semester of the contemporary novel. And since hard-pressed school administrators feel that anyone who can speak English can in a pinch teach it, the result is that many people are called upon to teach grammar whose knowledge of the subject is totally inadequate.

There is, in other words, a battle ahead of the new grammar. It will have to fight not only the apathy of the general public but the ignorance and inertia of those who count themselves competent in the field of grammar. The battle is already on, in fact. Those who try to get the concepts of the new grammar introduced into the curriculum are tagged as "liberal" grammarians—the implication being, I suppose, that one has a free choice between "liberal" and "conservative" grammar, and that the liberals are a bit dangerous, perhaps even a touch subversive. They are accused of undermining standards, of holding that "any way of saying something is just as good as any other," of not teaching the fundamentals of good English. I trust that the readers of this article will see how unfounded these charges are. But the smear campaign is on. So far as I know, neither religion nor patriotism has yet been brought into it. When they are, Professor Fries will have to say to Socrates, Galileo, Darwin, Freud, and the other members of the honorable fraternity of the misunderstood, "Move over, gentlemen, and make room for me."

NEW APPROACHES TO GRAMMAR   *Robert C. Pooley*

The long history of grammar has brought about very slight variation in the naming of parts of speech and the functions assigned to them. The same conservative influence is to be seen in the general scheme of grammar utilized in describing English. Terminology and the arrangement of elements have remained static over a period of two hundred years in which the organization and nomenclature

From *Teaching English Grammar* by Robert C. Pooley. Copyright © 1957 Appleton-Century-Crofts, Inc. Reprinted by permission of the publishers.

of almost every other subject of study have changed to a high degree. Only recently has the traditional scheme of grammar been challenged, and while the challenge has been received with respect by professional grammarians, it has not as yet influenced to any observable degree the teaching of grammar in schools and colleges.

Numerous grammarians have made minor alterations in nomenclature to improve what seemed to them to be deficient elements in the traditional system, but they have retained the basic organization. To illustrate: Henry Sweet in *A New English Grammar, Logical and Historical* (1925) accepts the usual classifications as conventionally useful, but coins new terms where he feels the system to be defective. The joining of two or more sentences together he calls a "complex" and adds these definitions: "A complex in which the principal clause is modified by a co-clause is called a co-complex, e.g., 'You shall walk and I shall ride.' " [1] "A complex in which the principal clause is modified by a sub-clause is called a *sub-complex*. . . . A complex which consists of more than two clauses is called an *extended complex*." [2] These and similar variations of nomenclature have almost never been adopted into the commonly taught grammar of the schools.

More extensive recommendations for changes in the traditional system were made by Otto Jespersen in *The Philosophy of Grammar* (1924) and in *Essentials of English Grammar* (1933).

Jespersen states his attitude toward grammar thus:

"Language is . . . a set of habits, of habitual actions. . . . The greater part of these actions are determined by what [the speaker] has done previously in similar situations. . . . But the speaker has to turn these habits to account to meet new situations . . . therefore he cannot be a mere slave to habits, but has to vary them to suit varying needs—and this in course of time may lead . . . to new grammatical forms and usages. Grammar thus becomes a part of linguistic psychology or psychological linguistics. . . ." [3]

Following out his statement that "No linguistic system, however, is either completely rigid or perfectly harmonious, and we shall see . . . that there are loopholes and deficiencies in the English gram-

---

[1] Henry Sweet, *A New English Grammar, Logical and Historical* (Oxford, Clarendon Press, 1925), p. 162.

[2] *Ibid.*, p. 164.

[3] Otto Jespersen, *The Philosophy of Grammar* (London, G. Allen and Unwin, Ltd., 1935), p. 29.

matical system," [4] he offers some improvements in definition and terminology. He lists five parts of speech:

(a) *substantives*
(b) *adjectives*
(c) *verbs*
(d) *pronouns,* in which he includes *pronominal adverbs* and the articles
(e) *particles,* in which he groups adverbs, prepositions, co-ordinating conjunctions, and subordinating conjunctions [5]

To account for the shifts in classification of words as they are used in combinations, he develops the concept of *ranks*. In the phrase *terribly cold weather* the three ranks are exhibited. *Weather,* the substantive is a *primary; cold,* the adjective is a *secondary; terribly,* the adverb, is a *tertiary*. These are the normal correspondences between word class and rank. However, because of the flexibility of English, *primaries* are not only substantives but frequently adjectives, adverbs, or pronouns. Similarly *secondaries* are not only adjectives, but substantives (a *garden* flower), pronouns, or adverbs. *Tertiaries,* generally adverbs, may also be substantives (come *home*), adjectives, or pronouns. Moreover, a whole phrase may be used as a primary, secondary, or tertiary: *Sunday afternoon* was fine; a *Sunday afternoon* concert; he slept all *Sunday afternoon.*

In addition to the rank terminology, Jespersen employs four other new terms: junction, nexus, adjunct, adnex. *Junction* is the joining of a secondary and a primary so closely "that they may be considered one composite name for what might in many cases just as well have been called by a single name." [6]

> *Examples:* a silly person = a fool
> the warmest season: summer
> a very tall person: a giant

The *adjunct* is the secondary: in the sentences above *silly, warmest,* and *tall* are adjuncts. *Nexus* is the joining of a secondary and a primary in such manner that "something new is added to the conception contained in the primary." [7] *Nexus* may be independent, as in *the dress is blue,* or dependent, as in I see *that the door is red.*

[4] Otto Jespersen, *Essentials of English Grammar* (New York, Henry Holt and Co., 1933), p. 16.
[5] *Ibid.,* pp. 66–69.
[6] *Ibid.,* p. 91.
[7] *Ibid.,* p. 95.

There is similar dependent nexus in the condensed structures: I painted the door *red;* I hear the dog *bark.* The secondaries in these sentences, *blue, red, bark,* are called *adnexes.*

Without discarding or altering the basic system of English grammar as traditionally taught, Jespersen sought to supply the deficiencies he found in the system. To this end he defined relationships and functions as he found them in the language and created terminology for his new concepts.

Rearrangement of Familiar Terms

Janet Rankin Aiken in *A New Plan of English Grammar* (1933) undertakes like Jespersen to improve the traditional system of English grammar. She begins, "The eight traditional parts of speech, the pillars of the grammatical arch, are seen under logical analysis to be shaky. One, the verb, is a really functional concept. The noun is not one but two functions (subject and complement) while the adjective and adverb together make one (modifier)." [8] She continues to show that prepositions and conjunctions perform one connective function, while the pronoun, traditionally called a part of speech, is really a list of specific words which fulfil any of the six grammatical functions with the exception of the verb. Her system does not abandon the terms *noun, pronoun, adjective,* and *adverb,* but recognizes their logical limitations. The heart of Aiken's system is her analysis of grammar into *unit* and *function.* She calls the main divisions of grammar *Syntax,* the study of word relations, and *Morphology,* the study of word forms.

Syntax has two main divisions: the *syntactical unit,* which is any word or word group performing a syntactical function; and the *syntactical function,* which is the part played by a unit in sentence structure. *Apposition* she classes by itself as a unit which repeats the function of another unit.

The syntactical units are:

    a. Sentence (a complete communication in words, containing a verb of independent rank, with its subject)

    b. Non-sentence (a complete communication in other than sentence form)

    c. *Clause* (a combination of subject, verb, and complement, or any two of these three)

---

[8] Janet Rankin Aiken, *A New Plan of English Grammar* (New York, Henry Holt and Co., 1933), preface, p. iii.

    d. Phrase (two or more words acting together but not constituting a clause)

    e. Word (a sound or combination of sounds used to convey a single concept or idea)

Aiken defines syntactical function as the work done by the five syntactical units above. These units perform the following functions:

a. Absolute   (independent)
b. Verb   (dependent)
c. Subject   (dependent)
d. Complement   (dependent)
e. Modifier   (dependent)
f. Connective   (dependent)

Any communication taken as a whole, she says, "is always in the form of a sentence or non-sentence performing an absolute function, and containing one or more units performing one or more of the other five functions. Thus, the absolute is an independent function performed by sentence or non-sentence, while the other five functions operate within the complete unit in a partial or dependent fashion." [9]

In Aiken's system, the exclamation *Not for a million dollars!* would be classified as an independent unit of non-sentence form, while *At the turn of the road he found an old mill which had been abandoned* would be classified as an independent unit (an absolute) in sentence form, containing such units as clauses, phrases, and words, which perform such functions as verb, subject, complement, modifier, and connective.

Another element of terminology in Aiken's system is the use of the word *verbid* to replace *verbal* as the group name for participles, gerunds, and infinitives. She says, "The only useful distinction between verb and verbid is one of idea or intent. The verbid does not convey the sense of completeness expressed by the full verb." [10] This definition is interesting because it places reliance upon the *meaning* of a word as a means of determining its grammatical classification. We shall see below that Fries attempts to discard meaning entirely in the analysis of the grammatical function of a unit of expression.

In summary, then, Aiken presents a well-thought-out arrangement of the traditional elements of English grammar with such new terminology as is necessary to rectify or supply such elements and rela-

[9] *Ibid.,* p. 6.
[10] *Ibid.,* p. 52.

tionships as she finds defective or lacking in the traditional system. In the twenty years since its publication, the sane and reasonable system of Aiken has made no observable impression upon the grammar of English as outlined in the school textbooks.

Some New Views of English Grammar

Fries

A direct challenge to the validity of the traditional scheme of English grammar is made by Fries.[11] Grammar as it is now taught, asserts Fries, is invalid for the true analysis of English. "From the point of view underlying this study, the principles, procedures, the definitions of 'formal grammar' are unsound. . . . Being falsely oriented, 'formal grammar,' as it is studied in relation to English, cannot be expected to provide any satisfactory insight into the mechanisms of our language or any grasp of the processes by which language functions." To proceed from traditional grammar to a scientific analysis of the structure of English, he adds, is no more feasible than to begin chemistry with alchemy or astronomy with astrology.

Utilizing the recorded speech of persons not aware of being recorded, Fries analyzes his data to find answers to such questions as these: What is a sentence? What kinds of sentences are there? What are parts of speech? How do they operate? What are the structural patterns of sentences? What are the "layers" of structure in sentences? The book, as a consequence, is a grammar of the English sentence on entirely new principles, derived exclusively from the observation and analysis of current American English, and organized in terms of a *rationale* derived from the material.

Fries points out that definitions of the English sentence as found in the traditional grammars are based upon meaning (a sentence is a group of words expressing a complete thought) or upon meaning plus grammatical form (a sentence is a meaningful group of words containing a subject and verb). Such definitions, he avers, do not describe what takes place in practical conversation. His analysis of recorded speech showed that the units of communication were one of these:

1. A single, minimum free utterance.
2. A single free utterance, but expanded, not minimum.
3. A sequence of two or more free utterances.

[11] Charles C. Fries, *The Structure of English* (New York, Harcourt, Brace and Co., 1952).

These observations lead to the author's definition: "We start then with the assumption that a sentence . . . is a single free utterance, minimum or expanded; i.e., that it is 'free' in the sense that it is not included in any larger structure by means of a grammatical device."

All speech consists of communicative utterances or noncommunicative utterances. Of the first type Fries finds three classifications:

> I. Utterances regularly eliciting "oral" responses only:
>   A. *Greetings*   B. *Calls*   C. *Questions*
> II. Utterances regularly eliciting "action" responses, sometimes accompanied by one of a limited list of oral responses: *requests* or *commands*.
> III. Utterances regularly eliciting conversational signals of attention to continuous discourse: *statements*.[12]

Noncommunicative utterances are those characteristic of situations such as surprise, sudden pain, prolonged pain, disgust, anger, sorrow.

Within an utterance of the communicative type, Fries finds two kinds of meaning; the lexical meaning, which is derived from the dictionary meaning of the words themselves; and the structural meaning, which is the set of signals which indicate such facts as the time of the action, the number of persons or things involved, and their relationship to each other. These devices which signal the structural meanings in an utterance constitute the grammar of a language. It is these devices which we learn unconsciously as we learn our language; without them we could not communicate intelligibly regardless of how many words we knew. "One of the earliest steps in learning to talk is this learning to use automatically the patterns of form and arrangement that constitute the devices to signal structural meaning."[13] Moreover, these devices operate in a system; the items of form and arrangement have signaling significance only as they are parts of patterns in a structural whole. Hence a sentence is a structure made up of form classes or parts of speech.

The structural framework of English, as Fries analyzes it, is made up of four parts of speech and fifteen groups of function words. These constitute the structural signals which convey grammatical meaning in a sentence. The parts of speech are:

> *Class 1:* words which fit into such frames as (The) _____ was good; (the) _____s were good; (the) _____ remembered the

---

[12] *Ibid.*, p. 41.
[13] *Ibid.*, p. 57.

_____; (the) _____ went there. In certain positions Class 1 words are used without an article; *Corn is good; he bought bread*

Class 2: words which fit these structural positions:

(The) ____1____ is/was _____

_____ remembered _____

_____ went there

Class 3: In the same frames, words which fit as below:

(The) *good* is/was *good*

The *good* _____s are/were

Class 4: (The)____3____ ____1____ is/was ____3____ *there*

(The) ____1____ remembered (the) ____1____ *clearly*

(The) _____ went *there rapidly.*[14]

These four parts of speech, Fries concludes, make up the bulk of the "words" in our utterances. It is important to recognize that although many words called "nouns" would fall into class 1, the two categories are not at all identical. In the sentence "The boy went home," *home* would conventionally be classified as a noun, but in Fries's analysis it would be a class 4 word.

In normal communication there is a collection of words fairly small (Fries finds 154 in his recorded materials) which are used with great frequency in English utterances and which are not included in the four parts of speech. These Fries calls "function words" and assorts them into fifteen groups. The first three groups are illustrated here.

Group A: all words for the position in which the word *the* occurs:

A   1   2   3

The concert was good

e.g., a, an, every, no, my, our, your, some, any, eighteen, etc.

Group B: words for the position occupied by *may* in this sentence frame:

A   1   B   2   3

The concert *may* be good

e.g., might, can, could, will, would, should, etc.

A   1   B   2

The _____ _____ moved

had, was, got

A   1   B   2

The _____ _____ moving

was, got, kept

[14] *Ibid.,* pp. 76–86.

```
    A     1        B
    The _____  _____ move
         had to    did
```

Group C: the word *not* in these constructions:

```
    A    1      B  C   2   3
    The concert may *not* be good
    A    1      2   C   3
    The concert was *not* good
```

Although the items of these groups are relatively few in number, they are used so frequently as to make up about one-third of the total bulk of the materials studied.[15] These words have also the characteristic of having very little independent lexical meaning, but have rather a meaning closely related to their structural functions.

Having classified the words in an utterance, Fries continues with the structural patterns of sentences. Since some utterances result in responses different from those of other utterances, there must be kinds of utterances which can be grouped by identifying characteristics. In classifying these groupings he comments,

> the structural signals are in the formal arrangements of the functioning units within the sentence itself. For these, the signals of the kind of sentence are, basically, contrasting arrangements of class 1 and class 2 words. Intonation contrasts are a part of these signals, but they do not often furnish the sole distinguishing feature of the kind of sentence. Certain function words, however, do play an important part in signaling the kinds of utterances we call questions.[16]

From the analysis of the primary elements of the sentence, Fries goes on to the functions performed by words within a sentence. These functions are traditionally described by the terms *subject, object,* and *modifier.* These terms, he insists, have no relationship to the actual facts of the real world, but are only names for particular formal structures within an utterance. Hence a *subject* "is simply that class 1 word that is bound to a class 2 word to form the basic arrangement of the sentence and is identified and distinguished from other class 1 words not by meaning but by certain contrastive arrangements." [17] By means of symbols the author demonstrates formulas which account for all the contrastive arrangements of class 1 words. He emphasizes that it is not the meanings of the words them-

15 *Ibid.,* p. 104.
16 *Ibid.,* p. 172.
17 *Ibid.,* p. 183.

selves but an intricate system of formal features which makes possible the grasp of what we generally call "meaning." "Train boy
house take" conveys no meaning; "The boy takes a train to his house"
is full of meaning. This meaning is not in the words themselves
but in the words as a pattern.

After the analysis of further functions, such as "modifier," Fries
describes "Sequence" sentences and "Included" sentences and deals
with "Layers of Structure." He is then able to present the ten steps
for the analysis of a present-day English sentence.[18] Such analysis
can be represented in symbols, e.g.:

$$D \quad 3 \quad 3 \quad 1^a \quad f \quad D \quad 1^b \quad 4 \quad 2 \quad D \quad 3 \quad 1^c \quad f \quad D \quad 1^d \quad f \quad 2 \quad f \quad 1^e$$

$$- \quad F \quad \qquad - \quad - \qquad \qquad - \quad F \qquad + \quad J \quad + \quad F \quad -$$

$$\text{it} \qquad \qquad \text{it} \qquad \qquad \qquad \text{it} \qquad \qquad \text{he} \quad \text{he} \qquad \qquad \text{it}$$

In this diagrammatic representation the numbers 1, 2, 3, 4 represent the four parts of speech; D is any "determiner," or Group A
form word; f represents a function word, and the capital letter under f, the particular group to which the function word belongs. The
letter exponents (1^a, 1^b, etc.) indicate the "referents" of the class 1
words. Words with the same exponent have the same referent. Of
this scheme of analysis Fries says, "For this type of analysis it is
not necessary to know the lexical meanings of the words nor to know
what the sentence is about. One must, however, in determining the
structure of class 1 words, either know whether the referent is the
"same" or "different," or have another special list of class 2 words." [19]

One of the principal challenges to traditional grammar which
Fries makes is with respect to the use of definitions derived from
meaning content rather than from form. He asserts, "That the precise lexical meanings of the 'words' are unnecessary [in linguistic an-
alysis] is proved from my use of formulas with symbols to represent
whole form classes." [20] As an example he cites the headline "Bus
Fares Badly in Emergency," pointing out that with *badly* recognized
as a class 4 word, *fares*, in the position it occupies in this utterance,
must be a class 2 word. The assumption that the classification may
be derived without the aid of lexical meaning seems overconfident.
By contrast, note this headline: "Doctor Stoops Low in Medic Meet."
Here there can be no assurance of classification until lexical meaning is known. *Is Stoops* a class 2 word? If so, then *Low* is a class 4

[18] *Ibid.*, pp. 267–268.
[19] *Ibid.*, p. 268.
[20] *Ibid.*, p. 294.

word. But if *Stoops* is a class 1 word, then *Low* must be a class 3 word. In such a combination it is impossible to derive the classification exclusively from structural signals. One must know or guess that *Stoops* is a name; i.e., make reference to lexical meaning, before he can ascertain accurately the structure.

In the author's example "Bus Fares Badly in Emergency" the classification of *Fares* as a class 2 word rests upon the formal signal *ly* of *Badly*, making it a class 4 word. But compare "Bus Crews Manly in Emergency"; note the *ly* signal which in the formal sense is identical with that of the preceding sentence but in this case *with the aid of lexical meaning only* can be called a class 3 word which in turn identifies *Crews* (also identical in form with *Fares)* as a class 1 word. Structural signals are significant, but apparently cannot be completely divorced from lexical meaning. How would Fries analyze by structural analysis alone the statement, "Professor Rakes Leaves after College Commencement"?

In addition to the doubt cast upon analysis by pure structural means free of lexical meaning, there seems to be a similar difficulty in the function words. In the utterance "The wind blew up the street," *up* is clearly group *F* of the function words (chiefly prepositions). From structure alone "The powder blew up the ship" would seem to demand a similar classification for *up*. How, apart from lexical meaning, can one show the absurdity of this analysis and prove that *up* is a class 3 word? It seems necessary that "meaning" be called upon to clarify structure.

The system of grammar presented by Fries has some very clear advantages. Identifying words in classes according to functional use avoids the "part of speech" problem inherent in the word *mile* in "He walked a mile." Conventional grammar must call *mile* a noun used as an adverb, an awkward explanation. Fries calls it simply a class 4 word. Thus the difficulties of classification arising from functional shift are done away with.

	Fries
I have a *run* in my stocking	Class 1
He can *run* fast	Class 2
The *running* water sparkles	Class 3
The boys came *running*	Class 4

Fries has done a thorough and workmanlike job with his analysis. Convinced that the orientation of traditional grammar is false and that his system provides the means to a scientific analysis of English

sentence structure, he has striven to make an objective and systematic description of the organization of English expression in terms
which are structural in character. Within the framework of his own
goals, he has succeeded admirably.

Whitehall

In his *Structural Essentials of English* [21] Harold Whitehall undertakes to describe the general structural design of English "with a view
to clarifying difficulties encountered in the writing of English." Starting from the viewpoint that serious written English is a rather artificial dialect of the current language, Whitehall offers an analysis of
its structural detail with attention to the ways this dialect differs
from less formal use of English. The principal features of his analysis are:

1. His definition of a word group to avoid the confusions connected with the traditional terms *phrase* and *clause*, and the division
of word groups into *headed* and *non-headed*. Headed word groups
contain a word identified as the *head* which can be used by itself in
all grammatical constructions open to the group. In the word group
five tall trees, the head word *trees* can stand grammatically wherever
the word group can be used. There are four types of headed groups:
noun group, verb group, modifier group, and verbal group. *Non-
headed* groups can be used in grammatical constructions not open to
any single expression within them. No part of the group can substitute
for the entire group and make sense. In the subject-verb group *he
talks*, neither *he* nor *talks* can substitute for the group; similarly in the
prepositional group *of words* neither part can be used for the group.
The analysis of the English sentence then rests upon the recognition
of the four headed groups, the two non-headed groups, plus headed
groups of more than one head *(he and I, John and Henry)*.

2. The relationship of rhythm to pattern in English by the factors
of relative voice loudness or *stress*, relative voice frequency or *tone*,
and interruption of the normal movement from one speech sound
to the next, or *juncture*. "Every normal speaker of English signals
the grammatical structure of his statements by the use of *tone, stress,*
and what is nowadays called *juncture*." [22] In written English it follows that the writer must be able to present the grammatical signals
that a speaker might use so that they are understandable to a reader.

[21] Harold Whitehall, *Structural Essentials of English* (New York, Harcourt,
Brace and Co., 1956).
[22] *Ibid.*, p. 20.

3. The analysis of sentence patterns into three classes of "sentence situations." Sentence situation I consists of subject and verb or verb group predicate; situation II is subject-verb-complement; situation III contains two complements, an *inner complement* and an *outer complement* added to subject and verb (example: The boys gave their sister (inner complement) a doll (outer complement). These patterns show the fixed word order which is characteristic of the English subject-verb sentence and may be summarized thus: "In the subject-predicate sentence, the subject, the verb, any inner complement, and any outer complement occur in a fixed 1, 2, 3, 4 order." [23]

4. His analysis of "word forms" (the surviving inflectional forms of English words) into three major functional approaches. Approach I is the study of the shapes of words (see, sees, saw; who, whom, etc). Approach II is called *substitution* and is the use of words or word groups as substitutes for preceding or following elements in a context (as, for example, the use of an appropriate pronoun in relation to a preceding noun). Approach III is called selection: it is the grammatical device by which one word or construction can dictate the choice of form in another (example: *John* is strong; *he* can lift *his* bicycle with *his* left hand). Selection affects number, gender, person, and case in the choice of forms.

These few items may serve to illustrate the use of structural linguistics which Whitehall employs in his analysis of the grammar of English and the freshness of approach which results. His analysis constantly rewards the reader with new insights into grammatical relationships not previously realized or at least not so clearly seen. By a happy blend of the resources of current linguistics with his own originality of analysis, he offers a most interesting, readable, and challenging approach to the study of English grammar.

Roberts

Of particular interest to high school teachers is Paul Roberts' *Patterns of English*.[24] In this book he attempts a bridge over that gap which exists between the work of the structural linguists and the traditionally trained high school teacher of English. He claims, with justice, to be the first to make a structural analysis of English for high school use. He says in his introduction,

[23] *Ibid.*, p. 40.
[24] Paul Roberts, *Patterns of English* (New York, Harcourt, Brace and Co., 1956).

I have no intention here of attacking or ridiculing the older ways of presenting the English language in the schools. . . . When I came in touch with linguistic science, I reacted against it and wished to defend the tradition. But when I tried to, I found the tradition largely indefensible. I found myself giving ground . . . until I was forced to the realization that the picture of the language I was giving my students was false . . . falsely grounded.[25]

In his analysis of the structure of English, Roberts reflects the influence of Fries, particularly in his use of four basic "form classes" and a cluster of "structure groups" which he classifies into three divisions: the determiners, the auxiliaries, and the intensifiers. So far as is possible Roberts uses the familiar grammatical nomenclature, though with specific restrictions to overcome the ambiguities of traditional definitions. Hence his four form classes are designated nouns, verbs, adjectives, and adverbs. These form classes are, of course, very large, containing thousands of words. In contrast the structure groups are small, some groups containing only a word or two. Nevertheless, it is the structure words which make the sentence "go"; this fact may be demonstrated in nonsense poems in which the form class words may all be novel, but the structure words must present a known pattern for the verse to hang together.

Roberts defines his form classes in terms of pattern: "a verb is a word that patterns like *sing, beautify,* or *arrive.* That is, it is a word which occurs in positions like those in which *sing, beautify,* and *arrive* occur." [26] His analysis of English grammar is the demonstration of the way in which form classes and structure words combine to create the patterns of English expression.

Especially interesting is the development of intonation and punctuation in Part Eight of the book. Here, like Whitehall, he analyzes the part that *stress, pitch,* and *juncture* play in our use of language, and the relationship between these elements of speech and their corresponding signals in written English. He points out that punctuation is often regularized by editors, and that it is well to let word structure guide the writer to punctuation wherever it will. But in those situations where word structure is not a good guide, knowledge of intonation patterns will help. After all, he points out that punctuation arose as a response to original speech intonations.

Patterns of English is a challenging invitation to the task of rewriting the grammar of English for use in secondary schools. In

[25] *Ibid.,* introduction, pp. 1, 2.
[26] *Ibid.,* p. 13.

his sensible and reasonable approach to the undertaking, Roberts will undoubtedly stand as a leader and pioneer in directing the work of all who will labor in the task of fitting the research of linguistic scholars to the needs of classroom English teachers.

Conclusions

How soon will the grammar of the schools reflect the new approaches to grammar as set forth in this chapter; particularly the schemes of Fries, Whitehall, Roberts, and those who will follow? The evidence from society and education in general is that the complete accomplishment of such a change will be slow. Generations of teachers must be trained in the new understandings and techniques; current school books will have to be abandoned or rewritten, and tests and other evaluative devices will have to be altered or replaced. Such things take time. The lag of inertia will be great. Nevertheless, there is without question an awakening of interest in structural linguistics and its applications to the teaching of English. Here and there at the present time are a few forward-looking and experimental teachers using the materials now available. They will create disciples. It is interesting to recall that the first half of the twentieth century has witnessed a notable change of attitude and teaching technique in the field of English usage. It seems probable that the second half of the century will witness the revolution in English grammar and its teaching which appears inevitable.

TRANSFORMATIONS   *H. A. Gleason, Jr.*

12.1 A favorite exercise in public school English has been the changing of sentences from one form to another. Thus from a sentence like

> *John is writing a letter.*

may be formed, among others, the following:

> *John isn't writing a letter.*
> *Is John writing a letter?*
> *A letter is being written by John.*

From *An Introduction to Descriptive Linguistics*, Revised Edition, by H. A. Gleason, Jr., copyright © 1955, 1961, Holt, Rinehart and Winston, Inc. Reprinted by permission.

Very little is ordinarily given by way of clearly formulated rules for these processes, yet students seem to learn the technique more or less readily. Given the same sentence to start with, and the same rather simple instructions (e.g., "Make this negative."), there will be a very high degree of agreement in the answer. All this would suggest that such exercises must reflect some significant structural relationships in the English language. If so, they are worth careful investigation and formal statement.

When such changes are discussed at all, it is generally in terms of the meanings of the sentences. But this cannot be very exact, and is seldom very helpful. For example, it is easy enough to label *Is John writing a letter?* as a question. But what is the meaning of a question? Indeed, we cannot even give a good definition of the word 'question.' There is, of course, nothing unusual in finding difficulties in describing meanings, or in making clear statements about language on the basis of meaning. But with questions, it seems particularly difficult and unsatisfactory.

On the other hand, a little examination will show that changes of the sorts illustrated above can be described structurally—that is, in terms of the addition of elements, the rearranging of elements, or the altering of the form of elements. What specific portions of the sentence are involved, and how, can be very exactly stated. This is done, not in terms of their meanings, but on the basis of their structural position within the sentence. Moreover, the descriptions so arrived at have very wide applicability. For example, almost any English sentence not already negative, may be made into a negative sentence in a way very similar to that shown. This can then be formulated into a rule of considerable power, precisely the kind of rule that we desire in grammars.

12.2 Not all changes are of this sort. Thus the same sentence might be altered to

John is penning an epistle.

Native speakers of English will recognize a very significant relationship between this sentence and its prototype. But they also sense that the relationship here is of an entirely different sort. The sentence structure is not changed; substitutions are made within the same structural framework. From a structural point of view

Mary is baking a cake.

is just as closely related to the original. There is a difference, of course. It lies in the fact that *penning* is a "synonym" of *writing*, whereas *baking* is not. Synonymy is not a precisely definable concept, nor indeed a structural concept. Changes of this sort are therefore not structurally describable. Moreover, they are of much more restricted scope. Clearly, not all operations of altering sentences to related sentences have the same linguistic interest. The ones involving structural changes stand apart from all the others. They will be called transformations.

12.3 A **transformation** is a statement of the structural relation of a pair of constructions which treats that relation as though it were a process. Hence, it is normally stated in the form of rules which may be applied to one of the pair—an **input**—altering it to produce the other—an **output**. Note that transformations are directional. Some can be described in either direction, though practically we must choose one. Others can be described effectively only in one way.

12.4 As an example we might consider the following set of sentence pairs. These are obviously a sample from a very much larger number.

1. *John is writing a letter.*	*John isn't writing a letter.*
2. *Jim has been trying to do it.*	*Jim hasn't been trying to do it.*
3. *James will come tomorrow.*	*James won't come tomorrow.*
4. *Ruth was a beautiful girl.*	*Ruth wasn't a beautiful girl.*
5. *Mary could have been there.*	*Mary couldn't have been there.*
6. *His father walked home.*	*His father didn't walk home.*
7. *My friends like chess.*	*My friends don't like chess.*
8. *The car runs well.*	*The car doesn't run well.*
9. *Sam started running immediately.*	*Sam didn't start running immediately.*

If we can find a single clearly statable rule to cover all of these, we may describe these nine sentence pairs as examples of a single transformation. The sentences seem to fall into two groups. For sentences 1 to 5 a simple rule is immediately evident: *—n't* is added as a suffix to the first word in the verb phrase. This is true whether the verb phrase consists of a single word as in 4, or several as in 2 and 5. There is a minor complication in 3: *will* + *–n't* yields *won't*. We can easily show that this is quite regular, a fact about the language which would have to be described in any case. Pairs 6 to 9 seem to follow a different rule. Before the *—n't* is added, *walked* is changed to *did walk* and comparable changes are made in the other cases. If we try applying the pattern of the first five pairs without this intermediate step we get such very strange outputs as

* His father walkedn't home.

These two rules may be combined into one, if certain conditions can be met. The first of these is that we find a clear conditioning which determines which applies. This we can do: *–n't* is never added to words like *walked*. Which of the two rules applies is determined by whether or not the first word is one of the small list (*is, are, was, has, can, might*—an English-speaking student can easily complete the list) to which *—n't* can be added. If not, it is changed to a verb phrase which starts with *did, do, does*. A second condition which must be met is to find a clear statement as to how this change, *walked* to *did walk*, etc., is to be described.

12.5 The following sentence pairs may help with this problem:

10.	*The boy ran away.*	*The boy didn't run away.*
11.	*The boy did run away.*	*The boy didn't run away.*

These present no difficulty for the rules just mentioned for the negative transformation. In 11 the verb phrase begins with *did*, and *—n't* is added directly. In 10 *ran* is a word to which *—n't* cannot be added; it is therefore changed to *did run*. The interesting feature is that the outputs in the two pairs SEEM to be identical. Actually this is something of an illusion. There are a number of different pronunciations for a writing like *The boy didn't run away*. Only one factor, the position of the sentence stress, needs to be noted here. There are at least the following pairs:

10.	a.	*The boy ran awáy.*	*The boy didn't run awáy.*
	b.	*The boy rán away.*	*The boy didn't rún away.*
	c.	*The bóy ran away.*	*The bóy didn't run away.*
11.		*The boy díd run away.*	*The boy dídn't run away.*

This seems clearly the natural way to match them up. The sentences in each pair have the sentence stress in the same place. *Did run* occurs in the input only when the sentence stress falls on *did*. (A sentence like *The boy did run awáy.* sounds at best extremely archaic, and certainly cannot be considered normal modern English.) It follows, then, that *did* occurs in such sentences ONLY either when *—n't* is suffixed or when it receives the sentence stress. There are other uses of *did,* but most of them fit into the same pattern. The auxiliary *did* occurs in English only where sentence structure demands it. It is never required by the meaning, and it never means anything at all. The difference between *The boy ran awáy.* and *The boy díd run away.* is not a matter of the presence or absence of *did,* only of the stress position. *Did* is there only to provide a meaningless carrier for that stress in the required position. If anything else were available, *did* would not occur. Compare

> *The boy will run awáy.*   *The boy wíll run away.*

Did, do, does, done (the verb *do* in all its forms) as auxiliaries are always completely meaningless—mere position makers. *Do* may also occur as a main verb, in which case it does have meaning: *I díd do my homework.*

The morphemes $\{-Z_3\}$ and $\{-D_1\}$ can occur only in the first word of a verb phrase. If that word ceases to be first by addition of $\{do\}$, these morphemes must shift to the new first word. Thus

walked $(= \{walk\} + \{-D_1\})$ becomes *did walk* $(= \{do\} + \{-D_1\}$
$+ \{walk\})$

like $(= \{like\})$ becomes *do like* $(\{= \{do\} + \{like\})$

runs $(= \{run\} + \{-Z_3\})$ becomes *does run* $(= \{do\} + \{-Z_3\}$
$+ \{run\})$

Both these rules (addition of *do* and position of $\{-Z_3\}$ and $\{-D_1\}$) are ones that will be needed anyway. They are not proposed merely to facilitate the definition of the negative transformation. This is, of course, the best possible recommendation of the result so far: All the rules are quite general. All the sentence pairs we have discussed can then be subsumed under one rule—the negative transformation—plus in some cases the operation of certain other rules, but these are also quite general.

12.6 We cannot speak of "the question transformation" in English, since there are a number of different ones, no one of which has any clear pre-eminence. But we can readily describe each of this rather heterogeneous family of transformations. Some are of considerable interest. Among them are

12. *John is writing a letter.*   *Who is writing a letter?*
13.   *Is John writing a letter?*
14.   *What is John writing?*
15.   *John is writing a letter, isn't he?*

Of these, number 12 seems the simplest. A question word (*who* or *what*) is merely substituted for the subject of the sentence. The intonation remains the same. This is a simple example of a transformation which can be described in only one direction. *Mary is writing a letter.*, *That old man over there is writing a letter.*, and many other input sentences all yield this same output. If the process is reversed, taking the question to be the input, how is the proper output to be selected from the multitude of sentences which are paired with it?

Number 13 is more complex. The first word in the verb phrase is transposed to the first position in the sentence. It must be one of the same list of forms as was found taking the suffix —*n't*. If it isn't, the verb phrase is first altered by the addition of a *do*, thus:

> *John wrote a létter.* → * *John did write a létter.* →
> *Did John write a létter?*

The intermediate stage is marked with * because it does not occur in that form in normal use. In pronunciation there is, of course, also a change in intonation. Commonly it is from /231↘/ to /233↗/.

Number 14 is also best described as involving a series of changes. First, the first word in the verb phrase is moved, as in number 13. Then a question word is substituted for some sentence element, and this is transposed to the initial position:

> *John is writing a letter.* → *Is John writing a letter?* →
> * *Is John writing what?* → *What is John writing?*

This illustrates another very common characteristic of transformations. When two or more apply in one sentence, it is usually easier to describe them in one fixed order; sometimes it is extremely difficult or impossible to use another order. Almost always the form in which the rules are stated must be changed if they are not applied in the same order.

Number 15 involves both change of the intonation (commonly to /232→/) and the addition of a second clause. This consists of only two words. The first is identical with the first word in the input's verb phrase, except that only one of the two must have the suffix —*n't*. The other word is the proper pronoun to substitute for the subject. This is pronounced with the intonation /233↗ /.

12.7 Describing various types of questions in this way does not merely elucidate their structure. It also provides a good basis for understanding some of the dialectal or stylistic variations which occur. The following two outputs from a single input will illustrate:

16. *John is writing to his mother.*   *To whom is John writing?*
17.   *Who is John writing to?*

Examined as they stand, these two results have quite different sentence structure. But looked at in terms of transformations, they are seen to be very much more similar. The intermediate steps are something like the following:

John is writing to his mother. → *Is John writing to his mother?*

→ * *Is John writing to* $\begin{cases} whom \\ who \end{cases}$ → $\begin{cases} \text{To whom is John writing?} \\ \text{Who is John writing to?} \end{cases}$

In the last stage they differ as to how much of the sentence is transposed. The transposition of a whole phrase, *to whom,* is found almost exclusively in literary and quite formal English. Colloquial usage very seldom transposes more than a single word. (Colloquial usage, including informal writing, is also much more likely to use *who* than *whom,* particularly when separated from its conditioning context.) The result is sentences with final prepositions and various other "errors." As is often the case, these "errors" are not the result of "loose grammar," but of very rigid and explicit patterns. Most colloquial English usage calls for transposition of the single question word, result what may.

In this discussion there is no desire to evaluate either pattern. The intention is rather to point out that much of our prescriptive grammar, and equally much of the rebellion against it, is vitiated by bad diagnosis. Linguistic description is neutral in such questions. Its task is to give a clear and significant description of usages which actually occur, and when usages differ, to make clear and significant statement as to how they differ. That is, descriptive linguistics can provide the diagnosis on the basis of which an evaluation can be made. Every thoughtful speaker must evaluate conflicting usages; he will do so more effectively with a clearer understanding of the facts. One of the strengths of a transformational description of this type of question is the clarity with which it sets forth this particular difference in usage.

12.8   In the process of operating these transformations we find that not only are words shifted around in sentences, but even affixes are moved from one word to another. Not infrequently this causes rather complex changes in forms. For example, applying two of the transformations we have just discussed in succession:

John will go. → *John won't go.* → *John won't go, will he?*

With the addition of *—n't*, the form of *will* was changed. Then in the second operation the *—n't* had to be removed, restoring the original form of *will*. This constant shifting of forms is awkward and wasteful. As long as every stage in our description is plagued with these operations, many of them only to be later undone, transformational description is unnecessarily complex.

One way around this difficulty is to operate not with sentences but with "strings" of morphemes, leaving the adjustment to the proper form to the last:

{John} {will} {go} → /²jâʜn+wìl+³gów¹\/ *John will go.*
↓

{John} {will} {—n't} {go} → /²jâʜn+wòwnt+³gów¹\/ *John won't go.*
↓

{John} {will} {—n't} {go} {will} {he}
→ /²ʸjâʜn+wòwnt+³gów²→²wíliy³↗/ *John won't go, will he?*

So described, there are two quite distinct sets of operations. The vertical arrows indicate transformations. They carry one string of morphemes into another. The horizontal arrows represent morphophonemic operations. They give any string of morphemes a phonemic shape. (Or, if a written language is being described, a comparable set of operations gives it a graphic shape.) Morphophonemic operations are described as applying only after all transformations have been completed. This, of course, will require some restatement of the transformational rules discussed above. It will also require a slight redefinition of transformation, since transformations do not alter one sentence into another, but one string of morphemes into another. These strings may be said to underlie the sentences which we used in the presentation above.

12.9 The word "string" might easily be misleading. We must certainly mean more than merely some assortment of morphemes arranged in some linear order. Several reasons for this should be apparent from the discussion above. Many of the transformations must be stated in terms of an operation performed on a certain element in a certain position in the string. For example, many of these we have discussed involve the first word in the verb phrase. But if a string were merely a sequence of elements in linear order, the only position we might define would be something like "second element" or "third from the end." Some of the question transformations involve substitution of a question word for a constituent. This might consist of a single morpheme, or of a considerable number. If transforma· tions are to apply to strings, strings must be assemblages of elements having constituent structure. When used in description in terms of transformations, "string" must mean a special sort of sequence of elements, which, because it is characterized by a constituent structure may be called a **structured string.**

Since transformations operate on structured strings, a grammar which is to describe transformations must first describe the construc· tion of a set of structured strings. This can best be done in terms of very much the same concepts as have been described in Chapter 10.

12.10   When carried out consistently, the ideas just sketched result in a grammar quite characteristic in its organization and form of statement. Such a description is called a **transformational grammar.** It is claimed by some linguists that this type of statement can attain to a degree of precision, completeness, and conciseness not possible in any other way—in fact, that this technique can overcome certain limitations which are inherent in any other known form of description. Needless to say, these claims are not universally accepted. Both the technique and the claims imply a certain distinctive general theory of linguistics. This differs from other descriptive linguistic theories in certain ways that produce characteristic features in grammatical statements. Certain of these should be pointed out:

1.   A transformational grammar is organized in three sections. The first of these describes certain strings of comparatively simple structure. The basic theory here is similar to that underlying all descriptions in terms of immediate constituents (see Chapter 10). For this reason, it is called the **constituent structure,** or by others, the **phrase structure,** segment of the grammar. The second, or **transformational** section, describes all the transformations by which the output strings of the first section of the grammar are carried into **terminal strings,** sufficient in number to underlie all of the sentences of the language. The third is the **morphophonemic** section. Here are described all of the processes by which terminal strings are given shapes which can be identified as utterances or portions of utterances. Any transforma-

tional grammar must have all three, but some individual sentences may involve no transformations. That is to say, the transformational section may be by-passed in some sentences; the other two cannot.

2. Since in such a scheme, no matter of phonemic (or orthographic) form comes in until the third, morphophonemic, portion of the grammar, the greater part of the statement, is properly in terms of quite abstract symbols. If the symbols used should have a form reminiscent of a familiar spelling or of a phonemic transcription, this is of no particular significance. In most instances the symbols are more or less arbitrary letters representing classes of structures, often with subscripts representing subclasses. Some of these symbols bear no obvious meaning, being selected merely for convenience. The use of such abstract symbols gives a thoroughgoing transformational grammar an algebraic appearance. This is often enhanced by the fact that the terminology and phraseology used in such grammars has been strongly influenced by that of mathematics. However, a transformational grammar is not properly any more mathematical than any other type of grammar in its basic features.

3. The statement is largely in the form of a set of rules. These are of two kinds. The first is of the form "X → Y + Z." This should be read as "X is to be rewritten as Y + Z." Such rules are referred to as **rewrite rules.** They have the effect of changing a symbolization, generally in the direction of making it more specific and explicit. For example, in one formulation of English grammar the starting point is the symbol S, roughly to be read as "sentence." The first rule is S → NP + VP. This substitutes for the very general representation, S, the more specific and explicit representation, NP + VP, roughly to be interpreted as "noun phrase plus verb phrase." This is not a statement that a sentence CONSISTS OF a noun phrase and a verb phrase. Many do, of course, but not all: e.g., *Come here!* lacks the noun phrase. Rather it is a statement that all sentences (or only one set if there is another rewrite rule that starts from S) must be DESCRIBED IN TERMS OF a noun phrase and a verb phrase. Subsequent rules may have the effect of cutting out some of these structures.

The rewrite rule applies to any string wherein the proper symbols are found. The second type of rule, the **transformational rule,** is similar in many respects, but operates only on certain symbols in certain places within a constituent structure. Thus a rewrite rule applying to NP, will apply to any NP. But a transformational rule may apply to certain NPs only. For example, a transformation involving the moving of an NP in object position relates the following pair of sentences:

18. *I saw John yesterday.*   *John I saw yesterday.*

But cannot apply to an NP in some other position:

19. *I gave the money to the man with John.*
    * *John I gave the money to the man with.*

4. Transformational grammars are generally very explicit about the conditions under which any given rule can be applied. Careful attention is given to the order of application of rules. An effort is made to distinguish clearly between **optional** and **obligatory** rules, and be-between **recursive** rules (ones that can be applied repeatedly) and **non-recursive** rules. Properly, this is not a peculiarity of transformational grammars as such, but of all grammars which attempt to be thoroughly rigorous in their description.

5. A key word in all transformational grammar is **generate.** This is used in a sense taken from mathematics.

$$(x - a)^2 + (y - b)^2 = c^2$$

may be said to generate a set of circles in a plane defined by x and y. That means that for any given a, b, and c this equation defines one specific circle. For all possible values of a, b, and c it defines all possible circles in the plane concerned. In the same way, a trans formational grammar consists of a set of statements which generate all possible sentences in a given language. Depending on the choices made wherever a choice is possible (whether to apply a certain optional rule, or which alternative to select when several are offered), it defines each specific sentence. In this sense, a particular running through of the grammar is not to be considered as CREATING a sentence, but more nearly as SELECTING a sentence from a pre-existing stock (the language) of all possible sentences. Thus the grammar might start with the symbol S and in a particular application of it end with /²jâʜɴ⁺wìl⁺³gów¹\/. But the last expression does not represent anything not represented by the first. Rather S stands for ALL sentences in the language, and thus represents, among others, /²jâʜɴ⁺wìl⁺³gów¹\/. The process of running through the grammar and making the required choices is a matter of singling out a specific sentence to replace the general symbol S. Nothing is created, increased, or added to; the meaning is instead very much narrowed. In much the same way $(x - 2)^2 + (y - 5)^2 = 3^2$ represents nothing not already completely covered by $(x - a)^2 + (y - b)^2 = c^2$, but only one specific instance out of the total set of circles. The selection is made by choosing values 2, 5, and 3 for a, b, and c.

12.11 At the beginning of this chapter a few transformations were described in terms of familiarly spelled sentences. Later it was shown that it would be preferable to work, not with sentences, but with structured strings. In the last section it was suggested that a transformational grammar, when formally stated would be quite different from the non-rigorous description above. Here will be given a more formal description of the pair of sentences with which the discussion began. Not all alternatives are stated at every step, but some are mentioned so that it will be clear where choices must be made and how it is that more than one sentence might come out. At each step the rule being applied is listed at the left and the form resulting from its application at the right. Braces around morpheme symbols have been omitted.

The description starts, of course, with the general expression for a sentence.

STEP 1.   S

The first rewrite rule is generally described as obligatory, that is, there is no other choice at this step:

STEP 2. S → NP + VP   NP + VP

There are a variety of ways in which the VP might be developed leading to a variety of sentence patterns: . . . *ran.*, . . . *is good.*, . . . *saw him.*, etc. At this point a choice of rewrite rules will determine which type, in the broadest sense, will result.

STEP 3. VP → Verb + NP   NP + Verb + NP

At the next step there are two alternatives, between which a choice must be made. In such a case a rewrite rule giving the alternatives can be stated in the following form:

STEP 4. NP → $\begin{Bmatrix} NP_{sing} \\ NP_{pl} \end{Bmatrix}$ NP_{sing} + Verb + NP

The import of this rule is to demand a choice between singular and plural for each NP. It must be applied twice, since there are two occurrences of NP in the form resulting from step 3. These must be considered as two separate steps, since they are quite independent of each other. Moreover, one basic principle of this sort of grammar is that each rewrite in the constituent structure must replace just one symbol.

STEP 5. $NP_{sing} + Verb + NP_{sing}$

STEP 6. Verb → Aux + V $NP_{sing} + Aux + V + NP_{sing}$

STEP 7. Aux → C(M) + (have + en) + (be + ing)
$$NP_{sing} + C + be + ing + V + NP_{sing}$$

The parentheses in this rule mean that a choice may be made. C must be used, M (which stands for *can, may, shall*, etc.) may be omitted, have + en and be + ing can be omitted. Of the optional elements only be + ing was selected. The next rule also presents some choices, but these are partly controlled by the context.

STEP 8. C → $\begin{Bmatrix} Z_3 \text{ in the context } NP_{sing} \\ \emptyset \text{ in the context } NP_{pl} \\ past \text{ in any context} \end{Bmatrix}$

$$NP_{sing} + Z_3 + be + ing + V + NP_{sing}$$

Next there are several alternatives for the rewriting of NP_{sing}, of which only two are listed here.

STEP 9. NP_{sing} → $\begin{Bmatrix} D + N + \emptyset \\ N_{prop} \\ etc. \end{Bmatrix}$

$$N_{prop} + Z_3 + be + ing + V + NP_{sing}$$

STEP 10. $N_{prop} + Z_3 + be + ing + V + D + N + \emptyset$

The $\emptyset$ in the last rule points out the lack of an inflectional suffix in contrast to $NP_{pl} \to D + N + Z_1$.

The result of step 10 is an expression consisting of some symbols for specific morphemes, either affixes like Z_3 or stems of function words like *be*, and some symbols standing for classes of stems or words. The next four steps consist of substituting an actual member of the class for each class symbol:

STEP 11. N_{prop} → Mary, John, Henry, . . .
John + Z_3 + be + ing + V + D + N + $\emptyset$

STEP 12. V   → write, read, take, . . .
John + Z_3 + be + ing + write + D + N + $\emptyset$

STEP 13. D   → the, this, a, . . .
John + Z_3 + be + ing + write + a + N + $\emptyset$

STEP 14. N   → ball, man, letter, . . .
John + Z_3 + be + ing + write + a + letter + $\emptyset$

The result of step 14 is a possible terminal string. Two courses of further development are open. We may apply certain transformations, or we may pass to the morphophonemic section of the grammar immediately. In the latter case there will be a variety of rules which must be applied, and no attempt will be made to give them in detail here. However, one type needs to be noticed. Certain affixes will regularly be combined with the following verbal element. In spelling the effect is as follows:

$$\text{John} + \underbrace{Z_3 + be}_{} + \underbrace{ing + write}_{} + a + \underbrace{letter + \emptyset}_{}$$
$$\text{John} \qquad is \qquad writing \qquad\quad a \qquad letter.$$

Or we may apply to the result of step 14 a transformation:

STEP 15. $\text{NP} + C + \begin{bmatrix} M \\ have \\ be \end{bmatrix} \ldots \rightarrow C + \begin{bmatrix} M \\ have \\ be \end{bmatrix} + \text{NP} \ldots$

$$\underbrace{Z_3 + be}_{} + \text{John} + \underbrace{ing + write}_{} + a + \underbrace{letter + \emptyset}_{}$$
$$Is \qquad\quad John \qquad writing \qquad\quad a \qquad letter?$$

Again, the morphophonemic steps are not given in detail, but only suggested by showing the final result in spelling. Much the same set of rules applies, however, as did above.

12.12 At first reading, the last section seems to be a very elaborate and complex way of describing a pair of quite simple sentences. But such an evaluation is not entirely appropriate. To be sure a very much more simple description is possible: In *John is writing a letter.*, the first word is *John,* the second word is *is,* the third word is *writing,* . . . . But such a description tells us very little if anything about the sentence. It might be possible to make a somewhat more sophisticated description of the same anecdotal sort, but however detailed this might be, it would tell nothing whatever about the grammar of the sentence. A sentence has a grammar only as it stands in relation to other sentences as part of a language. Any speaker of English immediately sees something of the grammar in a sentence like *John is writing a letter.* This is only possible because he knows the language, and can fit this sentence into its place within the language. The sentence *apko kya cahıye.* 'What do you want?' is just as grammatical, but the grammar is inaccessible to most readers of this book, simply because they cannot relate it to other sentences in Hindi. A grammatical description must place any given sentence in a framework which can be used to describe any sentence in the language, even though this requires making some statements which do not seem, superficially, to be of any great pertinence to the sentence at hand. Many features of the statement in the last section are not demanded by anything in the sentences being discussed, but by things in other (perhaps very many other) English sentences. At every point where a choice was presented, these two sentences were related to, and set off from, a host of other sentences. The statement did not merely describe the sentences in themselves, but rather put the two sentences into their place within the whole structure of the English language. The English language is an immensely complex thing, ramifying in many directions, and a description which does actually relate a single sentence to this complex structure cannot be very simple. One of the marvelous things about language is that any statement as short as that just given could in fact approach adequacy in relating these two sentences to the billions of billions of other sentences in the language.

In a statement of this sort, given with just two sentences in focus, the reasons for some of the features of the statement could not be made clear. To understand them, it would be necessary to trace out some of the consequences of other alternatives. An excerpt from a grammar cannot be as meaningful as a full grammar. To have given a full grammar of English, even if very much lacking in detail, would have been impossible here. What was given is a little like a full recounting of all the moves of the king's bishop in a championship chess game, mentioning the other pieces only when they fall directly in the path of the bishop.

There is another very important reason why the statement may seem unduly cumbersome. It attempted to state explicitly a number of things which are quite easily taken for granted. Every grammar leaves a great deal unsaid which the user must supply somehow from his "common sense" or "Sprachgefühl" or some other undefinable source. Much of this seems so obvious that to state it seems gratuitous. But research consists very largely of attempting to state the phenomena as explicitly as possible. Thus, Newton's law is traditionally said to have been found through dissatisfaction with treating the fall of an apple as simple and obvious, and was nothing more than an attempt to explain explicitly how it falls. Progress in linguistics must come largely by raising questions about the unstated phenomena, probing into them and attempting to make explicit statements in places where it had not previously been done. An explicit statement is not necessarily an acceptable statement. But it is often a testable statement. It always calls the attention of investigators to the question, and often provides a starting point toward a better formulation. Work on a transformational grammar of English has forced explicit statement at some points in the structure of the language and in general linguistic theory which had previously been passed by.

12.13 The introductory sections of this chapter centered around a small selection of sentence pairs related through a few transformations. The rules were not explicitly stated. Indeed, it would have been rather pointless to have given an explicit statement of the transformations without building this on an explicit statement of the underlying constituent structure. It should be pointed out, however, that a formal statement is possible. None of the sentences discussed would require the use of any very complex rules, and most of the rules would be quite general in application. Indeed, a proper writing of the rules might lead to a further step in generalization. For example, pairs 12 and 14 were described differently. But this is not necessary. Instead, the same sequence of transformational rules can be applied to produce both. The first fifteen steps in the generation are identical with that described in 12.11. Step 14 gives the string which, if taken directly through the morphophonemic rules, would give *John is writing a letter*. In the same way, the product of step 15 would yield *Is John writing a letter?*. As a string it is of the form:

STEP 15. Z_3 + be + John + ing + write + a + letter + $\emptyset$

The next step replaces an NP by a question word. There are two NPs in this string, *John,* and *a letter.* They belong to different classes, one which requires *who* as a substitute, and one that requires *what.*

STEP 16. Z_3 + be + who + ing + write + a + letter + $\emptyset$
OR Z_3 + be + John + ing + white + what

This is followed by an obligatory transformation which shifts any such question word to the initial position:

STEP 17.   who + Z_3 + be +   ing + write + a + letter + $\emptyset$
        what + Z_3 + be + John + ing + write

To these the same morphophonemic rules would apply. They would have the effect of taking them into a phonemic form familiarly associated with the spellings of examples 12 and 14:

Who	is		writing	a letter?
What	is	John	writing?	

The other transformations discussed can be formally stated in much the same way.

A complete transformational grammar of English would, of course, list many more transformations than this small sample. Some of them would be rather different in general form and effect. In the following sections a few more will be mentioned in order to show the range of possibilities. All are, of course, capable of formal statement. But for the present purpose, it will be better to revert to the less rigorous style of discussion in which sentences are compared rather than strings, and in which only certain outstanding features are mentioned.

12.14 One type of transformation uses two or more inputs, combining them into one output. A very simple case is the following:

20. *The car stopped suddenly.* *The car stopped suddenly and I*
    I was thrown against the *was thrown against the wind-*
    windshield. *shield.*

This particular transformation can be described in terms of nothing more than concatenation, the addition of a marker *and,* and appropriate adjustment of the intonation (or in writing of the punctuation). But the situation can be more complex:

21. *You have some bananas.* *If you have any bananas, I would*
    I would like about a dozen. *like about a dozen.*

At first sight, sentence 21 would seem to come from * *You have any bananas* and *I would like about a dozen.* But the first of these two sentences seems quite unnatural. A little investigation will show that there is a very special relation between *any* and *some.* The one occurs in certain types of sentences, the other in other types. An adequate set of transformational rules will have to include a rule which has the effect of substituting *any* for *some* to produce sentences like that in 21. This is not as special a rule as it might seem. Very much the same relationship is seen in other pairs of sentences, so that the same rule can be applied in the series of transformations which connect them.

22. *I have some bananas.* *I haven't any bananas.*
23. *You have some bananas.* *Have you any bananas?*

Another somewhat similar phenomenon is illustrated in the following:

24. *I will come.* *He said he would come.*

Only one of the two input sentences is shown here; the other will be discussed in 12.15. There is a change of *will* to *would*, and of *I* to *he*. These changes are conditioned by the occurrence of *said* and *he* in the first part of the sentence, as may be seen by comparing the set of sentences in 25, all having the same input:

25. *I will come.*   *He says he will come.*
                                        I said I would come.
                                        I say I will come.

Transformations which have the effect of putting two or more inputs together into one output involve a number of rules. There is the addition of various construction markers, *and, either . . . or, because, therefore, if . . . then,* etc.   There may be changes of certain specific items, *some → any, sometime → ever,* etc. Verb forms may be changed to bring them into the proper relationship. (Traditional grammar gives a partial treatment of these phenomena under the rules of "sequence of tenses.") Pronouns may undergo various changes. As all of these can be structurally defined, they belong in a grammar and can be formulated in transformational rules.

12.15 Example 24 illustrates another feature of some transformations. The other underlying sentence cannot easily be *He said.* Such a sentence does occur, but rather infrequently, and in a quite specialized situation. Rather it must come from something like *He said it.* In the transformation, *it* is replaced by *he would come.* This sort of transformation does not merely connect strings; it inserts one into another so that it becomes an element in the structure of the other. In doing so it removes and replaces some element. Sometimes it is fairly obvious what this replaced element must be. In other cases it is not clear from the final result what such an element should be considered to have been in the input. In this respect, such a transformation is exactly like some of the question transformations. In example 12, the transformation involved the substituting of *who* for *John.* Looking at the output alone, it would not be clear what nominal was involved. It might have been *Mary, the man, my neighbor who grows daffodils,* or innumerable other possibilities. But it could not be *the pen* or *that typewriter,* or many others, which would require the substitution of *what* rather than *who.* Perhaps it is just this uncertainty which lies behind calling a sentence like *Who is writing a letter?* a question. It is not possible to go from the output sentence backward and reconstruct in detail every step of the generation. But it is possible to know that *who* substitutes for an NP, and equally to know that *he would come* must substitute for an NP.

Another type of transformation which inserts one input into another is exemplified by the following two sentences:

26. *The man who drives the yellow Cadillac hit a lamppost yesterday.*
27. *The man who hit a lamppost yesterday drives the yellow Cadillac.*

Both these sentences can be generated from the same pair of inputs.

The man hit a lamppost yesterday.
The man drives the yellow Cadillac.

To be usable in this transformation, the two inputs must have some part in common, in this case, *the man.* For this constituent in one input may be substituted *who* or *which,* whereby the whole S becomes attributive to the matching noun in the other, and is inserted in the position after the noun. When the NP replaced by *who* or *which* is not initial, then additional changes have to be specified.

By means of various transformations of these types, it is possible to take care of all those sentence types which are traditionally labeled as "compound" or "complex." So conceived, the phrase structure sector of the grammar generates certain clauses, and the transformational sector unites these into sentences. In the light of this, it is not, strictly speaking, correct to read the symbol S at the start of 12.11 as meaning "sentence" as used in traditional grammar. Nor indeed is it necessarily much better to read it as meaning "clause" in the sense of traditional grammar, since some transformations will carry an S into some structure other than what is traditionally called either a "clause" or a "sentence." But this does not mean that S does not designate some real and significant unit, only that it is not a unit identical with any one of those defined in traditional grammar. It is better to consider S as a designation for a unit which is basic to English grammatical patterns as described by a transformational grammar. If read as "sentence" it means only "sentence" as understood in this kind of grammar. It should not be expected to match precisely any unit in any other statement of English grammar. A transformational grammar is not merely a restatement of, or a minor amendment to, a traditional grammar or an immediate constituent grammar, but a basically different approach to language structure. It must find different units.

12.16 Once it is recognized that transformations can be applied to a pair of input strings to reduce one to the status of an element within the other, a vast panorama of possibilities opens up. Certain types of what are traditionally labeled "phrases" seem quite similar in important ways to "subordinate clauses" and suggest that a similar treatment is possible. As examples the following sentences will serve:

28. *His coming and going like that gives me the willies.*
    from   *He comes and goes like that.*
29. *His continual drumming on the table makes me nervous.*
    from   *He continually drums on the table.*

These both have a great deal of the underlying sentence pattern still remaining, and therefore have a great deal that commends such treatment.

If it is permissible with sentences like 28 and 29, why not also with similar phrases with less of the sentence elements preserved? The following all seem to be related in some way to example 29, and should perhaps be treated as having the same origin:

30. *His continual drumming   makes me nervous.*
    His   drumming on the table makes me nervous.
    Continual drumming on the table makes me nervous.
    His   drumming   makes me nervous.
    Continual drumming   makes me nervous.
    Drumming on the table makes me nervous.
    Drumming   makes me nervous.

but not

   °*His continual   on the table makes me nervous.*, etc.

All of these differ from 29 only in the omission of certain parts. Any element or combination of elements can be omitted except *drumming*. They might accordingly be described in terms of a special type of transformation which merely deletes certain statable constituents.

This sort of transformation has a very wide usefulness, but it requires caution. It would be quite possible to generate 29 by a series of deletions from something like:

31. *His continual drumming on the table with his knife and fork while the toastmaster is introducing the speaker of the evening makes me nervous.*

But this is quite unnecessary. There seems to be no reason to start from the longer sentence. *He continually drums on the table.* is sufficient as an input. But if so, why not merely *He continually drums.* for the first sentence in 30? In this case a deletion transformation would be unnecessary. But this is not true of all these sentences.

The input may be *He continually drums.*, or *He drums on the table.*, or simply *He drums.*, but it must have *he* or some other NP in the subject position. Those sentences in 30 without *his* must be derived by the use of a deletion transformation if the *drumming* is to be gotten from the VP of an S. Unnecessary deletions are not justifiable, but some deletions are necessary in a transformational grammar of English.

12.17 One of the commonest criticisms of traditional school grammar has been directed at the use of "understood" sentence parts. For example, an imperative sentence like *Come here!* is commonly described as having as subject "*you* understood." *You* in such sentences is quite rare and exceptional. Some linguists reject the use of such "understood" elements in a grammatical statement. Here, as in many other instances, a transformational grammar parallels traditional grammar in some respects. This sentence can be derived by the same first rewrite rule as used in 12.11, S → NP + VP. If so, at a later point in the grammar, a deletion transformation must remove the NP. The question is, then, is it necessary to have the NP in the derivation? There is some evidence that it is. *Myself* occurs, generally speaking, only in sentences in which *I* occurs in subject position. *Yourself* occurs commonly in two kinds of sentences, those with *you* for the subject, and imperatives. All these facts can be brought under one rule if *you* could be the subject of imperative sentences at the point in their generation at which the rules introducing *yourself* apply. That is, if something like * *You go chase yourself!* were one stage in the generation of the imperative sentence *Go chase yourself!*

Within the framework of a transformational grammar deletion transformations seem to have a place when they are required to explain existing patterns. Unnecessary deletion transformations have no such place—no unnecessary rule of any kind can be tolerated. In other types of grammars the use of "understood" elements may be less easily justified, and whether they will be used or not is a decision which the linguist must make, just as he must decide which of several possible forms of statement he will follow. There is, however, one special danger in "understood" elements which explains, and at least partly justifies, the condemnation of many linguists. This is the use of "understood" elements in field linguistics. It requires a very profound knowledge of a language to be able to assess when such a device is justified by the structure of the language itself. The temptation in preliminary stages is to supply "understood" elements in order to bring the structure into line with that of some other language. For example, in Hebrew /ṭóob haaʔíiš/ 'The man is good.' /ṭóob/ means 'good' and /haaʔíiš/ means 'the man.' There is no direct equivalent to 'is,' though of course the sentence structure as a whole is in some way equivalent to the structure of the English sentence as a whole. Some grammarians have stated that 'is' is understood, or even that /haayáa/ is understood. (This is glossed in some dictionaries as meaning, among other things, 'to be.') But it is difficult to see how /haayáa/ can be "restored" to this sentence without utterly changing it. In no instance can there be any justification for "understood" elements or deletion transformations except in the STRUCTURE of the language. That "the meaning requires"—or the exigencies of translation, or any other ___ structural indication, real or imaginary—is totally irrelevant.

12.18 If individual words can be introduced into a sentence by means of a transformation combining two structured strings, it would seem possible to give a similar treatment to a great deal more of what has in the past been taken care of in the IC structure, or handled by traditional grammatical devices of various kinds. For example, it has been proposed that attributive adjectives can be introduced into noun phrases by this means.

32. *I see the house.* } *I see the red house.*
   The house is red. }

In favor of this suggestion is the fact that *I see the red house.* does seem to be related in some way to *I see the house which is red.* The latter clearly can be gotten from the inputs of 32. It is claimed that this procedure does result in a considerable simplification of description, but some linguists are less convinced of the value of such transformations than of those described earlier in this chapter.

Such a proposal seems to be pointing in the direction of making all of sentence structure a matter of transformations. But this is not the case. While it is easy enough to derive *red house* from an input *The house is red.*, it does not seem possible to generate *the house* in this way. Certainly it cannot be done in a strictly parallel way, since there is no sentence of the form * *House is the.* In any case, it would seem that there must be at least a small collection of sentences in the derivation of which no transformations are applied. Nevertheless, one of the important issues in regard to transformational grammars is determining the proper apportionment of the task of description between the phrase structure sector and the transformational sector of the description. Some would push the use of transformational description much farther than others.

The use of transformations in grammar, in any rigorous sense, has been a new development in the decade of the 1950's. Involving as it does a reorientation of linguistic theory and a significantly different technique of description, it has necessarily been the center of a vigorous controversy. At the time of writing, several of the issues are not as yet clearly defined. Not enough has been published in the way of transformational grammars of a variety of languages. It is, therefore, not yet possible to evaluate its potentialities adequately. It may be expected, however, that the theory will continue to play a significant role in the development of linguistics by virtue of having raised some important, previously overlooked issues, and perhaps by contributing to their solution.

THE STUDY OF LANGUAGE   *Leonard Bloomfield*

1. 1. Language plays a great part in our life. Perhaps because of its familiarity, we rarely observe it, taking it rather for granted, as we do breathing or walking. The effects of language are remarkable, and include much of what distinguishes man from the animals, but language has no place in our educational program or in the speculations of our philosophers.

There are some circumstances, however, in which the conventionally educated person discusses linguistic matters. Occasionally he debates questions of "correctness"—whether it is "better," for instance, to say *it's I* or *it's me*. His discussion of such things follows a fairly rigid pattern. If possible, he looks to the conventions of writing for an answer—as, say, for the question whether a *t* is to be pronounced in words like *often* or *soften*. Otherwise he appeals to authority: one way of speaking, he believes, is inherently right, the other inherently wrong, and certain learned men, especially the authors of grammars and dictionaries, can tell us which is which. Mostly, however, he neglects to consult these authorities, and tries, instead, to settle the matter by a kind of philosophical reasoning, which operates with terms such as "subject," "object," "predicate," and so on. This is the common-sense way of dealing with linguistic matters. Like much else that masquerades as common sense, it is in fact highly sophisticated, and derives, at no great distance, from the speculations of ancient and medieval philosophers.

It is only within the last century or so that language has been studied in a scientific way, by careful and comprehensive observation; the few exceptions will occupy us in a moment. *Linguistics,* the study of language, is only in its beginnings. The knowledge it has gained has not yet become part of our traditional education; the "grammar" and other linguistic instruction in our schools confines itself to handing on the traditional notions. Many people have difficulty at the beginning of language study, not in grasping the methods or results (which are simple enough), but in stripping off the preconceptions which are forced on us by our popular-scholastic doctrine.

1. 2. The ancient Greeks had the gift of wondering at things that other people take for granted. They speculated boldly and persistently about the origin, history, and structure of language. Our traditional lore about language is due largely to them.

Herodotus, writing in the fifth century B.C., tells us that King Psammetichus of Egypt, in order to find out which was the oldest nation of mankind (whatever this may mean), isolated two newborn infants in a park; when they began to speak, they uttered the word *bekos,* which turned out to be Phrygian for 'bread.'

In his dialogue *Cratylus,* Plato (427–347 B.C.) discusses the origin of words, and particularly the question whether the relation between things and the words which name them is a natural and necessary relation or merely the result of a human convention. This dialogue gives us a first glimpse into a century-long controversy between the *Analogists,* who believe that language was natural and therefore at bottom regular and logical, and the *Anomalists,* who denied these things and pointed out the irregularities of linguistic structure.

The Analogists believed that the origin and the true meaning of words could be traced in their shape; the investigation of this they called *etymology.* We may illustrate their theory by English examples. The word *blackbird* obviously consists of *black* and *bird:* the species was named for its color, and, indeed, blackbirds are birds and are black. In the same way, the Greeks would have concluded that there was some deep-seated connection between a *gooseberry* and a *goose:* it was the etymologist's task to find this connection. The word *mushroom* would have presented a more difficult problem. The components are often altered; thus, *breakfast,* in spite of the difference in sound, is evidently the meal by which we *break* our *fast,* and *manly* a shorter form of *man-like.*

In Greek, as in English, however, most words resist this kind of analysis. Thus, *early* ends like *manly,* but the rest of the word is obscure; *woman* resembles *man,* but what is the first syllable? Then there is a residue of short, simple words that do not resemble others—words such as *man, boy, good, bad, eat, run.* In such cases the Greeks and their pupils, the Romans, resorted to guesswork. For instance, they explained the Greek word *lithos* 'stone' as derived from the phrase *lian theein* 'to run too much,' because this is what a stone does *not* do. A Latin example of this sort has become proverbial: *lucus a non lucendo* 'a grove (*lucus*) is so named on account of its not being light (*lucendo*).'

These etymologies show us, at any rate, that the Greeks realized that speech-forms change in the course of time. In the systematic study of this change modern students have found the key to most linguistic problems. The ancients never settled down to any careful study of linguistic change.

The ancient Greeks studied no language but their own; they took it for granted that the structure of their language embodied the universal forms of human thought or, perhaps, of the cosmic order. Accordingly, they made grammatical observations, but confined these to one language and stated them in philosophical form. They discovered the parts of speech of their language, its syntactic constructions, such as, especially, that of subject and predicate, and its chief inflectional categories: genders, numbers, cases, persons, tenses, and modes. They defined these not in terms of recognizable linguistic forms, but in abstract terms which were to tell the meaning of the linguistic class. These teachings appear most fully in the grammars of Dionysius Thrax (second century B.C.) and of Apollonius Dyscolus (second century A.D.).

The Greeks made also some observations of detail, but this phase of their work, unfortunately, had less effect upon posterity. Their great epic poems, the *Iliad* and the *Odyssey,* which they viewed somewhat as sacred scriptures, were composed in an ancient and otherwise unknown kind of Greek. In order to understand these texts and to make correct copies, one had to study their language. Most famous in this work was Aristarchus (about 216–144 B.C.). Other works of Greek literature were composed in conventionalized forms of various regional dialects: the Greeks had the opportunity of comparing several divergent forms of their language. When the language of the great Athenian writers of the fourth century had become antiquated, it was made a special subject of study, since it represented the ideal form of written discourse. All this work demanded careful observation of details. Some of the later grammarians, notably Herodian, the son of Apollonius Dyscolus, assembled valuable information on such topics as the inflection and accent of ancient Greek.

1. 3. The Greek generalizations about language were not improved upon until the eighteenth century, when scholars ceased to view language as a direct gift of God, and put forth various theories as to its origin. Language was an invention of ancient heroes, or else the product of a mystical Spirit of the Folk. It began in man's attempts to imitate noises (the "bow-wow" theory), or in his natural sound-producing responses (the "ding-dong" theory), or in violent outcries and exclamations (the "pooh-pooh" theory).

In the etymological explanation of speech-forms there was no improvement. Voltaire is reported to have said that etymology is a science in which the vowels count for nothing and the consonants for very little.

The Romans constructed Latin grammars on the Greek model; the most famous of these, the work of Donatus (fourth century A.D.) and of Priscian (sixth century A.D.), remained in use as text-books through the Middle Ages. In the Middle Ages, when Latin was changing from its ancient shape into the forms which we know today as the Romance languages (French, Italian, Spanish, and so on), the convention remained of writing, as well as one could, in the ancient classical form of Latin. The medieval scholar, accordingly, in both the Latin countries and others, studied only classical Latin. The scholastic philosophers discovered some features of Latin grammar, such as the distinction between nouns and adjectives and the differences between concord, government, and apposition. They contributed much less than the ancients, who had, at any rate, a first-hand knowledge of the language they studied. The medieval scholar saw in classical Latin the logically normal form of human speech. In more modern times this doctrine led to the writing of *general grammars,* which were to demonstrate that the structure of various languages, and especially of Latin, embodies universally valid canons of logic. The most famous of these treatises is the *Grammaire générale et raisonnée* of the Convent of Port-Royal, which appeared in 1660. This doctrine persisted into the nineteenth century; it appears, for instance, in the classical scholar, Gottfried Hermann's work *De emendanda ratione Graecae grammaticae* (1801). It is still embodied in our school tradition, which seeks to apply logical standards to language. Philosophers, to this day, sometimes look for truths about the universe in what are really nothing but formal features of one or another language.

An unfortunate outgrowth of the general-grammar idea was the belief that the grammarian or lexicographer, fortified by his powers of reasoning, can ascertain the logical basis of language and prescribe how people ought to speak. In the eighteenth century, the spread of education led many dialect-speakers to learn the upper-class forms of speech. This gave the authoritarians their chance: they wrote *normative grammars,* in which they often ignored actual usage in favor of speculative notions. Both the belief in "authority" and some of the fanciful rules (as, for instance, about the use of *shall* and *will*) still prevail in our schools.

For the medieval scholar, language meant classical Latin, as it appears in books; we find few traces of interest in any other form of speech. The horizon widened at the time of the Renaissance. At the end of the Middle Ages, the study of Greek came back into fashion; soon afterward, Hebrew and Arabic were added. What was more important, some scholars in various countries began to take an interest in the language of their own time.

The era of exploration brought a superficial knowledge of many languages. Travelers brought back vocabularies, and missionaries translated religious books into the tongues of newly-discovered countries. Some even compiled grammars and dictionaries of exotic languages. Spanish priests began this work as early as in the sixteenth century; to them we owe a number of treatises on American and Philippine languages. These works can be used only with caution, for the authors, untrained in the recognition of foreign speech-sounds, could make no accurate record, and, knowing only the terminology of Latin grammar, distorted their exposition by fitting it into this frame. Down to our own time, persons without linguistic training have produced work of this sort; aside from the waste of labor, much information has been lost.

The increase of commerce and travel led also to the compilation of grammars and dictionaries for languages closer at hand. The linguistic horizon at the end of the eighteenth century can be surveyed in the glossary of 285 words in two hundred languages of Europe and Asia which P. S. Pallas (1741–1811) edited at the behest of Empress Catharine of Russia in 1786. A second edition of this, in 1791, added eighty more languages, including some African and American. In the years 1806 to 1817 there appeared a four-volume treatise under the title

Mithridates, by J. C. Adelung and J. S. Vater, which contained the Lord's Prayer in nearly five hundred languages.

The Renaissance turned the interest of a few scholars to the older records of their own languages. Franciscus Junius (1589–1677) accomplished an enormous amount of work in the study of the ancient documents of English and of the closely related languages, Frisian, Dutch, German, Scandinavian, and Gothic. This last—a language no longer spoken today—Junius knew from the famous Silver Codex, then recently discovered, a manuscript of the sixth century A.D. containing fragments of a Gospel translation; Junius published its text, together with that of the Anglo-Saxon Gospels. George Hickes (1642–1715) continued this work, publishing a Gothic and Anglo-Saxon grammar and a *Thesaurus* of miscellaneous information about the older stages of English and the sister tongues.

1. 4. The development so far outlined shows us what eighteenth-century scholars knew about language. They stated the grammatical features of language in philosophical terms and took no account of the structural difference between languages, but obscured it by forcing their descriptions into the scheme of Latin grammar. They had not observed the sounds of speech, and confused them with the written symbols of the alphabet. This failure to distinguish between actual speech and the use of writing distorted also their notions about the history of language. They saw that in medieval and modern times highly cultivated persons wrote (and even spoke) good Latin, while less educated or careless scribes made many mistakes: failing to see that this Latin-writing was an artificial and academic exercise, they concluded that languages are preserved by the usage of educated and careful people and changed by the corruptions of the vulgar. In the case of modern languages like English, they believed, accordingly, that the speech-forms of books and of upper-class conversation represented an older and purer level, from which the "vulgarisms" of the common people had branched off as "corruptions" by a process of "linguistic decay." The grammarians felt free, therefore, to prescribe fanciful rules which they derived from considerations of logic.

These misconceptions prevented scholars from making use of the data that were at hand: the modern languages and dialects, the records of ancient languages, the reports about exotic languages, and, above all, the documents which show us successive stages of one and the same language, as for instance of Anglo-Saxon (Old English) and modern English, or of Latin and the modern Romance languages. One knew that some languages resembled each other, but the doctrine of linguistic decay discouraged systematic study of this relation, since the changes which led, say, from Latin to modern French, were viewed as haphazard corruptions.

The illusion that Latin had lived on, unchanged, beside the Romance languages, led scholars to derive contemporary languages one from the other. Mostly they took Hebrew to be the language from which all others had sprung, but some thought otherwise, as, for example, Goropius Becanus of Antwerp, who patriotically derived all languages from Dutch.

It was plain that the more familiar languages of Europe fell into three groups by virtue of close resemblances within each group, resemblances such as appear in the following words:

GERMANIC GROUP	ROMANCE GROUP	SLAVIC GROUP	
'hand'			
English *hand*	French *main*	Russian	*ruka*
Dutch *hand*	Italian *mano*	Polish	*reka*
German *Hand*	Spanish *mano*		x
Danish *haand*		Bohemian	*ruka*
Swedish *hand*		Serbian	*ruka*
'foot'			
English *foot*	French *pied*	Russian	*noga*
Dutch *voet*	Italian *piede*	Polish	*noga*
German *Fuss*	Spanish *pie*	Bohemian	*noha*
Danish *fod*		Serbian	*noga*
Swedish *fot*			
'winter'			
English *winter*	French *hiver*	Russian	*zima*
Dutch *winter*	Italian *inverno*	Polish	*zima*
German *Winter*	Spanish *invierno*	Bohemian	*zima*
Danish *vinter*		Serbian	*zima*
Swedish *vinter*			
'drink'			
English *drink*	French *boire*	Russian	*pit'*
Dutch *drinken*	Italian *bere*	Polish	*pic'*
German *trinken*	Spanish *beber*	Bohemian	*piti*
Danish *drikke*		Serbian	*piti*
Swedish *dricka*			

There was apparent also a less striking resemblance between these groups; this wider resemblance extended to some other languages, such as, notably, Greek:

'mother': Greek *mētēr*, Latin *māter* (with its modern forms in the Romance languages), Russian *mat'* (genitive case *materi*—with similar forms in the other Slavic languages), English *mother* (with similar forms in the other Germanic languages);

'two': Greek *duo*, Latin *duo*, Russian *dva*, English *two;*

'three': Greek *treis*, Latin *trēs*, Russian *tri*, English *three;*

'is': Greek *esti*, Latin *est*, Russian *jest'*, English *is* (German *ist*).

1. 5. Outside the tradition of Europe, several nations had developed linguistic doctrines, chiefly on an antiquarian basis. The Arabs had worked out a grammar of the classical form of their language, as it appears in the Koran; on the model of this, the Jews in Mohammedan countries constructed a Hebrew grammar. At the Renaissance, European scholars became acquainted with this tradition; the term *root,* for instance, as a designation for the central part of a word, comes from Hebrew grammar. In the Far East, the Chinese had gained a great deal of antiquarian linguistic knowledge, especially in the way of lexicography. A Japanese grammar seems to have grown up independently.

It was in India, however, that there arose a body of knowledge which was destined to revolutionize European ideas about language. The Brahmin religion guarded, as sacred texts, some very ancient collections of hymns; the oldest of these collections, the Rig-Veda, dates in part, at a conservative estimate, from about 1200 B.C. As the language of these texts grew antiquated, the proper way of pronouncing them, and their correct interpretation, became the task of a special class of learned men. The antiquarian interest in language which arose in this way, was carried over into a more practical sphere. Among the Hindus, as among us, different classes of society differed in speech. Apparently there were forces at work which led upper-class speakers to adopt lower-class forms of speech. We find the Hindu grammarians extending their interest from the Scriptures to the upper-caste language, and making rules and lists of forms descriptive of the correct type of speech, which they called *Sanskrit*. In time they worked out a systematic arrangement of grammar and lexicon. Generations of such labor must have preceded the writing of the oldest treatise that has come down to us, the grammar of Pāṇini. This grammar, which dates from somewhere round 350 to 250 B.C., is one of the greatest monuments of human intelligence. It describes, with the minutest detail, every inflection, derivation, and composition, and every syntactic usage of its author's speech. No other language, to this day, has been so perfectly described.

It may have been due, in part, to this excellent codification that Sanskrit became, in time, the official and literary language of all Brahmin
India. Long after it had ceased to be spoken as anyone's native language, it remained (as classical Latin remained in Europe) the artificial
medium for all writing on learned or religious topics.

Some knowledge of Sanskrit and of the Hindu grammar had reached
Europe, through missionaries, in the sixteenth and seventeenth centuries. In the eighteenth century, Englishmen in India transmitted
more exact reports; round the beginning of the nineteenth century, the
knowledge of Sanskrit became part of the equipment of European
scholars.

1. 6. The Indian grammar presented to European eyes, for the first
time, a complete and accurate description of a language, based not
upon theory but upon observation. Moreover, the discovery of Sanskrit
disclosed the possibility of a comparative study of languages.

To begin with, the concept of related languages was strikingly confirmed by the existence, in far-off India, of a sister of the familiar
languages of Europe; witness, for example, the Sanskrit equivalents
of the words above cited:

    mātā 'mother,' accusative case *mātaram;*
    dvāu 'two';
    trayah 'three';
    asti 'he is.'

Even more important was the insight into linguistic structure which
one got from the accurate and systematic Hindu grammar. Until now,
one had been able to see only vague and fluid similarities, for the current grammars, built on the Greek model, did not clearly set off the
features of each language. The Hindu grammar taught Europeans to
analyze speech-forms; when one compared the constituent parts, the
resemblances, which hitherto had been vaguely recognized, could be
set forth with certainty and precision.

The old confused notions of linguistic relationship lived on for a
brief time in the opinion that the European languages were derived
from Sanskrit, but this opinion soon gave way to the obviously correct
explanation, namely, that Sanskrit, Latin, Greek, and so on, were divergent later forms of some one prehistoric language. This explanation
seems to have been first stated by Sir William Jones (1746–1794), the
first great European Sanskrit scholar, in an address delivered in 1786:
Sanskrit bears a resemblance to Greek and Latin which is too close to

be due to chance, but shows, rather, that all three "have sprung from some common source which, perhaps, no longer exists," and Gothic (that is, Germanic) and Celtic probably had the same origin.

In order to work out the comparison of these languages, one needed, of course, descriptive data for each one of them. The prospect of comparison, however, with all that it revealed about ancient speech-forms and tribal migrations and the origin of peoples and customs, proved so alluring that no one undertook the humdrum task of analyzing the other languages on the model of Sanskrit. European scholars had a sound knowledge of Latin and Greek; most of them spoke some Germanic language as their mother-tongue. Confronting a precise statement of Sanskrit grammar or a carefully analyzed lexical form, they could usually recall a similar feature from some of the more familiar languages. In reality, of course, this was a makeshift; often enough the comparer had to make a preliminary investigation to establish the facts, and sometimes he went astray for lack of methodically arranged data. If European scholars had possessed descriptions of the sister languages comparable to the Hindus' description of Sanskrit, the comparative study of the *Indo-European* languages (as they are now called) would have progressed far more speedily and accurately. Yet, in spite of poor equipment, and thanks to the energy of its workers, the historical and comparative study of the Indo-European languages became one of the principal enterprises, and one of the most successful, of European science in the nineteenth century.

The languages of Persia (the so-called Iranian languages) so closely resembled Sanskrit that their kinship was certain from the start. A similar relation, though less close, was found to exist between the Baltic languages (Lithuanian, Lettish, and Old Prussian) and the Slavic. Jones' surmise that the Germanic languages were related to Latin, Greek, and Sanskrit, at once proved true, as did later his surmise about Celtic (Irish, Welsh, Cornish, Breton, and the ancient language of Gaul). Later, Armenian and Albanese, and a few ancient languages known to us only from scant written records, proved also to belong to the Indo-European family.

Although there was some dispute as to details, the general pre-suppositions of historical and comparative language-study soon became clear. Languages change in the course of time. Apparent exceptions, such as the medieval and modern use of Latin (or, in India, of Sanskrit), amount only to this, that by long schooling people can be trained to imitate the language of ancient writings. This antiquarian feat is utterly different from the normal transmission of speech from parents to children. All writing, in fact, is a relatively recent invention, and has remained, almost to our day, the property of only a chosen few: the effect of writing upon the forms and the development of actual speech is very slight.

If a language is spoken over a large area, or thanks to migration, in several separate areas, then it will change differently in different places, and the result will be a set of related languages, like Italian, French, Spanish, Portuguese, Roumanian, and the other Romance dialects. We infer that other groups of related languages, such as the Germanic (or the Slavic or the Celtic), which show a similar resemblance, have arisen in the same way; it is only an accident of history that for these groups we have no written records of the earlier state of the language, as it was spoken before the differentiation set in. To these unrecorded parent languages we give names like *Primitive Germanic* (*Primitive Slavic, Primitive Celtic,* and so on).[1] In the same way, finding that all these languages and groups (Sanskrit, Iranian, Armenian, Greek, Albanese, Latin, Celtic, Germanic, Baltic, Slavic) resemble each other beyond the possibility of mere chance, we call them the *Indo-European family of languages,* and conclude, with Jones, that they are divergent forms of a single prehistoric language, to which we give the name *Primitive Indo-European.*

The method of comparison, too, was clear from the start. In general, any feature that is common to all or to several of the related languages, must have been present in their common antecedent stage, in the "parent language." Thus, from the above cited forms of the word for 'mother,' it is clear that in Primitive Indo-European this word must have begun with the sound which we indicate in writing by means of the letter *m*. Where the related languages do not agree, some or all of them must have made some change. Thus, it is clear that the second consonant in the word for 'mother' was in Primitive Indo-European a *t*-sound, and that the *th*-sound in English (as well as the earlier *d*-sound in the Old English form, *mōdor*) must be due to change.

1.7. The beginning of a systematic comparison of the Indo-European languages was a treatise on the inflectional endings of verbs in Sanskrit, Greek, Latin, Persian, and Germanic, published in 1816 by Franz Bopp (1791–1867). In 1818 Rasmus Kristian Rask (1787–1832)

---

[1] The word *primitive* is here poorly chosen, since it is intended to mean only that we happen to have no written records of the language. German scholars have a better device in their prefix *ur-* 'primeval,' with which they form, for this purpose, names like *urgermanisch, urslavisch, urkeltisch.*

showed that the words of the Germanic languages bear a regular formal relation in matters of sound, to the words of the other Indo-European languages. For instance, where the others have *p*, the Germanic languages have *f*, as in *father:* Latin *pater, foot:* Latin *pēs, five:* Greek *pente, few:* Latin *paucī.* In 1819 Jakob Grimm (1787–1863) published the first volume of his *Deutsche Grammatik,* which was not, as the title nowadays would indicate, a German grammar, but a comparative grammar of the Germanic languages (Gothic, Scandinavian, English, Frisian, Dutch, and German). In the second edition, in 1822, of this volume, Grimm presented a systematic exposition of the correspondences of consonants between Germanic and the other Indo-European languages; since then, these correspondences have been known to English-speaking scholars as *Grimm's Law.* These correspondences are a matter of historical detail, but their significance was overwhelming, since they showed that human action, in the mass, is not altogether haphazard, but may proceed with regularity even in so unimportant a matter as the manner of pronouncing the individual sounds within the flow of speech. Grimm's comparison of the Germanic languages remains to this day unrivaled; three more volumes appeared in 1826, 1831, and 1837; a fifth volume, which was to complete the syntax, never appeared.

In 1833 Bopp began the publication of a comprehensive treatise, a comparative grammar of the Indo-European languages. In the years 1833 to 1836 there appeared the first edition of the *Etymological Investigations* of August Friedrich Pott (1802–1887). The term *etymology,* here as in all modern discussions, has taken on a precise meaning: the etymology of a speech-form is simply its history, and is obtained by finding the older forms in the same language and the forms in related languages which are divergent variants of the same parent form. Thus, to state the etymology of the English word *mother* is to say that this form is the modern version of the ninth-century Old English *mōdor;* that this is related to Old Norse *mōðer,* Old Frisian *mōder,* Old Saxon *mōdar,* Old High German *muoter* (these are the forms in our oldest records of the respective languages), in the sense that all these are divergent variants of a single Primitive Germanic word, which we symbolize as **mōder;* and that these Germanic forms are in turn related to ("cognate with") Sanskrit *mātā,* Avestan (Old Iranian) *mātā,* Old Armenian *mair,* ancient Greek *mētēr,* Albanese *motrε* (which, however, means 'sister'), Latin *māter,* Old Irish *māthir,* Lithuanian *motē* (which means 'wife'), Old Bulgarian (Slavic) *mati,* and with the other corresponding forms in each of the groups of languages here illustrated, in the sense that all these are divergent later forms of a single Primitive Indo-European word, which we symbolize as * *mātēr*. As this example shows, etymologies, in the modern sense, do not necessarily show us an older, more transparent meaning of words. Our modern etymologies in the Indo-European languages are due largely to the researches of Pott.

During the following decades progress was so rapid that both smaller treatises and the great handbooks rapidly became antiquated. Of the latter, Bopp's, in spite of new editions, was superseded in 1861 by the *Compendium of the Comparative Grammar of the Indo-European Languages* of August Schleicher (1823–1868). In 1886 Karl Brugmann (1849–1919) and Berthold Delbrück (1842–1922) began the publication of their *Outline of the Comparative Grammar of the Indo-European Languages;* the standard work of reference today is the second edition of this, which appeared from 1897 to 1916.

As the work went on, other, more detailed treatises were devoted to the separate branches of the Indo-European family, in the manner of Grimm's great treatise on Germanic. Friedrich Diez (1794–1876) began the serious study of the Romance languages in his *Grammar of the Romance Languages* (1836–1844); Johann Kaspar Zeuss (1806–1856) opened the field of the Celtic languages in his *Grammatica Celtica* (1853); Franz von Miklosich (1813–1891) wrote a *Comparative Grammar of the Slavic Languages* (1852–1875).

1. 8. These studies could not fail to throw light upon many an aspect of history and archaeology, but their immediate interest lay in what they told about human speech. Although the various Indo-European languages had a common origin, their later careers were independent: the student had now a vast collection of details concerning the changes in human speech, which enabled him to generalize on the manner of this change.

To draw the conclusions as to the way in which languages change, was to replace the speculation of earlier times by the results of scientific induction. William Dwight Whitney (1827–1894), an American scholar, wrote *Language and the Study of Language* (1867) and *The Life and Growth of Language* (1874). These books were translated into several European languages; today they seem incomplete, but scarcely antiquated, and still serve as an excellent introduction to language study. In 1880 there appeared the *Principles of Linguistic History* by Hermann Paul (1846–1921), which, in its successive editions (the fifth appeared in 1920), became the standard work on the methods of historical linguistics.

Paul's book of *Principles* illustrates, with a wealth of examples, the process of linguistic change which had been revealed by Indo-European studies. Not so well written as Whitney's, but more detailed and methodical, this book exercised a great influence on linguistic studies; students of a more recent generation are neglecting it, to their disadvantage. Aside from its very dry style, Paul's *Principles* suffers from faults that seem obvious today, because they are significant of the limitations of nineteenth-century linguistics.

One of these faults is Paul's neglect of descriptive language study. He admitted that descriptions of languages were necessary, but confined his actual discussion to matters of linguistic change. This shortcoming he shares with his epoch. We can study linguistic change only by comparing related languages or different historical stages of the same language. For instance, by noting the similarities and differences of English, Frisian, Dutch, German, Scandinavian, and Gothic, we can get a notion of the older language ("Primitive Germanic") from which they have differentiated in the course of time, and we can then study the changes which have occurred in each of these later languages. Or else, by comparing our records of Old English (say, in the writings of King Alfred) with modern English, we can see how English has changed in the last thousand years. Evidently our power of making this comparison depends upon our knowledge of the things to be compared. For example, our knowledge about the compounding of words (as in *blackbird* or *footsore*) in the several Germanic languages is decidedly incomplete; therefore we cannot go very far with a comparative study of this matter, which would tell us how words were compounded in Primitive Germanic, and how these habits have changed in the subsequent history of each Germanic language. The historical language students of the nineteenth century suffered under these limitations, but they seem not to have grasped the nature of the difficulty.

The other great weakness of Paul's *Principles* is his insistence upon "psychological" interpretation. He accompanies his statements about language with a paraphrase in terms of mental processes which the speakers are supposed to have undergone. The only evidence for these mental processes is the linguistic process; they add nothing to the discussion, but only obscure it. In Paul's book and largely to the present day, linguistics betrays its descent from the philosophical speculations of the ancient Greeks. Paul and most of his contemporaries dealt only with Indo-European languages and, what with their neglect of descriptive problems, refused to work with languages whose history was unknown. This limitation cut them off from a knowledge of foreign types of grammatical structure, which would have opened their eyes to the fact that even the fundamental features of Indo-European grammar, such as, especially, the part-of-speech system, are by no means universal in human speech. Believing these features to be universal, they resorted, whenever they dealt with fundamentals, to philosophical and psychological pseudo-explanations.

1. 9. Alongside the great stream of historical research, there ran, however, a small but accelerating current of general linguistic study. The Hindu grammar of Sanskrit was never quite forgotten; while many pupils used its result without knowing of its existence, the masters, who knew the antecedents of their science, appreciated its value. For the less-known Indo-European languages descriptive studies could not be avoided. It is surely no accident that the best of these, in the field of the Slavic and Baltic languages, were furnished by August Leskien (1840–1916), a scholar who took a leading part in laying the foundations of historical methods of research.

For the most part, however, descriptive studies did not merge with the main stream of historical work. Some students were attracted by the structural peculiarities of languages outside the Indo-European group, even though the history of these languages was unknown. Other students examined a variety of languages in order to get a philosophical survey of human speech; in fact, much of the older descriptive work is almost unintelligible today because it is pervaded by philosophical notions that are no longer familiar to us.

The first great book on general linguistics was a treatise on the varieties of human speech by Wilhelm von Humboldt (1767–1835), which appeared in 1836. H. Steinthal (1823–1899), beside more general writings on the fundamentals of language, published in 1861 a treatise on the principal types of language structure. G. von der Gabelentz' (1840–1893) work on the science of language (1891) is much less philosophical. This direction of study culminated in a great work on language by the philosopher and psychologist, Wilhelm Wundt (1832–1920), which appeared in 1900 as the first part of a treatise on social psychology. Wundt based his psychology of speech upon any and all accessible descriptions of languages. It is interesting today to read the Indo-Europeanist Delbrück's critique and Wundt's rejoinder, both of which appeared in the following year. Delbrück objects to Wundt's use of languages whose history is unknown; for him the only aspect of language worth studying is its change in the course of time. Wundt, on the other hand, insists upon the importance of psychological interpretation in terms of his system, while Delbrück says that it does not matter what particular system of psychology a linguist may choose.

Meanwhile some students saw more and more clearly the natural relation between descriptive and historical studies. Otto Böhtlingk (1815–1904), who made the modern European edition of Pāṇini, applied the descriptive technique to a language of totally different structure, the Yakut of Asiatic Russia (1851). Friedrich Müller (1834–1898) published an outline of linguistic science (1876–1888) which contained brief sketches of the languages of the world, regardless of whether a historical treatment was possible. Franz Nikolaus Finck (1867–1910), both in a theoretical essay (1905) and in a little volume (1910) in which he analyzed descriptively eight unrelated languages, insisted upon descriptive study as a basis for both historical research and philosophical generalization. Ferdinand de Saussure (1857–1913) had for years expounded this matter in his university lectures; after his death, they were published in book form (1915).

Most convincing in this respect was the historical treatment of language families other than the Indo-European. On the one hand, the need of descriptive data as a prerequisite for comparative work was here self-evident; on the other hand, the results showed that the processes of linguistic change were the same in all languages, regardless of their grammatical structure. The comparative study of the Finno-Ugrian languages (Finnish, Lappish, Hungarian, and their kin) began as early as 1799, and has been greatly elaborated. The second volume of Humboldt's great treatise founded the comparative grammar of the Malayo-Polynesian language family. Today we have comparative studies of other families, such as the Semitic family and the Bantu family in Africa. Students of American languages could indulge in no self-deception as to the need of descriptive data: north of Mexico alone there are dozens of totally unrelated groups of languages, presenting the most varied types of structure. In the stress of recording utterly strange forms of speech one soon learned that philosophical prepossessions were only a hindrance.

The merging of these two streams of study, the historical-comparative and the philosophical-descriptive, has made clear some principles that were not apparent to the great Indo-Europeanists of the nineteenth century, as represented, say, by Hermann Paul. All historical study of language is based upon the comparison of two or more sets of descriptive data. It can be only as accurate and only as complete as these data permit it to be. In order to describe a language one needs no historical knowledge whatever; in fact, the observer who allows such knowledge to affect his description, is bound to distort his data. Our descriptions must be unprejudiced, if they are to give a sound basis for comparative work.

The only useful generalizations about language are inductive generalizations. Features which we think ought to be universal may be absent from the very next language that becomes accessible. Some features, such as, for instance, the distinction of verb-like and noun-like words as separate parts of speech, are common to many languages, but lacking in others. The fact that some features are, at any rate, widespread, is worthy of notice and calls for an explanation; when we have adequate data about many languages, we shall have to return to the problem of general grammar and to explain these similarities and divergences, but this study, when it comes, will be not speculative but inductive.

As to change in language, we have enough data to show that the general processes of change are the same in all languages and tend in the same direction. Even very specific types of change occur in much the same way, but independently, in the most diverse languages. These things, too, will some day, when our knowledge is wider, lend themselves to a systematic survey and to fruitful generalization.

LINGUISTICS, THE SCIENCE
OF LANGUAGE   W. Nelson Francis

From the linguistic point of view there is not much to be said about language in the abstract. People don't speak language; they speak languages. Some people—a relatively small number—are capable of speaking more than one language, but nobody can speak more than one at a time. To the neurologist investigating the cerebral circuits used in speech, or to the otolaryngologist observing the mechanism of the vocal bands in producing voice, it is of no moment what language is being spoken. But for the linguist, whose subject of observation is the articulate sounds themselves, it is essential to begin, at least, with a single language. Time enough when he knows a great deal about a large number of languages to make statements about language in general.

Before we go on to describe how the linguist operates, it would be well to make clear just what we mean by **linguistics** and **linguist**. To

From W. Nelson Francis, *The Structure of American English,* The Ronald Press Co., New York, 1958.

begin with, linguistics is a science. It is, in fact, often called **linguistic science** in order to emphasize this point. This will occasionally happen in this book, most likely at those places where the scientific nature of linguistics must be emphasized. But in general the shorter term, analogous as it is to *mathematics* and *physics,* is sufficient. Now a form of study or a body of knowledge if it is to call itself a science must conform to certain generally recognized requirements. They are these:

1. A science directs its attention to a coherent body of facts, entities, or events which can be separated from the rest of the universe by consistent and clearly statable definitions. This is its *subject matter.* The subject matter of geology, for instance, is the earth, especially its crust, and all nonliving things found within it. It is bounded on the one side by the subject matter of astronomy, and on the other by that of biology.

2. A science directs upon its subject matter a close and unprejudiced scrutiny and attempts to record the results of this scrutiny in such a manner that they can be verified by any competent observer. It produces, in short, *careful objective descriptions.*

3. A science further attempts to put together the results of its descriptions in such a way that they form orderly and systematic patterns which display the relationships that exist within its subject matter. In brief, it *makes generalizations.*

4. A science tests its generalizations by applying them to parts of its subject matter not used in forming the generalizations. In other words, it *makes predictions.*

5. Finally, a science examines the outcome of its predictions and, in the light of their success or failure, corroborates or revises its generalizations. If the corroboration is satisfactory, it may call its generalizations *laws,* which are simply statements of predictable behavior.

In any active science, all five of these processes are going on at the same time. Science is constantly redefining its subject matter, refining its observations, restating and revising its generalizations. It may also occupy itself in working out practical applications of its discoveries, but this is by no means a necessary or even typical part of science. Science as such has fulfilled its function when it has produced laws upon which accurate predictions may be based.

Let us now apply these criteria to linguistic science.

1. The *subject matter* of linguistics is all the systems of articulated sounds used today by humans in the carrying on of their affairs, that is, all living languages. It further includes records, in writing and in such media as phonograph records and magnetic tapes, of languages that have been used at some time in the past.

2. The methods of observation used by linguistics are various, including simple listening, phonetic transcription, and the use of various instruments, such as oscillographs, sound-spectrographs, and kymographs. Records made in these ways constitute various kinds of *objective description*.

3. The kinds of *generalization* made by linguistics are primarily statements about the systematic selection and arrangement of significant sounds and groups of sounds which are actually used by native speakers. Other kinds of generalization include statements about the changes which have taken place in specific languages in the past and about the genetic and other relationships between languages both at present and in the past.

4. The *predictions* made by linguistics are principally of the nature of grammars and dictionaries, which say, in effect, "If you use these sounds and groups of sounds in the patterns of arrangement here described, native speakers of this language will understand you and will respond in the predicted way."

5. Since linguistics is a very active science just now, it is constantly engaged in revising and overhauling all parts of its methods, findings, and generalizations. In fact, so rapidly is it moving that parts of this book may well be out of date by the time it is printed. This would also be true of a textbook in physics, chemistry, or, indeed, any other active science.

A person who engages in the methodical exercise of some or all of these five pursuits is a **linguist**. Not all such people are wholly content with this term, because it has another well-established meaning: "a person who knows several languages and uses them with facility; a person who learns languages easily." Linguists in the scientific sense are usually, but not necessarily, linguists in this sense as well. But linguists in the popular sense are seldom linguists in the scientific sense; they may be travelers, cosmopolitan playboys, waiters, diplomats, international business men, students of literature, or just plain citizens with a fondness for languages. In this book, *linguist* invariably means "linguistic scientist"; if it is necessary to refer to the person who knows many languages, some such term as *polyglot* will be used.

Linguistics in Relation to Other Studies

Just as we felt it necessary to find the place of language in the total scheme of things, so it seems wise at this point to place linguistics among the other branches of study. We must certainly do this before we can decide what it can and cannot do, before, that is, we can answer the question, "What use is it?" From another point of view, we want to know in at least general terms what its boundaries are so that we can avoid straying out of its territory into the domain of some neighboring discipline. As anyone knows, it is not always easy to draw precise boundaries between two branches of learning. Sometimes the subject matter becomes ambiguous at the borderline, as, for example, in the case of certain single-celled organisms that can be assigned equally well to the provinces of botany and zoology. But border areas of this sort do not disturb us; either we draw an arbitrary line somewhere, as we do in making political boundaries, or else we create separate, over-lapping fields whose very names often indicate their nature, such as biochemistry, physical chemistry, and economic geography.

Language, which we have stated to be the subject matter of linguistics, is such an ever-present and multipurposed form of human behavior that it turns up as part, at least, of the subject matter of many other disciplines beside linguistics. Some sort of linguistic factor is involved in most of the things we humans do. It may be only an unimportant and chiefly irrelevant accompaniment, as in golf, where the only essential use made of language is to yell "Fore!" Or it may be one of the most important and central parts of the activity, as in praying or political campaigning. This means, in turn, that people who study and teach the many hundreds of human activities must devote a part, at least, and sometimes a pretty large part, of their attention to the related uses of language. This seems very obvious, and indeed it is, as a general rule. But a good many mistakes have been made and continue to be made by people who do not take it sufficiently into account. For this reason, and because some important points about linguistics depend upon it, we must here labor the obvious a bit more.

First, we might look at the large field of activity that we can call by some such general term as "special skills." Here belong games, like golf, bridge, and baseball; occupational techniques, like carpentry, automobile mechanics, and gardening; useful acquirements of varied application, like driving a car, dressmaking, and first aid; social graces, like dancing, ballroom etiquette, and formal entertaining. The list could be greatly extended, but enough examples have been cited to make it obvious that each of these skills has its own linguistic accompaniment, which the beginner must learn as he masters the activity itself. Usually the language element is a vocabulary of terms designating objects and the manner of manipulating them, as in "clutch," "throttle," "steering wheel," "put on the brake." Less often it may consist of a collection of utterances that may be repeated in certain circumstances, such as "I pass," "Come on, seven!" and "I've had a delightful evening." In any case, the person who simply learns and teaches these special areas of language is not thereby engaging in linguistics. But a person who collects these special vocabularies and subjects them to observation, objective description, and generalization is acting in accordance with scientific method and is, therefore, to some degree at least a linguist.

Next, we might consider a group of human activities which use language not as an accompaniment to more important nonlinguistic actions, but as the actual medium in which actions are conducted. This is a vast field indeed. It includes almost all of what we call "thinking," which I shall not attempt to define. It therefore includes all the branches of study that have thinking as their subject matter: a good part of philosophy and psychology. It also includes a large part of all the branches of learning which study (that is, think about) all the other subject matters, simply because one of the most important ways they have of carrying on their thinking and expressing its results is by using language. There are, of course, other ways—mathematics, diagrams, and manipulative experiments—but language is always there too. No matter what a branch of study may be, in addition to its laboratories it always has its textbooks and lecture-rooms. Furthermore this large field includes those activities which use language as a medium of artistic creation and performance. Here belong rhetoric, literature, oratory, storytelling, and part, at least, of acting and singing. A fourth area in which language is central is religion, since language is the medium of prayer and for much of ritual. Still another great area of human activity uses language as a medium of social, political, and economic manipulation and control. Here fall advertising, propaganda, pedagogy, political caucusing and campaigning, and a large part of what we loosely call "human relations." Finally, though not exhaustively, we might mention a few miscellaneous activities which use language as their main medium in varied and interesting ways, such as psychoanalysis, games like "Twenty Questions" and "Scrabble," polite conversation, journalism, criticism of all sorts, hypnotism, magic and incantation generally, and the desultory interchange of personal reminiscences, prejudices, and bits of information which serves to fill an idle silence and is variously known as "chat," "gossip," or "shooting the breeze."

All these multifarious activities are deeply concerned with language, and their practitioners spend a good deal of their time studying, thinking about, and discussing various qualities, phases, uses, and kinds of language. But they must all be excluded from the field of linguistics proper, for one or both of two reasons. Either they fail to make language itself, as we have defined it, their total subject matter, or they fail to use the methods of science as we have previously described them, or both. A few examples will make this clear. Logic, for instance, might seem to qualify because it deals in a scientific manner with language as a tool of thought. But those last five words rule it out; its subject matter is not language but thought, which does not consist of "a system of articulated sounds," though it may depend on one for its existence. Similarly rhetoric, which studies the use of language as a means of effective communication and persuasion, is disqualified because its subject matter is not language pure and simple, but language as a means to some ultra-linguistic end.

It would be an instructive exercise to go over the list we have just given and see the detailed reasons why each of these language-employing activities must be ruled out of our definition of linguistic science. The reader is urged to do so. He may sometimes have trouble putting his finger on the disqualifying element. In fact, many linguists occasionally or habitually venture into one or more of these fields, and they are not always aware that in so doing they cease to be linguists in the precise sense of the word. We shall undoubtedly do so ourselves many times in this book, because many of these fields are closely related to linguistics, and many of them are areas where linguistics can either learn something of help to itself, or be of service to some other discipline.

Fields and Aspects of Linguistics

As with all the other sciences in our day, it is not possible for any one man to take all linguistics for his province. Therefore linguistics has many subdivisions, representing various ways in which the subject matter can be cut up. We may recognize three groups of these divisions, which can be called *fields, aspects,* and *branches*.[1]

The various **fields** of linguistics are arrived at by dividing the total subject matter (which, you will remember, is all language, present and past) into various language groups, language families, and individual languages. Thus we can speak of Indo-European, Semitic, or Algonkian linguistics, all of which deal with large language families. Or the field may be progressively narrowed. Our field, American English,

---

[1] These are not standard terms, but are introduced by the author in the meanings used here. Linguists, like other scientists, sometimes disagree over both the subdivision and the nomenclature of their science.

belongs in the largest sense to Indo-European linguistics. This includes many lesser fields, among them Germanic, which in turn includes English. By restricting ourselves to American English, we limit our field to only part of a single language. At that we shall have more than we can do.

The **aspects** of linguistics are divisions of the subject matter on the basis of time or point of view. Here the fundamental distinction is between *synchronic* and *diachronic* linguistics. **Synchronic**, a term also used in other fields such as anthropology, means "dealing with the state of affairs at a given point of time." It takes no account of history, in other words. On the other hand, **diachronic**, also used in other sciences, means "dealing with changes that occur in time." History is its material. This distinction between synchronic and diachronic linguistics is very important because many mistakes and fallacies result from overlooking it. Let us then pause briefly in our subdividing of linguistics in order to take a closer look at this distinction and the way it influences the kinds of description and generalization that a linguistic scientist can make.

In the first place, since everything in this time-bound world of ours changes from year to year, even from moment to moment, this distinction recognizes two fundamental ways of looking at and describing almost anything. We usually mix them together in our descriptions of things. Thus *Webster's New International Dictionary,* under the entry "Unitarian," makes the following statements (somewhat abbreviated here):

> The churches of the Unitarian denomination are congregational in polity, except in Hungary where they are organized under a bishop. They have never issued any authoritative confession of faith, one of their most distinctive principles being the right of private judgment in theological matters. They formerly differed widely among themselves. . . . Later there came to be virtual unity on the broad basis of [certain] doctrines . . . but the denomination now includes in its ministry as well as its membership a number of nontheistic humanists.

It is obvious that this paragraph contains both synchronic and diachronic statements. What is more, the synchronic statements do not all deal with the same point in time. Thus the first sentence makes a synchronic statement about the Unitarian denomination "now," that is at the time of writing (presumably shortly before 1934, when the dictionary was published). The first part of the next sentence, as far as the comma, makes a diachronic statement covering the whole history of the denomination. The second half of that sentence is ambiguous; from one point of view it is synchronic ("one of their most distinctive principles *is . . .*"); from another it is diachronic ("one of their most distinctive principles *has always been . . .*"). Probably the latter was intended. The next sentence is also ambiguous, depending on how we interpret *formerly*. If we take it to mean "at an unnamed point of time in the past," the statement is a synchronic one; if we take it to mean "during a good part of their past history," it is diachronic. The first part of the next sentence is clearly diachronic because of the verb *came*, which describes a process going on in time. Finally, the last sentence returns to a synchronic statement of the time of writing, as is clearly indicated by the words *now includes*.

It is, of course, quite proper for the two kinds of statement to be mingled in this paragraph since people who look for information about the Unitarian denomination in the dictionary undoubtedly are interested not only in what it is now but also in how it got that way. But when we are dealing with statements about language, particularly if they are precise enough statements to warrant being called scientific, it is of considerable importance to keep our synchronic and our diachronic statements separate. This usually is not difficult; it simply involves being aware of the distinction and being careful about making it. Let us look at a few examples from familiar linguistic material.

Coming across "this was the most unkindest cut of all" in Shakespeare's *Julius Caesar*, I can make several statements about it. I can say, for instance, "About the year 1600 an exceedingly popular playwright at a critical point in a serious play put into the mouth of an important and dignified character an expression involving a double superlative." This is an objective description and it is a purely synchronic statement. It is not evidence enough to permit a generalization, but if I searched about I would find some more examples, such as "the calmest and most stillest night" (*2 Hen. IV*, III.i.28); "this most bravest vessel of the world" (*Cym.*, IV.ii.319); "the basest and most poorest shape" (*Lear*, II.iii.7). I might eventually feel justified in saying, "The double superlative was a rather rare but perfectly acceptable construction in the standard English of the late sixteenth century." This is a generalization, still synchronic. After observing the usage of some of my educated friends, and relying somewhat on my own knowledge as a native speaker of English, I might make another generalization: "The double superlative is not used by cultivated speakers of present-day English." This is also a synchronic statement, but about a different point of time than the preceding one. But if I say, "The double superlative has disappeared from cultivated use since Shakespeare's time," I have made a diachronic generalization because I have described a change taking place in the course of time.

There are, of course, other statements that I might make. I might say, for instance, "It is all right to use a double superlative because Shakespeare did," or, "Even Shakespeare made mistakes, witness his use of the double superlative, which is not permissible in English." It may be seen at once that both these statements are utterly unscientific, and hence from the point of view of linguistics they are worthless, whatever may be their value as indications of the speaker's prejudices. One reason they are unscientific is that they are neither synchronic nor diachronic. One bases a generalization about present-day English on observation of late sixteenth-century English; the other reverses the process and bases a conclusion about Shakespeare's English upon a generalization about present-day English.

Sometimes the distinction between synchronic and diachronic is not so easy to observe. Take, for instance, two ways of describing the relationship between the English words *agree* and *agreement*: (1) "*agreement* was formed from *agree* by adding the noun-forming suffix *-ment*"; (2) "*agree* and *agreement* differ in that *agreement* has the noun-suffix *-ment*, otherwise they are alike." At first glance these seem to be merely two slightly different ways of saying the same thing. But closer scrutiny reveals that the first is a diachronic statement because it assumes that *agree* existed first and that *-ment* was added to it. This is a statement about a change taking place in time; hence, by definition it is diachronic. The second statement, on the other hand, simply describes a state of affairs that exists at the present time; hence, it is synchronic.

The study of language in its diachronic aspect is often called **historical linguistics**. This is a perfectly acceptable term, of course, since history is indeed the description of changes taking place in time. Likewise, the study of language in its synchronic aspect is often called **descriptive linguistics**. This, however, is much less acceptable, because by definition all linguistics is basically descriptive. Hence, this term is misleading. It once enjoyed quite a vogue, however, and is still used, so the student should know about it. But he should avoid using it and stick to *synchronic* as the more accurate term.

One minor point might be mentioned here because it might create occasional difficulties. This is that a truly synchronic description as we have defined it is an impossibility because there is no such thing as "a point of time." Actually, a synchronic statement may cover a duration of time of months or even years. Lorenzo Dow Turner's study of the Gullah dialect spoken in the Sea Islands of Georgia and South Carolina occupied him for fifteen years. Yet it contains a description of this dialect which can quite properly be called synchronic. The reader is frankly told about the time involved in collecting and studying the material and can make adjustments accordingly. On the other hand a statement covering a much shorter span, or even appearing to be confined to a point of time, may be diachronic if it describes a process rather than a state of affairs. For instance, the statement "the verb *contact* is well on the way to being accepted in cultivated English" is really a diachronic statement, because it says, in effect, "the verb *contact* was once not accepted at all in cultivated English, but it is accepted by a good number of cultivated speakers now, and I predict that it will be accepted by the large majority of them in the future."

There is another kind of statement we can make about language, which, in effect, means there is another aspect under which we can study it. If we return to Shakespeare's "most unkindest cut of all," it is apparent that we can make a statement of this sort: "The double superlative was used in Shakespeare's English, but it is not used in the English of the twentieth century." What has been done here is to *compare* two synchronic statements about two points of time. The comparison may suggest a diachronic conclusion, but it does not state it. There are many other kinds of comparative statements that can be made, such as "the Germanic dative survives in German but has disappeared in English" (comparison of two diachronic statements about different but related languages), or, "the German definite article is inflected, but the English one is not" (comparative synchronic statements about two languages at the same point of time) and so on. The study of language from this point of view is **comparative linguistics.** It is always based on a foundation of synchronic or historical linguistics, or both, simply because comparisons are impossible without something to compare.

Finally, before we take leave of this rather lengthy discussion of the subdivision of linguistics according to aspect, we should take note of the term **structural linguistics.** This is used to denominate the kind of linguistics which is primarily interested in discovering and describing as concisely and accurately as possible the interrelationships and patterns which make up the intricate structures of languages. In a way, structural linguistics can be called the mathematics of language study because it is likely to be rather abstract and preoccupied with methods. It is the most rigorously scientific form of linguistics, and its practitioners sometimes claim to be the only true linguists, just as mathematicians sometimes claim to be the only pure scientists. The structural linguists may be indulged in this claim because they have developed methods and standards of procedure that have contributed more than anything else to making linguistics the most scientific of the social sciences. It is largely owing to their work during the last three decades that the study of language has taken on new vitality and interest in our day.

Branches of Structural Linguistics

The third method by which the subject matter of linguistics can be subdivided is on the basis of the various parts, or layers of structure, which go to make up speech. This gives us the various **branches** of linguistics, which are listed on pages 195–96. But first we must look more closely at the principle of division, because it is not so immediately obvious as the division by fields and aspects.

Language, as we shall see in detail later on, is a highly organized affair. Now most highly organized things exhibit various degrees, levels, or layers of organization, whereby the original smallest units are built into larger units, which in turn are built into larger ones, until the largest desired unit is reached. In our political organization, for instance, the unit is the individual citizen. If the citizen is a city dweller, he is grouped with his neighbors into a precinct, a group of precincts are organized into a ward, a group of wards make a city, a group of cities and townships make a county, counties are organized into states, and states into the largest unit we recognize, the nation. The world is at present trying to find a satisfactory way to organize nations into even larger political units. Perhaps the very survival of the human race depends on the success of this effort. Other examples of organization by layers will come to mind readily, such as the military, which builds individual soldiers into squads, squads into platoons, and so on through company, battalion, regiment, division, and army. Here, too, our country has added one more degree of organization by creating a Department of Defense to bring together all the branches of the military into one unit.

This method of organizing things is not man made; it is Nature's way. "What a piece of work is a man!" Hamlet said. A knowledge of modern science would certainly have confirmed him in his opinion, though today he might say instead, "What a miracle of organization is a man!" A relatively small variety of unit particles—charges of electricity, bundles of energy, or what you will—are organized into a somewhat larger number of types of atoms, which in turn are organized into a very large variety of molecules. Selections of these are organized into cells, the cells into organs, and the organs into the total man, who walks about like a single thing (our very word *individual* comes from Latin elements meaning "not to be divided up"), totally unconcerned by the fact that he is a complex of at least five layers of organization.

Before we go on to see how all this applies to language, we should note two facts about this kind of organization:

1. The old axiom from Euclid, "the whole is equal to the sum of all its parts," does not apply to *organized* wholes. An organized whole is always *greater* than the sum of all its parts, because it is equal to the sum of its parts *plus the way they are organized*. Everybody knows that water, H_2O, is made up of hydrogen and oxygen. But one could not put two tanks of hydrogen and one of oxygen into a sealed room, open the valves, and expect to come back an hour later to find a room full of water. The hydrogen and oxygen would be there in the right proportions, but they would be simply *mixed*, not *organized*. In the same way both an army and a rabble are wholes made up of the sum of many individual persons, but because it is organized, the army has many properties which the rabble has not.

2. As a result of this principle, the person who studies or uses material which is organized in this way may move up and down from one level to another, and as he does so, he may treat what is a collection of parts on one level as a unit on the next higher level. A general may manipulate regiments in much the same way a squad leader manipulates individual men. Similarly, as we move up the scale of the organization of the universe, we find the nuclear physicist preoccupied with the smallest units, the subatomic particles; then the chemist, studying atoms and molecules; the structural geologist, studying various kinds of rocks and their organization; and finally, the astronomer, whose units are stars, galaxies, and supergalaxies. Another chain would take us from the chemist to the cytologist, who studies cells, to the histologist, who studies tissues, to the anatomist, who studies organs. All these scientists are to a large degree concerned with studying patterns of organization, or structures, and how they affect the behavior of all the many things to be found in this fascinating universe. In fact, if one were asked to name the most characteristic feature of science at the middle of the twentieth century, he would be bound to reply, "its preoccupation with *structure*." Here, as we have already seen, linguistics is no exception; whatever may be the other interests of modern linguistic science, its heart and center is an interest in the *structure of language*.

We shall have a good deal to say about the details of linguistic structure later on. For the present we need only take a quick look at it in order to see how its various levels become the subject matter of the various branches of linguistics. When we hear a person say something in a language we understand, such as, for instance, "It's going to rain this afternoon," spoken with a rather heavy stress on *rain* and a descending intonation from there to the end, we are subconsciously aware of a good many things at once. We recognize, for instance, that the speaker is expressing an *opinion*. This we gather from the over-all structure of what is said. A change in this structure, such as giving the intonation an upward turn at the end, or changing the beginning to "Is it," would change our interpretation of the whole utterance from an opinion to a question. We further are aware that the over-all structure is made up of smaller structures we call *words*. We may also be aware that these in turn are made up of *sounds* (or, if we are highly literate, we may think of *letters*). This is about as far as the ordinary person goes in his thinking about language structure; it corresponds to about the H_2O level of thinking about chemical structure. But a bit of closer scrutiny will reveal that some of the sounds are important—of structural significance—and some are not. We can pronounce *rain* in a good many different ways before somebody thinks we are saying "run," or "ran," or "ruin." Finally, even closer scrutiny will reveal that the various sounds are themselves structures made up of various features, such as whether we are talking through our nose, as in the last part of *rain,* or through our mouth, as in the first part of *afternoon,* and so forth. These **features** or **qualities** of sounds are, in the present state of linguistics at least, the atoms of speech.

To reverse the process and start from the small end, we may say that in an act of speech, features are organized into sounds, these are selected and organized into significant groups, these in turn are organized in various combinations into words and parts of words, which in turn are organized into an utterance. Each level of organization in this process, which we all perform at incredible speed every time we speak, is the subject matter of a branch of structural linguistics. For our purposes in this book, four branches may be recognized. They are:

Phonetics, whose subject matter is sound-features or qualities and their organization into speech-sounds, or **phones.**

Phonemics, whose subject matter is the organization of phones into groups or families, called **phonemes,** whose members are the *significant* sounds of speech.

Morphemics, whose subject matter is the organization of phonemes into meaningful groups called **morphs.** It is also concerned with the organization of these morphs into family groups, called **morphemes,** and the combination of morphemes into *words.*

Grammar, whose subject matter is the organization of words into various combinations, often representing many layers of structure, such as phrases, sentences, and complete utterances.

Beyond this, linguistics does not at present go. Further levels of organization, such as the paragraphs, sections, and chapters of this book, are the province of rhetoric, which, as we have seen, is not a part of linguistics.

Three more terms which are often used in structural linguistics should be mentioned here. **Phonology** is a cover term embracing phonetics and phonemics. It is sometimes convenient, for example, to speak of "the phonology of English," meaning all matters relating to the sound-system of English. **Morphology** and **Syntax** are subdivisions of grammar; the former deals with the structure of words, the latter with the structure of word groups. Thus, a discussion of how English plurals are formed would belong to morphology, while a discussion of prepositional phrases would belong to syntax.

The Subdivisions of Linguistics (Summary)

The various subdivisions of linguistics may be summarized in outline form, as follows:

I. Fields of Linguistics
    A. Language families: Indo-European, Semitic, etc.
    B. Individual languages: French, English, etc.
    C. Subdivisions of languages: Canadian French, American English, etc.

II. Aspects of Linguistics
    A. Synchronic (or Descriptive)
    B. Diachronic (or Historical)
    C. Comparative
    D. Structural

III. Branches of Linguistics
    A. Four main branches of Structural Linguistics
        1. Phonetics

2. Phonemics
3. Morphemics
4. Grammar
    a) Morphology
    b) Syntax
B. Four kinds of Applied Linguistics
    1. Semantics
    2. Graphics
    3. Linguistic Geography (Area Linguistics, Dialectology)
    4. Lexicography

WHAT IS A SENTENCE?   Charles C. Fries

More than two hundred different definitions of the sentence confront the worker who undertakes to deal with the structure of English utterances. The common school grammars continue to repeat the familiar definition, "A sentence is a group of words expressing a complete thought," although this ancient definition (which antedates Priscian c. 500 A.D.) quite evidently does not furnish a workable set of criteria by which to recognize sentences. In actual practice we often ignore the definition with its "complete thought" as a criterion. If, for example, a reader attempts to count the number of sentences that occur on this or any other page of print, he usually does not stop to decide whether each group counted expresses a "complete thought." In fact he may not read a single word of the material nor even attempt to discover what the discourse is about. He simply gives attention to the marks of end punctuation and to the capital letters with which, in our conventions of writing, we begin sentences. The practical definition used to count the number of sentences in any written material would thus be phrased as follows: A sentence is a word or group of words standing between an initial capital letter and a mark of end punctuation or between two marks of end punctuation.

The student, however, very often finds his writing condemned because of his "sentence fragments" and "comma splices." His teachers insist that the groups of words he has marked with capital letters at the beginning and periods at the end are not "sentences" in that they do not contain a "thought." Sometimes they insist that these marks for the boundaries of some sentences include too much material for

From *Structure of English* by C. C. Fries, copyright, 1952, by Harcourt, Brace & World, Inc. and reprinted with their permission.

one sentence and should therefore be changed to indicate the several "sentence" thoughts "spliced" together in the larger group. Sometimes they insist that the word groups marked off with the signs of "end" punctuation, although they are not "sentence fragments" as such, in that they do contain a "thought," still are "insignificant" sentences, and need to be joined in order to make a "complete" thought.

To remedy such pupil practices teachers give their students vague admonitions to develop "a sentence sense" and "to feel out" the sentences they have written in order to determine "whether the thought is complete or not."

> The best way to tell whether our sentences are complete or not is to "feel them out." Incomplete sentences do not make sense. . . . It is really not difficult to tell a fragment from a complete sentence. We seem to "feel" instinctively when a thought is stated completely. . . . Another very common error in pupils' themes is the "comma splice" . . . they sometimes join two of their sentences together with a comma. If you have learned to "feel out" the complete sentence unit, you will not be likely to make this error. . . . The best way to find such errors is to read one's own sentences aloud "feeling" carefully whether the thought is complete or not.[1]

If the following paragraph is read aloud with normal intonation to a group of teachers, and these teachers are asked to record simply the number of sentence units to be marked by the punctuation, there will be considerable disagreement. Usually with a dozen or more teachers the count will vary surprisingly; every number from three to nine will be indicated.

> Behind all of them lay two fundamental causes, which most Germans have persistently refused to admit. One was the failure of the will to do; the other was the almost organized abandonment of the currency to its fate. This is why I have all along maintained in these columns that there has never been anything vitally wrong with the country itself. Her soil is as productive as ever. The bosom of her earth is still a treasure house of coal and iron. The people have not lost their craft or cunning. The country escaped war ravage. The only concrete thing that went to pot was the currency.

Teachers have never succeeded in agreeing upon a set of criteria to determine just what and how much can be put into a word-group punctuated as a single sentence.

[1] F. G. Walcott, C. D. Thorpe, and S. P. Savage, *Growth in Thought and Expression* (Chicago: Benjamin H. Sanborn and Co., 1940), II, 31, 32, 35, 37.

On the other hand, the student in his reading finds single words punctuated as sentences and word groups that consist of hundreds of words. The 1943 report of the President of Columbia University contains one word-group, punctuated as a single sentence, which fills eleven pages and consists of 4,284 words.[2] Within this one sentence ten paragraph divisions are marked. As a matter of actual practice most of the consideration given to the sentence in the schools centers upon the punctuation of written material.

> Of course, our only difficulty with complete sentences comes when we write. We usually speak in complete sentence units without much difficulty, but when we write, we have so many other things to think about that we get lost.[3]

Theoretically many teachers would disagree with this statement and insist not only that conversation abounds in sentence "fragments" but that one of most important objectives of school English is to develop in students "the ability to speak, in conversation, in complete sentences, not in broken phrasing." [4] Practically, however, they devote their time to the sentences as marked off by punctuation in their students' writing. Discussions of the sentence, for students and for teachers, deal with "the types of sentences that appear in good prose." Sometimes these discussions take note of fragmentary sentences, but these are always the "fragmentary sentences" that appear in writing.

> Modern writers are making increasingly greater use of snatches of phrases and subordinate clauses set off as sentences even when the missing elements are not always immediately apparent. They do this particularly in situations in which they are concerned with communicating the psychological processes governing the minds of their characters.[5]

It is writing and the writer's practice of using graphic devices to mark off units of his writing which are the objects of the teacher's consideration. The rhetorical sentences of written composition rather than the grammatical sentences of living speech have occupied the atten-

[2] Report of the President of Columbia University for the Year Ending June 30, 1943. 44th Series #3, December 2, 1943, pp. 5–16.

[3] Walcott, Thorpe, and Savage, op. cit., p. 34.

[4] C. S. Pendleton, The Social Objectives of School English (Nashville, 1924), p. 36. Of the 1,581 objectives listed and ranked in order of importance according to the judgments of a large body of experienced teachers of English this objective was in second place of all those that were put into the group of "the greatest importance," "outcomes to be attained at all costs."

[5] Russell H. Barker, The Sentence (New York: Rinehart and Company, 1939), p. 8.

tion of most teachers in their search for some rule, some specific directions, that would furnish students a clear and definite guide for the
use of "starters and stoppers"—the punctuation to mark the beginnings and ends of sentences.

For these guides they have turned to the theoretical discussions
of the sentence as these have appeared in the grammars and in the
books that have dealt with the definitions of the sentence unit. Some
of the two hundred-odd definitions have attempted to indicate quantitative limits for the material that a sentence should or could include.
Examples of these statements are the following:

> 1. Speech is made up of separate sayings, each complete in it-
> self . . . these sayings are sentences. Any complete meaning is a sen-
> tence.[6]

But how much must one know in order to have a "complete"
meaning? Is it enough to know that a particular identified book is
red in color? Or must I know that this red book contains accounts,
and that these accounts are those of a particular family, and that
they are accounts of income, and that the income is that of three
years ago, and that the head of this family is charged with income-
tax evasion, and that this particular book has been lost and that there
is a reward for its recovery, and that the red color is the only mark
of identification for the account book of this particular year? How
much of all this is necessary for a "complete" meaning and how many
complete meanings or sentence meanings are there in all?

> 2. A "complete" thought, or what we may call a *sentence-thought*
> is therefore any idea or group of ideas that is felt as answering to one
> impulse of attention. Not the amount of meaning but its being felt as
> *directed* is what makes it complete. . . . The only limit to the possible
> length of the sentence is the number of ideas that can be grasped in
> their relations in one act of attention.[7]
>
> 3. The completeness or incompleteness of a communication is
> wholly a matter of the intent or idea in the mind of the speaker.[8]
>
> 4. A sentence is an utterance which makes just as long a com-
> munication as the speaker has intended to make before giving himself
> a rest.[9]

[6] Alexander Bain, *A Higher English Grammar* (London, 1879), p. 8.

[7] Alfred D. Sheffield, *Command of Sentence Patterns* (Chicago: Scott, Foresman
and Co., 1924), pp. 34, 37.

[8] Janet Rankin Aikin, *A New Plan of English Grammar* (New York: Henry Holt
and Co., 1933), p. 14.

[9] Allan H. Gardiner, *Theory of Speech and Language* (Oxford: Clarendon Press,
1932), p. 208.

This search for definite quantitative limitations of content for the sentence unit has not produced acceptable and workable criteria.

More frequently the effort to define the sentence has turned to attempts to indicate the *constituents* of a sentence thought, and teachers have sought in the identification of these constituents the criteria for completeness. For centuries [10] it has been insisted that, for completeness, every sentence must have a word representing a person, place, or thing, and also a word "asserting" or "saying something" about that person, place, or thing. There must be a "subject" and a "predicate." This statement of the parts which a sentence must contain occurs in most school texts that deal with grammar in any way.

> Here then is the secret of every sentence: first we always name some object or place or person or thing; and then, second, we say something about that object or place or person or thing. Unless we do these two things, we are not making complete sentences. . . . The subject will always be the object, place, person, or thing that is being talked about. The predicate will always be what is said about that object, place, person, or thing.[11]

> Two elements are necessary to the expression of a complete thought: (1) a subject which names a person or thing or idea about which a statement is made; and (2) a predicate which makes a statement about the subject.[12]

It is certainly true that many of the English expressions that we call sentences have the parts indicated in these quotations. But difficulties arise when we state this descriptive fact as a definition and then assume that its terms furnish adequate criteria for identifying and separating sentences from nonsentence word-groups. Use of only these criteria would make us accept as sentences many expressions we now usually call nonsentences. A situation such as that in which a dog is making the noise called *barking* can be expressed by the utterance *the dog is barking*. This expression we accept as a sentence. It fulfills the criteria indicated above—the word *dog* represents an animal, the word *barking* an action, and the action is attributed to the dog as performer. But the word-group *the barking dog*, expressing the same situation, also contains all the indicated criteria. An animal

---

[10] Cf. the following from the thirteenth century: "*Ad perfectionem locutionis duo sunt necessaria scilicet suppositum et appositum. (Suppostitum est illud, de quo fit sermo, appositum est illud, quod dicitur de supposito.)*" Quoted from Delbrück: see Eugen Seidel, *Geschichte und Kritik der wichtigsten Satzdefinitionen* (Jena: Jenaer Germanistische Forschungen [Bd. 27], 1935).

[11] Walcott, Thorpe, and Savage, *op. cit.*, I, 61, 62.

[12] Barker, *The Sentence, op. cit.*, p. 4.

is named, the *dog;* an action, *barking,* is ascribed to this animal, the *dog,* as performer. Nothing in the criteria contained in the definition above will serve to guide us to accept *the dog is barking* as a sentence, and to exclude *the barking dog* as a nonsentence. The same is true of such word-groups as *the red book, a beautiful white dress with a wide lace hem, who the man is, why he will come.* The statements in these textbook definitions quite obviously do not furnish the actual criteria we use practically in such a situation.

These statements fail us, not only when we assume that every utterance having the two constituents can be accepted as a sentence, but also when we assume that unless an utterance contains both a "subject" *and* a "predicate" it is not a sentence. Such an assumption would make us exclude most requests or commands. The materials examined for this book abound in such expressions as:

> come over soon
> send me a memorandum
> wait a minute

In respect to these expressions it is usually insisted that additional words are "understood." We must supply the "subject" word *you.* If, however, these expressions are to be accepted as fulfilling the requirements of the definition above on the ground that we must *supply words that are not there but "understood,"* then certainly by the same procedure many other expressions must be accepted as sentences. Nothing in the criteria furnished in these definitions gives us any indication of a limit to the number or the kind of words that may be "understood."

Actual expression as heard	Expression with possible words "understood"
Congratulations	I offer you my congratulations
Fire	The building is on fire
Hands up	You put your hands up
Tomorrow	(When are you going) I'm going tomorrow
Down with the King	You let us dethrone (cast down) the King

The following newspaper headlines would also be filled out to make complete sentences with words "understood."

Headline	To be supplied
Wedding Bells for Student and Japanese Bride	ring
New Charge against Doctor———	is made

| Three Fraternities on Probation after Party | are put |
| Strike Called in Protest to King Leopold | is |

By means of supplying words "understood," practically any expression can be made to fit the requirements set up in the definitions. Clearly these definitions as they stand do not furnish all the criteria needed nor all that are actually used in practice by teachers in the schools to determine whether any particular collocation of words is a sentence.

Much labor has thus, over a period of many years, been devoted to the problem of defining the sentence. Collected evidence of this labor appears in the books that have, during the last twenty years, reviewed and criticized the former definitions and attempted to state anew the essential features of the sentence. John Ries, for example, subjects some 140 of the different definitions to much sound and searching criticism and then adds to the number by creating a new one. (The English here is my translation.) [13]

> A sentence is a grammatically constructed smallest unit of speech which expresses its content with respect to this content's relation to reality.

In 1935 Eugen Seidel [14] published his history and criticism of some eighty of the most important definitions, and in 1941 Karl Sundén published his *Linguistic Theory and the Essence of the Sentence*.[15] Sundén also devotes special attention to a critical evaluation of the more recent treatments of the sentence, especially those of Ries, Gardiner, and Jespersen, and then finds the "essence of the sentence" in what he calls its modal function—its stating that the thing meant by the sentence "has reality even if it belonged to the world of the imagination." His conclusion is embodied in his definition:

> A sentence is a portion of speech that is putting forward to the listener a state of things (a thing meant) as having validity, i.e., as being true.[16]

Practically all of this tremendous labor which has concerned itself with defining the sentence as a grammatical unit has approached the

---

[13] John Ries, *Was ist ein Satz?* first published at Marburg in 1894, and then revised and published at Prague in 1931 (*Beiträge zur Grundlegung der Syntax,* Heft 3). "Ein Satz ist eine grammatisch geformte kleinste Redeeinheit, die ihren Inhalt im Hinblick auf sein Verhältnis zur Wirklichkeit zum Ausdruck bringt."

[14] Seidel, *op. cit.*

[15] Karl F. Sundén, *Linguistic Theory and the Essence of the Sentence* (Göteborgs högskolas årsskrift) 47 (1941), No. 5.

[16] *Ibid.*, p. 40.

problem of analysis *by way of the meaning or thought content*. Most of those who have sought to define the sentence, under whatever term used—*λόγος, oratio, propositio, phrase, thèse,* Satz—have tried to find universal characteristics of meaning content for this speech unit— characteristics that could not only be identified in the utterances of all languages, but would serve also as defining criteria of the sentence in any language. They have assumed that "language is a 'reflection' of thought," and that grammar, which was assumed to be the "laws of language," must therefore represent the laws of human thought. Sometimes it has been explicitly asserted that "the human mind thinks in sentences," "understands in sentences." Therefore, it is argued, the basic characteristics of the sentence, the "essence of the sentence," must be something common in the utterances of all languages. The very fact, however, that the many attempts to grasp the "essence of the sentence" by this type of subtle reasoning and analysis have not given us a satisfactorily acceptable or workable set of criteria to make an acceptable definition (shown by the continual argument and dispute, and the varied attempts to form new definitions) seems to indicate that we must approach the problem from a different point of view.

The more one works with the records of the actual speech of people the more impossible it appears to describe the requirements of English sentences in terms of meaning content. It is true that whenever any relationship is grasped we have the material or content with which a sentence can be made. But this same content can be put into a variety of linguistic forms, some of which can occur alone as separate utterances and some of which always occur as parts of larger expressions. As indicated above, a situation in which a dog is making the noise called *barking* can be grasped either by the linguistic form *the dog is barking*, which can occur as an utterance separated from any other speech, or the same situation can be grasped in the form *the barking dog*, a form which, except as an answer to such a question as "What frightened the burglar away?" occurs only as a part of some larger expression, such as *the barking dog protected the house*. In similar fashion a situation in which a mother provides a home for her boy may be expressed either in the linguistic form *the mother supports him* or in the form *his mother's support*. In both expressions the relationship that has been grasped is the same. The form of the first is that which might appear entirely by itself in a separate utterance; the form of the second might appear as a part of a larger unit such as *his mother's support enabled him to devote himself to music*. A situation in which water is mixed with some solution to weaken it may be grasped in the form *the water diluted the solution,* which might occur as a separate utterance, or in the slightly different form *the water diluted solution,* which would occur only as part of a larger expression such as *the water diluted solution was too weak to be effective.*

In other words, the characteristics which distinguish those expressions which occur alone as separate utterances and those which occur only as parts of larger units are not matters of content or meaning, but matters of form. These formal matters are not the same from language to language. Each language has its distinct patterns of formal arrangements for utterances which occur alone as separate expressions. The one thing in which various languages do agree is the fact that, in all the languages that we know, there are utterances that stand alone, that are separate from other utterances, that occur with silence before and after the utterance. This common fact has been made the basis of some of the definitions of the sentence. Jespersen, for example, framed his definition in this way.

> A sentence is a (relatively) complete and independent human utterance—the completeness and independence being shown by its standing alone or its capability of standing alone, i.e., of being uttered by itself.[17]

Somewhat similar, and earlier, the definition by Meillet furnished the base upon which others have built.

> . . . the sentence can be defined [as follows]: a group of words joined together by grammatical agreements [relating devices] and which, not grammatically dependent upon any other group, are complete in themselves.[18] [The English here is my translation.]

Bloomfield used that part of Meillet's definition which touched formal features.

> A sentence is a construction (or form) which, in the given utterance, is not part of any larger construction.[19]

---

[17] Otto Jespersen, *Philosophy of Grammar* (New York: Henry Holt and Co., 1924), p. 307.

[18] A. Meillet, *Introduction à l'étude comparative des langues indo-européenes* (Paris, 1903), p. 326 (3d ed., 1912, p. 339). *". . . la phrase peut être définie: un ensemble d'articulations liées entre elles par des rapports grammaticaux et qui, ne dépendent grammaticalement d'aucun autre ensemble, se suffisent à elles-mêmes."*

[19] Leonard Bloomfield, "A Set of Postulates for the Science of Language," *Language,* 2 (1926), 156. See also Bloomfield's review of Ries's *Was ist ein Satz?* in *Language,* 7 (1931), 204.

The following quotation will help to make clear the significance of Bloomfield's definition.

> In any utterance, a linguistic form appears either as a constituent of some larger form, as does *John* in the utterance *John ran away*, or else as an independent form, not included in any larger (complex) linguistic form, as, for instance, *John* in the exclamation *John!* When a linguistic form occurs as part of a larger form, it is said to be in *included position;* otherwise it is said to be in *absolute position* and to constitute a *sentence. . . .*
>
> An utterance may consist of more than one sentence. This is the case when the utterance contains several linguistic forms which are not by any meaningful, conventional grammatical arrangement (that is, by any construction) united into a larger form, e.g., *How are you? It's a fine day. Are you going to play tennis this afternoon?* Whatever practical connection there may be between these three forms, there is no grammatical arrangement uniting them into one larger form: the utterance consists of three sentences.
>
> It is evident that the sentences in any utterance are marked off by the mere fact that each sentence is an independent linguistic form, not included by virtue of any grammatical construction in any larger linguistic form.[20]

In this book we shall accept as our general definition of the sentence—our starting point—the words of Bloomfield.

> Each sentence is an independent linguistic form, not included by virtue of any grammatical construction in any larger linguistic form.

The basic problem of the practical investigation undertaken here is not solved simply by accepting Bloomfield's definition of a sentence. As one approaches the body of recorded speech which constitutes the material to be analyzed[21] (or any body of recorded speech), just how should he proceed to discover the portions of an utterance that are not "parts of any larger construction"? How can he find out the "grammatical constructions" by virtue of which certain linguistic forms are included in larger linguistic forms? What procedure will enable him to decide which linguistic forms can "stand alone as independent utterances"?

Answers to these questions had to be found early in the investigation.[22]

[20] Leonard Bloomfield, *Language, op. cit.*, p. 170.
[21] See *The Structure of English*, Chapter I, p. 3, for a description of these materials.
[22] Very few investigators have tried to discover answers to such questions as these. Roy G. Curtis reported the results of his study in a dissertation entitled *An*

We started first with the term *utterance*. Although the word *utterance* appears frequently in linguistic discussions and has occurred a number of times in this chapter, there has been nothing to indicate how much talk an "utterance" includes. The definition that "an act of speech is an utterance" [23] doesn't furnish any quantitative measure of either "an act of speech" or of "an utterance." Bernard Bloch calls attention to this vagueness but finds it unnecessary for his purpose to give the term more definiteness.

> A single act of speech is an *utterance*. It is true that this definition, like Bloomfield's, leaves the limits of an utterance completely vague, and therefore fails to tell us just how much of speech an utterance is supposed to include. For our purpose, however [phonemic analysis], the length or inclusiveness of utterances can be ignored.[24]

For the purposes of this investigation, however, which aimed to discover and describe the significant features of "sentences" as they occur in the records of actual conversation, it was necessary to start with some unit of talk that could be marked off with no uncertainty. These units were to be collected from the materials, and then compared and classified.

The recorded conversations provided the suggestion for the first step. The easiest unit in conversation to be marked with certainty was the talk of one person until he ceased, and another began. This unit was given the name "utterance." In this book, then, the two-word phrase *utterance unit* will mean any stretch of speech by one person before which there was silence on his part and after which there was also silence on his part. Utterance units are thus those chunks of talk that are marked off by a shift of speaker. As indicated above, it was necessary to find some way of deciding what portions of speech could "stand alone," what constituted independent or free expressions—free, in that they were not necessarily bound to other

---

Investigation of Some of the Structures of Independent Utterances in Modern English (Ann Arbor: University of Michigan, 1947). He studied the spontaneous responses of one thousand native English-speaking informants to a carefully prepared page of printed material consisting of a succession of words in which various types of sequence were "planted," but in which appeared no marks to separate any groups or sequences. He attempted to record the responses of these informants in order to determine which sequences would be reacted to as units that could occur alone in their natural English speech—i.e., units that could, in their own practical conversation, normally occur with silence on their part, before and after the utterance.

[23] Bloomfield, "A Set of Postulates . . ." *op. cit.*, p. 154.

[24] B. Bloch, "A Set of Postulates for Phonemic Analysis," *Language*, 24 (1949), 7.

expressions to make a single unit. It seemed obvious that in a conversation in which two speakers participate, the stretch of speech of
one speaker at one time can be taken as a portion that does stand
by itself, unless, of course, that speaker has been so completely interrupted that he stops because of the interruption.[25] The first step,
then, in the procedure to determine the linguistic forms that can stand
alone as independent utterances was thus to record the utterance units
as marked off by a change of speaker.

These utterance units exhibited great variety both in length and
in form. It was a basic assumption of our approach, however, that all
the utterances that appeared in the recorded materials were pertinent
to the investigation. It was not our task arbitrarily to include some
and to exclude others as unworthy of consideration. The great range
of actual variety in these utterance units was thus an accepted factor
of the problem before us. The following conversation, consisting of
sixteen utterance units, shows something of the variety of the units
marked off by this first step of our procedure.[26]

1. [A—— I don't know whether you let B—— go out during the week do you suppose he could come over tonight
   while we go out to dinner]
2. [Well the difficulty is J—— that he got back in his lessons]
3. [Oh|oh]
4. [And in his last report about two weeks ago he was down
   in two subjects his father hasn't been letting him do
   anything]
5. [Well that's a good idea]
6. [I'm awfully sorry]

[25] These interruptions which stop the speaker can be recognized by certain matters of "external" evidence. Among these are: (1) The speech activities of two or
more persons overlap. The records reveal the beginning of the speech of a second
speaker while the first is still speaking and sometimes the beginning of the new
speaker is so loud that it makes the continued speech of the first speaker difficult or
impossible to hear and understand. (2) Certain utterance forms occur only in
situations in which there is evidence of such breaking in of a second speaker. (3)
Statistically the situations were very few in which it was impossible to hear all of
an utterance unit, or rather such an utterance as would fit into the classification
groups of Chapter III.

[26] It is perhaps unnecessary to remind the reader that the body of material
which furnished the basis for this study was living speech mechanically recorded,
not writing. Punctuation, therefore, has no part in our descriptive treatment of the
sentence. The final chapter, however, dealing with "Practical Applications," does
contain some discussion of the punctuation of sentences in written material. Quotations from the materials will use conventional spelling but no punctuation.
Sometimes intonation marks will be necessary.

7. [Well that's all right thanks A—— to tell you the truth
   I don't want awfully badly to go you know what I mean]
8. [M|hm]
9. [Well how's the garden]
10. [Oh it's much worse than yours I imagine the only thing
    that looks decent at all is the strawberries]
11. [Yes I know but you know they're not going to be any
    good unless they get some sun and dry weather]
12. [No well there's still time for them isn't there]
13. [Yes I know]
14. [I've got strawberries started have you]
15. [What]
16. [Some of the berries have started on my plants]

Because the recorded materials were all of practical conversations,
not lectures, nor sustained narratives, the utterance units marked by
a shift of speaker were limited in length. Even so, it could not be
assumed that each of these utterance units contained only one unit
that could stand alone. We could not take for granted that these
utterance units contained only a single free utterance, nor that they
were minimum free utterances. We could assume, however, that each
utterance unit if not interrupted must be one of the following:

1. A single minimum free utterance.
2. A single free utterance, but expanded, not minimum.
3. A sequence of two or more free utterances.

We start then with the assumption that a sentence (the particular
unit of language that is the object of this investigation) is a single free
utterance, minimum or expanded; i.e., that it is "free" in the sense that
it is not included in any larger structure by means of any grammatical
device.

LINGUISTICS IN THE CLASSROOM   *Sumner Ives*

Anyone who has been reading periodicals for English teachers or
who has been attending conventions of English teachers must be aware
of the controversy over linguistics and its relevance to the teaching
of composition. As one whose research is primarily in descriptive lin-

From *College English*, December, 1955. Reprinted with the permission of The
National Council of Teachers of English, and of the author.

guistics, but whose teaching includes at least one composition class each semester, I have a personal interest in the interaction of linguistics and the practical use of language. I am somewhat disturbed by what appears to be a conflict between linguists and teachers of writing when I can detect no valid reason for such a conflict.

I suspect, both from reading the exchanges and from listening to the discussions, that much of the disagreement comes from misunderstanding. I observe arguments which promote linguistics without showing an exact appreciation of the significance of its findings; I notice defences of positions which linguistics, properly understood, does not attack. Moreover, although many composition teachers have come to believe that traditional grammar is a very poor description of English structure, some of the more judicious have complained, rightly, that the arguments of the linguists have been largely negative, that they have given little to replace that which they have attacked. This, then, is the situation with which this paper deals.

In order to accomplish its purpose, the discussion must be both general and specific, for the usefulness of linguistics is two-fold. One contribution is a valid and useful theory of what language is and how it works. The other is a description of the specific forms and constructions which are used in a particular language for the expression of meaning.

In general academic usage, the term linguist includes those who teach the language courses in an English or other modern language department. However, the criticisms of traditional grammar have come chiefly from those who have made particular study of descriptive or structural linguistics, and the counterattacks have been made against this group. In this discussion, therefore, linguistics means descriptive linguistics, and linguists are those who work in this branch of language study. In his study of language, the linguist uses the standard methods of observation and classification common to all systematic studies of human behavior and the natural world. In describing the structure of a language, he is guided by the forms of words and their characteristic patterns of use. His criteria of definition and classification are therefore very much the same as those of the anthropologist or the chemist.

The major aims of the linguist are the discovery of the principles true of all living languages and the accumulation of detailed and systematic descriptions of the phonology and the grammar of these languages. Both these major goals have relevance to promoting facility in the native language and to teaching the use of a second language.

Hence, as a methodology of investigation, linguistics is one of the social sciences, but the nature of its subject matter and the application of its results give it primary association with the humanities. The study of the forms of language is a science; the proper and effective use of language is an art.

The difficulty which many persons trained in the humanities seem to have with linguistics is due primarily to our intellectual climate. Most of the notions which underlie our common vocabulary for talking about language are survivals from a pre-objective period of language study. The words in our vocabulary reflect an orientation on language matters which is very different from that which is derived through direct observation of individual languages. When a non-linguist reads what a linguist has written about language, there is often a break-down in the communication, even when familiar terms are used, for the non-linguist is often interpreting the discussion in a frame of reference which differs from that in which it was written. This difficulty is compounded when the linguist uses terms from the technical jargon of his field. Yet such a technical vocabulary is necessary and is no more exotic than those in other fields. Physicians, for example, no longer use such terms as "humorous" and "sanguine" in their medieval sense, for these terms reflect a theory of disease which they no longer hold.

The consequences of this misunderstanding, which is often greater than either party realizes, are most easily observed in the extrapolations from linguistics which persons without training in its methods attempt to make. Any statement in any field is only a partial expression; it must be interpreted within the restrictions imposed by the nature of what is talked about, by the context, and by all the assumptions, postulates, and qualifications which are part of the accumulated knowledge in the field. This does not mean that linguists talk only with each other, though they are as prone to this as anyone, but it does mean that the statements of linguists should be accepted and applied only to the extent that they are explicit, that conclusions should be drawn only within the limits of the primary statements and only about that aspect of the subject concerning which they are made. When, for example, a linguist uses stretches of actual speech as material for grammatical analysis, his purpose does not include the establishment of a standard dialect, and his results apply only to his sample.

Aside from this difficulty, which is concomitant to every major advance in fundamental knowledge, linguistics is not a hard subject. Its subject matter is all around us. Ordinary people have mastered and use quite easily all the forms, constructions, and sound patterns it deals with. Its results, whenever a particular language is described, can be checked by any native speaker who will believe what he observes and not what he has been taught to expect. And any native speaker who has the necessary perseverance and mental discipline can learn and use its methods to extend his conscious understanding of the form and constructions of his own language.

But at the present time, direct provision for the development of an adequate theory of language and for the accumulation of knowledge about the actual constructions of English is seldom made in the training of English teachers. Virtually all their upper division and graduate courses are in literature. When language courses are required, and they are seldom taken unless required, they generally consist of reading more literature, this time in a stage of the language which is no longer current, or they consist primarily of tracing individual sound changes, with some attention to resulting changes in morphology, and some checking on etymologies. This language program undoubtedly has cultural value, but it has little direct bearing on the teaching of composition. It is possible for a student to go through such a program with excellent marks and yet remain basically ignorant of the nature of language as a socially directed activity, unaware of the difference yet interaction between a language and its written symbolization, blind to the operation of its grammatical devices, and unprepared even to read many of the basic publications which describe the current characteristics of his own language or to analyze that language for himself.

This has not been said in any spirit of superiority or condemnation. It is the simple truth. Any blame is general. It is up to linguists to relate their findings to the larger aims of education. But they have the same right to attention and trust as the zoologist, the political-scientist, or the specialist in the pastoral elegy. The problem is the familiar one of cultural lag. A solution will come only with time, careful explanations, and a decent regard for human feelings and fallibility on all sides.

Much of the misunderstanding about what the linguist does and says comes from his insistence on two of his basic principles and their corollaries. One of these is the primacy of speech as the language, with writing as a secondary and derivative manifestation of speech. The other is the dynamic changing nature of language, with its corollaries about stability and standardization. Both principles are derived from studying languages as physically observable structures; neither is a threat to the basic aims of the composition course—namely, to teach students to write their own language as clearly and effectively as they can and with full regard for the conventions of usage observable in the products of recognized masters.

In explaining his attention to speech, the linguist points out that all systems of writing are based on the prior existence of speech, that all alphabetic systems depend ultimately on the sound system of the language, even though, as in English, the correspondence between sound and spelling is very complex and difficult to describe. The linguist realizes that the writing system, even with its marks of punctuation, never quite symbolizes all the components which contribute to meaning in speech. He comes to see the teaching that English has five vowels as nonsense and the mother of error, and the designation of long and short vowels in English as little better. And he learns to dismiss such questions as whether English is a phonetic language as meaningless. These lessons may not have direct bearing on the teaching of good composition, but they are vital if one is to understand the relationship of writing to the language, of spelling to pronunciation, or of reading to speaking.

On the other hand, distinct from the alphabetic representation of words on paper, speaking and writing are different but interacting activities. They are not the same, do not follow all of the same conventions, and are not done for the same list of purposes. Neither is finally and fully determinative for the other. No competent linguist would suggest that the teacher of written English should accept in student writing all of the conventions and the same characteristics of style as are customary in speech, even that of the most cultivated. The notion that linguists make speech determinative for writing is one of the false extrapolations made by people who interpret the findings of linguistics without knowing what they mean. They are failing to distinguish between writing as a graphic representation of a linguistic expression (which is secondary to speech) and writing as a special kind of communicative activity (which differs in style and purpose from speech).

The fundamental reason why the linguist gives his primary attention to speech is the fact that only in speech does he find all the signals which convey information. For example, the two phrases, "a stone wall" and "a race horse," are not spoken with the same patterns of stress. In the first phrase, "stone" is functionally an adjective, just as "high" would be in the same place. In the second, "race" is functionally a part of a compound noun, in spite of the orthography, like "black-" in "blackberry." It is the difference in the patterns of stress which makes the grammar clear. With the grammatical importance of stress in mind, read the following sentences aloud and then parse "drinking" and "water" in all of them. (1) Our drinking water fortunately remained fresh. (2) Drinking water from our canteens rather than from open streams kept us from getting dysentery. (3) Drinking water rather than wine made the boys healthy.

Another practical result of investigation into these "supra-segmental" characteristics of speech is the recognition of the relationship between pitch patterns and structural unity. In ordinary prose, the ends of statements and of most questions are marked by a quick rise in pitch, followed by a quick drop to a level below that of the bulk of the sentence. A sentence which has the word order of a statement can be made into a question by a quick rise of pitch at the end. When there is a quick rise and then a drop back to the basic level, a shift in constructions within a sentence is marked. These pitch signals mark the places where punctuation decisions are to be made if the speech is set down in writing. A student can often clarify his constructions and rectify his punctuation simply by reading his themes aloud, for he will generally find that an unEnglish construction cannot be read with the English supra-segmental patterns—what are popularly called intonation patterns—and he has used these since childhood.

For these reasons, any analysis of English grammar which is not based ultimately on the signals of speech is necessarily incomplete. The other basic principle which is sometimes misunderstood is corollary to the fact that language is a social institution with the same counteracting tendencies towards stability and adaptability as other social institutions.

A typical expression of the linguist's view is found on page 177 of W. D. Whitney's *Language and the Study of Languages*, published as long ago as 1867. "Language is an institution founded in man's social nature, wrought out for the satisfaction of his social wants; and hence, while individuals are ultimate agents in the formation and modification of every word and every meaning of a word, it is still the community that makes and changes its language."

The relevance which this principle has for the composition teacher is its bearing on the formation and continuity of the conventions which he should teach as part of the standard language. That dialect of English which we now call edited written English is the product of changes resulting from the interaction of individuals as agents of the community. The dialect whose modern development we teach originally had no discernible virtues as a language which made it superior to other local forms of English. Its selection for cultivation was almost surely the result of socio-economic factors. Nonetheless its fortuitous origin does not invalidate its claim to superiority today. But these claims rest in part on the growth and refinement of special vocabularies, in part on the great store of literature which is written in it, in part to the social prestige which is granted to those who use it, and in part to the size and importance of the territory over which it is spread. These reasons are fully adequate to demand that it be taught as a school subject.

Yet, this standard English cannot be exactly defined, nor does it remain constantly the same, in spite of the factors which give it stability. No complete, definitive, and final dictionary of English usage can be made so long as English is in active use, although the list of disputed usages is never large at any one time. A teacher of writing simply has to maintain the same kind of contact with changes in his basic material as that maintained by doctors and lawyers.

A special problem in dealing with usage is the presence of shibboleths. So long as overt marks of social and educational status are considered useful by society, some of these will be linguistic. For example, the adequacy of one's education is often judged by his ability to spell, or by whether he splits infinitives, or by whether he says "eyether" or "eether." It is in the area of shibboleths that the purist feels most authority, for he is usually their custodian. To the linguist, however, most of these have the status of myth, as the term is used in sociology. Nevertheless, a rather large part of one's acceptance in society is his adjustment to myths of this type. Hence, it is, I think, the duty of the school teacher to point out the current shibboleths, for they change, and to advise how much they are observed and by which people.

Language is thus a social institution. It has the same kind of stability and adaptability as other social institutions, from table manners to democratic government, and its conventions are just as obligatory while they last. The scholar should remember that the major purpose of language is not to preserve for the future, but to serve the exigencies of now. To ask for a static language makes just as much sense, and no more, as to ask for a static society. There are, of course, people who do this. To put the language in the hands of a self-appointed few is just as reasonable, and no more, as to put the regulation of government in the hands of a similarly appointed group. There are people who want to do this too.

These principles constitute the major elements in a theory of language which is valid and which should assist the composition teacher to deal more intelligently with his basic subject matter. The major tool which linguists can give to the teachers of composition is a true and adequate description of the forms and constructions which are used in English for the expression of grammatical meaning, in short, an English grammar. Such a grammar will retain some of the categories and their terms which are in traditional grammar, but its methods of classification and definition will be fundamentally different.

When we attempt to relate the terminology, with its implied classification, of traditional grammar to the actual forms of English and their behavior, at least four major defects appear. Some terms, e.g., grammar, have more than one referent; some terms, e.g., passive voice and tense, have referents which are not, by their very nature, susceptible to sharp definition in English; some terms, e.g., adverb and pronoun, are in use without a genuine referent (the supposed referents of these terms lack identity as single classes or categories of items); finally, some terms, e.g., noun and verb, are identified, not by definitions, but by statements which may well be true, but which do not name the particularizing characteristics of the classes which the terms refer to.

In traditional grammar, an adverb is defined as a word which modifies a verb, adjective, or other adverb. However, the "adverbs" *quite* and *very* simply do not obey the same rules of syntax as the "adverbs" *usually* and *soon*, for *quite* and *very* do not modify verbs. Another false classification is that which includes *he* and *few* in the same category, for one is inflected and the other is not, one can be modified by *very* and the other cannot, and one has a noun antecedent and the other does not. It is true that both can act as subjects, but then, so can adjectives. The concept of tense in traditional grammar is complicated by the fact that verb phrases made with *will* are called a future tense, yet these phrases have the same formal characteristics as those made with *must* and other modal auxiliaries.

I am, admittedly, judging a grammatical description according to criteria of form and usefulness. To be valuable in teaching a language or in promoting facility in its use, a description of its grammar should isolate those classes about which statements need to be made. These statements may be rules for word order, for the formation of phrases, for derivational change, for functional change, for inflectional concord, and so on. There is obviously very little which one can say about word order which will be true of both *very* and *soon,* of both *he* and *few.*

A classification must select out and associate in identity a group of items which, so far as the purpose of the classification is concerned, are equivalent. These items must be, within the purpose for which the class is isolated, freely substitutable for each other. In defining this class, a property must be named which is tangible, which is present in all members of the class, and which is absent from all items not in the class. If this definition is part of a taxonomy, it must be one of a set. The definitions in a set must contrast with each other and must conjointly exhaust all items in the same division and level of analysis. These sets must each have a common factor which excludes members of other sets, and so on until the entire classification is complete. A properly developed taxonomy, therefore, has the outward design of a genetic tree.

In framing definitions, one must enumerate a list of attributes generally agreed upon, or one must name one or more characteristics whose presence or absence can be verified by direct observation. Many of the terms in literary criticism, e.g., "romanticism," rest upon agreement to associate the term with a list of attributes. Other terms, such as those in the taxonomy of botany, are defined by direct appeal to nature. Anyone who has good eyesight and the proper instruments can count the cotyledons in a seed. One may have more trouble with "hirsute" and "pubescent," but the degree of fuzziness which they denote can be easily distinguished after a little experience. Since Linnaeus, the botanists have had a way to bring order to the apparently limitless variety of nature; they had a classification system for what is, to the layman, infinite discreteness. The objective of the descriptive grammarian is to do for the forms of individual languages what the botanist has done for plant life.

In popular usage, grammar is often considered to be a crystallization of human logic, a set of concepts and distinctions in terms of which all languages should be described, a set of formal characteristics and correspondences to which all languages should conform. In this view, which is that implied in some recent articles and found in most older books on language, the most convenient expression of grammar is one based on Latin. When it was shown that a knowledge of traditional grammar had little correlation with an ability to use English correctly and effectively, the result was a belief that grammar need not be studied as a prerequisite to training in composition. This view is, I think, wrong. I think that, on the contrary, an adequate knowledge of the forms of English and of the rules for their use should be a very valuable prerequisite to instruction in composition. Arguments based on current experience are irrelevant, for the grammar has not been English grammar.

Now the linguist studies a language by analyzing, in turn, its levels of complexity. These correspond only roughly to the levels indicated by the common terms phonology, morphology, and syntax. In this division into levels, that which deals with the combination of the smallest meaningful units into the largest self-sufficient and independent constructions is grammar. These smallest meaningful units are called morphemes. They may be affixes like *-ness, -ed,* and *non-;* they may be words like *kind, his,* and *the;* they may be stress patterns like those which make a word like *subject* into a noun or into a verb. Every utterance consists of segmental morphemes, like words, stems, and affixes, and of supra-segmental morphemes, which include what the layman means by intonation. Grammar classifies these morphemes into groups according to similarities of form and grammatical meaning. It includes the rules by which morphemes are combined into constructions and the rules governing the formation of still larger constructions until the ultimate limit of strict structural relationship has been reached. The units at the limit of strict structural relationship are sentences.

Grammar as conformity to the conventions of the standard dialect becomes a matter of comparative grammar. The dialects of English which comprise vulgate English all have grammars, as the term is defined in the preceding paragraph, but the rules and forms of these grammars differ in some ways from those of the standard dialect. The teaching problem is the correlation of equivalent expressions and the substitutions of standard for nonstandard forms and constructions. The only inherent source of confusion is the presentation by the teacher of conventions which differ from those which the student observes in his academic reading.

A more serious cause for confusion is a failure to distinguish between grammar and style. The rules which govern the combination of morphemes into sentences are imposed on the individual; the words and constructions which he uses, out of those which conform to the rules, are matters of choice. This area of language choice is style, or rhetoric. For example, after "individual," just above, I could have used a period or a semicolon, for both show the boundary between structurally complete units. But I could not have used either mark before that word, for it is grammatically related to those which immediately precede. Such matters as the selection of words and constructions, the length of sentences and their complexity, and the organization of the total expression are matters of style. Such matters as consistency in parallel structure, reference of pronouns, and agreement of subject and verb are matters of grammar. These matters of grammar are finite; they can be discovered and described.

An example of confusion arising from a failure to make this distinction clear is the trouble students have with "sentence recognition." The customary definition of the sentence as the verbal expression of a complete thought does not, by itself, separate the sentence from the paragraph or from larger sections which are supposed to have unity. As the term is applied in most handbook discussions of punctuation, it designates a unit in style but not necessarily in grammar. The crucial information—that there is an identifiable unit in grammar, that, in conected prose, the juxtapositions of these units must be marked, and that one of the ways to make these juxtapositions is with a period—does not follow from the traditional definition.

In English structure, the sentence, the independent unit in connected discourse, has the following characteristics: (1) it must contain at least one finite verb or verb phrase; (2) all words must be structurally related; (3) it must not, as a unit, have a grammatical function in a larger construction. There are three types of such units in English. In the statement, the subject normally precedes the verb, unless it begins with a word of the class of "never." In the question, the subject is normally inserted inside the verb phrase. (If the verb is not a phrase, it is made into one with a form of "do.") In the request, there is no subject. The verb may come first, or it may be preceded by a word to get attention or to show courtesy.

There are two other types of constructions which are marked by end punctuation or intonation. One is the response; the other is the exclamation. Both of these constructions get their "incompleteness" from something which has been said or is physically close enough to be pointed out by a gesture. Thus, we can use a construction which is structurally not a sentence when we reply to a question, stated or implied, or when we react to an automobile accident, or when we point to something and comment on it.

The most common error in student themes is the failure to mark the juxtapositions of structurally complete units, or the habit of marking as sentences groups of words which are not structurally units. But difficulty with "sentence recognition" can be virtually eliminated by teaching what is in the preceding paragraphs, listing the devices for marking the juxtapositions, and giving the following suggestions. At the beginning of a sentence, structural relationship points forward; at the end it points backward. If the student reads what he has written, aloud and phrase by phrase, he can detect the point where there is a break, where the shift from backward to forward relationship occurs. "Sentence fragments" ordinarily result from one of two causes. One is the insertion of an end sign where no structural end exists; the other is the failure to keep the structural patterns clear enough so that a structural unit can be isolated. In this case, a break in communication will almost be noticed. It has been my experience that native speakers of English can determine the presence or absence of grammatical relationship even when they cannot give a name to the type which exists.

In so far as their academic functions are concerned, linguists and composition teachers are related in somewhat the same way as botanists and gardeners are related in raising plants. Their duties do not conflict; they complement. The botanist identifies plants, groups them in families, analyzes their physiology, and observes the ecological factors which promote or retard growth. The gardener uses such information and adds to it his knowledge of the virtues of different fertilizers and methods of cultivation. If he has good soil and healthy stock, he may get good results regardless of how little he knows. But if his soil is not good, his stock is poor, or his experience is little, there is much he can learn from the botanist, although the botanist cannot teach him all he needs to know. There is, of course, nothing to prevent the botanist from becoming a gardener or to keep the gardener from gaining through experience a great deal of useful but uncoordinated knowledge.

What this means is that the students whose environment has provided them with habitual use of good English are likely to do well whether their teacher knows much about language or not. On the other hand, in so far as the students do not have these habits, the teacher will find useful what the linguist has to say. Even if he does not have this preparation for formal and systematic teaching, he may still get acceptable results with some students by requiring practice, making corrections, and insisting on revision, provided he is himself a reasonably competent craftsman.

I should confess, nay insist, that linguistics simply gives the teacher additional or more effective tools and a better understanding of what he is working with. Any improvement he makes in his knowledge of language, any details he learns about the actual forms and constructions of English, will make him a more expert instructor. But at the present time, although linguists know and can teach information which is more accurate than the traditional notions, they still have to learn much about the details of English, and some of what they have learned is not ready for publication. Moreover, the field itself does not cover all the things that the composition teacher needs to know. There is still no royal road to good writing, no magic method that will turn out skilled writers, and neither linguistics nor any other field is likely to provide one.

SECTION IV

USAGE:
THE EMPLOYMENT
OF LANGUAGE

"Words strain,
Crack and sometimes break, under the burden,
Under the tension, slip, slide, perish,
Decay with imprecision, will not stay in place,
Will not stay still."

—T. S. Eliot *

In his sensible and measured statement in the opening essay of this section Porter Perrin makes it clear that the problem of usage is neither the problem of linguistics nor the problem of style. Although the data needed for a competent discussion of all three of these areas must be discovered by an examination of the six categories that Perrin lists, it is important for the purposes of clarity to remember that usage can be simply defined as the accumulation of specific incidents of the way in which people use pronunciation, word forms, word groups, sentences, vocabulary, and the conventions of writing. Investigations in all these areas by modern students of our language have led to a vigorous and undecided controversy over the problem of usage. The extent of the value of this section for the student may very well be in the appreciation he receives from his reading of the selections of the depth and seriousness of the controversy. Certainly there are no easy or pleasant solutions to the problems of usage.

The controversy is not over the fact of usage: that language changes constantly and that this kind of change is normal would seem to be admitted by most scholars. It is in trying to describe the implications of usage and to determine the relation of values to the facts that the problems can be discerned. For example, John Kenyon, although deeply appreciative of what previous scholars have accomplished, feels it necessary to correct earlier notions by objecting to the way "level" has been applied to usage. Instead he offers what he considers a more logical and apt method by distinguishing between "cultural levels" and "functional varieties." One of the keys to his essay is his explanation of why the label "colloquial" is finally inadequate.

Margaret Schlauch, as a keen observer of language usage, uses "levels" in a slightly different sense than the one criticized by Kenyon. Her concern is with social "levels" and, depending upon both experience and history, she attempts to demonstrate that language, as the metaphorical clothing of man in society, reveals social variations especially evident in class, taboos, and politics. The principle of usage is, of course, at the base of her observations about subjects as diverse as the language of the underworld, the taboos on death, and the slogans of the politician.

That the problem of usage remains a lively one was made apparent by the publication of the *Merriam-Webster's Third International Unabridged Dictionary* in 1961. This major publishing event was greeted by charges and countercharges. At the base of the argument over the value of Webster III was a fundamental disagreement over the principle of usage, well illustrated in the debate included in this section between Wilson Follett and Bergen Evans. Follett argues that the shortcomings of the third edition can be explained by the fact that the editors have accepted the notion that all usage is relative and have thereby abdicated their responsibility as dictionary makers. He is particularly disturbed by the disappearance of "colloquial" as a label. The method of the editors, he argues, forces them to "whittle away" at traditional controls by destroying "every criterion for distinguishing between better usages and worse." Bergen Evans, in the spirit of the majority of professional linguists, contends that change is constant and normal, that correctness finally can rest only upon usage, and that all usage is relative. The principles upon which Evans bases his argument are those enunciated by the Commission on the English Curriculum for the National Council of Teachers of English in the first volume of *The English Language Arts*. Thus, his position has a certain amount of "official" pedagogical approval.

An attempt at resolving this problem of usage is the substance of Morton Bloomfield's essay. He begins by clearly defining the outside edges of the two camps: "anything goes" vs. the prescriptionist. What he adds to the debate that is so important is the idea that the opposing views really represent a "philosophic problem of the first magnitude," the problem of the relation of fact and value. The question, for Bloomfield, is not merely linguistic, for the problem of value is with us no matter what grammatical system we finally adopt. It is important to note that he does not defend the more-or-less traditional grammatical description of English. He is very clear in stating that "the key to the whole problem . . . is the doctrine of usage." While freely admitting that language changes and that this change is normal, he argues with the ideas that correctness rests solely upon usage and that all usage is relative. Finally, although he states clearly that the facts of language set a limit to our application of values, he thinks that some choice in favor of a prudent prescriptivism must be made on the grounds of value.

The number and extent of the disagreements evident from the reading of the essays in this section should not lead the student into a position of linguistic confusion or anarchy. Diversity of viewpoint is something that the student must recognize and understand; perhaps at this stage of the great debate over usage, essential enlightenment might be said to consist in an appreciation of the dimensions of this unresolved problem.

USAGE   *Porter G. Perrin*

The view presented in this book is that there are three emphases in the study of current English—on linguistics, on style, and on usage. The same materials are studied and the methods have much in common, but there are characteristic differences in the three emphases, particularly in purposes. *Linguists* are chiefly concerned with the objective observation and analysis of the language—primarily of the spoken language—in order to discover and describe its system or "structure." Students of *style* examine specific examples of language—in our culture especially of written literature—primarily to find the qualities of language that are the source of a listener's or reader's impressions. Students of *usage* observe specific items in the language—both spoken and written—primarily to ascertain their currency and appropriateness in speech and writing of various sorts.

Some would regard style and usage simply as divisions of linguistics, but while linguistics furnishes much of the data and methods of the other two, and will do so increasingly, style and usage involve some consideration of social attitudes and responses usually not the concern of linguistics. An analysis made by a linguist will usually be more detailed than a student of usage requires, and often more detailed even than a student of style needs. Many linguists are sensitive to qualities of style and are excellent judges of the appropriateness of usage, but they seldom consider these their primary concern and probably feel that too much preoccupation with such questions may interfere with their scientific purpose. Although all people working with current English need a good deal of the same basic training, some division of labor, based on a recognition of the different purposes of the three emphases, will work not only for simplicity but for efficiency.

1. *The varying emphases of usage, style, and linguistics.* The data of usage can be grouped under six headings. Comparing under these six headings the concerns of usage with those of style and linguistics will illustrate some of the differences among the three studies.

From *Writer's Guide and Index to English,* Third Edition, by Porter G. Perrin. Copyright © by Scott, Foresman and Company, Chicago.

a) Pronunciation. *Usage*—the pronunciation of words and phrases, and, where pronunciations vary, the relative currency and standing of differing pronunciations. *Style*—the qualities of the sounds, their harmony or contrast, and features such as alliteration, assonance, and rhythm. *Linguistics*—phonetic and especially phonemic analysis (developed in detail and perhaps the foundation of the science).

b) Word forms. *Usage*—the parts of speech and their forms, the modifications for plurals, past tenses, and so on, with special attention to differences between Standard and Nonstandard forms and to differences within Standard English. *Style*—choices among forms is a minor concern; more important is predominance of one of the parts of speech in number or in qualitative emphasis. *Linguistics*—the form classes and their affixes and other modifications.

c) Word groups. *Usage*—the typical patterns of phrases and clauses, specific idioms, such as fixed prepositions with certain nouns, adjectives, or verbs, and idioms that do not conform to the general system of the language. *Style*—the dominance of noun-headed or verb-centered constructions, long or short constructions, and so on. *Linguistics*—the basic combinations of morphemes into syntactical units, usually determined by and described in terms of intonation.

d) Sentences. *Usage*—the favorite and minor types of sentence, with special attention to the patterns and variety of written sentences, in general from the point of view of clarity and effective communication. *Style*—variations in length and in arrangement of sentence elements, qualities of emphasis. *Linguistics*—the basic sentence patterns, with relatively little attention to the combination of these in the elaborated sentences of discourse.

e) Vocabulary. *Usage*—the meanings and qualities of words, especially their conventional uses and their range in the varieties of English. *Style*—the qualities of the words, especially their associations and connotations, imagery, and figurative use. *Linguistics*—not so much attention to individual words; semantics, the contribution of linguistics to the study of meaning, not yet very fully elaborated.

f) Conventions of writing. *Usage*—the conventions of spelling, punctuation, capitalization bulk rather large. *Style*—they are of minor importance. *Linguistics*—they are of very little importance except as the means by which the spoken language is represented in writing.

Beyond these primarily observational categories, usage is concerned with questions of "standards," style with literary effects and effectiveness, and linguistics with the understanding of language as an aspect of human behavior and other theoretical questions.

2. *The study of usage.* The study of usage helps to answer the question: Should I say or write this in this situation? Such a question comes usually either from lack of knowledge of what people say or write in a particular variety of English or from uncertainty because of differing practices. Since people are usually less at home in writing than in speaking, their questions often relate to written usage.

The study of usage has the general structure of the language as its frame, but it involves even more an accumulation of specific instances. It depends on wide observation of what people say and write in various situations as a basis for judgment of the standing of particular words, forms, and constructions. No one person can cover thoroughly this vast field, though he can amass a considerable body of data. However, since many people make special studies of individual points and present them in articles—in *American Speech,* the "Current English Forum" of *College English, Word Study,* and other periodicals—considerable reliable information accumulates. Three important books on usage are worth studying for their method, data, and conclusions:

C. C. Fries in *American English Grammar* (1940) discusses the usage found in a large group of letters and considers it in relation to the education and social position of the writers. Mr. Fries' study made clear that educated writers of Standard English show more variation in usage than was commonly thought.

George Summey, Jr., in *American Punctuation* (revised 1949) discusses the practices in punctuation he discovered from studying a large body of printed material. Although Mr. Summey discovered considerable range, he found prevailing practices that could be safely followed by individual writers.

Albert H. Marckwardt and Fred G. Walcott in *Facts About Current English Usage* (1938) present not so much a record of actual usage as of attitudes toward it. They include the results of the Leonard questionnaire to editors, teachers, and businessmen asking their judgment of a number of debatable items and add the record of dictionaries on individual words. They give recommendations representing this data.

As a result of these and other usage studies we now have a more accurate picture of what educated users of English say and, more especially, write. Such studies, presenting not a "liberal" but simply a more accurate picture of the language in use, have done a good deal to limit the puristic tendencies of texbooks on grammar and usage.

But recording usage by itself is not enough, partly because there is so much variety, especially in the very matters that are likely to raise questions. Relative frequency of occurrence is an important fact, but it gives only the range of usage. Reasoning on the data and further study are needed. Dictionaries record what their files show on particular words and phrases and give "usage labels" for many, designating them as colloquial or slang or restricted to some occupation. Such books are useful but are likely to be rather traditional. The stylebooks of publishers, such as the *United States Government Printing Office Style Manual* or the Associated Press *Stylebook*, give the choices their publishers have made for printed matter and should be taken into account. The history of a word or construction, in the *Oxford English Dictionary* or a history of the language, is often instructive (shall—will, don't), because such histories reveal that a good many of the more puristic strictures on usage are of relatively recent origin. Another source of information is the explicit or incidental comments by writers, defending their own preferences or lamenting others'.

It must be remembered that people's attitudes toward usages as well as actual usage are important. *Disinterested* is widely used in the sense of "uninterested" and is so recorded in dictionaries, but many people object to it; the same is true of like as a conjunction, the construction "the reason is because," and many others. Actual use of *shall* and *will* has not materially changed in recent years, but the attitudes toward the usage have changed. In fact, most questions are concerned not with differences between Standard and Nonstandard English (*ain't*, the double negative) but with matters of divided usage within Standard English. A student of usage, then, has not only to observe widely what is said and written but also to note the attitudes of people toward particular items.

And finally he has to use his judgment, based on his accumulated data. Judgments will vary somewhat, depending on the range of the individual's information and to a certain extent on his preferences in language. The best safeguard against avoidable bias is awareness of some principles of selection.

3. *Amateur students of usage.* In a sense any speaker of a language is an amateur student of usage. Unconsciously or perhaps consciously he notes and imitates things he hears. Children amass their stock of language in this way. Later most people's attention seems not to focus on the details of language—they become so accustomed to the steady flow of speech around them that they don't notice the details. Even though their circumstances may change and call for different or at least new elements of language, they often keep on speaking and writing as they did before.

Although we should not be too conscious of our language, it would be well to cultivate our observation occasionally and to become students of usage at least on a small scale. And anyone professionally concerned with English or anyone who wants to make it a hobby, should make some systematic study, to sharpen his observation, so that he won't have to be dependent on dictionaries or handbooks. He might concentrate on a few topics, such as sentence patterns, or idioms, or constructions like the prepositions used with *different*.

The easiest way to keep track of usage items is to have a file of 3x5 or 4x6 cards. The slips should be labeled at the top with the name of the particular point dealt with. Exact reference should be made to the source of the quotation, or to the speaker and place and circumstances of speaking. Even a small collection will allow you to make accurate judgments about some items of usage and will provide you with good evidence to back them up. And your collection may not only give you confidence in the particular item studied but show something of the way the language in general goes.

CULTURAL LEVELS AND FUNCTIONAL
VARIETIES OF ENGLISH   *John S. Kenyon*

The word *level*, when used to indicate different styles of language, is a metaphor, suggesting higher or lower position and, like the terms *higher* and *lower*, figuratively implies 'better' or 'worse,' 'more desirable' or 'less desirable,' and similar comparative degrees of excellence or inferiority in language.

The application of the term *level* to those different styles of language that are not properly distinguished as better or worse, desirable or undesirable, creates a false impression. I confess myself guilty of this error along with some other writers. What are frequently grouped together in one class as different levels of language are often in reality false combinations of two distinct and incommensurable categories, namely, *cultural levels* and *functional varieties*.

Among *cultural levels* may be included, on the lower levels, illiterate speech, narrowly local dialect, ungrammatical speech and writing, excessive and unskilful slang, slovenly and careless vocabulary and construction, exceptional pronunciation, and, on the higher level, lan-

From *College English*, October, 1948. Reprinted with the permission of The National Council of Teachers of English.

guage used generally by the cultivated, clear, grammatical writing, and pronunciations used by the cultivated over wide areas. The different cultural levels may be summarized in the two general classes *substandard* and *standard*.

Among *functional varieties* not depending on cultural levels may be mentioned colloquial language, itself existing in different degrees of familiarity or formality, as, for example, familiar conversation, private correspondence, formal conversation, familiar public address; formal platform or pulpit speech, public reading, public worship; legal, scientific, and other expository writing; prose and poetic belles-lettres. The different functional varieties may roughly be grouped together in the two classes *familiar* and *formal* writing or speaking.

The term *level*, then, does not properly belong at all to functional varieties of speech—colloquial, familiar, formal, scientific, literary language. They are equally "good" for their respective functions, and as classifications do not depend on the cultural status of the users.

The two groupings *cultural levels* and *functional varieties* are not mutually exclusive categories. They are based on entirely separate principles of classification: *culture* and *function*. Although we are here principally concerned with the functional varieties of standard English (the highest cultural level), yet substandard English likewise has its functional varieties for its different occasions and purposes. Thus the functional variety colloquial English may occur on a substandard cultural level, but the term *colloquial* does not itself indicate a cultural level. So the functional variety formal writing or speaking may occur on a lower or on a higher cultural level according to the social status of writer or speaker, and sometimes of reader or audience. It follows, for instance, that the colloquial language of cultivated people is on a higher cultural level than the formal speech of the semiliterate or than some inept literary writing.

Semiliterate formal speech is sometimes heard from radio speakers. I recently heard one such speaker solemnly announce, "Sun day will be Mother's Day." Because the speaker, in his ignorance of good English, thought he was making himself plainer by using the distorted pronunciation *sun day* instead of the standard pronunciation *sundy*, he actually was misunderstood by some listeners to be saying, "Some day will be Mother's Day." About forty years ago the great English phonetician Henry Sweet used this very example to show that "we cannot make words more distinct by disguising them." [1] He was re-

[1] Henry Sweet, *The Sounds of English* (Oxford, 1910), p. 78.

ferring to the use, in this instance, of the full sound of vowels in un-
accented syllables where standard English has obscure vowels. On
the same page Sweet gives another example of the same blunder:
"Thus in the sentence *I shall be at home from one to three* the substitution of **tuw** for **tə** [ə=the last sound in *sofa*] at once suggests a confusion between the preposition and the numeral." This was also verified on the radio. Not long ago I heard a radio speaker announce
carefully, "This program will be heard again tomorrow from one two
three." I have also recorded (among many others) the following such
substandard forms from the radio: *presidEnt* for the standard form
presidənt, the days of the week ending in the full word *day* instead of
the standard English syllable *-dy, ay man,* for the correct *man, cahn-
sider* for *cənsider, tooday* for *təday, too go* for *tə go, Coalumbia* for
Cəlumbia, etc. This is merely one sort among many of substandard
features in the formal speech of the semiliterate.[2]

To begin my strictures at home, in *American Pronunciation* (9th
ed., 4th printing, p. 17), I use the page heading "Levels of Speech."
This should be "Functional Varieties of Standard Speech," for the
reference is solely to the different uses of speech on the one cultivated
level. Similarly, in the Kenyon-Knott *Pronouncing Dictionary of American English* (p. xvi, §2), I carelessly speak of "levels of the colloquial"
where I mean "styles of the colloquial," as three lines above. For
though there are different cultural levels of colloquial English, the
reference here is only to standard colloquial.

S. A. Leonard and H. Y. Moffett, in their study, "Current Definition
of Levels in English Usage," [3] say (p. 348): "The levels of English usage
have been most clearly described in Dr. Murray's Preface ["General
Explanations," p. xvii] to the *New English Dictionary.* I have varied
his diagram a little in order to illustrate better the overlapping between
the categories." It appears to me that Leonard and Moffett have so
varied the diagram as to obscure Murray's intention. For he is not
here primarily exhibiting levels of speech but is showing the 'Anglicity,'
or limits of the English vocabulary for the purposes of his dictionary.[4]
The only topical divisions of his diagram that imply a cultural level are
"slang" and "dialectal," and the only statement in his explanation of the
diagram that could imply it is, "Slang words ascend through colloquial
use." This may imply that slang is on a lower cultural level than

---

[2] See further *American Speech*, VI, No. 5 (June, 1931), 368–72.

[3] *English Journal*, XVI, No. 5 (May, 1927), 345–59.

[4] The word *Anglicity* is a coinage of the *Oxford Dictionary.* They define it as
'English quality, as of speech or style; English idiom.'

"colloquial, literary, technical, scientific, foreign." We may also safely
infer that Murray would place "Dialectal" on a lower level than colloquial and literary if he were here concerned with cultural levels.
Murray's diagram rests consistently on the same basis of classification
throughout ('Anglicity'), and he emphasizes that "there is absolutely
no defining line in any direction [from the central nucleus of colloquial
and literary]." Moreover, Murray's exposition here concerns only vocabulary, with no consideration of the other features that enter so
largely into "levels" of language—grammatical form and structure, pronunciation, spelling, and meaning—of styles, in short, only so far as
they are affected by vocabulary. These he treats of elsewhere but
without reference to levels.

It is not quite clear just how far Leonard and Moffett intend their
grouping "literary English," "standard, cultivated, colloquial English,"
and "naïf, popular, or uncultivated English" to be identical with what
they call Murray's "levels," his description of which they commend.
But it is clear that they call their own grouping "three levels of usage"
(p. 357) and classify them together as a single descending scale (cf. "the
low end of the scale," p. 358). The inevitable impression that the average reader receives from such an arrangement of the scale is: Highest
level, literary English; next lower level, colloquial English; lowest level,
illiterate English; whereas, in fact, the first two "levels" are functional
varieties of the one cultural level standard English, while the third
("illiterate or uncultivated," p. 358) is a cultural level.

Krapp has a chapter on "The Levels of English Speech," [5] in which
he reveals some awareness of the confusion of cultural levels with
functional varieties. He says:

> Among those who pay any heed at all to convention in social rela-
> tionships, a difference of degree is implicit in all use of English. This
> difference of degree is usually thought of in terms of higher and lower,
> of upper levels of speech appropriate to certain occasions of more
> formal character, of lower levels existing, if not necessarily appropriate,
> among less elevated circumstances. These popular distinctions of level
> may be accepted without weighting them too heavily with significance
> in respect of good, better, and best in speech. A disputatious person
> might very well raise the question whether literary English, ordinarily
> regarded as being on a high level, is really any better than the spoken
> word, is really as good as the spoken word, warm with the breath of the
> living moment.

[5] George Philip Krapp, *The Knowledge of English* (New York, 1927), pp.
55–76.

At the risk of having to own the hard impeachment of being disputa-
tious, I must express the fear that the logical fallacy in treating of levels,
which Krapp rather lightly waves aside, is having a serious effect on
general ideas of speech levels, and especially of the significance of colloquial English in good usage. Krapp's grouping, frankly on a scale of
"levels" throughout, constitutes a descending scale from the highest,
"Literary English," through "Formal Colloquial," "General Colloquial,"
"Popular English," to the lowest, "Vulgar English." Here the fallacy
is obvious: Literary English, Formal Colloquial, and General Colloquial
are not cultural levels but only functional varieties of English all on the
one cultural level of standard English. The last two, Popular English
and Vulgar English, belong in a different order of classification, cultural
levels, without regard to function.

So in his succeeding discussion *level* sometimes means the one,
sometimes the other; now a functional variety of standard English, and
now a cultural level of substandard or of standard English. It is functional on page 58 ("a choice between two levels") and on page 60 ("level
of general colloquial"), cultural on page 62 ("popular level" and "cultivated level") and on pages 63–64 ("popular level," "level of popular
speech"), functional on page 64 ("general colloquial level"), cultural
again on the same page ("popular level," "still lower level"), cultural on
page 67 ("vulgar . . . level of speech," "applying the term 'vulgar' to it
at certain levels"), cultural on page 68 ("its own [popular] level"), cultural and functional in the same phrase on page 68 ("speakers from the
popular and the general colloquial level meet and mix"), and so on
most confusingly to page 75.

The same kind of mixture of cultural levels and functional varieties
is thrown into one apparently continuous scale by Kennedy: "There is
the formal and dignified language of the scholarly or scientific address
or paper. . . . The precision and stateliness of this uppermost level
. . . is a necessary accompaniment of thinking on a high plane." [6]
Next in order he mentions colloquial speech, which he refers to as "the
second level, . . . generally acceptable to people of education and
refinement." Clearly this is not a cultural level but a functional variety
of standard English, like the "uppermost level." The third level is,
however, a cultural one: "the latest slang," workmen's "technical slang
and colloquialisms which other persons cannot comprehend," "grammatical solecisms." "The speech of this third level can fairly be ranked
as lower in the social scale." His fourth level is also cultural: "At the

[6] Arthur G. Kennedy, *Current English* (Boston, 1935), pp. 15–17: "Speech
Levels."

bottom of the scale is the lingo, or cant, of criminals, hobos, and others of the lowest social level."

Finally, Kennedy fixes the false mental image of a continuous and logically consistent descent from "the cold and lonely heights of formal and highly specialized scientific and scholarly language" to "the stupid and slovenly level of grammatical abuses and inane slang." In reality there is no cultural descent until we reach his third "level," since "formal and dignified language" and "colloquial speech" are only functional varieties of English on the one cultural level of standard English.

A clear instance of the inconsistent use of the term *level* is found in Robert C. Pooley's *Teaching English Usage* (New York, 1946), chapter iii, "Levels in English Usage." He names five levels: (1) the illiterate level; (2) the homely level; (3) standard English, informal level; (4) standard English, formal level; and (5) the literary level. In (1) and (2) *level* has an altogether different meaning from that in (3), (4), and (5). In the first two *level* plainly means 'cultural level'; in the last three it just as plainly means 'functional variety of standard English,' all three varieties being therefore on the one cultural level of standard English. So *level* in the two groups belongs to different orders of classification. All misunderstanding and wrong implication would be removed from this otherwise excellent treatment of levels if the last three groups were labeled "Standard English Level, Informal Variety"; "Standard English Level, Formal Variety"; and "Standard English Level, Literary Variety." Pooley's groups contain three cultural levels (illiterate, homely, standard) and three functional varieties of the standard cultural level (informal, formal, literary).

The misapplication to colloquial English of the term *level*, metaphorically appropriate only to cultural gradations, is especially misleading. We often read of English that is "on the colloquial level." For example, Krapp writes: "*Who do you mean?* . . . has passed into current spoken use and may be accepted on the colloquial level."[8] This implies that colloquial English is on a different cultural level from formal English (literary, scientific, etc.), and a too frequent assumption, owing to this and other misuses of the term *colloquial*, is that its cultural level is below that of formal English. This supposition, tacit or explicit, that colloquial style is inferior to formal or literary style, leads inescapably to the absurd conclusion that, whenever scientists or literary artists turn from their formal writing to familiar conversation with their friends, they thereby degrade themselves to a lower social status.

[8] *A Comprehensive Guide to Good English* (New York, 1927), p. 641.

This misuse of *level* encourages the fallacy frequently met with of contrasting colloquial with standard English, logically as fallacious as contrasting white men with tall men. For instance, Mencken writes: "'I have no doubt *but* that' . . . seems to be very firmly lodged in colloquial American, and even to have respectable standing in the standard speech." [9] This contrast, not always specifically stated, is often implied. For example, Kennedy writes: "Colloquial English is, properly defined, the language of conversation, and especially of familiar conversation. As such it may approximate the standard speech of the better class of English speakers, or it may drop to the level of the illiterate and careless speaker." [10] *May approximate* should be replaced by *may be on the level of.*

Similarly, on page 440: "Some measure words [are] still used colloquially without any ending in the plural . . . ; but most of these are given the *s* ending in standard English usage." Here *standard* is confused with *formal.*

Kennedy (pp. 534, 616) several times contrasts colloquial English with "standard literary English." This implies that colloquial English is not standard, while literary English is. If he means to contrast standard colloquial with standard literary, well and good; but I fear that most readers would understand the contrast to be of colloquial with standard. [11]

The term *colloquial* cannot properly designate a substandard cultural level of English. It designates a functional variety—that used chiefly in conversation—and in itself says nothing as to its cultural level, though this discussion, and the dictionary definitions, are chiefly concerned with cultivated colloquial, a functional variety of standard English. When writers of such standing as those I have mentioned slip into expressions that imply lower cultural status of colloquial English, it is not surprising that colloquialisms should not be represented as standard American speech. But the context of the statement indicated that its author was using *colloquialism* in the sense of 'localism.' I could

[9] H. L. Mencken, *The American Language* (4th ed.; New York, 1936), p. 203.
[10] Kennedy, *op. cit.*, p. 26.
[11] Greenough and Kittredge in *Words and Their Ways in English Speech* (New York, 1909), Chap. VII, only apparently treat literary English as the sole standard form: "What is the origin of standard or literary English?" (p. 80). They use *standard* in a special sense for their particular purpose, calling it "the common property of all but the absolutely illiterate," "the language which all educated users of English speak and write" (therefore including colloquial). For the usual current meaning, see the definitions of *standard* quoted in *American Pronunciation* (6th and subsequent eds.), pp. 14–15.

hardly believe how frequent this gross error is, until I heard it from a well-known American broadcaster.[12]

The best dictionaries, at least in their definitions, give no warrant for the various misuses of *colloquial, colloquially, colloquialism, colloquiality*. I urge the reader to study carefully the definitions in the *Oxford English Dictionary* with its many apt examples from standard writers, and in *Webster's New International Dictionary, Second Edition*, with its quotations from George Lyman Kittredge. Kittredge's views on the standing of colloquial English are well known. It is said that somebody once asked him about the meaning of the label "Colloq." in dictionaries. He is reported to have replied, "I myself speak 'colloke' and often write it." I cannot verify the story, but it sounds authentic.

It seems to me inevitable that the frequent grouping of so-called "levels" such as "Literary, Colloquial, Illiterate," and the like, will lead the reader to suppose that just as Illiterate is culturally below Colloquial, so Colloquial is culturally below Literary. While I can scarcely hope that my humble remonstrance will reform all future writing on "levels of English," I believe that writers who confuse the meaning of the term *level* must accept some part of the responsibility for the popular misunderstanding of the true status of colloquial English; for I cannot avoid the belief that the popular idea of colloquial English as something to be looked down upon with disfavor is due in part to the failure of writers on the subject to distinguish between *cultural levels of English* and *functional varieties of standard English*.

SOCIAL ASPECTS:
CLASS, TABOOS, POLITICS   Margaret Schlauch

Language Like Clothing

Speculating on the function of clothes in society, and what they have done to us, Carlyle at one point of *Sartor Resartus* asks us to imagine the functioning of "government, legislation, property, police, and civilized society" if all persons were abruptly forced to appear in public without any clothing whatsoever. We are so accustomed to reliance on badges, buttons, styles, and materials in judging our fellow-men, he argues, that august institutions would dissolve in "wails and howls"

---

[12] Leonard and Moffett also mention the frequency of this blunder (*op. cit.,* p. 351, n. 5).

From *The Gift of Language* by Margaret Schlauch. Copyright 1942 by Margaret Schlauch. Reprinted by permission of The Viking Press, Inc.

without them. These are the signs of rank and class; we deplore their artificiality, but we need them. "Lives the man," he asks, "that can figure a naked Duke of Windlestraw addressing a naked House of Lords? Imagination, choked as in mephitic air, recoils on itself, and will not forward with the picture. . . ." It is the wig, squirrel-skins, and plush gown that announce the judge; without them he would be no more by day than he is by night, only "a forked Radish with a head fantastically carved."

But Carlyle is wrong. Even with the badges and uniforms stripped away, something would remain as a guide, as sure if less ponderable, to the social position of each forked radish. Even a naked Duke of Windlestraw, upon opening his mouth, would speak the English language with a certain air, an accent and intonation inextricably associated with his rank and authority. An untrained impostor from the lower levels of society would be detected by his speech, although appearing as one nude radish among many. Of course, his speech could be faked for this occasion; but so could his clothes, for other occasions. Both types of deception have been practiced. It is a pity that Carlyle did not turn his attention to language as a metaphorical clothing of man in society.

Class Dialects

The existence of different manners of speech for persons in various ranks is a familiar fact. We are constantly sorting and classifying people according to them. A variation of any national language according to social levels is called a *class dialect*. Even within the class dialect there may be many variations and minor divisions. For instance, the younger members of a privileged class who attend special schools sometimes develop a special jargon among themselves which is almost incomprehensible to outsiders. Yet it is clearly an offshoot of the general "upper-class" dialect of their parents. Poorer youngsters also develop a kind of tribal school jargon as local and esoteric as the other. Even families and other restricted groups develop special jargons mystifying to an outsider. But these are even more clearly recognized and assigned to the general class dialects to which they belong.

When we talk, then, we tell much more about ourselves than the factual statements we are making. The sum total of small nuances will indicate much about our training, environment, economic position, and even profession. In conversation we are unconsciously providing a rich commentary about ourselves which supplements the clothing and outward possessions we gather.

Cockney English

Not all European languages offer the same number of levels contrasted with equal sharpness. Within the English-speaking world the sharpest contrast is probably to be found between Cockney London dialect on the one hand and "upper-class" speech on the other. Londoners are not skittish about admitting this contrast; they are very frank about the existence of class levels in speech. The attitude of most observers is that Cockney is intrinsically humorous, and can be appreciated—at best—only by a condescending tolerance. Of course this is a result of the social connotations of the speech. In an early play, *Captain Brassbound's Conversion* (written before his better known *Pygmalion*), George Bernard Shaw experimented with the use of Cockney for dramatic purposes involving class distinctions. One of his problems was the difficult task of recording the vowel sounds of his low-class character, Drinkwater. This is what the attempt looked like on the printed page. Drinkwater, an engaging ne'er-do-well, finds himself entertaining Sir Howard Hallam, a judge before whom he once appeared as defendant:

Drinkwater *(placing the chair for Sir Howard)*. Awskink yr pawdn for the libbety, Sr Ahrd.

Sir Howard *(looking at him)*. I have seen you before somewhere.

Drinkwater. You ev, Sr Ahrd. But aw do assure yer it were hall a mistake.

Sir Howard. As usual. *(He sits down.)* Wrongfully convicted, of course.

Drinkwater *(with sly delight)*. Naow, gavner. *(Half whispering, with an ineffable grin.)* Wrongfully hacquittid!

Sir Howard. Indeed! That's the first case of the kind I have ever met.

Drinkwater: Lawd, Sr Ahrd, wot jagginses them jurymen was! You an me knaowed it too, didn't we?

Sir Howard. I daresay we did. I am sorry to say I forget the exact nature of the difficulty you were in. Can you refresh my memory?

Drinkwater. Owny the aw [high] sperrits o youth, y'lawdship. Worterloo Rowd kice. Wot they calls Ooliganism. . . . Nime [name] giv huz pore thortless leds baw, a gent on the Dily Chrorncile. . . . Awll eng [hang] abaht within ile [hail], gavner, hin kice aw should be wornted.

In this conversation, it will be observed, the only attempts at phonetic writing are limited to the speech of the Cockney. Sir Howard Hallam's speech is given in conventional (that is, highly unphonetic) spelling. As Shaw admits, this procedure is quite inconsistent, but it has the merit of convenience. When educated persons, for instance professional people, read a printed page each assumes that the unreal orthography stands for his own special form of "acceptable" English. It would be too complicated for a dramatist to indicate every shading (even if he could) within that very inclusive territory. Shaw finds many attractive features in the Cockney dialect, and is particularly impatient with the snobbish contempt of outsiders for the so-called "misplaced aitch" which is one of its characteristics. "Roughly speaking, I should say that in England he who bothers about his *h*'s is a fool, and he who ridicules a dropped *h* a snob."

Yet persons with social ambitions have spent much time and suffered real distress in an effort to achieve conformity with their "betters" in details such as this. The matter has been treated with solemnity in a novel by May Sinclair, *The Divine Fire,* which was widely read about a generation ago. The hero was supposed to be a gifted poet born with the soul of ancient Greece lodged in a Cockney bosom: "The child of 'Ellas and 'Ollywell Street—innocent of—er—the rough breathing," [1] as one of the London literati puts it. Later his "innocence" of that minor phoneme when under emotional stress causes him the most excruciating social agonies. It is amusing to remember that at a certain time in ancient Rome it was considered very *chic* to insert unhistorical *h*-sounds before words normally beginning with vowels. It gave a fashionable Greekish flavor to ordinary everyday Latin. Catullus tells us in one of his poems that the fops of his day were saying *hinsidiae* for *insidiae* ("hambushes" for "ambushes"). It was the obverse of the Cockney poet's failing. So relative are the social connotations of a single sound!

Levels of Speech

The existence of an accepted upper-class dialect associated with those who govern a country and man its professions has some amusing consequences. The sociological implications have never been adequately explored. For one thing, the levels will not be clearly preserved if historical change is moving rapidly, as at the time of the French Revolution. And even where change has been slow and barriers are clearly marked, the rise and fall of individuals brings about incongruities—a lack of harmony, let us say, between the physical clothing and the garment of speech.

[1] This is the term used in Greek grammars to designate initial [h].

It is only human for people in a stratified society to want to appear more smart and elegant than they are by birth and training. This is true if the society does leave some opportunities for personal advancement from the lower ranks. When people are over-eager to climb, they adopt a speech of uneasy and self-conscious gentility. One of its obvious characteristics is an excess of zeal for correctness: zeal to "talk good grammar," as it is sometimes called. This solicitude produces what we call hypercorrect forms.

Hypercorrectness

For instance, a person may have been drilled in school to correct his native speech in the matter of present participles: to "pronounce the final g," as the unscientific saying is, in words like "ringing, singing, eating." The drill embarrasses him into self-consciousness, and he tends, for safety's sake, to substitute the syllable [ɪŋ] for all final [ɪn]'s in his speech. So he says "curting," "garding," "ruing" for "curtain," "garden," "ruin." Or it may be that in triumph at having corrected errors like "Him and me get along fine" into "He and I get along well," the rising individual produces sentences like "It's a secret between him (he) and I."

The *arriviste* in language is also apt to gloat in the use of perfect tenses and to overdo them. "It was a great pleasure *to have met you*." Excessive self-consciousness about adverbial endings produces "finely" or "fastly" if the speaker has recently learned to avoid "He works good." A preposition is doubled in sentences like "It's the man for whom I was waiting for" when the speaker is just unlearning "who I was waiting for."

Another more refined vice of the self-consciously correct person is the refusal to use unstressed forms of articles or prepositions, as if they were always vulgar. He pronounces "the man and the girl" with painful distinctness, as if he were still in first grade struggling over individual words under a teacher's strict eye. He says [ði: mæn ænd ði: gɔɹl], pedantically; and yet it is the best speakers, those at home in cultured English, who say: [ðə mæn ən ðə gɔːl]. In accepted English, too, there is a clear difference between "to" [tə] and "too" [tu:]. The man at ease in society says: "I'm about to come too" as [aɪm ə'baʊt tə 'kʌm 'tu:] not the hypercorrect [aɪ 'æm ə'baʊt 'tu: 'kʌm 'tu:], which is in fact a bad self-betrayal. A mistaken snobbishness prompts this schoolroom isolation of words. Yet the most snobbish of snobs, the man poised with inherited confidence, is the one who freely permits slurred forms—provided, of course, they are the "right" slurred forms, hallowed by general usage in his "set."

Underworld Speech

There is another type of class dialect more baffling to the uninitiated: the argot of the underworld of great cities. Here the normal sub-standard speech is deliberately and frequently modified by slang peri-phrases to keep outsiders from understanding. Thus it is that jewels become "ice," and stolen jewels, the object of police questing, become, quaintly enough, "hot ice." Drugs like heroin and cocaine become "snow." A whole vocabulary has developed around the use of the for-bidden "reefers" of marihuana by "vipers" (addicts). It is interesting to note that American argot has had its influence on the underworld of foreign cities. Paris, rich in its own special language, shows in addition some loans from American gangster speech. In fact the word "gang-ster" has been taken over unchanged save for accent. Collaborated rob-bery is called "American robbery" or *vol à l'américaine*. If three work together they are called *le leveur* ("lifter"), *l'Américain* and *l'utilité* ("utility-man"). If there are two, one is designated by an American-English phrase, *le contact-man,* and the other is *le banquier* ("the banker"). Professions more or less related to a robber's life are also designated by picturesque English loans. The woman who works for a *souteneur* is called by many words, including an English one: *biftek* ("beefsteak"). A prostitute's work is called by another English term. *le bizness.* The underworld shows a certain measure of interna-tionalism in its vocabulary. For the most part, however, it relies on metaphor and semantic shifts in native words.

Courtly and Polite Forms

In English we show our social levels primarily by choice of words and general style. One method used by other languages is unknown to us: the multiplication of personal pronouns to express various social attitudes towards the person addressed. We say "you" when talking to someone, whether he is a haughty superior, a friendly equal, or a subservient inferior. In this one pronominal respect English may be said to be classless. Other European languages make differences which seem formal or exclusive or arrogant or groveling to us users of the simple "you." In addressing a child or an intimate or (strangely enough) one for whom he feels contempt, a German says *du.* In addressing a stranger, he uses *Sie*, which is identical in form as well as origin with the word for "they"—a tribute to the distance and importance (plurality) of the person addressed. If he wishes to be deferential he uses a third-person noun while he looks straight at the person addressed. Thus, "Did the lady (or the gracious lady) sleep well? Has the gentleman finished his coffee?" Other languages use the third person similarly for cautious and reserved address. A Dane will say *"Har Fruen tabt sin Bog?"* and a Frenchman *"Est-ce que Madame a perdu son livre?"* ("Has madam lost her book?") But both use such forms more sparingly, I think, than the polite German.

In courtly circles it was formerly quite customary to use (usually feminine) abstract nouns like "Excellency" or "Your Excellency" in speaking directly to a person of rank. The pronoun which might be substituted for this abstract noun, in languages with grammatical gender, was naturally "she." The contemporary Spanish word for "you" comes from a feminine noun with distinctly courtier-like connotations. *Usted* is a contraction of *vuestra merced*, which means "your mercy" or "your graciousness." A touch of the ancient formality of a sixteenth-century Spanish grandee hangs about the word.

Nothing in Europe, however, corresponds to the elaboration of pronominal snobbishness in some Eastern languages. In Malay a whole series of social levels are stratified in the pronouns of address. Nobody can simply and blithely say "you" without further reflection. He must stop to think: "How far is this man above or below me on the social ladder?" And according to the relative positions on that ladder, he will modify not only the "you" but also "I" and "we." The following table will indicate how many forms a Malay speaker must choose among, according to the social positions of the three possible persons to be designated. The choice involves not only words for "you" but *all* pronouns; and there are ten levels:

Person speaking	"I, we"	"thou, you"	"he, she, they"
Peasants to one another	*aku;* pl. *kita*	*ĕngkau*	*ia, dia*
Superior pointedly to inferior	*aku;* pl. *kita*	*ĕngkau*	*ia, dia*
Superior ordinarily to inferior	*sahaya,* pl. *kita*	*kamu, awak* [diff. dialect]	
Superior with affected modesty to equals	*hamba (tuan)*	*tuan (hamba)*	*tuan (hamba)*

All classes to Europeans	*sahaya; kita*	*tuan*	*tuan*
Malay gentry to one another	*kami*	*ĕnche', tuan*	*ĕnche', tuan*
Commoner to chief	*hamba (dato') sahaya (dato')*	*dato'*	*dato'*
Commoner to rajah; lesser to greater rajahs	*patek*	*tĕngku; ĕngku*	*tĕngku; ĕngku raja*
Subject to sultan	*patek*	*tuan-ku*	*yam-tuan; tuan-ku*
Literary	*beta*	*sahabat beta*	[name and title]

In Japanese, according to Von der Gabelentz, politeness forbids a speaker to use the simple active voice in referring to high-class people, as if they were obliged to engage in activity themselves. So the speaker chooses the causative voice, giving them the role of persons acting mediately, by command—or the passive voice, as if the action were happening by itself. The Koreans are unequaled in this respect, since they express through the *verbal* form whether a higher personage is talking to a lower, a lower to a higher, or one equal to another; and, moreover, whether this is happening in a comparatively reverential, contemptuous, or indifferent manner. This would, properly speaking, yield 3x3x3 or 27 modal forms. Thus voice and other verbal inflections may also be determined by sociological relations—titles and income, in short. The Algonquian language is said to possess complex stratified forms of polite locution also.

Regional Dialects

It is customary to distinguish class dialects from local or regional dialects. The latter include the ways of speech which mark people off according to the province, village, or region from which they come. "Everyone who does not speak a Regional dialect," says Henry Cecil Wyld, "speaks a Class dialect." Yet the matter is not quite so simple as that. The two dialect types cannot be so completely separated.

In America, for instance, we have several varieties of regional dialect. A citizen of Louisiana is said to speak Southern American;

one from Massachusetts, New England American (English). A few tricks of pronunciation of vowels and many niceties of sentence tempo and intonation betray the regional origins of the two. The former will say "po'k" [po:k] for "pork"; the latter, [pɔ:k]. Each one, in fact, may tend to jeer at the other with entire good nature because of these perceptible differences, minor though they may be. But although the educated, traveled, and affluent Southerner may share some of these traits with poor cotton-pickers and mill workers, there are other ways of speech quite as marked which separate the two groups within the confines of the very same regional dialect. Comparative analyses are still lacking. It is probable, however, that the study of the levels *within* such a regional dialect would show two things: that the individual sounds were very much alike throughout the region, regardless of class, but that the syntax (grammatical structure) of sentences was different. In saying "He doesn't like me any more," speakers of all levels would agree on the vowel sounds in "like" [la:k] and "more" [mo:], and they might have the same deliberate and agreeable speech melody; but the mill worker would change the verbal agreement and use a double negative as Chaucer often did: "He don't like me no more." In this he would agree with many persons of the same class in other parts of the country.

Dialect and Governmental Power

Where the governmental and economic power have been associated with one place and one dialect, the use of regional language may be a social or class handicap. The overlapping is clear in England, where the broad Lancashire dialect, for all its venerable history, is a label of class as well as region for a person wishing to rise in the social scale. According to English writers, the speech of the "better class" is heard with practically no variation all over the country: it is "Public School English," and all else—"the vulgar English of the towns, and the English of the Villager who has abandoned his native Regional Dialect"—is Modified Standard. In compiling his *English Pronouncing Dictionary* Daniel Jones tells us that he recorded what is "most usually heard in everyday speech in the families of Southern English persons who have been educated at the great public boarding schools. . . . The pronunciation may also be heard, to an extent which is considerable though difficult to specify, from educated people in the South of England who have not been educated at these schools." It is assumed, however, that the linguistic influence radiates from them.

The Lancashire manufacturer may despair of changing his own speech, but he will probably see to it that his children learn Public School English. Even Scots dialect, with its distinguished literary history, has been regarded as a handicap. J. M. Barrie's play, *What Every Woman Knows*, presents the efforts of an ambitious politician who, with his wife's help, is at some pains to smooth out of his speech the local flavor which might hamper his career. In ancient Greece, the Attic dialect became the accepted "superior" language because it was used in the powerful city-state of Athens and particularly was employed in the writings of a splendid galaxy of writers in the fifth and fourth centuries B.C. As a consequence Attic speakers began to look down their noses at "countrymen" who used other local dialects. The only exception was perhaps Ionian, which also represented political power and had an early, distinguished literature. A politician hampered by a "countryman's" dialect has always been a subject of unkind jests by his enemies.

Politics and American "Provincial" Speech

In the early days of the American republic our ancestors were sensitive about the minor differences of pronunciation and vocabulary which already marked us off perceptibly from British speakers. Political independence seems to have converted the uneasy sense of inferiority into a truculent claim upon "superiority," as might be expected. Ardent patriots hoped that a new day had dawned for the English language in America. They wished to see differences recognized and accelerated. On the other hand, British writers tended to sharpen their attitude of disapproval towards American "provincialisms." Some of the Founding Fathers carried on a lively discussion on the desirability of showing the world by means of our language that we had become an independent, proudly republican state. English was supposed to be "purer" in the land of freedom, at the very time when British critics were making contemptuous remarks about it.

Frontier Life

As a matter of fact, some of the very "provincialisms" cited in early dictionaries of American speech, and condemned by British purists, give a lively picture of frontier life and struggles. They make up a colorful creation—an unconscious linguistic record of early American

ways of living. Here are a few of them, classified according to the
pioneers' occupations:

Farm Life

to make a bee-line
to have a long row to hoe
to fly off the handle
to sit on the fence
to have an ax to grind
to go haywire [origin in doubt]
to have a chip on the shoulder
to fork over
to have the wrong end of the stick

Hunting and Gunmanship

to make the fur fly
to knock the spots out of
to draw a bead [i.e., to take aim]
to bark up the wrong tree
to get on one's own hook
to be up a tree

Warfare (Indian style)

to scalp
to walk Indian file
to bury the hatchet
to put on war-paint

Pioneering

to make tracks
to blaze a trail
to jump a claim
to pull up stakes
to peter out
to be as easy as rolling off a log
to clear out
to spark [to woo a girl]
to have the latchstring out
to be stumped
to swap horses in mid-stream

For all their vividness, however, it may be imagined that these expressions redolent of frontier life would be regarded as low barbarisms
in the sophisticated coffee houses and drawing rooms of eighteenth-
century London, and would therefore be a social handicap to the user
of them.

Lower-class Speech in Earlier Times

The lower ranks of society had a dialect of their own in past ages too. Feudal England gives an especially clear case of linguistic division on class lines. For a certain period of time after 1066, as we have observed, government, courts, and local administration were in the hands of persons speaking a tongue foreign to the native English: French as opposed to Anglo-Saxon. The situation was solved more quickly, it now appears, than earlier historians supposed. But out of the original division came the tendency still noticeable in English to use Anglo-Saxon words for homely, intimate, and even ugly or indecent things, and to use French words for the loftier ideas (or to conceal the ugly ones).

With the development of town life and commerce, lower-class speech was further diversified. It was not merely the language of the peasant as opposed to that of the knight. It included the language of guildsmen and artisans, of retainers, clerks, and hangers-on of the aristocracy; of beggars, thieves, sharpers, and peddlers. Each trade had its own cant. Most diverting was the speech of the last group.

Robert Greene, Shakespeare's contemporary, wrote a series of satirical pamphlets describing the tricks of sharpers and cheats in the London underworld. They give us most valuable material on substandard urban locutions during the reign of Elizabeth. From dictionaries and other sources we can then trace the underworld language through the seventeenth and eighteenth centuries. Thievery created a list of metaphors which were not only esoteric—for trade use—but also poetic. Here are a few, taken from a dictionary compiled in the reign of William and Mary:

> *bacon:* skin; body. "He saved his bacon," meaning "he escaped."
> *bracket-face:* ugly, homely, ill-favored
> *briers:* trouble. "To be in the briers," to be in trouble
> *bess:* an instrument to crack open a door
> *jenny:* "an instrument to lift up a grate, and whip anything out of a shop-window."
> *dead men:* empty bottles
> *dub:* a pick-lock key
> *fork:* a pickpocket. "Let's fork him" is thus glossed: "Let us Pick that man's Pocket, the newest and most dexterous way: It is, to thrust the Fingers, strait, stiff, open and very quick into the Pocket, and so closing them, hook what can be held between them."
> *green-bag:* a lawyer

milch-kine: "a term us'd by Gaolers, when their Prisoners will bleed freely to have some Favor, or be at large."

mill: to rob, steal, break open. "Milling the Gig with a Betty, c[ant for] Breaking open the Door with an Iron-Crow, milling the Glaze, c. Breaking open the Window."

queer birds: "such as having got loose, return to their old Trade of Roguing and Thieving."

Spanish-money: "fair words and Compliments"

splitter-of-causes: a lawyer

unrig: to strip the clothes off someone—whether for stealing or amorous purposes.

Metaphors of Slang

One fact emerges clearly from the study of disreputable slang, both past and present. No one impulse explains its creation and its peculiar qualities. It results from specialization, like any other trade dialect; also from a need for secrecy, for economy of expression; but certainly also from humor, delight in metaphor, and a quite uneconomic playfulness. Both conciseness and a pleasing contempt for conciseness will be found operative in the slang of the more respectable traders as well.

No occupation is more rushed, for example, than quick-lunch counter service at high noon. Hundreds of thousands of busy, nervous Americans besiege these dispensaries of pabulum every noon-time. Above the clamor of dishes and public conversation can be heard the cries of waiters and chefs calling and repeating orders for food in a language as special, mysterious, and playful as any thieves' cant. Surely here, you would suppose, the feverish tempo of service would make economy the paramount virtue of speech. And some expressions, like "B.T." for "bacon and tomato sandwich," are in fact a kind of spoken short-hand designed to clip a second or two off the necessary communication. Others are graphic as well as brief: *fizz* for "carbonated water"; *freezone* for "chocolate frosted milk"; *one-down* (referring to the electric toaster) for "an order of toast"; and *sparkle one* for "an order of Bromo-Seltzer." But what shall we say of the gay wastefulness of the following delightful expressions:

Adam's ale: Water
Clean up the kitchen: Hamburger; *also* hash
Coney Island bloodhounds: Frankfurters
Dough well done with cow to cover: Bread and butter

Draw one in the dark: Black coffee
Hudson River ale: Water
Noah's boy with Murphy carrying a wreath: Ham and potatoes with
cabbage
Shot out of the blue bottle: Bromo-Seltzer
Slab of moo—let him chew it: Rare rump steak
Twelve alive in a shell: A dozen raw oysters
Yesterday, today, and forever: Hash

They ignore the requirements of economy but provide verbal entertainment.

Taboo on Death

Another social attitude reflected in our language is the existence of all sorts of forbidden subjects which must be avoided or carefully disguised when we speak. The reasons for fear in connection with certain words and names are deep-lying and complicated. The use of such words presumably gives the speaker an exposed and vulnerable feeling, due ultimately to the magic powers originally attributed to language. (See chapter 1.) To name death, disease, and wounds was felt, and indeed, is still felt, to be a way of inviting their presence. Hence elaborate phrases are to be found among many types of people, civilized and uncivilized, to avoid use of the simple words "die" or "be sick." We use them too. The very persons who protest that death is a fortunate release into a happier hereafter, or that disease is a negligible inconvenience easily conquered, are most wary about using the simple straightforward words to describe these aspects of our mortality. They use euphemisms like "passing on" or "passing away" or "being taken away." They also use noncommittal terms about someone who is seriously ill. Of course it is true that another element appears in the situation when politeness impels us to avoid direct reference to topics unpleasing to the listener. This may or may not be true among all peoples, but we certainly pride ourselves on this motive so far as we ourselves are concerned. Nevertheless it is very likely that some of the old fear of spirits and demons lurks within us still. Rational as we may think we are, we can still feel for the peasant of the fairy tales who cries out carelessly: "May the Devil take this stubborn mule of mine"—and at once beholds the Old Man himself at his elbow, smiling and saying "Always ready to oblige!" We still feel in some obscure way that to name is to summon.

Nationalism

Language and politics offer a combination somewhat easier to investigate than language and indecency. Nevertheless we seldom stop to reflect upon the great import of language in political issues such as the conflict of nations. Many bloody struggles have centered about claims and oppressions which used languages as symbols. When people engage in agitation for political independence, one very appealing issue is the demand to use a native tongue for official purposes, and to have it taught in the schools. It is usually felt by the most indifferent of observers that a real grievance is endured by any people when foreign officials, supported by a foreign army, take over a school system and suddenly forbid the use of a language hitherto officially accepted, as well as dear and familiar, to the children. Suppressed patriotism frequently centers about the determination of families to maintain the despised language within the home, no matter what may happen to it in the courts and schools.

A conspicuous example is the faithful preservation of Polish as a national language when the country had been divided by three empires in the eighteenth century. A language is also a rallying point for peoples who have never enjoyed the privileges of nationhood in the modern sense. In Ireland the Gaelic speech was consistently repressed for centuries, and a child who inadvertently slipped into native idiom in the (exclusively English) schools was severely punished, according to nineteenth-century reports. Parallel situations may be found all over the world, especially in colonies and semi-colonial countries. Here the native peoples frequently have no access to any schools except those founded and maintained by an outside group, a linguistic minority who have established themselves by military or commercial invasion.

Today, when conquest succeeds conquest with terrifying rapidity, the shifts in official speech must be confusing in the extreme to young students. If there were time in the midst of world affairs, it would be very enlightening to have a study by trained psychologists on the emotional and mental difficulties engendered in students by some of the recent political shifts of territory. In some Central American countries the situation is very complex for different reasons. The Indian populations have quietly and faithfully retained the indigenous dialects as their primary speech; Spanish, the official language, is still regarded as the imposed dialect of a conquering minority. But Spanish itself now finds competition in English, employed by resident company officials, higher paid employees, wives, children, and teachers connected with the small "colony" of American business enterprises. If Spanish is still resented by many natives, it would be curious to know what attitude is being built up towards English, the super-language of rulers.

So strong is the feeling for language in relation to nationality that it is quite possible to resurrect a language long since dead and re-establish it among the living. Hebrew is an example in point. The tongue of the Bible had become extinct so far as everyday life is concerned, but the zeal of Jewish re-settlers in Palestine has made it once more a living and expanding medium.

In the conflict of nations, enthusiasts for one side or another sometimes claim superiority for their special language. They affirm that their cause must be right because their language is "naturally" better than that of the opponent. Such statements are based rather on emotion than scientific judgment. An over-patriotic German will claim that his language is superior because it has such qualities as *Innerlichkeit* and *Tiefe*—and he will prove this to you triumphantly by pointing to idioms carefully chosen for the purpose. On the other hand the complacent Frenchman, sure that civilization and France are co-extensive, will claim for his language a monopoly of lucidity: *"Tout ce qui est clair est français!"* It should be remembered, however, that the best scholars carefully avoid these extravagant and unscientific claims. The German *Literaturblatt* has frequently reproved linguistic flag-wavers for their excesses, with exemplary scientific honesty, and the French sins of a similar nature have been most devastatingly satirized by French-speaking scholars like Daniel Mornet, Charles Bally, and Ferdinand Brunot.

Undeveloped Languages

But, someone may urge, some languages *are* limited in one way or another. They may at this given moment have an inadequate vocabulary for modern needs, or their traditional syntax may be needlessly elaborate, or they may lack the use of simple common nouns like "tree" or "table" without which one cannot conceive of the philosophical "tree-in-general." Hence they can never rise to the abstractions of lofty Western European philosophy, with its tradition of abstract thought reaching back to Plato. If this is so, perhaps we are justified, after all, in thinking of such languages as really inferior, since they are handicapped by their very structure in comparison with our own.

We have touched on this question before, but it is so important that a bit of repetition is not out of place.

Let us grant that at this particular moment in world history some languages, remote from major currents of events, are less developed than others in the directions required by a dominant civilization based on industry and machines. The grammar may employ cumbersome, repetitious constructions to express simple relations. Nevertheless even these languages are dynamic, not static. Change is always going on, rapidly or slowly according to the stimulus of cultural change. The complex syntax may be simplified; the needed words borrowed or created by compounding. Even sentence structure is modified with the ages. Useless distinctions are sloughed off when the need for them has died. If this has occurred unconsciously, for the most part, in the past, it is increasingly done with conscious direction today.

Under kindly tutelage directed toward the people's cultural advancement, a backward language can be speedily adapted, out of its own potential resources, to meet the requirements of modern civilization. Franz Boas reports how young Indian students can be introduced to the concept of Platonic universals even though their language traditionally lacks unmodified common nouns. They can easily be taught to isolate the term "house" out of expressions meaning "that-house-yonder," "my-house-here," and "the-house-made-of-wood." In the same way medieval scholastics created abstractions like "quiddity" when they felt the need for them. At first the natives may feel that they are doing violence to their language, since traditional syntax demands that every noun must have a modifier; but once they have been made to feel the intellectual need for the bare term "house," they will accept the usage—and thus push the language ahead a thousand years in one generation. A minority may first avail itself of the development, but there is no inherent reason why its use may not become general. The potentiality was always there; all that was needed was to elicit its application in a new situation.

Unfortunately people speaking undeveloped languages have hitherto encountered more developed idioms in a highly unpleasant manner. It was difficult to appreciate the virtues of a more economic speech when fellow-tribesmen had just been massacred in large numbers by those using it. The results may be quite different when a more fraternal spirit prevails. When the emissaries of a modern culture arrive with no intent to exploit or deceive or oppress, and without any arrogant assumption of superiority, they may obtain quite a different reception. There will be no sullen resistance to linguistic instruction, we may assume, when there is no resentment or fear. Under such happy circumstances a backward language can surmount structural handicaps in a very short time. Deficiencies in vocabulary have never presented serious difficulties. There is no reason why such adaptations should be left to slow and bungling processes as in the past. Conscious direction may be desirable in this situation as in others where an interchange occurs between one culture and another. Rarely, in fact, is the debt exclusively on one side when two languages meet on such a basis, even if one is more "advanced" than the other.

Slogans

Of course there is no aspect of man's social life which is not reflected in his language. Politics too offers material for the linguist. He may amuse himself by collecting the metaphors engendered in a lively campaign, or analyzing the special vocabulary of modern war, or tabulating the semantic shifts which accompany a change like the French Revolution. Upsetting movements like that of 1789 create a new terminology, elevating humble terms and hurling ancient ones into the discard, to the perturbation of conservatives. Back in 1799 an irate opponent of *Liberté, Egalité, Fraternité* expressed his disapproval of the new order by publishing anonymously in Venice a satirical Dictionary—really a political tract—called *Nuovo Vocabolario Filosofico-Democratico*, "indispensable," as the title page announces, "for all who wish to understand the new revolutionary language." Among the clichés the author denounced were: "ally, alliance," which, he said, "is used by Democrats only when they plan deceit"; "hypocrisy," a term applied to Napoleon and his followers for flirting with religion after denouncing it; "perfection, to perfect" an optimistic formula of Enlightenment expressing the hope of human progress, here stigmatized by the author as the immoral and irreligious slogan of assassins. Other expressions to be found in the alphabetical index are: "celibate," "civic guard," "gazette," "regeneration," "revolution," and "tribunal." Political slogans that have been cordially loved have also been cordially hated, until in many cases the intellectual content (if any) has been submerged by emotional inundations.

The linguistic aspect of demagogy and political spellbinding deserves more study than it has hitherto received. The Institute of Propaganda Analysis has done useful work in exposing the psychologi-

cal devices employed. The rhetoric is just as interesting. For instance, archaisms are used, along with iteration, sound effects, epithets,
and so forth, to play on the feelings of the listeners. A Biblical flavor-
ing of seventeenth-century language will reinforce the appeal. Here
it is still possible to use extinct pronouns like "ye, thou, thee" or verbal
endings long since discarded, or constructions no longer understood
like "Woe worth the day!" Such phrases affect people all the more
because they are mysterious and unclear, with sacred connotations.
Likewise the figures of speech are kept archaic when appeal is made
to feeling rather than reason. Orators will speak of defending the
gates or the walls of the city even when none exist, as everyone knows.
Certain undefined terms like "free enterprise" or "rugged individual-
ism" are used in a manner to suggest incantations more readily than
reasoned exposition. Perhaps no department of human expression
justifies more clearly the cynical statement that the chief function of
language is to conceal thought.

Social Values of Clarity

Nevertheless we still use it, hopefully, to understand one another.
By becoming aware of limitations we begin to circumvent them.
Since language is so eminently social there is no end to the problems
interrelating society and language. Amateurs may provide themselves
with unending diversion if they wish to extend their original observation of language behavior into various special aspects of the subjects here indicated, and to others as well. In a living medium there
are always new developments, significantly indicative to the trained
listener. You will find that the correlation of social tendencies and
language will deepen your understanding of both: what you say and
the milieu in which you say it.

In language as in many other things awareness is the first step
towards intelligent adaptation and change. Laymen as well as professional linguists can have the fun and also the benefits of awareness.
A pencil, a notebook, and an alert ear are all you need. You will
learn much about yourself and your fellow man if you jot down striking phenomena connected with social concerns important for all of
us: not only those here surveyed, but others. And you may very possibly be ready in a short time to make an original contribution concerning your discoveries. Language is the heritage of all of us, and so
there is no reason why all of us may not be critical students of it—or
even creators in the use of it.

SABOTAGE IN SPRINGFIELD:
WEBSTER'S THIRD EDITION   *Wilson Follett*

Of dictionaries, as of newspapers, it might be said that the bad ones are too bad to exist, the good ones too good not to be better. No dictionary of a living language is perfect or ever can be, if only because the time required for compilation, editing, and issuance is so great that shadows of obsolescence are falling on parts of any such work before it ever gets into the hands of a user. Preparation of *Webster's Third New International Dictionary of the English Language* began intensively in the Springfield establishment of G. & C. Merriam Company in 1936, but the century was nine months into its seventh decade before any outsider could have his first look at what had been accomplished. His first look is, of course, incompetent to acquaint him with the merits of the new work; these no one can fully discover without months or years of everyday use. On the other hand, it costs only minutes to find out that what will rank as the great event of American linguistic history in this decade, and perhaps in this quarter century, is in many crucial particulars a very great calamity.

Why should the probable and possible superiorities of the Third New International be so difficult to assess, the shortcomings so easy? Because the superiorities are special, departmental, and recondite, the shortcomings general and within the common grasp. The new dictionary comes to us with a claim of 100,000 new words or new definitions. These run almost overwhelmingly to scientific and technological terms or meanings that have come into existence since 1934, and especially to words classified as ISV (belonging to the international scientific vocabulary). No one person can possibly use or even comprehend all of them; the coverage in this domain, certainly impressive to the nonspecialist, may or may not command the admiration of specialists. It is said that historians of the graphic arts and of architecture were displeased with the 1934 Webster, both for its omissions and for some definitions of what it included in their fields. Its 1961 successor may have disarmed their reservations; only they can pronounce.

But all of us may without brashness form summary judgments about the treatment of what belongs to all of us—the standard, staple, traditional language of general reading and speaking, the ordinary vocabu-

From *The Atlantic Monthly*, January, 1962. Reprinted with the permission of the author.

lary and idioms of novelist, essayist, letter writer, reporter, editorial writer, teacher, student, advertiser; in short, fundamental English. And it is precisely in this province that Webster III has thrust upon us a dismaying assortment of the questionable, the perverse, the unworthy, and the downright outrageous.

Furthermore, what was left out is as legitimate a grievance to the ordinary reader as anything that has been put in. Think—if you can—of an unabridged dictionary from which you cannot learn who Mark Twain was (though **mark twain** is entered as a leadsman's cry), or what were the names of the apostles, or that the Virgin was Mary the mother of Jesus of Nazareth, or what and where the District of Columbia is!

The disappointment and the shock are intensified, of course, because of the unchallenged position earned by the really unabridged immediate predecessor of this strange work. *Webster's New International Dictionary,* Second Edition (1934), consummated under the editorship of William Allan Neilson, at once became the most important reference book in the world to American writers, editors, teachers, students, and general readers—everyone to whom American English was a matter of serious interest. What better could the next revision do than extend the Second Edition in the direction of itself, bring it up to date, and correct its scattering of oversights and errata?

The 1934 dictionary had been, heaven knows, no citadel of conservatism, no last bastion of puristical bigotry. But it had made shrewd reports on the status of individual words; it had taken its clear, beautifully written definitions from fit uses of an enormous vocabulary by judicious users; it had provided accurate, impartial accounts of the endless guerrilla war between grammarian and anti-grammarian and so given every consultant the means to work out his own decisions. Who could wish the forthcoming revision any better fortune than a comparable success in applying the same standards to whatever new matter the new age imposed?

Instead, we have seen a century and a third of illustrious history largely jettisoned; we have seen a novel dictionary formula improvised, in great part out of snap judgments and the sort of theoretical improvement that in practice impairs; and we have seen the gates propped wide open in enthusiastic hospitality to miscellaneous confusions and corruptions. In fine, the anxiously awaited work that was to have crowned cisatlantic linguistic scholarship with a particular glory turns out to be a scandal and a disaster. Worse yet, it plumes itself on its faults and parades assiduously cultivated sins as virtues without precedent.

Examination cannot proceed far without revealing that Webster III, behind its front of passionless objectivity, is in truth a fighting document. And the enemy it is out to destroy is every obstinate vestige of linguistic punctilio, every surviving influence that makes for the upholding of standards, every criterion for distinguishing between better usages and worse. In other words, it has gone over bodily to the school that construes traditions as enslaving, the rudimentary principles of syntax as crippling, and taste as irrelevant. This revolution leaves it in the anomalous position of loudly glorifying its own ancestry—which is indeed glorious—while tacitly sabotaging the principles and ideals that brought the preceding Merriam-Webster to its unchallengeable preeminence. The Third New International is at once a resounding tribute of lip service to the Second and a wholesale repudiation of it—a sweeping act of apology, contrition, and reform.

The right-about-face is, of course, particularly evident in the vocabulary approved. Within a few days of publication the new dictionary was inevitably notorious for its unreserved acceptance as standard of *wise up, get hep* (it uses the second as a definition of the first), *ants in one's pants, one for the book, hugeous, nixie, passel, hepped up* (with *hepcat* and *hepster*), *anyplace, someplace,* and so forth. These and a swarm of their kind it admits to full canonical standing by the suppression of such qualifying status labels as *colloquial, slang, cant, facetious,* and *substandard*. The classification *colloquial* it abolishes outright: "it is impossible to know whether a word out of context is colloquial or not." Of *slang* it makes a chary occasional use despite a similar reservation: "No word is invariably slang, and many standard words can be given slang connotations or used so inappropriately as to become slang." *Cornball* is ranked as slang, *corny* is not.

The overall effect signifies a large-scale abrogation of one major responsibility of the lexicographer. He renounces it on the curious ground that helpful discriminations are so far beyond his professional competence that he is obliged to leave them to those who, professing no competence at all, have vainly turned to him for guidance. If some George Ade of the future, aspiring to execute a fable in slang, were to test his attempt by the status labels in Webster III, he would quickly discover with chagrin that he had expressed himself almost without exception in officially applauded English. With but slight exaggeration we can say that if an expression can be shown to have been used in print by some jaded reporter, some candidate for office or his speech writer, some potboiling minor novelist, it is well enough credentialed for the full blessing of the new lexicography.

This extreme tolerance of crude neologisms and of shabby diction generally, however, is but one comparatively trifling aspect of the campaign against punctilio. We begin to sound its deeper implications when we plunge into the definitions and the copious examples that illustrate and support them. Under the distributive pronoun *each* we find, side by side: "(each of them is to pay his own fine) (each of them are to pay their own fine)." Where could anyone look for a neater, more succinct way to outlaw the dusty dogma that a pronoun should agree in number with its antecedent? Here is the same maneuver again under another distributive, *everybody:* "usu. referred to by the third person singular (everybody is bringing his own lunch) but sometimes by a plural personal pronoun (everybody had made up their minds)." Or try *whom* and *whomever:* "(a . . . recruit whom he hoped would prove to be a crack salesman) (people . . . whom you never thought would sympathize) . . . (I go out to talk to whomever it is) . . . (he attacked whomever disagreed with him)." It is, then, all right to put the subject of a finite verb in the accusative case—"esp. after a preposition or a verb of which it might mistakenly be considered the object."

Shall we look into what our dictionary does with a handful of the more common solecisms, such as a publisher might introduce into a cooked-up test for would-be copy editors? Begin with *center around* (or *about*). It seems obvious that expressions derived from Euclidean geometry should make Euclidean sense. A center is a point; it is what things are around, not what is around them; they center *in* or *on* or *at* the point. The Second Edition defined the Great White Way as "That part of Broadway . . . centering about Times Square"—patently an oversight. Is it the same oversight that produces, in the Third: "heresy . . . 3: a group or school of thought centering around a particular heresy"? We look up *center* itself, and, lo: "(a story to tell, centered around the political development of a great state) . . . (more scholarship than usual was centered around the main problems)," followed by several equivalent specimens.

Here is *due to.* First we come on irreproachable definitions, irreproachably illustrated, of *due* noun and *due* adjective, and we think we are out of the woods. Alas, they are followed by the manufacture of a composite preposition, *due to*, got up solely to extenuate such abominations as "the event was canceled due to inclement weather." An adjective can modify a verb, then. And here is a glance at that peculiarly incriminating redundancy of the slipshod writer, *equally as:* "equally opposed to Communism as to Fascism." The intolerable *hardly than* or *scarcely than* construction is in full favor: "hardly had the birds dropped than she jumped into the water and retrieved them." The sequence *different than* has the double approbation of editorial use and a citation: conjunctive *unlike* means "in a manner that is different than," and a passage under *different* reads "vastly different in size than it was twenty-five years ago." Adjectival *unlike* and conjunctive *unlike* both get illustrations that implicitly commend the unanchored and grammarless modifier: "so many fine men were outside the charmed circle that, unlike most colleges, there was no disgrace in not being a club man"; "unlike in the gasoline engine, fuel does not enter the cylinder with air on the intake stroke."

This small scattering should not end without some notice of that darling of the advanced libertarians, *like* as a conjunction, first in the meaning of *as,* secondly (and more horribly) in that of *as if.* Now, it is well known to the linguistic historian that *like* was so used for a long time before and after Langland. But it is as well known that the language rather completely sloughed off this usage; that it has long been no more than a regional colloquialism, a rarely seen aberration among competent writers, or an artificially cultivated irritant among defiant ones. The *Saturday Evening Post,* in which *like* for *as* is probably more frequent than in any other painstakingly edited magazine, has seldom if ever printed that construction except in reproducing the speech or tracing the thoughts of characters to whom it might be considered natural. The arguments for *like* have been merely defensive and permissive. Not for centuries has there been any real pressure of authority on a writer to use *like* as a conjunction—until our Third New International Dictionary decided to exert its leverage.

How it is exerted will appear in the following: "(impromptu programs where they ask questions much like I do on the air) . . . (looks like they can raise better tobacco) (looks like he will get the job) (wore his clothes like he was . . . afraid of getting dirt on them) (was like he'd come back from a long trip) (acted like she felt sick) . . . (sounded like the motor had stopped) . . . (the violin now sounds like an old masterpiece should) (did it like he told me to) . . . (wanted a doll like she saw in the store window) . . . (anomalies like just had occurred)."

By the processes represented in the foregoing and countless others for which there is no room here, the latest Webster whittles away at one after another of the traditionary controls until there is little or nothing left of them. The controls, to be sure, have often enough been overvalued and overdone by pedants and purists, by martinets and bigots; but more often, and much more importantly, they have worked as aids toward dignified, workmanlike, and cogent uses of the wonderful language that is our inheritance. To erode and undermine them is to convert the language into a confusion of unchanneled, incalculable williwaws, a capricious wind blowing whithersoever it listeth. And that, if we are to judge by the total effect of the pages under scrutiny—2720 of them and nearly 8000 columns of vocabulary, all compact in Times Roman—is exactly what is wanted by the patient and dedicated saboteurs in Springfield. They, if they keep their ears to the ground, will hear many echoes of the despairing cry already wrung from one editorial assistant on a distinguished magazine that still puts its faith in standards: "Why have a Dictionary at all if anything goes?"

The definitions are reinforced, it will have been conveyed, with copious citations from printed sources. These citations occupy a great fraction of the total space. They largely account for the reduction in the number of entries (from 600,000 to 450,000) and for the elimination of the Gazetteer, the Biographical Dictionary, and the condensed key to pronunciation and symbols that ran across the bottoms of facing pages—all very material deprivations. Some 14,000 authors, we are told, are represented in the illustrative quotations—"mostly from the mid-twentieth century."

Can some thousands of authors truly worth space in a dictionary ever be found in any one brief period? Such a concentration can hardly fail to be, for the purposes of a dictionary, egregiously overweighted with the contemporary and the transient. Any very short period, such as a generation, is a period of transition in the history of English, and any great mass of examples drawn primarily from it will be disproportionately focused on transitional and ephemeral elements. To say that recording English *as we find it today* is precisely the purpose of a new dictionary is not much of a retort. For the bulk of the language that we use has come down to us with but minor, glacially

slow changes from time out of mind, and a worthy record of it must
stand on a much broader base than the fashions of yesterday.

It is, then, a mercy that among the thousands of scraps from recent
authors, many of them still producing, we can also find hundreds from
Shakespeare, the English Bible, Fielding, Dickens, Hawthorne, Mel-
ville, Henry James, Mark Twain, and so on. But the great preponder-
ance of latter-day prose, little of it worth repeating and a good deal
of it hardly worth printing in the first place, is likely to curtail by years
the useful life of the Third New International.

So much is by the way. When we come to the definitions proper
we face something new, startling, and formidable in lexicography.
The definitions, all of them conformed to a predetermined rhetorical
pattern, may be products of a theory—Gestaltist, perhaps?—of how the
receiving mind works. The pattern, in the editor's general preface, is
described as follows: "The primary objective of precise, sharp defining
has been met through development of a new dictionary style based
upon completely analytical one-phrase definitions throughout the book.
Since the headword in a definition is intended to be modified only by
structural elements restrictive in some degree and essential to each
other, the use of commas either to separate or to group has been
severely limited, chiefly to elements in apposition or in series. The
new defining pattern does not provide for a predication which conveys further expository comment."

This doctrine of the strictly unitary definition is of course formulated and applied in the interest of a logical integrity and a simplification never before consistently attained by lexical definitions. What
it produces, when applied with the rigor here insisted on, is in the first
place some of the oddest prose ever concocted by pundits. A typical
specimen, from the definition of the simplest possible term: "**rabbit
punch . . . :** a short chopping blow delivered to the back of the neck
or the base of the skull with the edge of the hand opposite the thumb
that is illegal in boxing." When the idea, being not quite so simple,
requires the one-phrase statement of several components, the definition
usually turns out to be a great unmanageable and unpunctuated blob
of words strung out beyond the retentive powers of most minds that
would need the definition at all. Both theory and result will emerge
clearly enough from a pair of specimens, the first dealing with a
familiar everyday noun, the second with a mildly technical one:

> **groan . . . 1:** a deep usu. inarticulate and involuntary often stran-
> gled sound typically abruptly begun and ended and usu. indicative

of pain or grief or tension or desire or sometimes disapproval or
annoyance

kymograph . . . **1:** a recording device including an electric motor
or clockwork that drives a usu. slowly revolving drum which carries a
roll of plain or smoked paper and also having an arrangement for
tracing on the paper by means of a stylus a graphic record of motion
or pressure (as of the organs of speech, blood pressure, or respiration)
often in relation to particular intervals of time.

About these typical definitions as prose, there is much that any
good reader might well say. What must be said is that the grim suppression of commas is a mere crotchet. It takes time to read such
definitions anyway; commas in the right places would speed rather
than slow the reading and would clarify rather than obscure the sense,
so that the unitary effect—largely imaginary at best—would be more
helped than hurt. In practice, the one-phrase design without further
expository predication lacks all the asserted advantages over a com-
petently written definition of the free conventional sort; it is merely
more difficult to write, often impossible to write well, and tougher to
take in. Compare the corresponding definitions from the Second
Edition:

groan . . . A low, moaning sound; usually, a deep, mournful sound
uttered in pain or great distress; sometimes, an expression of strong
disapprobation; as, the remark was received with *groans.*

kymograph . . . **a** An automatic apparatus consisting of a motor revolving a drum covered with smoked paper, on which curves of pressure, etc., may be traced.

Everyone professionally concerned with the details of printed English can be grateful to the new Webster for linking the parts of various
expressions that have been either hyphenated compounds or separate
words—*highlight, highbrow* and *lowbrow, overall, wisecrack, lowercase* and *uppercase,* and so on. Some of the unions now recognized
were long overdue; many editors have already got them written into
codes of house usage. But outside this small province the new work
is a copy editor's despair, a propounder of endless riddles.

What, for example, are we to make of the common abbreviations
i.e. and *e.g.?* The first is entered in the vocabulary as **ie** (no periods,
no space), the second as **e g** (space, no periods). In the preliminary
list, "Abbreviations Used in This Dictionary," both are given the customary periods. (Oddly, the list translates its *i.e.* into "that is," but

merely expands *e.g.* into "exempli gratia.") Is one to follow the vocabulary or the list? What point has the seeming inconsistency?

And what about capitalization? All vocabulary entries are in lowercase except for such abbreviations as ARW (air raid warden), MAB (medical advisory board), and PX (post exchange). Words possibly inviting capitalization are followed by such injunctions as *cap, usu cap, sometimes not cap, usu cap 1st A, usu cap A&B.* (One of the small idiosyncrasies is that "usu.," the most frequent abbreviation, is given a period when roman, denied it when italic.) From **america,** adjective—all proper nouns are excluded—to **american yew** there are over 175 consecutive entries that require such injunctions; would it not have been simpler and more economical to capitalize the entries? A flat *"cap,"* of course, means "always capitalized." But how often is "usually," and when is "sometimes"? We get dictionaries expressly that they may settle such problems for us. This dictionary seems to make a virtue of leaving them in flux, with the explanation that many matters are subjective and that the individual must decide them for himself—a curious abrogation of authority in a work extolled as "more useful and authoritative than any previous dictionary."

The rock-bottom practical truth is that the lexicographer cannot abrogate his authority if he wants to. He may think of himself as a detached scientist reporting the facts of language, declining to recommend use of anything or abstention from anything; but the myriad consultants of his work are not going to see him so. He helps create, not a book of fads and fancies and private opinions, but a Dictionary of the English Language. It comes to every reader under auspices that say, not "Take it or leave it," but rather something like this: "Here in 8000 columns is a definitive report of what a synod of the most trustworthy American experts consider the English language to be in the seventh decade of the twentieth century. This is your language; take it and use it. And if you use it in conformity with the principles and practices here exemplified, your use will be the most accurate attainable by any American of this era." The fact that the compilers disclaim authority and piously refrain from judgments is meaningless: the work itself, by virtue of its inclusions and exclusions, its mere existence, is a whole universe of judgments, received by millions as the Word from on high.

And there we have the reason why it is so important for the dictionary maker to keep his discriminations sharp, why it is so damaging if he lets them get out of working order. Suppose he enters a new definition for no better reason than that some careless, lazy, or uninformed scribbler has jumped to an absurd conclusion about what a word means or has been too harassed to run down the word he really wanted. This new definition is going to persuade tens of thousands that, say, *cohort,* a word of multitude, means one associate or crony "(he and three alleged housebreaking cohorts were arraigned on attempted burglary charges)" or that the vogue word *ambivalence,* which denotes simultaneous love and hatred of someone or something, means "continual oscillation between one thing and its opposite (novels . . . vitiated by an ambivalence between satire and sentimentalism)." To what is the definer contributing if not to subversion and decay? To the swallower of the definition it never occurs that he can have drunk corruption from a well that he has every reason to trust as the ultimate in purity. Multiply him by the number of people simultaneously influenced, and the resulting figure by the years through which the influence continues, and a great deal of that product by the influences that will be disseminated through speech and writing and teaching, and you begin to apprehend the scope of the really enormous disaster that can and will be wrought by the lexicographer's abandonment of his responsibility.

BUT WHAT'S A DICTIONARY FOR?   *Bergen Evans*

The storm of abuse in the popular press that greeted the appearance of *Webster's Third New International Dictionary* is a curious phenomenon. Never has a scholarly work of this stature been attacked with such unbridled fury and contempt. An article in the *Atlantic* viewed it as a "disappointment," a "shock," a "calamity," "a scandal and a disaster." The New York *Times,* in a special editorial, felt that the work would "accelerate the deterioration" of the language and sternly accused the editors of betraying a public trust. The *Journal* of the American Bar Association saw the publication as "deplorable," "a flagrant example of lexicographic irresponsibility," "a serious blow to the cause of good English." *Life* called it "a non-word deluge," "monstrous," "abominable," and "a cause for dismay." They doubted that "Lincoln could have modelled his Gettysburg Address" on it—a concept of how things get written that throws very little light on Lincoln but a great deal on *Life.*

From *The Atlantic Monthly,* May, 1962. Reprinted with the permission of the author.

What underlies all this sound and fury? Is the claim of the G. & C. Merriam Company, probably the world's greatest dictionary maker, that the preparation of the work cost $3.5 million, that it required the efforts of three hundred scholars over a period of twenty-seven years, working on the largest collection of citations ever assembled in any language—is all this a fraud, a hoax?

So monstrous a discrepancy in evaluation requires us to examine basic principles. Just what's a dictionary for? What does it propose to do? What does the common reader go to a dictionary to find? What has the purchaser of a dictionary a right to expect for his money?

Before we look at basic principles, it is necessary to interpose two brief statements. The first of these is that a dictionary is concerned with words. Some dictionaries give various kinds of other useful information. Some have tables of weights and measures on the flyleaves. Some list historical events, and some, home remedies. And there's nothing wrong with their so doing. But the great increase in our vocabulary in the past three decades compels all dictionaries to make more efficient use of their space. And if something must be eliminated, it is sensible to throw out these extraneous things and stick to words.

Yet wild wails arose. The *Saturday Review* lamented that one can no longer find the goddess Astarte under a separate heading—though they point out that a genus of mollusks named after the goddess is included! They seemed to feel that out of sheer perversity the editors of the dictionary stooped to mollusks while ignoring goddesses and that, in some way, this typifies modern lexicography. Mr. Wilson Follett, folletizing (his mental processes demand some special designation) in the *Atlantic,* cried out in horror that one is not even able to learn from the Third International "that the Virgin was Mary the mother of Jesus"!

The second brief statement is that there has been even more progress in the making of dictionaries in the past thirty years than there has been in the making of automobiles. The difference, for example, between the much-touted Second International (1934) and the much-clouted Third International (1961) is not like the difference between yearly models but like the difference between the horse and buggy and the automobile. Between the appearance of these two editions a whole new science related to the making of dictionaries, the science of descriptive linguistics, has come into being.

Modern linguistics gets its charter from Leonard Bloomfield's *Language* (1933). Bloomfield, for thirteen years professor of Germanic philology at the University of Chicago and for nine years professor of linguistics at Yale, was one of those inseminating scholars who can't be relegated to any department and don't dream of accepting established categories and procedures just because they're established. He was as much an anthropologist as a linguist, and his concepts of language were shaped not by Strunk's *Elements of Style* but by his knowledge of Cree Indian dialects.

The broad general findings of the new science are:

1. All languages are systems of human conventions, not systems of natural laws. The first—and essential—step in the study of any language is observing and setting down precisely what happens when native speakers speak it.

2. Each language is unique in its pronunciation, grammar, and vocabulary. It cannot be described in terms of logic or of some theoretical, ideal language. It cannot be described in terms of any other language, or even in terms of its own past.

3. All languages are dynamic rather than static, and hence a "rule" in any language can only be a statement of contemporary practice. Change is constant—and normal.

4. "Correctness" can rest only upon usage, for the simple reason that there is nothing else for it to rest on. And all usage is relative.

From these propositions it follows that a dictionary is good only insofar as it is a comprehensive and accurate description of current usage. And to be comprehensive it must include some indication of social and regional associations.

New dictionaries are needed because English has changed more in the past two generations than at any other time in its history. It has had to adapt to extraordinary cultural and technological changes, two world wars, unparalleled changes in transportation and communication, and unprecedented movements of populations.

More subtly, but pervasively, it has changed under the influence of mass education and the growth of democracy. As written English is used by increasing millions and for more reasons than ever before, the language has become more utilitarian and more informal. Every publication in America today includes pages that would appear, to the purist of forty years ago, unbuttoned gibberish. Not that they are; they simply show that you can't hold the language of one generation up as a model for the next.

It's not that you mustn't. You *can't*. For example, in the issue in which *Life* stated editorially that it would follow the Second International, there were over forty words, constructions, and meanings which are in the Third International but not in the Second. The issue of the New York *Times* which hailed the Second International as the authority to which it would adhere and the Third International as a scandal and a betrayal which it would reject used one hundred and fifty-three separate words, phrases, and constructions which are listed in the Third International but not in the Second and nineteen others which are condemned in the Second. Many of them are used many times, more than three hundred such uses in all. The Washington *Post*, in an editorial captioned "Keep Your Old Webster's," says, in the first sentence, "don't throw it away," and in the second, "hang on to it." But the old Webster's labels *don't* "colloquial" and doesn't include "hang on to," in this sense, at all.

In short, all of these publications are written in the language that the Third International describes, even the very editorials which scorn it. And this is no coincidence, because the Third International isn't setting up any new standards at all; it is simply describing what *Life*, the Washington *Post*, and the New York *Times* are doing. Much of the dictionary's material comes from these very publications, the *Times*, in particular, furnishing more of its illustrative quotations than any other newspaper.

And the papers have no choice. No journal or periodical could sell a single issue today if it restricted itself to the American language of twenty-eight years ago. It couldn't discuss half the things we are interested in, and its style would seem stiff and cumbrous. If the editorials were serious, the public—and the stockholders—have reason to be grateful that the writers on these publications are more literate than the editors.

And so back to our questions: what's a dictionary for, and how, in 1962, can it best do what it ought to do? The demands are simple. The common reader turns to a dictionary for information about the spelling, pronunciation, meaning, and proper use of words. He wants to know what is current and respectable. But he wants—and has a right to—the truth, the full truth. And the full truth about any language, and especially about American English today, is that there are many areas in which certainty is impossible and simplification is misleading.

Even in so settled a matter as spelling, a dictionary cannot always be absolute. *Theater* is correct, but so is *theatre*. And so are *traveled* and *travelled*, *plow* and *plough*, *catalog* and *catalogue*, and scores of other variants. The reader may want a single certainty. He may have

taken an unyielding position in an argument, he may have wagered in
support of his conviction and may demand that the dictionary "settle"
the matter. But neither his vanity nor his purse is any concern of the
dictionary's; it must record the facts. And the fact here is that there
are many words in our language which may be spelled, with equal
correctness, in either of two ways.

So with pronunciation. A citizen listening to his radio might notice
that James B. Conant, Bernard Baruch, and Dwight D. Eisenhower
pronounce *economics* as ECKuhnomiks, while A. Whitney Griswold,
Adlai Stevenson, and Herbert Hoover pronounce it EEKuhnomiks.
He turns to the dictionary to see which of the two pronunciations is
"right" and finds that they are both acceptable.

Has he been betrayed? Has the dictionary abdicated its responsibility? Should it say that one *must* speak like the president of Harvard
or like the president of Yale, like the thirty-first President of the
United States or like the thirty-fourth? Surely it's none of its business
to make a choice. Not because of the distinction of these particular
speakers; lexicography, like God, is no respecter of persons. But because so widespread and conspicuous a use of two pronunciations
among people of this elevation shows that there *are* two pronunciations. Their speaking establishes the fact which the dictionary must
record.

Among the "enormities" with which *Life* taxes the Third International is its listing of "the common mispronunciation" *heighth*. That
it is labeled a "dialectal variant" seems, somehow, to compound the
felony. But one hears the word so pronounced, and if one professes to
give a full account of American English in the 1960s, one has to take
some cognizance of it. All people do not possess *Life's* intuitive perception that the word is so "monstrous" that even to list it as a dialect
variation is to merit scorn. Among these, by the way, was John
Milton, who, in one of the greatest passages in all literature, besought
the Holy Spirit to raise him to the "highth" of his great argument.
And even the *Oxford English Dictionary* is so benighted as to list it,
in full boldface, right alongside of *Height* as a variant that has been
in the language since at least 1290.

Now there are still, apparently, millions of Americans who retain,
in this as in much else, some of the speech of Milton. This particular
pronunciation seems to be receding, but the *American Dialect Dictionary* still records instances of it from almost every state on the
Eastern seaboard and notes that it is heard from older people and

"occasionally in educated speech," "common with good speakers," "general," "widespread."

Under these circumstances, what is a dictionary to do? Since millions speak the word this way, the pronunciation can't be ignored. Since it has been in use as long as we have any record of English and since it has been used by the greatest writers, it can't be described as substandard or slang. But it is heard now only in certain localities. That makes it a dialectal pronunciation, and an honest dictionary will list it as such. What else can it do? Should it do?

The average purchaser of a dictionary uses it most often, probably, to find out what a word "means." As a reader, he wants to know what an author intended to convey. As a speaker or writer, he wants to know what a word will convey to his auditors. And this, too, is complex, subtle, and forever changing.

An illustration is furnished by an editorial in the Washington *Post* (January 17, 1962). After a ringing appeal to those who "love truth and accuracy" and the usual bombinations about "abdication of authority" and "barbarism," the editorial charges the Third International with "pretentious and obscure verbosity" and specifically instances its definition of "so simple an object as a door."

The definition reads:

> a movable piece of firm material or a structure supported usu. along one side and swinging on pivots or hinges, sliding along a groove, rolling up and down, revolving as one of four leaves, or folding like an accordion by means of which an opening may be closed or kept open for passage into or out of a building, room, or other covered enclosure or a car, airplane, elevator, or other vehicle.

Then follows a series of special meanings, each particularly defined and, where necessary, illustrated by a quotation.

Since, aside from roaring and admonishing the "gentlemen from Springfield" that "accuracy and brevity are virtues," the *Post's* editorial fails to explain what is wrong with the definition, we can only infer from "so simple" a thing that the writer takes the plain, downright, man-in-the-street attitude that a door is a door and any damn fool knows that.

But if so, he has walked into one of lexicography's biggest booby traps: the belief that the obvious is easy to define. Whereas the opposite is true. Anyone can give a fair description of the strange, the

new, or the unique. It's the commonplace, the habitual, that challenges definition, for its very commonness compels us to define it in
uncommon terms. Dr. Johnson was ridiculed on just this score when
his dictionary appeared in 1755. For two hundred years his definition
of a network as "any thing reticulated or decussated, at equal dis-
tances, with interstices between the intersections" has been good for
a laugh. But in the merriment one thing is always overlooked: no
one has yet come up with a better definition! Subsequent dictionaries
defined it as a mesh and then defined a mesh as a network. That's
simple, all right.

Anyone who attempts sincerely to state what the word *door* means
in the United States of America today can't take refuge in a log cabin.
There has been an enormous proliferation of closing and demarking
devices and structures in the past twenty years, and anyone who tries
to thread his way through the many meanings now included under
door may have to sacrifice brevity to accuracy and even have to employ words that a limited vocabulary may find obscure.

Is the entrance to a tent a door, for instance? And what of the
thing that seals the exit of an airplane? Is this a door? Or what of
those sheets and jets of air that are now being used, in place of old-
fashioned oak and hinges, to screen entrances and exits. Are they
doors? And what of those accordion-like things that set off various
sections of many modern apartments? The fine print in the lease
takes it for granted that they are doors and that spaces demarked by
them are rooms—and the rent is computed on the number of rooms.

Was I gypped by the landlord when he called the folding contrap-
tion that shuts off my kitchen a door? I go to the Second International, which the editor of the *Post* urges me to use in preference to
the Third International. Here I find that a door is

> The movable frame or barrier of boards, or other material, usually
> turning on hinges or pivots or sliding, by which an entranceway into a
> house or apartment is closed and opened; also, a similar part of a piece
> of furniture, as in a cabinet or bookcase.

This is only forty-six words, but though it includes the cellar door, it
excludes the barn door and the accordion-like thing.

So I go on to the Third International. I see at once that the new
definition is longer. But I'm looking for accuracy, and if I must sacrifice brevity to get it, then I must. And, sure enough, in the definition
which raised the *Post's* blood pressure, I find the words "folding like

an accordion." The thing *is* a door, and my landlord is using the word in one of its currently accepted meanings.

We don't turn to a work of reference merely for confirmation. We all have words in our vocabularies which we have misunderstood, and to come on the true meaning of one of these words is quite a shock. All our complacency and self-esteem rise to oppose the discovery. But eventually we must accept the humiliation and laugh it off as best we can.

Some, often those who have set themselves up as authorities, stick to their error and charge the dictionary with being in a conspiracy against them. They are sure that their meaning is the only "right" one. And when the dictionary doesn't bear them out they complain about "permissive" attitudes instead of correcting their mistake.

The New York *Times* and the *Saturday Review* both regarded as contemptibly "permissive" the fact that one meaning of one word was illustrated by a quotation from Polly Adler. But a rudimentary knowledge of the development of any language would have told them that the underworld has been a far more active force in shaping and enriching speech than all the synods that have ever convened. Their attitude is like that of the patriot who canceled his subscription to the *Dictionary of American Biography* when he discovered that the very first volume included Benedict Arnold!

The ultimate of "permissiveness," singled out by almost every critic for special scorn, was the inclusion in the Third International of *finalize*. It was this, more than any other one thing, that was given as the reason for sticking to the good old Second International—that "peerless authority on American English," as the *Times* called it. But if it was such an authority, why didn't they look into it? They would have found *finalize* if they had.

And why shouldn't it be there? It exists. It's been recorded for two generations. Millions employ it every day. Two Presidents of the United States—men of widely differing cultural backgrounds—have used it in formal statements. And so has the Secretary-General of the United Nations, a man of unusual linguistic attainments. It isn't permitting the word but omitting it that would break faith with the reader. Because it is exactly the sort of word we want information about.

To list it as substandard would be to imply that it is used solely by the ignorant and the illiterate. But this would be a misrepresentation: President Kennedy and U Thant are highly educated men, and both are articulate and literate. It isn't even a freak form. On the contrary, it is a classic example of a regular process of development in English, a process which has given us such thoroughly accepted words as *generalize, minimize, formalize,* and *verbalize.* Nor can it be dismissed on logical grounds or on the ground that it is a mere duplication of *complete.* It says something that *complete* doesn't say and says it in a way that is significant in the modern bureaucratic world: one usually *completes* something which he has initiated but *finalizes* the work of others.

One is free to dislike the word. I don't like it. But the editor of a dictionary has to examine the evidence for a word's existence and seek it in context to get, as clearly and closely as he can, the exact meaning that it conveys to those who use it. And if it is widely used by well-educated, literate, reputable people, he must list it as a standard word. He is not compiling a volume of his own prejudices.

An individual's use of his native tongue is the surest index to his position within his community. And those who turn to a dictionary expect from it some statement of the current status of a word or a grammatical construction. And it is with the failure to assume this function that modern lexicography has been most fiercely charged. The charge is based on a naïve assumption that simple labels can be attached in all instances. But they can't. Some words are standard in some constructions and not in others. There may be as many shades of status as of meaning, and modern lexicography instead of abdicating this function has fulfilled it to a degree utterly unknown to earlier dictionaries.

Consider the word *fetch,* meaning to "go get and bring to." Until recently a standard word of full dignity ("Fetch me, I pray thee, a little water in a vessel"—I Kings 17:10), it has become slightly tainted. Perhaps the command latent in it is resented as undemocratic. Or maybe its use in training dogs to retrieve has made some people feel that it is an undignified word to apply to human beings. But, whatever the reason, there is a growing uncertainty about its status, and hence it is the sort of word that conscientious people look up in a dictionary.

Will they find it labeled "good" or "bad"? Neither, of course, because either applied indiscriminately would be untrue. The Third International lists nineteen different meanings of the verb *to fetch.* Of these some are labeled "dialectal," some "chiefly dialectal," some "obsolete," one "chiefly Scottish," and two "not in formal use." The primary meaning—"to go after and bring back"—is not labeled and hence can be accepted as standard, accepted with the more assurance because the many shades of labeling show us that the word's status has been carefully considered.

On grammatical questions the Third International tries to be equally exact and thorough. Sometimes a construction is listed without comment, meaning that in the opinion of the editors it is unquestionably respectable. Sometimes a construction carries the comment "used by speakers and writers on all educational levels though disapproved by some grammarians." Or the comment may be "used in substandard speech and formerly also by reputable writers." Or "less often in standard than in substandard speech." Or simply "dial."

And this very accurate reporting is based on evidence which is presented for our examination. One may feel that the evidence is inadequate or that the evaluation of it is erroneous. But surely, in the face of classification so much more elaborate and careful than any known heretofore, one cannot fly into a rage and insist that the dictionary is "out to destroy . . . every vestige of linguistic punctilio . . . every criterion for distinguishing between better usages and worse."

Words, as we have said, are continually shifting their meanings and connotations and hence their status. A word which has dignity, say, in the vocabulary of an older person may go down in other people's estimation. Like *fetch*. The older speaker is not likely to be aware of this and will probably be inclined to ascribe the snickers of the young at his speech to that degeneration of manners which every generation has deplored in its juniors. But a word which is coming up in the scale—like *jazz*, say, or, more recently, *crap*—will strike his ear at once. We are much more aware of offenses given us than of those we give. And if he turns to a dictionary and finds the offending word listed as standard—or even listed, apparently—his response is likely to be an outburst of indignation.

But the dictionary can neither snicker nor fulminate. It records. It will offend many, no doubt, to find the expression *wise up*, meaning to inform or to become informed, listed in the Third International with no restricting label. To my aging ears it still sounds like slang. But the evidence—quotations from the *Kiplinger Washington Letter* and the *Wall Street Journal*—convinces me that it is I who am out of step, lagging behind. If such publications have taken to using *wise up* in serious contexts, with no punctuational indication of irregularity, then it is obviously respectable. And finding it so listed and supported, I can only say that it's nice to be informed and sigh to realize that I am becoming an old fogy. But, of course, I don't have to use it (and I'll be damned if I will! "Let them smile, as I do now, At the old forsaken bough Where I cling").

In part, the trouble is due to the fact that there is no standard for standard. Ideas of what is proper to use in serious dignified speech and writing are changing—and with breathtaking rapidity. This is one of the major facts of contemporary American English. But it is no more the dictionary's business to oppose this process than to speed it up.

Even in our standard speech some words are more dignified and some more informal than others, and dictionaries have tried to guide us through these uncertainties by marking certain words and constructions as "colloquial," meaning "inappropriate in a formal situation." But this distinction, in the opinion of most scholars, has done more harm than good. It has created the notion that these particular words are inferior, when actually they might be the best possible words in an informal statement. And so—to the rage of many reviewers—the Third International has dropped this label. Not all labels, as angrily charged, but only this one out of a score. And the doing so may have been an error, but it certainly didn't constitute "betrayal" or "abandoning of all distinctions." It was intended to end a certain confusion.

In all the finer shades of meaning, of which the status of a word is only one, the user is on his own, whether he likes it or not. Despite *Life's* artless assumption about the Gettysburg Address, nothing worth writing is written *from* a dictionary. The dictionary, rather, comes along afterwards and describes what *has been* written.

Words in themselves are not dignified, or silly, or wise, or malicious. But they can be used in dignified, silly, wise, or malicious ways by dignified, silly, wise, or malicious people. *Egghead,* for example, is a perfectly legitimate word, as legitimate as *highbrow* or *long-haired.* But there is something very wrong and very undignified, by civilized standards, in a belligerent dislike for intelligence and education. *Yak* is an amusing word for persistent chatter. Anyone could say, "We were just yakking over a cup of coffee," with no harm to his dignity. But to call a Supreme Court decision *yakking* is to be vulgarly insulting and so, undignified. Again, there's nothing wrong with *confab* when it's appropriate. But when the work of a great research project, employing hundreds of distinguished scholars over several decades and involving the honor of one of the greatest publishing houses in the world, is described as *confabbing* (as the New York *Times* editorially described the preparation of the Third International), the use of this particular word asserts that the lexicographers had merely sat around and talked idly. And the statement becomes undignified—if not, indeed, slanderous.

The lack of dignity in such statements is not in the words, nor in the dictionaries that list them, but in the hostility that deliberately seeks this tone of expression. And in expressing itself the hostility frequently shows that those who are expressing it don't know how to use a dictionary. Most of the reviewers seem unable to read the Third International and unwilling to read the Second.

The *American Bar Association Journal*, for instance, in a typical outburst ("a deplorable abdication of responsibility"), picked out for special scorn the inclusion in the Third International of the word *irregardless*. "As far as the new Webster's is concerned," said the *Journal*, "this meaningless verbal bastard is just as legitimate as any other word in the dictionary." Thirty seconds spent in examining the book they were so roundly condemning would have shown them that in it *irregardless* is labeled "nonstand"—which means "nonstandard," which means "not conforming to the usage generally characteristic of educated native speakers of the language." Is that "just as legitimate as any other word in the dictionary"?

The most disturbing fact of all is that the editors of a dozen of the most influential publications in America today are under the impression that *authoritative* must mean *authoritarian*. Even the "permissive" Third International doesn't recognize this identification—editors' attitudes being not yet, fortunately, those of the American people. But the Fourth International may have to.

The new dictionary may have many faults. Nothing that tries to meet an ever-changing situation over a terrain as vast as contemporary English can hope to be free of them. And much in it is open to honest, and informed, disagreement. There can be linguistic objection to the eradication of proper names. The removal of guides to pronunciation from the foot of every page may not have been worth the valuable space it saved. The new method of defining words of many meanings has disadvantages as well as advantages. And of the half million or more definitions, hundreds, possibly thousands, may seem inadequate or imprecise. To some (of whom I am one) the omission of the label "colloquial" will seem meritorious; to others it will seem a loss.

But one thing is certain: anyone who solemnly announces in the year 1962 that he will be guided in matters of English usage by a dictionary published in 1934 is talking ignorant and pretentious nonsense.

THE PROBLEM OF FACT AND VALUE
IN THE TEACHING OF ENGLISH

Morton W. Bloomfield

The increase of accurate knowledge about the history of the English language and of linguistic processes in general during the last hundred years has begun only recently to have its impact upon the teaching of English, and especially of grammar, in the schools. Greater and more accurate knowledge is bound to affect the attitudes toward and the aims of any academic subject as well as its content. It is therefore proper to consider just what changes are called for in the teaching of English on the basis of our enlarged knowledge.

Some linguists in America during the last two decades have become exercised over the traditional prescriptionist attitude toward grammar which has long been one of the chief factors contributing to the conviction held by a vast majority of Americans that the "rules" of grammar are laws, in the same sense as the regularities of nature were laws in nineteenth-century eyes, or moral imperatives on a level with the Ten Commandments. Some, in disgust, have been led to the extreme of suggesting that "anything goes," that one should leave one's language alone, and that all teaching of English should be confined to a description of the state of the language or to its history. Very recently, in American cultural and literary journals, there have been disputes between these ardent linguists and those who favor some kind of prescriptionist approach. At the same time, one hears over and over again, in the teaching and other professions, the wail that young people do not know how to read and write their own language.

Embedded in these disputes and complaints is a philosophic problem of the first magnitude of which many participants do not seem to be aware—the relation of fact to value. In the background are tacit assumptions about this relationship which, if they cannot be simply solved, should at least be thrust into the light. The purpose of this ar-

From *College English*, October, 1953. Reprinted with the permission of the National Council of Teachers of English, and of the author.

ticle is to point up some of these basic issues in their bearing on the teaching of English in the schools.

The problem of what to teach to youngsters in English is first of all a question of value not of fact. As Professor Northrop has written: "The characteristic of a problem of value . . . is that, in part at least, it raises a question concerning what ought to be, rather than what is, the case." [1] The question of the relation of fact to value is an exceedingly complex one. That facts have some bearing on value is clear. What man ought to do is at least limited by what he is; the values set up or discovered cannot violate his nature. On the other hand, the mere presence of certain facts does not make them valuable. Possibly more than 50 per cent of humanity desire to steal, at least on occasion, but this "fact" does not mean that stealing is a value. When Hegel wrote that whatever is is right, what he meant was that everything has a reason, that is, is capable of rational explanation. He did not necessarily approve of whatever is. Some social scientists and linguists, however, follow Hegel's dictum to the letter.

The problem of value impinges on the science of linguistics on various levels, but it is not my intention here to discuss the general philosophical issues involved but to limit myself to their bearing on the subject of teaching English. There is, for example, the problem of value involved in the very subject matter of the science. The question of what language is must be answered, implicitly or explicitly, before the subject matter of linguistics can be properly delimited and understood. This involves general values, but they shall not be my concern here.[2] I shall start with the assumption—not completely agreed upon—that we know what language is and what its facts are.

In relation to the teaching of English the question of what ought to be taught about the language to students cannot be completely answered by a knowledge of the facts of the language (or by linguists as linguists), because, first, value questions are never completely answered by the facts and, second, facts and values from areas other than language must be taken into consideration. Furthermore, the aim of education is not a linguistic question.

In order to decide what ought to be taught in elementary English classes, we not only have to find out what are the facts of language but what are the facts of society and man, problems which are difficult and which involve from the very beginning value questions. We are

[1] *The Logic of the Sciences and the Humanities* (New York, 1947), p. 20.
[2] For my views on this subject see "Some Problems of Method in Linguistics," *Studium Generale,* V (August, 1952), 437–43.

concerned with what we want to do for a child; with the desirability of advocating norms in the speaking and writing of English and with educational aims generally. Everyone who argues what ought to be taught in English classes—even those who believe that nothing should be recommended—has made certain value judgments as to the nature of man, society, and education and as to what a command of language means. Ultimately, the question which we must basically consider in dealing with the teaching of English is what kind of men we want to make of our students. This cannot be solved by a knowledge of the history of the English language.

The general picture of man behind the pure descriptionist's recommendation is a completely passive one. Having discovered that language is always changing and that past attempts to fix it have failed,[3] he concludes that language should be left alone. It will change anyway; usage determines correctness; all will work out well. This argument is on the level of another: All men must die eventually; therefore, when you are sick, do not go to the doctor.

But man is not a purely passive creature of circumstance. Circumstances help to make him, but he also makes circumstances. He is limited by historical, biological, and psychological forces, but within these limits he can do a great deal—with language as with other instruments and structures. The picture of the purely passive man acted upon by forces over which he has no control is not only untrue but dangerous—and an out-of-date picture of the human personality to boot.

The key to the whole problem as regards English is the doctrine of usage. We must recognize today that usage is sovereign in the long run; but man determines usage, whether consciously or unconsciously, and the long run can make a lot of difference. In the long run we will all be dead, but this need not lead us to commit suicide.

Is there any value in the relative stability which grammatical norms can give a language? The question cannot be answered from the history of language alone. Other factors must be considered. The eighteenth century had a genuine point when it foolishly tried to "ascertain" the language. It did not realize how impossible it was because of its lack of knowledge, but it did know how useful a relative stability could be in making for clarity, exactitude, and an understanding of the

---

[3] Not always true, incidentally, in the short range. The schoolmarm reintroduced the [ŋ] sound at the end of the present participles in formal and informal levels of English usage. In the long run, however, the generalization is true, although the long run may be very long.

past. To slow down the rate of language change—putting the eighteenth-century desire into modern terms—is a desirable goal.

What are the reasons for teaching some kind of prescriptionist grammar on a formal and informal level in the schools? Why must we decide that this is a value? I do not necessarily approve of the present methods of teaching grammar, nor do I think that old-fashioned drill and rules are the most satisfactory method, but I do think some choice on the side of prescription must be made. Why?

1. *Social utility.*—It is a fact that society as a whole, however mistaken, believes that there is a correct grammar and will judge our students by it. Ultimately this attitude may be changed but certainly not in the foreseeable future. The honest teacher is as responsible for teaching the static in language as he is for teaching the dynamic. His task is neither to hinder nor to hurry change—but to teach realities. A certain amount of standardization in practice is also useful and valuable.

2. *Aid in understanding the past.*—The quicker language changes the sooner the literature and documents of the past become unreadable to the majority of the American people. With the precarious situation of the humanities in America, those who believe in the spiritual value of the humanities must not labor to make them even more difficult and strange to our students.

3. *Aesthetics.*—The beauty and value of the literature of the past and present are lost to those who speak only vulgate English (the language of the majority). Vulgate English has an advantage over the other levels only in vigor, when vigor is appropriate, as in the obscene, but in almost every other sense—in subtlety, sonorousness, ambiguity, cleverness, breadth—it is deficient. A person who cannot recognize the superior beauty of "Forever wilt thou love and she be fair" to "I ain't got no dough" is not fit to be teaching English.

4. *Intellectual breadth.*—Speakers limited to vulgate cannot discuss a variety of ideas because they do not have the vocabulary and grasp of linguistic structure for ideas beyond those of a most primitive type. It is most improbable that one who speaks and has command only of vulgate English could write a book on leaving one's language alone. A whole range of ideas is inaccessible to him. He cannot even talk about his talking vulgate in vulgate.

For these reasons, most of which are independent of the facts of linguistics, we can defend some form of study of formal and informal English (the language of the educated) on some kind of prescriptionist level.

The problem facing the teacher and supervisors of English is similar to that facing the teacher of civics. To the political scientist qua scientist, all political constitutions are of equal importance, all come down to the level of facts and per se no fact is more important than any other fact. To him as scientist the political constitution of Tibet— if there is one—is as important as that of the U.S.A. But in the schools and universities we emphasize the constitution of the U.S.A. and ignore, for all practical purposes, the constitution of Tibet. For teaching purposes a value judgment is made on grounds other than those provided by the facts of political science. On utilitarian grounds we recognize that the student is an American who will presumably become an adult citizen of America and will exercise his democratic rights here. A knowledge of his government is most desirable. Also, on philosophical grounds, we assume that intrinsically the American Constitution is a more profound and more satisfactory constitution than that of Tibet. But, as a science, political science says nothing of this at all. Similarly, as a science, linguistics cannot favor formal and informal English (or for that matter Bantu) to vulgate English. All linguistic facts are per se of equal importance or of equal unimportance. But on other grounds we can and must choose our values and say that we can justifiedly teach a type of prescriptive grammar and emphasize formal and informal English in the schools. Majorities in language matters are not necessarily decisive. For five hundred years at least the contraction "ain't" has been used by, I'm sure, a majority of English-speaking people, but it still is not used in formal and higher informal discourse. The fact that a majority of the people may be dishonest does not mean that we should teach dishonesty in the schools, though we may, of course, be concerned to understand the ways in which dishonesty originates or to describe dishonesty so that it can be recognized.

But, the question arises, what good then is a knowledge of linguistics and an awareness of the doctrine of usage? Is the great increase in linguistic knowledge of no value or use in teaching English? I think it is of great value, though in a different way from that in which many regard it.

The facts of language set a limit to our application of values. In a negative sense they make us aware of where prescription dare not tread. They make us more open-minded, more willing to accept divided usage, more willing to give up unimportant battles (as, e.g., over "contact" as a noun.) They contribute to the peace of mind of the teacher and thereby to that of the pupil. If the teacher recognizes that the "rules" of grammar are not heaven-sent, he can with more equanimity discuss with his students the problems involved. He will be more apt to avoid mechanical drill and avoid the *odium grammaticum*. He can make grammar and language study more pleasant and exciting by giving a sense of the past to his drive toward the present and future. He can create a sense of the excitement of linguistic awareness and language study. And, above all, he can keep the prescriptions down to a minimum, stress usage as the final arbiter, and concentrate on style, which is certainly even more important than grammar.

Some of the new work in structural linguistics may be of practical value in actually teaching the structure of present-day English. We are not necessarily tied to the traditional grammatical analysis of English which is largely based on that of Latin and Greek. In fact, the categories laid down in a recent work by Charles Fries [4] may prove to be more useful in teaching English. We are not necessarily committed to the traditional approach. But the problem of value is still with us, no matter what system we may adopt. It is never solved merely by reference to the internal facts of a subject. More is needed, and the teacher or supervisor must face the problem if he is to be successful in his task.

[4] *The Structure of English: An Introduction to the Construction of English Sentences* (1952).
I myself am not convinced that this work, which considers English almost completely in oral terms, which is based on behavioristic psychology, which plays down the basic characteristic of language—meaning—and which introduces categories as complicated and probably as inconsistent as the present system is really what we need. The book, however, has opened new perspectives in the practical analysis of our language and is an important contribution to its understanding. However, some kind of prescriptionist commitment such as I am advocating here is not tied to any particular type of language analysis—even the traditional one.

SECTION V

METALINGUISTICS:
LANGUAGE IN ITS RELATIONS

"Man is man by virtue of language."

—Wilhelm von Humboldt

Language in and of itself is a genuine subject for study, truly one of the liberal arts. It is necessary for the man who would be educated to have some sense of its nature and history, to appreciate the facts and speculations of the grammarian and linguist, and to understand the implications of the great principle of usage. And yet, the study of language inevitably leads the student beyond language itself into a consideration of language in its relations. When one takes this step beyond language, he is in the area of metalinguistics. The student of almost any of the principal human disciplines will himself be at one time or another concerned with language. This section brings to your attention essays by a number of "non-linguists" as an illustration of this point. What happens is a kind of mutual dependence. The non-linguist depends upon scientific information taught him by the linguist, and the linguist, in going beyond linguistic materials alone, seeks whatever help concerning language that can be given by the psychologist, sociologist, anthropologist, literary critic, philosopher, or theologian.

John Carroll, a psychologist, introduces the linguistic *Weltanschauung* problem by discussing the way in which a language system organizes human experiences. Without committing himself, he raises the point made by Benjamin Whorf, a pioneering speculator, that linguistic structures and categories influence man's modes of thought, determining in a sense what the user of a language *can* perceive. This is a startling view because of its implications, the chief being that linguistic expression determines a culture wholly and completely because language determines and controls what it is possible to think. It is appropriate at this point for Carroll to consider the work of Alfred Korzybski and his popularizer S. I. Hayakawa—both semanticists—because Whorf's point is at the heart of semantic thinking. Hayakawa speaks for himself in the parable of the two towns, which illustrates from the semanticist's point of view a sample of language in action. The inference that the reader is supposed to make from the parable is that disagreements happen between people because of their linguistic habits. These habits, in turn, with their accompanying prejudices are the result of unconscious attitudes toward language. Expose these attitudes, and, a semanticist would contend, the prejudices may disappear. Special habits which are a part of a cultural pattern may, in this view, obviously be altered or modified if language habits are altered or modified. Though he shares the semanticist's concern that men should understand one another, Richard Weaver objects to the basic facts of their position, facts which shape and direct their approach to human problems. It is Weaver's point that language always has an "inclination"; remove it, and you destroy the essence of language. When finally he discusses the symbolic power of language, he concludes that it is extremely important to use language exactly and accurately, but precisely because it is such a rich and various thing—emotive, directive, and tendentious.

The famous anthropologist, Franz Boas, does not accept the Whorfian notion that language is an important determinant of culture. He contends, rather, that a culture acts to determine the development of a vocabulary. "Language is a reflex of culture," and there are everywhere sufficient linguistic devices which enable a language to follow the demands of a cultural pattern. He admits that the available grammatical categories exert a limited influence on a culture, but that influence is definitely limited; culture is the prime and powerful determinant, not language. C. S. Lewis, noted literary critic, next discusses the emotional aspects of language, what Weaver had called the "inclination" of language and what the semanticists would most object to in language. This kind of language is seen especially in imaginative literature, a vital and necessary language that is paradoxically most effective when it is not solely emotional. The reader should pay special attention to Lewis' discussion of the proper function of pejorative words as a clear illustration of his basic point.

Two subtle and penetrating philosophic essays conclude the section. Jacques Maritain, eminent Thomistic philosopher, contributes an essay that might be said to be a development of the quotation by von Humboldt which opened this section: "Man is man by virtue of language." Since it is Maritain's point that the keystone of the life of the mind is the sign, he discusses at length the meaning of sign, distinguishing, for instance, between natural and conventional signs. He cites Karl von Frisch's famous analysis of the "language" of the bees in order to make his own notion of language clear. It is not the use of a conventional sign or signs that defines language; it is the awareness of the relation of signification. In short, to use language, properly speaking, one must not only use signs, but be aware of the fact that they are signs. In the essay which concludes the section and the volume Ruth Nanda Anshen asserts that language is not mere mechanism, but something much more than mechanism. Recognizing this, we can then learn something of its sacredness, meaning, and power. One of the key passages in her essay is crucial for our understanding of language: "Language and 'word' are not synonymous. Because of this, languages may be differentiated morphologically. There are, however, evolutions and mutations of words, words which are learned. But at the same time they constitute the varying symbols of the same living reality which is synonymous with the infinite capacity of the human mind."

Language is the distinctive mark of man. It is indispensable for the world of thought and for the world of perception. It allows man to communicate with others and to express himself; and by its power of "naming" it makes it possible for man to orient himself to the universe and all it contains. The broader implications of the science of linguistics, as developed by the writers included in this section, should remind us that language "is the mysterious bridge between what is beyond time and what is within time."

THE LINGUISTIC
WELTANSCHAUUNG PROBLEM
John Carroll

There exists in linguistic science, though as yet in a poorly defined way, a topic or a possible area of study which for want of a better term may be called the *linguistic Weltanschauung* ("world-view") problem. Some linguists have described the problem as one of "metalinguistics," but if we accept Trager's definition of metalinguistics (1949),[1] this problem is only a part of that branch of linguistics, which is here referred to as exolinguistics.

The linguistic *Weltanschauung* problem concerns the way in which a language system organizes human experience. To give a simple and somewhat trite example, the normal human organism is sensitive to a certain band of wavelengths of electromagnetic energy, that band of wavelengths which we refer to as *light*. In English, we have a certain series of terms applied to various parts of that spectrum, normally *red, orange, yellow, green, blue,* and *violet*. (Textile-manufacturers find it necessary to concoct all sorts of other words for special shades and tints, but these terms often change from year to year and may have no fundamental significance in our language.) Our language thus provides certain verbal symbols in terms of which we habitually classify colors. It is quite possible to conceive other languages (and there are such languages) which break the spectrum into different groupings of wavelengths. For example, instead of there being a special word for the color of orange, that color might be grouped with yellow and qualified as reddish. Now, the reader may say that this has little to do with one's world view or *Weltanschauung*, and I would agree. This example is only a paradigm.

The admirable articles written by the late Benjamin Lee Whorf (1939, 1940a, 1940b, 1941)[2] will provide us with somewhat more convincing demonstrations.

[1] For notes on the references in this selection, see pp. 291–92.

In English we divide most of our words into two classes, which have different grammatical and logical properties. Class 1 we call nouns, e.g., "house," "man"; Class 2, verbs, e.g., "hit," "run." . . . Our language thus gives us a bipolar division of nature. But nature herself is not thus polarized. If it be said that strike, turn, run, are verbs because they denote temporary or short-lasting events, i.e., actions, why then is fist a noun? It also is a temporary event. Why are lightning, spark, wave, eddy, pulsation, flame, storm, phase, cycle, spasm, noise, emotion, nouns? They are temporary events. . . . It will be found that an "event" to *us* means "what our language classes as a verb" or something analogized therefrom. And it will be found that it is not possible to define event, thing, object, relationship, and so on, from nature, but that to define them always involves a circuitous return to the grammatical categories of the definer's language.

In the Hopi language, lightning, wave, flame, meteor, puff of smoke, pulsation, are verbs—events of necessarily brief duration cannot be anything but verbs. Cloud and storm are at about the lower limit of duration for nouns. Hopi, you see, actually has a classification of events (or linguistic isolates) by duration of type, something strange to our modes of thought. On the other hand, in Nootka, a language of Vancouver Island, all words seem to us to be verbs, but really there are no classes 1 and 2; we have, as it were, a monistic view of nature that gives us only one class of word for all kinds of events.

Linguistics must imply a sort of Copernican revolution if what Whorf writes has any validity:

When linguists became able to examine critically and scientifically a large number of languages of widely different patterns, their base of reference was expanded; they experienced an interruption of phenomena hitherto held universal, and a whole new order of significances came into their ken. It was found that the background linguistic system (in other words, the grammar) of each language is not merely a reproducing instrument for voicing ideas but rather is itself the shaper of ideas, the program and guide for the individual's mental activity, for his analysis of impressions, for his synthesis of his mental stock in trade. Formulation of ideas is not an independent process, strictly rational in the old sense, but is part of a particular grammar and differs, from slightly to greatly, as between different grammars. We dissect nature along lines laid down by our native languages. The categories and types that we isolate from the world of phenomena we do not find there because they stare every observer in the face; on the contrary, the world is presented in a kaleidoscopic flux of impressions which has to be organized by our minds—and this means largely by the linguistic systems in our minds. We cut nature up, organize it into concepts, and ascribe significances as we do, largely because we are parties to an agreement to organize it in this way—an agreement that holds throughout our speech community and is codified in the patterns of our language. The agreement is, of course, an implicit and unstated one, *but its terms are absolutely obligatory;* we cannot talk at all except by subscribing to the organization and classification of data which the agreement decrees. (Whorf, 1939, p. 231; reprinted from *The Technology Review,* edited at the Massachusetts Institute of Technology.) [3]

In the words of Edward Sapir (1921, p. 105): [4]

It is almost as though at some period in the past the unconscious mind of the race had made a hasty inventory of experience, committed itself to a premature classification that allowed of no revision, and saddled the inheritors of its language with a science that they no longer quite believed in nor had the strength to overthrow. Dogma, rigidly prescribed by tradition, stiffens into formalism. Linguistic categories make up a system of surviving dogma—dogma of the unconscious. They are often but half real as concepts; their life tends ever to languish away into form for form's sake.

In principle, the idea that linguistic structure and categories in some way influence our modes of thought is an attractive one. Whorf was by no means the first to call attention to it; such eminent scholars of older generations as W. von Humboldt (1836–1839) [5] and Baudouin de Courtenay (1929) [6] have also written on the subject. For various reasons, however, this notion has never become one of the generally accepted doctrines of general linguistic theory. In the writer's talks with a number of contemporary American linguists, he encountered a considerable skepticism. One individual characterized Whorf's propositions as "untested generalizations." Many linguists think Whorf's ideas represent too much of an extrapolation from available data. Nevertheless, one can find everywhere an interest in these questions. Their possible contemporary importance is attested by the fact that the linguistic staff of the Foreign Service Institute in the Department of State has had several of Whorf's papers reprinted for use in its training program for foreign-service officers (Whorf, 1949). [7]

In order to put the linguistic *Weltanschauung* problem to empirical test, we must follow, as a preliminary step, two lines of analysis. First, we must assemble more information on a variety of linguistic structures, with particular reference to grammatical categories, inflectional systems, and form classes; in addition, we must know more about the manner in which various languages express different kinds of abstract relations, for example, relations having to do with causality, quantity, quality, time, and space. It might be convenient to draw up a standard list of about a hundred concepts to be investigated in an equal number of languages. Such a job, obviously, is one for a well-trained linguist. The results would be helpful in the second line of analysis, namely, the formulation of hypotheses about the influence of linguistic structure on behavior. These hypotheses must be stated in a way which will make them amenable to experimental test. An extremely liberal interpretation of the *Weltanschauung* problem would lead to the hypothesis that linguistic categories actually influence what the user of a language *can* perceive—to the extent that he can perceive some things and *cannot* perceive others. It seems improbable that such a hypothesis would be sustained. A more conservative hypothesis is that linguistic structure predisposes the individual to pay attention to some things more than others, or to perceive things in one mode rather than in others, even though with respect to his general perceptual capacities he is no different, on the average, from users of other languages. For example, by virtue of the fact that English uses the adjective *hot* in referring to pepper, the native speaker of English may perceive more readily a relation between the sensation of heat and a peppery taste, but his actual sensations probably differ in no way from those of a speaker of one of the many languages which do not apply a word for "hot" to pepper. Experiments on the *Weltanschauung* problem must be designed in such a way as to control the effect of individual differences and of cultural differences which may be incidentally correlated with linguistic differences. It goes without saying that at least some of the experiments must be *cross-linguistic*, that is, they must involve the comparison of the responses of native speakers of different languages.

One reservation that we may have about the *Weltanschauung* problem, particularly in the positive form in which Whorf states it, is that although language provides a mold in which statements are made by a speaker, it does not necessarily have any bearing on the "truth" of those statements, nor on the logical "correctness" of the speaker's thought processes. One world-view is as good as another, for all we know, and for that matter different world-views and logics *can* be expressed in the same language, as is demonstrated by the very fact that English permits us to speak about the varying ways in which Hopi, Nootka, and other linguistic systems describe experience. In general (that is, aside from differences arising from culture and technology), contrary to the popularly held misconception, anything that can be said in one language can be said in any other language. There is no guarantee that our thought habits would be improved by the use of an improved language, or of a different language. It is probably not true that the speakers of some languages (for example, Japanese, we are sometimes told) must necessarily think illogically because their language forces them to do so. In the face of these facts, it is nevertheless true that the study of what is termed here the linguistic *Weltanschauung* problem may in the long run help us to improve our thinking by drawing our attention to the linguistic foundations of our perceptions and thought processes.

Many writers have pointed out the need to examine the relation of language to reality. General semantics, as developed by Korzybski (1933) [8] and his students, claims to be concerned with this problem and its implications. Korzybski emphasized his conviction that language is a finite system of abstractions from the infinitely differentiated sense impressions of reality. The word *chair,* for example, is an abstraction from a manifold set of immediate experiences related to objects with certain characteristics. We can in no way avoid the fact that from this point of view "there is a fundamental lack of correspondence between the structure of our language and the structure of reality" (Wendell Johnson, 1946, p. 115).[9] General semanticists declare that lack of full awareness of the ways in which language abstracts reality can lead to errors in thinking (Hayakawa, 1949) [10] and even to personal maladjustments and speech disorders (Johnson, 1946).[11] Now, language structure as conceived by general semanticists is something quite different from linguistic structure as defined in linguistic science, but it would certainly include the kinds of phenomena noted by Sapir and Whorf. General semantics has recognized the existence of problems relating to the effect of formal linguistic categories, but to my knowledge it has not developed any detailed investigations of these problems.

The linguistic *Weltanschauung* problem, therefore, has thus far received very little attention in America. Among the few papers which reflect a preoccupation with this problem we may cite those of Dorothy Lee (1943, 1950a, 1950b) [12] and Thompson (1950).[13] Basson and O'Connor (1947),[14] in England, have attempted to investigate the influences of linguistic structure upon logic and philosophy. Kluckhohn and Leighton (1946) [15] have described possible relations between Navaho language and Navaho culture, and in a careful study the linguist Hoijer (1951)[16] adduces evidence of these relations in at least two important respects: *(a)* The verb system emphasizes the reporting of "eventings" which are very concretely linked to the motions and resting states of objects; this seems associated with the nomadic character of the culture and the thematic "restlessness" found in the mythology. *(b)* The linguistic structure divides objective reality "into a number of sharply defined object classes in motion or at rest"; thus, "both movement and position . . . are inherent in and specific to an object class; they are not extraneously produced by an actor, nor imposed as a force on a goal." One is tempted to think, from this evidence, that the Navaho views his world as something which is not subject to manipulation by human beings, and in which human actions get somehow involved as an almost incidental function of Nature, which is regarded as being more powerful than Man. But one may rightly remain skeptical as to whether this evidence truly demonstrates any fundamental relation between linguistic structure and world-view.

Bibliographical Note to "The Linguistic Weltanschauung Problem," by John Carroll

1. George L. Trager, *The Field of Linguistics* (Norman, Oklahoma, 1949).
2. Cf. John B. Carroll, ed., *Language, Thought, and Reality: Selected Writings of Benjamin Lee Whorf* (Cambridge, Mass., 1956).
3. Cf. "Science and Linguistics," *ibid.*, pp. 212–14.
4. *Language: An Introduction to the Study of Speech* (New York, 1921).
5. Wilhelm von Humboldt, *Über die Kawi-Sprache auf der Insel Java, nebst einer Einleitung über die Verschiedenheit des menschlichen Sprachbaues und ihren Einfluss auf die geistige Entwickelung des Menschengeschlechts.* 3 vols. (Berlin, 1836–39).
6. Jan Baudouin de Courtenay, *Einfluss der Sprache auf Weltanschauung und Stimmung* (Warsaw, 1929).
7. Benjamin Lee Whorf, *Four Articles on Metalinguistics* (Washington, D.C., 1949).
8. Alfred Korzybski, *Science and Sanity* (Lancaster, Pa., 1933).
9. Wendell Johnson, *People in Quandaries* (New York, 1946).
10. S. I. Hayakawa, *Language in Thought and Action* (New York, 1949).
11. Johnson, *op. cit.*
12. Cf. the following: "The Linguistic Aspect of Wintu Acculturation," *American Anthropologist*, XLV (1943), 435–40; "Notes on the Conception of the Self among the Wintu Indians," *Journal of Abnormal*

and *Social Psychology*, XLV (1950), 538–43; "Lineal and Nonlineal Codifications of Reality," *Psychosomatic Medicine*, XII (1950), 89–97.

13. Laura Thompson, "Science and the Study of Mankind," *Science*, CXI (1950), 559–63.

14. A. H. Basson and D. J. O'Connor, "Language and Philosophy: Some Suggestions for an Empirical Approach," *Philosophy*, XXII (1947), 49–65.

15. Clyde Kluckhohn and Dorothea Leighton, *The Navaho* (Cambridge, Mass., 1946).

16. Harry Hoijer, "Cultural Implications of some Navaho Linguistic Categories," *Language*, XXVII (1951), 111–20.

A SEMANTIC PARABLE   S. I. Hayakawa

Once upon a time (said the Professor), there were two small communities, spiritually as well as geographically situated at a considerable distance from each other. They had, however, these problems in common: Both were hard hit by a depression, so that in each of the towns there were about one hundred heads of families unemployed. There was, to be sure, enough food, enough clothing, enough materials for housing, but these families simply did not have money to procure these necessities.

The city fathers of A-town, the first community, were substantial businessmen, moderately well educated, good to their families, kindhearted, and sound-thinking. The unemployed tried hard, as unemployed people usually do, to find jobs; but the situation did not improve. The city fathers, as well as the unemployed themselves, had been brought up to believe that there is always enough work for everyone, if you only look for it hard enough. Comforting themselves with this doctrine, the city fathers could have shrugged their shoulders and turned their backs on the problem, except for the fact that they were genuinely kindhearted men. They could not bear to see the unemployed men and their wives and children starving. In order to prevent starvation, they felt that they had to provide these people with some means of sustenance. Their principles told them, nevertheless, that if people were given something for nothing, it would demoralize their character. Naturally this made the city fathers even more unhappy, because they were faced with the horrible choice of (1) letting the unemployed starve, or (2) destroying their moral character.

The solution they finally hit upon, after much debate and soul-searching, was this. They decided to give the unemployed families relief of fifty dollars a month; but to insure against the pauperization of the recipients, they decided that this fifty dollars was to be accompanied by a moral lesson, to wit: the obtaining of the assistance would be made so difficult, humiliating, and disagreeable that there would be no temptation for anyone to go through the process unless it was absolutely necessary; the moral disapproval of the community would be turned upon the recipients of the money at all times in such a way that they would try hard to get off relief and regain their self-respect. Some even proposed that people on relief be denied the vote, so that the moral lesson would be more deeply impressed upon them. Others suggested that their names be published at regular intervals in the newspapers, so that there would be a strong incentive to get off relief. The city fathers had enough faith in the goodness of human nature to expect that the recipients would be grateful, since they were getting something for nothing, something which they hadn't worked for.

When the plan was put into operation, however, the recipients of the relief checks proved to be an ungrateful, ugly bunch. They seemed to resent the cross-examinations and inspections at the hands of the relief investigators, who, they said, took advantage of a man's misery to snoop into every detail of his private life. In spite of uplifting editorials in A-town *Tribune* telling them how grateful they ought to be, the recipients of the relief refused to learn any moral lessons, declaring that they were "just as good as anybody else." When, for example, they permitted themselves the rare luxury of a movie or an evening of bingo, their neighbors looked at them sourly as if to say, "I work hard and pay my taxes just in order to support loafers like you in idleness and pleasure." This attitude, which was fairly characteristic of those members of the community who still had jobs, further embittered the relief recipients, so that they showed even less gratitude as time went on and were constantly on the lookout for insults, real or imaginary, from people who might think that they weren't as good as anybody else. A number of them took to moping all day long, to thinking that their lives had been failures; one or two even committed suicide. Others found that it was hard to look their wives and kiddies in the face, because they had failed to provide. They all found it difficult to maintain their club and fraternal relationships, since they could not help feeling that their fellow citizens despised them for having sunk so low. Their wives, too, were unhappy for the same reasons and gave up their social activities. Children whose parents were on relief felt inferior to classmates whose parents were not public charges. Some of these children developed inferiority complexes which affected not only their grades at school, but their careers after graduation. Several other relief recipients, finally, felt they could stand their loss of self-respect no longer and decided, after many efforts to gain honest jobs, to earn money by their own efforts, even if they had to go in for robbery. They did so and were caught and sent to the state penitentiary.

The depression, therefore, hit A-town very hard. The relief policy had averted starvation, no doubt, but suicide, personal quarrels, unhappy homes, the weakening of social organizations, the maladjustment of children, and, finally, crime, had resulted. The town was divided in two, the "haves" and the "have-nots," so that there was class hatred. People shook their heads sadly and declared that it all went to prove over again what they had known from the beginning, that giving people something for nothing inevitably demoralizes their character. The citizens of A-town gloomily waited for prosperity to return, with less and less hope as time went on.

The story of the other community, B-ville, was entirely different. B-ville was a relatively isolated town, too far out of the way to be reached by Rotary Club speakers and university extension services. One of the aldermen, however, who was something of an economist, explained to his fellow aldermen that unemployment, like sickness, accident, fire, tornado, or death, hits unexpectedly in modern society, irrespective of the victim's merits or deserts. He went on to say that B-ville's homes, parks, streets, industries, and everything else B-ville was proud of had been built in part by the work of these same people who were now unemployed. He then proposed to apply a principle of insurance: If the work these unemployed people had previously done for the community could be regarded as a form of premium paid to the community against a time of misfortune, payments now made to them to prevent their starvation could be regarded as insurance claims. He therefore proposed that all men of good repute who had worked in the community in whatever line of useful endeavor, whether as machinists, clerks, or bank managers, be regarded as citizen policyholders, having claims against the city in the case of unemployment for fifty dollars a month until such time as they might again be employed. Naturally, he had to talk very slowly and patiently, since the idea was entirely new to his fellow aldermen. But he described his plan as a "straight business proposition," and finally they were persuaded. They worked out the details as to the conditions under which citizens should be regarded as policyholders in the city's social insurance plan to everybody's satisfaction and decided to give checks for fifty dollars a month to the heads of each of B-ville's indigent families.

B-ville's claim adjusters, whose duty it was to investigate the claims of the citizen policyholders, had a much better time than A-town's relief investigators. While the latter had been resentfully regarded as snoopers, the former, having no moral lesson to teach but simply a business transaction to carry out, treated their clients with businesslike courtesy and got the same amount of information as the relief investigators with considerably less difficulty. There were no hard feelings. It further happened, fortunately, that news of B-ville's plans reached a liberal newspaper editor in the big city at the other end of the state. This writer described the plan in a leading feature story headed "B-VILLE LOOKS AHEAD. Great Adventure in Social Pioneering Launched by Upper Valley Community." As a result of this publicity, inquiries about the plan began to come to the city hall even before the first checks were mailed out. This led, naturally, to a considerable feeling of pride on the part of the aldermen, who, being boosters, felt that this was a wonderful opportunity to put B-ville on the map.

Accordingly, the aldermen decided that instead of simply mailing out the checks as they had originally intended, they would publicly present the first checks at a monster civic ceremony. They invited the governor of the state, who was glad to come to bolster his none-too-enthusiastic support in that locality, the president of the state university, the senator from their district, and other functionaries. They decorated the National Guard armory with flags and got out the American Legion Fife and Drum Corps, the Boy Scouts, and other civic organizations. At the big celebration, each family to receive a social insurance check was marched up to the platform to receive it, and the governor and the mayor shook hands with each of them as they came trooping up in their best clothes. Fine speeches were made; there was much cheering and shouting; pictures of the event showing the recipients of the checks shaking hands with the mayor, and the governor patting the heads of the children, were published not only in the local papers but also in several metropolitan picture sections.

Every recipient of these insurance checks had a feeling, therefore, that he had been personally honored, that he lived in a wonderful little town, and that he could face his unemployment with greater courage and assurance, since his community was back of him. The men and women found themselves being kidded in a friendly way by their acquaintances for having been "up there with the big shots," shaking hands with the governor, and so on. The children at school found themselves envied for having had their pictures in the papers. All in all, B-ville's unemployed did not commit suicide, were not haunted by a sense of failure, did not turn to crime, did not get personal maladjustments, did not develop class hatred, as the result of their fifty dollars a month. . . .

At the conclusion of the Professor's story, the discussion began:

"That just goes to show," said the Advertising Man, who was known among his friends as a realistic thinker, "what good promotional work can do. B-ville's city council had real advertising sense, and that civic ceremony was a masterpiece . . . made everyone happy . . . put over the scheme in a big way. Reminds me of the way we do things in our business: as soon as we called horse-mackerel tuna-fish, we developed a big market for it. I suppose if you called relief 'insurance,' you could actually get people to like it, couldn't you?"

"What do you mean, 'calling' it insurance?" asked the Social Worker. "B-ville's scheme wasn't relief at all. It *was* insurance. That's what all such payments should be. What gets me is the stupidity of A-town's city council and all people like them in not realizing that what they call 'relief' is simply the payment of just claims which those unemployed have on a community in a complex interdependent industrial society."

"Good grief, man! Do you realize what you're saying?" cried the Advertising Man in surprise. "Are you implying that those people had any *right* to that money? All I said was that it's a good idea to *disguise* relief as insurance if it's going to make people any happier. But it's still relief, no matter what you *call* it. It's all right to kid the public along to reduce discontent, but we don't need to kid ourselves as well!"

"But they *do* have a right to that money! They're not getting something for nothing. It's insurance. They did something for the community, and that's their prem—"

"Say, are you crazy?"

"Who's crazy?"

"You're crazy. Relief is relief, isn't it? If you'd only call things by their right names . . ."

"But, confound it, insurance is insurance, isn't it?"

(Since the gentlemen are obviously losing their tempers, it will be best to leave them. The Professor has already sneaked out. When last heard of, not only had the quarrelers stopped speaking to each other, but so had their wives—and the Advertising Man was threatening to disinherit his son if he didn't break off his engagement with the Social Worker's daughter.)

This story has been told not to advance arguments in favor of "social insurance" or "relief" or for any other political and economic arrangement, but simply to show a fairly characteristic sample of language in action. Do the words we use make as much difference in our lives as the story of A-town and B-ville seems to indicate? We often talk about "choosing the right words to express our thoughts," as if thinking were a process entirely independent of the words we think in. But is thinking such an independent process? Do the words we utter arise as a result of the thoughts we have, or are the thoughts we have determined by the linguistic systems we happen to have been taught? The Advertising Man and the Social Worker seem to be agreed that the results of B-ville's program were good, so that we can assume that their notions of what is socially desirable are similar. Nevertheless, they *cannot agree.*

Alfred Korzybski, in his preface to *Science and Sanity* (which discusses many problems similar to those discussed in this book), asks the reader to imagine what the state of technology would be if all lubricants contained emery dust, the presence of which had never been detected. Machines would be short-lived and expensive; the machine age would be a dream of the distant future. If, however, someone were to discover the presence of the emery, we should at once know *in what direction to proceed* in order to release the potentialities of machine power.

Why do people disagree? It isn't a matter of education or intelligence, because quarreling, bitterness, conflict, and breakdown are just as common among the educated as the uneducated, among the clever as the stupid. Human relations are no better among the privileged than the underprivileged. Indeed, well-educated people are often the cleverest in proving that insurance is *really* insurance and that relief is *really* relief—and being well educated they often have such high principles that nothing will make them modify their position in the slightest. Are disagreements then the inevitable results of the nature of human problems and the nature of man? Possibly so—but if we give this answer, we are confessing to being licked before we have even started our investigations.

The student of language observes, however, that it is an extremely rare quarrel that does not involve some kind of *talking*. Almost invariably, before noses are punched or shooting begins, *words are exchanged*—sometimes only a few, sometimes millions. We shall, therefore, look for the "previously undetected emery dust" (or whatever it is that heats up and stops our intellectual machinery) in *language*—that is to say, *our linguistic habits* (how we talk and think and listen) and *our unconscious attitudes toward language*. If we are even partially successful in our search, we may get an inkling of the *direction in which to proceed* in order to release the now imperfectly realized potentialities of human co-operation.

P.S. Those who have concluded that the point of the story is that the Social Worker and the Advertising Man were "only arguing about different names for the same thing," are asked to reread the story and explain what they mean by (1) "only" and (2) "the same thing."

THE POWER OF THE WORD   *Richard M. Weaver*

> *The corruption of man is followed by the corruption of language.*—EMERSON

After securing a place in the world from which to fight, we should turn our attention first to the matter of language. The impulse to dissolve everything into sensation has made powerful assaults against the forms which enable discourse, because these institute a discipline and operate through predications which are themselves fixities. We have sought an ultimate sanction for man's substance in metaphysics, and we must do the same for his language if we are to save it from a similar prostitution. All metaphysical community depends on the ability of men to understand one another.

At the beginning I should urge examining in all seriousness that ancient belief that a divine element is present in language. The feeling that to have power of language is to have control over things is

From *Ideas Have Consequences*, University of Chicago Press, Chicago, 1948. Reprinted with permission from the publisher.

deeply imbedded in the human mind. We see this in the way men gifted in speech are feared or admired; we see it in the potency ascribed to incantations, interdictions, and curses. We see it in the legal force given to oath or word. A man can bind himself in the face of contingencies by saying Yea or Nay, which can only mean that words in common human practice express something transcending the moment. Speech is, moreover, the vehicle of order, and those who command it are regarded as having superior insight, which must be into the necessary relationship of things. Such is the philosophic meaning of great myths. "And out of the ground the Lord God formed every beast of the field, and every fowl of the air; and brought them unto Adam to see what he would call them, and whatever Adam called every living creature, that was the name thereof." This story symbolizes the fact that man's overlordship begins with the naming of the world. Having named the animals, he has in a sense ordered them, and what other than a classified catalogue of names is a large part of natural science? To discover what a thing is "called" according to some system is the essential step in knowing, and to say that all education is learning to name rightly, as Adam named the animals, would assert an underlying truth. The sentence passed upon Babel confounded the learning of its builders.

As myth gives way to philosophy in the normal sequence we have noted, the tendency to see a principle of divinity in language endures. Thus we learn that in the late ancient world the Hebrew *memra* and the Greek *logos* merged, and in the Gospel of John we find an explicit identification:

> In the beginning was the Word, and
> the Word was with God, and the Word was God.
> The same was in the beginning with God.

A following verse declares that *logos* as god lies behind the design of the cosmos, for "without him was not anything made that was made." Speech begins to appear the principle of intelligibility. So when wisdom came to man in Christ, in continuation of this story, "the Word was made flesh and dwelt among us." The allegory need give no difficulty; knowledge of the prime reality comes to man through the word; the word is a sort of deliverance from the shifting world of appearances. The central teaching of the New Testament is that those who accept the word acquire wisdom and at the same time some identification with the eternal, usually figured as everlasting life.

It seems that man, except in periods of loss of confidence, when skepticism impugns the very possibility of knowledge, shows thus an incurable disposition to look upon the word as a means of insight into the noumenal world. The fact that language is suprapersonal, uniting countless minds which somehow stand in relationship to an overruling divinity, lies at the root of this concept. If, as Karl Vossler has observed, "Everything that is spoken on this globe in the course of ages must be thought of as a vast soliloquy spoken by the human mind, which unfolds itself in millions of persons and characters, and comes to itself again in their reunion," language must somehow express the enduring part. Certainly one of the most important revelations about a period comes in its theory of language, for that informs us whether language is viewed as a bridge to the noumenal or as a body of fictions convenient for grappling with transitory phenomena. Not without point is the cynical observation of Hobbes that "words are wise men's counters—they do but reckon by them—but they are the money of fools." Doctrines thus sharply defined can tell us whether a period is idealistic or pragmatic. Because this circumstance concerns the problem of restoration at a critical point, it becomes necessary to say something about contemporary theories of language.

The most notable development of our time in the province of language study is the heightened interest in semantics, which seems to stem from a realization that words, after all, have done things on their own, so to express it. I shall review briefly the state of the question. The problem of the word was argued with great acuteness by the Middle Ages, and one of the first major steps in the direction of modern skepticism came through the victory of Occam over Aquinas in a controversy about language. The statement that *modi essendi et subsistendi* were replaced by *modi significandi et intelligendi,* or that ontological referents were abandoned in favor of pragmatic significations, describes broadly the change in philosophy which continues to our time. From Occam to Bacon, from Bacon to Hobbes, and from Hobbes to contemporary semanticists, the progression is clear: ideas become psychological figments, and words become useful signs.

Semantics, which I shall treat as an extreme outgrowth of nominalism, seems inspired by two things: a feeling that language does not take into account the infinite particularity of the world and a phobia in the face of the autonomous power of words.

The semanticists are impressed with the world as process, and, feeling with Heraclitus that no man can step in the same river twice, they question how the fixities of language can represent a changeful reality. S. I. Hayakawa, one of the best-known popularizers of the subject, tells us that "the universe is in a perpetual state of flux." [1] Alfred Korzybski has declared that the use of the word "is," in the sense condemned in his system of semantics, so falsifies the world that it could endanger our sanity. Such men work laboriously to show by categories of referents all the things a single term can mean, and, at the same time, they take into account the circumstances of the user, apparently in an effort to correlate him with the world of becoming. (This should recall the earlier tendency of Romanticism to regard a work of art as expressive of the artist's emotional condition at the moment of its execution.) They desire language to reflect not conceptions of verities but qualities of perceptions, so that man may, by the pragmatic theory of success, live more successfully. To one completely committed to this realm of becoming, as are the empiricists, the claim to apprehend verities is a sign of psychopathology. Probably we have here but a highly sophisticated expression of the doctrine that ideals are hallucinations and that the only normal, sane person is the healthy extrovert, making instant, instinctive adjustments to the stimuli of the material world. To such people as these, Christ as preacher of the Word, is a "homosexual paranoiac." In effect, their doctrine seems part of the general impulse to remove all barriers to immediate apprehension of the sensory world, and so one must again call attention to a willingness to make the physical the sole determinant of what is.

In recognizing that words have power to define and to compel, the semanticists are actually testifying to the philosophic quality of language which is the source of their vexation. In an attempt to get rid of that quality, they are looking for some neutral means which will be a nonconductor of the current called "emotion" and its concomitant of evaluation. They are introducing into language, in the course of their prescriptions, exactly the same atomization which we have deplored in other fields. They are trying to strip words of all meaning that shows tendency, or they are trying to isolate language from the noumenal world by ridding speech of tropes.

Let us consider an illustration from Hayakawa's *Language in Action*, a work which has done much to put the new science before the public. It is easy to visualize a social situation, the author tells us, in which payment to unemployed persons will be termed by one group of citizens "relief" and by another "social insurance." One can admit

---

[1] *Language in Action*, p. 121.

the possibility, but what lies behind the difference in terminology? The answer is: a conception of ends which evaluates the tendency of the action named. The same sort of thing is encountered when one has to decide whether the struggle of the American colonists against Great Britain should be termed a "rebellion" or a "war for independence." In the first case, the bare existential thing, the payment of money to needy persons (and it will be noted that this translation does not purify the expression of tendency) is like anything else neutral as long as we consider it solely with reference to material and efficient causes. But, when we begin to think about what it represents in the totality, it takes on new attributes (emotional loading, these may be called) causing people to divide according to their sentiments or their metaphysical dream.

It is in such instances that the semanticists seem to react hysterically to the fear of words. Realizing that today human beings are in disagreement as never before and that words serve to polarize the conflicting positions, they propose an ending of polarity. I have mentioned, earlier, people who are so frightened over the existence of prejudice that they are at war with simple predication. The semanticists see in every epithet a prejudice.

The point at issue is explained by a fundamental proposition of Aquinas: "Every form is accompanied by an inclination." Now language is a system of forms, which both singly and collectively have this inclination or intention. The aim of semantics is to dissolve form and thereby destroy inclination in the belief that the result will enable a scientific manipulation. Our argument is that the removal of inclination destroys the essence of language.

Let us look more closely at the consequence of taking all tendentious meaning from speech. It is usually supposed that we would then have a scientific, objective vocabulary, which would square with the "real" world and so keep us from walking into stone walls or from fighting one another over things that have no existence. Actually the result would be to remove all teleology, for language would no longer have *nisus,* and payment to the needy would be neither "relief" nor "social insurance" but something without character, which we would not know how to place in our scheme of values. (The fact that equalitarian democracy, to the extent that it makes leadership superfluous or impossible, is repudiating teleology must not be overlooked here. Teleology enjoins from above; equalitarian democracy takes its counsel without point of reference. The advantage of semantics to equalitarian democracy is pointed out by some semanticists.)

Hayakawa has said further that "arguments over intensional mean-ing can result only in irreconcilable conflict." [2] With the proper quali-fications, this observation is true. Since language expresses tendency, and tendency has direction, those who differ over tendency can re-main at harmony only in two ways: (1) by developing a complacency which makes possible the ignoring of contradictions and (2) by refer-ring to first principles, which will finally remove the difference at the expense of one side. If truth exists and is attainable by man, it is not to be expected that there will be unison among those who have differ-ent degrees of it. This is one of the painful conditions of existence which the bourgeoisie like to shut from their sight. I see no reason to doubt that here is the meaning of the verses in Scripture: "Suppose ye that I am come to give peace on earth? I tell you, Nay; but rather division" and "I bring not peace, but a sword." It was the mission of the prophet to bring a metaphysical sword among men which has been dividing them ever since, with a division that affirms value. But amid this division there can be charity, and charity is more to be relied on to prevent violence than are the political neofanaticisms of which our age is signally productive. Positivism cannot grant theology's basis of distinction, but neither can it provide a ground for charity.

When we look more narrowly at the epistemological problem raised by the semanticists, we conclude that they wish to accept patterns only from external reality. With many of them the notion seems im-plicit that language is an illusion or a barrier between us and what we must cope with. "Somewhere bedrock beneath words must be reached," is a common theme. Some talk about achieving an infinite-valued orientation (this last would of course leave both certitude and the idea of the good impossible). Mr. Thurman Arnold, who seems to have assimilated most of the superficial doctrines of the day, takes a stand in the *Folklore of Capitalism* even against definition. He argues that every writer on social institutions "should try to choose words and illustrations which will arouse the proper mental associations with his readers. If he doesn't succeed with them, he should try others. If he is ever led into an attempt at definition, he is lost." On the same footing of ingenuousness is another observation in this work: "When men begin to examine philosophies and principles as they examine atoms and electrons, the road to the discovery of the means of social control is open." The author of *Political Semantics*, fearful of the in-tervention of abstractions, suggests that the reader, too, add something

2 *Ibid.*, p. 63.

to the definition given, a notion savoring strongly of progressive education. "Possibly the reader himself should participate in the process of
building up a definition. Instead of being presented with finished
summary definitions he might first be introduced to an array of examples arranged in such a way as to suggest the 'mental picture' in
terms of which the examples were chosen." [3] There is just enough
here to suggest the Socratic method; but the true implication is that
there are no real definitions; there are only the general pictures one
arrives at after more or less induction. The entire process is but a
climbing-down of the ladder of abstraction.

Now whether it is profitable to descend that ladder is certainly not
a question to be begged. Semanticists imagine, apparently, that the
descent is a way out of that falsity which universality imposes on all
language. Do we know more definitely what a horse is when we are
in a position to point to one than when we merely use the name
"horse" in its generic significance? This concerns one of the most fundamental problems of philosophy—one on which we must take a stand;
and I am ready to assert that we can never break out of the circle of
language and seize the object bare-handed, as it were, or without some
ideational operation.

It must surely be granted that whatever is unique defies definition.
Definition then must depend on some kind of analogical relationship
of a thing with other things, and this can mean only that definition
is ultimately circular. That is to say, if one begins defining a word
with synonyms, he will, if he continues, eventually complete a circuit
and arrive at the very terms with which he started. Suppose we
allow Korzybski, who has been especially restive in what appears to
him the imprisoning net of language, to testify from his experiments:
"We begin by asking the 'meaning' of every word uttered, being satis-
fied for this purpose with the roughest definition; then we ask the
'meaning' of the words used in the definition, and this process is continued for no more than ten to fifteen minutes, until the victim begins
to speak in circles as, for instance, defining 'space' by 'length' and
'length' by 'space.' When this stage is reached, we have usually come
to the *undefined* terms of the given individual. If we still press, no
matter how gently, for definitions, a most interesting fact occurs.
Sooner or later, signs of affective disturbance appear. Often the face
reddens; there is body restlessness—symptoms quite similar to those
seen in a schoolboy who has forgotten his lessons, which he 'knows'

[3] Norman H. Hinton, *Political Semantics*, p. 68.

but cannot tell. . . . Here we have reached the bottom and the foundation of all *non-elementalistic* meanings, the meanings of *undefined* terms, which we 'know' somehow but cannot tell."

Taking the experiment as Korzybski recounts it, I would wish to ask whether this schoolboy who has forgotten his lessons is not every man, whose knowledge comes by a process of recalling and who is embarrassed as by ignorance when he can no longer recall? He is here frustrated because he cannot find any further analogues to illustrate what he knows. Any person, it seems, can be driven back to that knowledge which comes to him by immediate apprehension, but the very fact of his possessing such knowledge makes him a participant in the communal mind. I do not desire to press the issue here, but I suspect that this is evidence supporting the doctrine of knowledge by recollection taught by Plato and the philosophers of the East. If we can never succeed in getting out of the circle of definition, is it not true that all conventional definitions are but reminders of what we already, in a way, possess? The thing we have never heard of is defined for us by the things we know; putting these together, we discover, or unbury, the concept which was there all the while. If, for example, a class in science is being informed that "ontogeny recapitulates phylogeny," it is only being asked to synthesize concepts already more or less familiar. Finding the meaning of the *definiendum* is finding what emerges naturally if our present concepts are put together in the right relation. Even empirical investigations of the learning process bear this out. Such conclusions lead to the threshold of a significant commitment: ultimate definition is, as Aristotle affirmed, a matter of intuition. Primordial conception is somehow in us; from this we proceed as already noted by analogy, or the process of finding resemblance to one thing in another.[4]

---

[4] It may be objected at this point that I have chosen to deal only with the popularizers of semantics, with men who have cheapened or distorted the science. Because this work is a study in social consequences, it is necessary to look at the form in which these doctrines reach the public. There is, of course, a group of serious philosophers who are working at language with caution and a sense of responsibility and who believe that they are erecting for us important safeguards against error. But, when I look into the writings of these men, I find, alas, that their conclusions march in the same direction as those of the popularizers. The Darwinian link is acknowledged, and semantics resembles, as much as before, behaviorism imported into language. Thus Charles W. Morris in *Foundations of the Theory of Signs* stresses the importance of semantics because "it has directed attention more closely to the relation of signs to their users than had previously been done and has assessed more profoundly than ever before the relevance of this relation in understanding intellectual activities." Language is spoken of as if it were some curious development of sense which enables an organism to take into

All this has bearing on our issue with semantics because words, each containing its universal, are our reminders of knowledge. For this reason it seems to me that semanticists are exactly wrong in regarding language as an obstruction or a series of pitfalls. Language, on the contrary, appears as a great storehouse of universal memory, or it may be said to serve as a net, not imprisoning us but supporting us and aiding us to get at a meaning beyond present meaning through the very fact that it embodies others' experiences. Words, because of their common currency, acquire a significance greater than can be imparted to them by a single user and greater than can be applied to a single situation. In this way the word is evocative of ideal aspects, which by our premises are the only aspects constituting knowledge. On this point I shall call as my witnesses two men as far apart as Shelley and a contemporary psychologist. The poet writes in *Prometheus Unbound:*

> Language is a perpetual Orphic song,
> Which rules with Daedal harmony the throng
> Of thoughts and forms, which else senseless and shapeless were.

Wilbur Marshall Urban declares in *Language and Reality:* "It is part of my general thesis that all meaning is ultimately linguistic and that although science, in the interests of purer notation and manipulation, may break through the husk of language, its nonlinguistic symbols must again be translated back into natural language if intelligibility is to be possible." [5]

The community of language gives one access to significances at which he cannot otherwise arrive. To find a word is to find a meaning; to create a word is to find a single term for a meaning partially disturbed in other words. Whoever may doubt that language has this power to evoke should try the experiment of thinking without words. It has been necessary to make these observations because our subject is the restoration of language, and semantics has appeared to some a

---

account objects not perceptually present. The determination of the scientist to see all reality as process appears later in the same work when Morris collapses the notion of "meaning" by making it purely a function of relationships. That is to say, nothing is, intrinsically, but each thing is, in terms of the process as a whole. The significant implication follows that concepts are not entities but are, rather, highly selective processes "in which the organism gets indications as to how to act with reference to the world in order to satisfy its needs or interests."

[5] *Language and Reality*, p. 241.

promising departure toward scientific reconstruction. In its seeking of objective determination, however, it turns out to represent a further flight from center. It endeavors to find the truth about reality in an agglomeration of peripheral meanings, as can be seen when its proponents insist on lowering the level of abstraction. This is only an attempt to substitute things for words, and, if words stand, in fact, for ideas, here is but the broadest aspect of our entire social disintegration. Here would be a vivid example of things in the saddle riding mankind. For the sake of memory, for the sake of logic—above all, for the sake of the unsentimental sentiment without which communities do not endure—this is a trend to be reversed. Those who regard the synthesizing power of language with horror are the atomists.

The opposition here indicated brings us necessarily to the important topic of symbolism. The attack upon the symbolic operations of language by positivists is only part of the general attack upon symbolism under way ever since it was widely agreed that there is but one world and that it is the world which is apparent to the senses. The logic is unexceptionable; since the symbol is a bridge to the other, the "ideational" world, those who wish to confine themselves to experience must oppose symbolism. In fact, the whole tendency of empiricism and democracy in speech, dress, and manners has been toward a plainness which is without symbolic significance. The power of symbolism is greatly feared by those who wish to expel from life all that is nonrational in the sense of being nonutilitarian, as witness the attack of Jacobins upon crowns, cassocks, and flags. As semanticists wish to plane the tropes off language, so do reformers of this persuasion wish to remove the superfluous from dress. It is worth recalling how the French Revolution simplified the dress of the Western world. At the time of this writing there appeared a report that during a leftist revolution in Bolivia the necktie was discarded as "a symbol of servility and conformity." The most tenacious in clinging to symbolic apparel have been the clerical and military callings, which we have already characterized as metaphysical; and now even the military service is under pressure to abandon its symbolic distinction in dress.

The same tendency is manifesting itself in the decay of honorifics. To the modern mind there is something so artificial and so offensive in titles of any kind that even "doctor" and "professor" are being dropped, though the military services cling grimly to their titles of rank. (There is a further lesson to be drawn from the fact that practitioners of the applied science of medicine have been allowed to keep theirs.) Honorifics are often mere flummery, to be sure, but one must not overlook the truth that they represent an effort to distinguish between men and men of parts. When not abused, they are an explicit recognition of distinction and hierarchy, a recognition that cannot be dispensed with where highly organized effort is required. The impulse to disorganize succeeds where it makes dress and language stand for just what is before us and not for transcendental attributes or past attainments— makes us see people in an instant of time, as does the camera.[6]

The well-known fondness of the Japanese for honorific expression is but an aspect of the highly symbolic character of their culture. Naturally this symbolism becomes a target for those who imagine they should re-educate the Japanese. Nothing would give the West a more complete sense of victory over the East than the abolishment of its taboos and ritualistic behavior. In this light I think we are to understand a curious press dispatch of March, 1946, which declared that MacArthur's headquarters "had suggested to the Japanese motion picture industry that kissing scenes in the movies would be a step toward democratization." We may expect many other attacks, inspired by good will and ignorance, upon the symbolic world picture of the Japanese, especially with reference to their religion and their emperor.

We return now to consider what is indicated by command over the symbolistic power of language. It is, as even primitives know, a wonderful thing to have the gift of speech. For it is true historically that those who have shown the greatest subtlety with language have shown the greatest power to understand (this does not exclude Sophists, for Plato made the point that one must be able to see the truth accurately in order to judge one's distance from it if he is practicing deception). To take a contemporary example which has statistical support: American universities have found that with few exceptions students who display the greatest mastery of words, as evidenced by vocabulary tests and exercises in writing, make the best scholastic records regardless of the department of study they enter. For physics, for chemistry, for engineering—it matters not how superficially unrelated to language the branch of study may be—command of language will prognosticate aptitude. Facility with words bespeaks a capacity to learn relations and grasp concepts; it is a means of access to the complex reality.

---

[6] I feel certain that the Reverend John Robinson had a similar thought in mind when he enjoined the Plymouth Pilgrims to look upon their civil leaders "not beholding in them the ordinarinesse of their persons, but God's ordinance for your own good."

Evidently it is the poet's unique command of language which gives him his ability to see the potencies in circumstances. He is the greatest teacher of cause and effect in human affairs; when Shelley declared that poets are the unacknowledged legislators of mankind, he merely signified that poets are the quickest to apprehend necessary truth. One cannot help thinking here of the peculiar fullness with which Yeats and Eliot—and, before them, Charles Péguy—foretold the present generation's leap into the abysm, and this while the falsehoods of optimism were being dinned into all ears. A poem of Eliot, "difficult" or "meaningless" in 1927, becomes today almost pat in its applications. The discourse of poetry is winged; the nominal legislators plod along empirically on foot. What can this mean except that the poet communes with the mind of the superperson? At the other extreme, those who confine their attention to the analysis of matter prove singularly inept when called upon to deal with social and political situations. If we should compile a list of those who have taught us most of what we ultimately need to know, I imagine that the scientists, for all the fanfare given them today, would occupy a rather humble place and that the dramatic poets would stand near the top.

It is difficult, therefore, to overrate the importance of skill in language. But for us there is the prior problem of preserving language itself; for, as the psyche deteriorates, language shows symptoms of malady, and today relativism, with its disbelief in truth, has made the inroads we have just surveyed upon communication. We live in an age that is frightened by the very idea of certitude, and one of its really disturbing outgrowths is the easy divorce between words and the conceptual realities which our right minds know they must stand for. This takes the form especially of looseness and exaggeration. Now exaggeration, it should be realized, is essentially a form of ignorance, one that allows and seems to justify distortion. And the psychopathic mind of war has greatly increased our addiction to this vice; indeed, during the struggle distortion became virtually the technique of reporting. A course of action, when taken by our side, was "courageous"; when taken by the enemy, "desperate"; a policy instituted by our command was "stern," or in a delectable euphemism which became popular, "rugged"; the same thing instituted by the enemy was "brutal." Seizure by military might when committed by the enemy was "conquest"; but, if committed by our side, it was "occupation" or even "liberation," so transposed did the poles become. Unity of spirit among our people was a sign of virtue; among the enemy it was a proof of incorrigible devotion to crime. The list could be prolonged indefinitely. And such always happens when men surrender to irrationality. It fell upon the Hellenic cities during the Peloponnesian War. Thucydides tells us in a vivid sentence that "the ordinary acceptation of words in their relation to things was changed as men thought fit."

Our situation would be sufficiently deplorable if such deterioration were confined to times of military conflict; but evidence piles up that fundamental intellectual integrity, once compromised, is slow and difficult of restoration. If one examines the strikingly different significations given to "democracy" and "freedom," he is forced to realize how far we are from that basis of understanding which is prerequisite to the healing of the world. To one group "democracy" means access to the franchise; to another it means economic equality administered by a dictatorship. Or consider the number of contradictory things which have been denominated Fascist. What has happened to the one world of meaning? It has been lost for want of definers. Teachers of the present order have not enough courage to be definers; lawmakers have not enough insight.

The truth is, as we have already seen, that our surrender to irrationality has been in progress for a long time, and we witness today a breakdown of communication not only between nations and groups within nations but also between successive generations. Sir Richard Livingstone has pointed out that the people of the Western world "do not know the meaning of certain words, which had been assumed to belong to the permanent vocabulary of mankind, certain ideals which, if ignored in practice under pressure, were accepted in theory. The least important of these words is Freedom. The most important are Justice, Mercy, and Truth. In the past we have slurred this revolution over as a difference in 'ideology.' In fact it is the greatest transformation that the world has undergone, since, in Palestine or Greece, these ideals came into being or at least were recognized as principles of conduct." [7] Drift and circumstance have been permitted to change language so that the father has difficulty in speaking to the son; he endeavors to speak, but he cannot make the realness of his experience evident to the child. This circumstance, as much as any other, lies behind the defeat of tradition. Progress makes father and child live in different worlds, and speech fails to provide a means to bridge them. The word is almost in limbo, where the positivists have wished to consign it.

[7] *The Future in Education* (Cambridge University Press, England), pp. 109–10.

LANGUAGE AND CULTURE   *Franz Boas*

The question of interrelation between language and culture has been much discussed and the opinion is still widely held that language is an important determinant of culture. I little doubt that this opinion is strongly supported by our emotional attitude towards our mother tongue and the ease with which our most intimate thoughts find expression in our native speech. There are certainly few poets who have been able to express themselves with equal ease and force in their mother tongue and in an acquired language.

Other attempts at an evaluation of language as a means of expressing thought are based on the ground that it is difficult to formulate an abstract and logical thought in the languages of people of lower, perhaps even of an alien culture.

The problem has to be looked at from two angles, the one, in how far does language fulfill the needs of communication and of thought in a given culture; the other, in how far does language influence the line of thought, in how far does it help or hinder the development of culture.

The former question is not difficult to answer. An examination of the vocabularies of people of various types of culture shows that words exist for everything that is essential in the culture and that elaborate distinctions are found that reflect the importance of objects and activities in the lives of the people. We may observe this most readily in our own languages. The development of electrical power, of the automobile, of modern science, of new political devices, of new economic organizations, have enriched our vocabulary with terms for new experiences and objects without number. Language has supplied our needs of new symbols, even though our linguistic technique is so feeble that we had to resort to combinations of letters of the alphabet, like FDR, CIO, BMT, to convey complex groups of ideas or attitudes. The reverse of this phenomenon is our lack of knowledge of the specific vocabulary of aspects of our culture with which we are not familiar. Occupational vocabularies are on the whole confined to occupational groups and only a few words of such a vocabulary become common property. Conversely we lose the vocabulary of occupations that go out of use, and of vanishing conditions like that of falconry, of the feudal system, of weapons no longer in use. These may survive in

From *Studies in the History of Culture: The Disciplines of the Humanities*, 1942. Reprinted with permission from the American Council of Learned Societies.

the minds of those familiar with history, but they are no longer parts of the living vocabulary of the people.

In every culture the vocabulary reflects the relation of man to his natural environment and gives testimony of the kind of life he leads. The Eskimo uses many terms for snow: snow falling, snow on the ground, snowdrift, drifting snow, soft snow; for all these aspects are of importance in his life. These terms must be ancient, for they are not derived from a common root, but distinct in origin. The seafaring Oceanian and the inhabitants of the northwest coast of America have many terms for the sea in its various aspects as well as for canoe and canoe-building. On the other hand the modern Aztec has lost every trace of the terms related to his ancient religion. To give another example: the potlatch system of the northwest coast of America has given rise to a large vocabulary relating to borrowing, loaning, interest at various rates, indebtedness incurred in contracting marriages or in the destruction of property for the purpose of rising in social rank. A large vocabulary exists also to designate rank. In all these cases of development of a special vocabulary we may judge of its antiquity by the number of independent, specific stems. More modern terms will be found often to be derived from stems in wider use. Thus the Kwakiutl terms for rank may be of moderate antiquity, since all are derivatives of existing stems, although the grammatical form of many of them is not easily understood. The chief is "standing at the head alone," or "being at the head," the chieftainess "lifting her blanket," namely when giving a great feast when she tries to have her blanket not soiled by grease, the chief's son "the one standing in front" (of his father); the chief's daughter "the one sitting still in the house." A chief's wife of lower rank is designated by a term that cannot easily be equated with other terms but seems to be related to the term for "wealth."

This view of a correlation between the use of terms that can be derived from older stems and the relative newness of the cultural feature so designated can be supported by the frequent reluctance of speakers of native languages to adopt terms of foreign languages the general connotation of which they do not understand, and to substitute new derivatives which describe those characteristics that strike them as significant. Thus a telegraph may be called "talks along a line," an automobile "stubnose vehicle," a horse "wonderful dog," if the dog was the only domesticated animal known.

Of course, it ought not to be assumed that the etymology of such new terms remains conscious for any length of time. Proof of this is that words of this type wear down rapidly and that knowledge of their etymology is lost to the speakers. This is proved by numerous cases in which by metathesis or other phonetic processes the etymology is obscured. The words become symbols like all others which are tokens of concepts regardless of their historic origin.

I think on the basis of such data we may infer that languages are able to supply terms for new ideas as they arise and that culture determines the course of development of the vocabulary.

While this will be conceded for concrete objects, the question arises whether abstract ideas can be readily expressed in primitive languages and whether the lack of devices adapted to their formation may not hinder the development of abstract concepts.

In regard to this question we ought to consider that a great many of our abstract concepts are not an outgrowth of the language of the common people, but have arisen among the educated and have gradually found their way into the common language, not without losing in many cases their function as tokens of abstract thought. Such words as *existence, essence, character, religion, quality, quantity,* originated among literary persons and came to be adopted with the increasing complexity of culture. There are others of different character: *love, hatred, friendship, freedom, envy, thought.* Have primitive languages their equivalent? The conditions of primitive culture are such that the absolute abstract term itself can hardly ever be the subject of conversation or the object of activities. The situations talked about are always concrete. I may talk of my love, hatred, or friendship in regard to a person, but I do not talk about these attitudes in an absolute sense. Therefore, if corresponding words exist they can occur only in possessive relations. If the structure of a language permits I can say "my sympathy for his pitiable condition is great," but I cannot say sympathy is the attitude of having pity. Still, when conditions arise which require the expression of the absolute noun, grammatical devices taken from more concrete situations are generally available which make it possible to create a word, at the time of its creation unidiomatic, that will adequately express the absolute idea. The Eskimo can form an abstract noun from any verb: goodness, pity, love; but it does not occur in everyday conversation except in reference to some tangible object. In languages of different structure the abstract noun may even exist as subject acting upon a person, as "hunger acts upon me," where it is open to question whether hunger is felt an animate actor or not; or "I have pains" where it is equally uncertain whether pains are felt as an object possessed, although the grammatical forms require such formal interpretation. The endeavors of missionaries to render the many abstract terms they require, show how unidiomatic terms may be created and come to be accepted—although for one acquainted with the language they may not render in the least the thought to be expressed—and become accepted tokens when the ideas are grasped more fully.

As a matter of fact etymological investigation shows in many cases that the fundamental ideas expressed in stems are so general that they appear to us as highly abstract. Thus we have languages that have a stem meaning "movement," and all specific forms of movement, like to walk, to fly, to swim, etc., are derived from it. "To say, to wish, to think" may all be derived from the same stem, meaning "the formulation of a thought process by spoken or unspoken language." This does not mean that the generalized notions which we derive by analysis are present in the minds of the speakers for whom the words, as they exist now, are merely tokens of specific actions. It seems not unlikely that in very early times such sound complexes of very vague connotation existed and that languages as we know them now were built up on the foundation of such elements.

I think our general experience in the field of linguistic data proves that language is a reflex of culture and that there are everywhere linguistic devices that enable the language to follow the demands of culture.

There is, however, another aspect from which our problem has to be considered. We have so far spoken only of words and their relation to culture. It is another question in how far the categories of grammar and the general classification of experience may control thought. To give an example: In our speech the category of time is all-important. Whether an action was done in the past, in the present, or in the future must be expressed. We must express whether we speak about a definite or indefinite object. We must state whether we mean singular or plural. These are obligatory categories, and although a child expresses itself in the early stages of speech development without them, the adult speaker cannot omit them, except by a forced experiment, or when he has to speak a foreign language the structure of which he does not know. This condition is found in many trade jargons.

The obligatory categories of languages differ fundamentally. As just stated, number, definiteness or indefiniteness of noun, time, are obligatory in most European languages. Some Indian languages either lack the obligatory category of number, or substitute for it distributive, collective, or other similar ideas; they may lack the obligatory category of time, which is expressed when needed by devices which fulfill the functions of our adverbs; they also lack (like Latin) the obligatory category of definiteness. On the other hand, they may require a much more rigid localization than is required in our language. Location near me, you, or him may be obligatory; the source of knowledge, whether something is known by one's own sense-experience, by evidence, or by hearsay; numerous time aspects, not tenses, such as "to be in a condition, to get into a position, to be discontinually in a condition, to be repeatedly in a condition, to terminate a condition," or the corresponding terms for action, all these may be obligatory in one language or another. It is obvious that the mental picture aroused by a spoken sentence will be fundamentally different according to these categories. We could read our newspapers with much greater satisfaction if our language would compel them to say whether their reports are based on self-experience, inference, or hearsay! The strict localization of some languages creates a much more vivid picture than our indifference to localization. If I say "the children are playing," an Indian of a certain tribe could not get a clear picture of what I have in mind, because he would have to say, for instance, "children (or child) whom I see here, are (or is, were or was) playing in the woods which I see here." The speaker must be definite as to locality, but he is indefinite as to how many children there are and when they were playing. When hearing the statement the picture conveyed to him may be entirely different from the one the speaker wishes to convey. It is an exaggeration of the conditions prevailing in our own language when we are conversing. The form of our grammar compels us to select a few traits of the thought we wish to express and suppresses many other aspects which the speaker has in mind and which the hearer supplies according to his fancy, so that the more generalized the obligatory categories, the more we are apt to find differences between the complete idea the speaker wishes to convey and the situation which the hearer recreates from the speaker's utterance. In different languages some emphasize one group of categories, others others.

There is little doubt that thought is thus directed in various channels. If I say "the father built a new house for his son" and the Indian says "the son was the reason for his father's housebuilding," we stress purpose, the Indian causality. Such a tendency pervading the language may well lead to a different reaction to the incidents of everyday life and it is conceivable that in this sense the mental activities of a people may be in part directed by language. I should not be inclined to overestimate this influence, because devices for expressing finality as over against causality are ever-present, and may rise into idiomatic use.

The morphological structure of words may have a similar influence. Although the complete words are merely tokens of concepts, their structure may direct thought in certain directions. Some Indian languages emphasize in all activities the means by which the action is performed—with the hand, the mouth, by means of an instrument such as a knife, or by pulling, pushing, etc. Further, they may indicate the form of the object acted upon as long, round, flat, rope-like, etc. Although the categories may not be intensely felt, they direct the thought in certain channels when handling experiences and may in this way exert a partial control over actions.

In this sense, we may say that language exerts a limited influence upon culture. It may, however, be safely said, that when changes of culture demand new ways of expression, languages are sufficiently pliable to follow new needs. Furthermore, under new conditions, the categories that are discovered by etymological analysis become more and more mere symbols and their etymological value does no longer elicit the consciousness of the category that the analysis reveals.

Under modern conditions culture controls the growth of language; the opposite influence is slight.

All this does not touch upon the obscure problem of the processes that may have existed in the earliest formation of languages. If we may trust morphological analysis, the fundamental categories of languages were very varied and we may assume on the basis of what we observe now, that cultural activities determined largely the development of these categories. It is intelligible that forms of objects, their physical qualities, their availability for human use, should have become the basis of generalization, or that activities should have been grouped according to the parts of the body or other instrumentalities used, or that a roving people may have differentiated movements according to the character of the country traversed—but it seems impossible to determine the conditions that led to the particular variety of categories found in a given language.

AT THE FRINGE OF LANGUAGE   C. S. Lewis

Language exists to communicate whatever it can communicate. Some things it communicates so badly that we never attempt to communicate them by words if any other medium is available. Those who think they are testing a boy's 'elementary' command of English by asking him to describe in words how one ties one's tie or what a pair of scissors is like, are far astray. For precisely what language can hardly do at all, and never does well, is to inform us about complex physical shapes and movements. Hence descriptions of such things in the ancient writers are nearly always unintelligible. Hence we never in real life voluntarily use language for this purpose; we draw a diagram or go through pantomimic gestures. The exercises which such examiners set are no more a test of 'elementary' linguistic competence than the most difficult bit of trick-riding from the circus ring is a test of elementary horsemanship.

Another grave limitation of language is that it cannot, like music or gesture, do more than one thing at once. However the words in a great poet's phrase interinanimate one other and strike the mind as a quasi-instantaneous chord, yet, strictly speaking, each word must be read or heard before the next. That way, language is as unilinear as time. Hence, in narrative, the great difficulty of presenting a very complicated change which happens suddenly. If we do justice to the complexity, the time the reader must take over the passage will destroy the feeling of suddenness. If we get in the suddenness we shall not be able to get in the complexity. I am not saying that genius will not find its own ways of palliating this defect in the instrument; only that the instrument is in this way defective.

One of the most important and effective uses of language is the emotional. It is also, of course, wholly legitimate. We do not talk only in order to reason or to inform. We have to make love and quarrel, to propitiate and pardon, to rebuke, console, intercede, and arouse. 'He that complains', said Johnson, 'acts like a man, like a social being.' The real objection lies not against the language of emotion as such, but against language which, being in reality emotional, masquerades —whether by plain hypocrisy or subtler self-deceit—as being something else.

From *Studies in Words*, by C. S. Lewis, Cambridge University Press, 1960.

All my generation are much indebted to Dr. I. A. Richards for having fully called our attention to the emotional functions of language. But I am hardly less indebted to Professor Empson for having pointed out that the conception of emotional language can be very easily extended too far. It was time to call a halt.

We must obviously not call any utterance 'emotional' language because it in fact arouses, even because it must arouse, emotion. 'It is not cancer after all', 'The Germans have surrendered', 'I love you'—may all be true statements about matter of fact. And of course it is the facts, not the language, that arouse the emotion. In the last, the fact communicated is itself the existence of an emotion but that makes no difference. Statements about crime are not criminal language; nor are statements about emotions necessarily emotional language. Nor, in my opinion, are value-judgements ('this is good', 'this is bad') emotional language. Approval and disapproval do not seem to me to be emotions. If we felt at all times about the things we judge good the emotion which is appropriate, our lives would be easier. It would also be an error to treat 'I am washed in the blood of the Lamb' as emotional language. It is of course metaphorical language. But by his metaphor the speaker is trying to communicate what he believes to be a fact. You may of course think the belief false in his particular case. You may think the real universe is such that no fact which corresponded to such a statement could possibly occur. You may say that the real cause which prompts a man to say things like that is a state of emotion. But if so an emotion has produced erroneous belief about an impossible fact and it is the fact erroneously believed in which the man is stating. A man's hasty belief that the Germans had surrendered (before they did) might well be caused by his emotions. That would not make 'The Germans have surrendered' a specimen of emotional language. If you could find a man nowadays capable of believing, and saying, 'The Russians have all been annihilated by magic', even this would not be emotional language, though his belief in magic might be a belief engendered by emotion.

All this is fairly plain sailing. We reach something harder in the things said by poets. For there the purpose of the utterance would be frustrated if no emotion were aroused. They do not merely, like the sentences cited above, arouse emotion in fact; it is their purpose—at any rate, part of their purpose—to do so. But we must be very careful here. Having observed that a poetical utterance in fact arouses emotion, and is intended to arouse emotion, and that if taken as a statement about reality—or even about the make-believe 'realities' of a fictitious narrative—it would be nonsensical or at least false, can we conclude that it communicates nothing but emotion? I think not.

Nothing will convince me that 'My soul is an enchanted boat'[1] is simply a better way—however much better—of doing what might be done by some exclamation like 'Gee!' Asia has risen from the dark cave of Demogorgon. She is floating upwards. She is saluted as 'Life of Life!' The reversed temporal process in ll. 97–103 ('We have passed Age's icy caves' etc.), borrowed from Plato's *Politicus* (269ᶜ *sq.*), marks the fact that at this moment the whole cycle is reversed and cosmos begins anew. She is undergoing apotheosis. What did it feel like? The poet says to us in effect 'Think of going in a boat. But quite effortless' ('Like a sleeping swan' gliding with the current, he adds in the next line), 'Like a boat without sail or oar; the motive power undiscoverable. Like a magic boat—you must have read or dreamed of such things—a boat drawn on, drawn swiftly on, irresistibly, smoothly, by enchantment.' Exactly. I know now how it felt for Asia. The phrase has communicated emotion. But notice how. By addressing in the first instance my imagination. He makes me imagine a boat rushing over waves, which are also identified with sounds. After that he need do no more; my emotion will follow of itself. Poetry most often communicates emotions, not directly, but by creating imaginatively the grounds for those emotions. It therefore communicates something more than emotion; only by means of that something more does it communicate the emotion at all.

Burns compares his mistress to 'a red, red rose'; Wordsworth his to 'a violet by a mossy stone Half hidden from the eye'. These expressions do communicate to me the emotion each poet felt. But it seems to me that they do so solely by forcing me to imagine two (very different) women. I see the rose-like, overpowering, midsummer sweetness of the one; the reticent, elusive freshness, the beauty easily overlooked in the other. After that my emotions may be left to themselves. The poets have done their part.

This, which is eminently true of poetry, is true of all imaginative writing. One of the first things we have to say to a beginner who has brought us his MS. is, 'Avoid all epithets which are merely emotional. It is no use *telling* us that something was "mysterious" or "loathsome" or "awe-inspiring" or "voluptuous". Do you think your readers will believe you just because you say so? You must go quite a different way to work. By direct description, by metaphor and simile, by

[1] *Prometheus Unbound* II, v, 72.

secretly evoking powerful associations, by offering the right stimuli to
our nerves (in the right degree and the right order), and by the very
beat and vowel-melody and length and brevity of your sentences, you
must bring it about that we, we readers, not you, exclaim "how mysterious!" or "loathsome" or whatever it is. Let me taste for myself, and
you'll have no need to *tell* me how I should react to the flavour.'

In Donne's couplet

> Your gown going off, such beautious state reveals
> As when from flowry meads th'hills shadow steales [2]

beautious is the only word of the whole seventeen which is doing
no work.

There are exceptions to this principle. By very successful placing,
a great author may sometimes raise such words to poetic life. Wordsworth's lines are a specimen:

> Which, to the boundaries of space and time,
> Of melancholy space and doleful time,
> Superior— [3]

Here we have almost the reverse of the process I have been describing. The object (space and time) is in one way so familiar to our
imaginations and in another so unimaginable—we have read so many
tedious attempts to exalt or over-awe us with mere superlatives or
even with simple arithmetic—that nothing can be made of it. This
time, therefore, the poet withdraws the object (the ground for emotion) altogether and appeals directly to our emotions; and not to the
quite obvious ones. Another exception is naturally to be found in
drama or very dramatic lyric, where the poet—with discretion and a
proper use of illusion—imitates the speech of people in some highly
emotional situation—even, at need, their inarticulate cries. This in
its purity, which purity a good poet never sustains for long, belongs to
poetry not in so far as poetry is a special use of language but in so
far as poetry is *mimesis*. In themselves the 'Ah! Ah!' or 'Otototoi' or
'Iou! Iou!' of characters in a Greek tragedy are not specimens of poetry
any more than the 'Bé, bé' of the lamb or the 'Au! Au!' of the dog
in Aristophanes.

In general, however, the poet's route to our emotions lies through
our imaginations.

[2] *Elegy* xix, 13.
[3] *Prelude* vi, 134.

We must also exclude from the category 'emotional language' words such as I have taken *supernatural* to be. The class of things which they refer to may be bound together chiefly by a common emotion; but the purpose of using the words is to assign something to that class, not merely to communicate the emotion which led to the classification.

Having thus narrowed the field, we can now make a new start. It will be noticed that I have throughout used the word *emotional* rather than *emotive*. This is because I think the latter word applicable to only one aspect of emotional language. For an 'emotive word' ought to mean one whose function is to arouse emotion. But surely we ought to distinguish utterances which arouse, from those which express, emotion? The first is directed towards producing some effect on a (real or imagined) hearer; the second discharges our own emotion, cleanses our stuffed bosom of some perilous stuff.

The distinction will seem straw-splitting if we have in mind the language of love. For, as Samson says, 'love seeks to have love', and it would be hard to say whether endearments serve more as expressions of love in the speaker or incitements to it in the beloved. But that tells us more about the nature of love than about the nature of language. One of my old headmasters once wisely said it was a pity that *amare* was the first Latin verb we all learn. He thought this led to an imperfect grasp of the difference between the active and the passive voice. It might be better to begin with *flagellare*. The difference between flogging and being flogged would come home to the business and bosoms of schoolboys far more effectively than that of loving and being loved. On the same principle, we can best see the distinction between the stimulant and the expressive functions of emotional language in a quarrel; and best of all where the same word performs both. The man who calls me a low hound both expresses and (actually or intentionally) stimulates emotion. But not the same emotion. He expresses contempt; he stimulates, or hopes to stimulate, the almost opposite emotion of humiliation.

Again, in the language of complaint we often find the expressive without the stimulant. When two people who have missed the last train stand on the silent platform saying 'Damn' or 'Bloody' or 'Sickening', they neither intend nor need to stimulate each other's disappointment. They are just 'getting it off their chests'.

The vocabulary of endearment, complaint, and abuse, provides, I think, almost the only specimens of words that are purely emotional, words from which all imaginative or conceptual content has vanished, so that they have no function at all but to express or stimulate emotion, or both. And an examination of them soon convinces us that in them we see language at its least linguistic. We have come to the frontier between language and inarticulate vocal sounds. And at that frontier we find a two-way traffic going on.

On the one hand we find inarticulate sounds becoming words with a fixed spelling and a niche in the dictionary. Thus English *heigh-ho* and Latin *eheu* are clearly formalised imitations of the sigh; *ah*, of the gasp; *tut-tut*, of the tongue clicked against the hard palate. These are general. In particular situations the 'verbification' of the inarticulate may occur *ad hoc*. A voluntary scream may become a cry for mercy. A voluntary groan, from a wounded man, uttered to attract the attention of the stretcher-bearers, may be the equivalent of a sentence ('There is a ~ounded man in this ditch').

But we also see the frontier being crossed in the opposite direction. In the vocabulary of abuse and complaint we see things that once were words passing out of the realm of language (properly so called) and becoming the equivalents of inarticulate sounds or even of actions; of sighs, moans, whimperings, growls, or blows.

The 'swear-words'—*damn* for complaint and *damn you* for abuse— are a good example. Historically the whole Christian eschatology lies behind them. If no one had ever consigned his enemy to the eternal fires and believed that there were eternal fires to receive him, these ejaculations would never have existed. But inflation, the spontaneous hyperboles of ill temper, and the decay of religion, have long since emptied them of that lurid content. Those who have no belief in damnation—and some who have—now damn inanimate objects which would on any view be ineligible for it. The word is no longer an imprecation. It is hardly, in the full sense, a word at all when so used. Its popularity probably owes as much to its resounding phonetic virtues as to any, even fanciful, association with hell. It has ceased to be profane. It has also become very much less forceful. You may say the same of *sickening* in its popular, ejaculatory, use. There are alarms and disappointments which can actually produce nausea, or, at least, emotions which we feel to be somehow similar to it. But the man who says *sickening!* when he has missed the train is not thinking about that. The word is simply an alternative to *damn* or *bloody*. And of course far weaker than it would be if it still carried any suggestion of vomiting.

So with abusive terms. No one would now call his schoolfellow or next door neighbour a *swine* unless someone had once used this word to make a real comparison between his enemy and a pig. It is

now a mere alternative to *beast* or *brute* or various popular unprint-
able words. They are all interchangeable. *Villain*, as we know, once
really compared your enemy to a *villein*. Once, to call a man *cad* or
knave assigned to him the status of a servant. And it did so because,
earlier still, these words meant 'boy' or 'junior' (you address a slave as
'boy' in Greek and a waiter as *garçon* in French).

Thus all these words have come down in the world. None of
them started by being *merely* abusive, few of them by being abusive
at all. They once stimulated emotion by suggesting an image. They
made the enemy odious or contemptible by asserting he was like
somebody or something we already disliked or looked down on. Their
use was a sort of passionate parody of the syllogism: pigs (or servants
or my juniors) are contemptible—John is like a pig (or servant or adolescent)—therefore John is contemptible. That was why they really
hurt; because hurting was not the whole of what they did. They
stimulated emotion because they also stimulated something else; imagination. They stimulated emotion in the particular case because they
exploited emotions which already existed towards whole classes of
things or persons. Now that they are nothing whatever but emotional
stimulants, they are weak emotional stimulants. They make no particular accusation. They tell us nothing except that the speaker has
lost his temper.

And even this they do not tell us linguistically, but symptomati-
cally; as a red face, a loud voice, or a clenched fist, might do equally
well. The fact of the other person's anger may hurt or frighten us;
hurt us if we love him, or frighten us if he is larger and younger than
ourselves and threatens violence. But his language as such has very
little power to do the only thing it is intended to do. It would have
been far more wounding to be called *swine* when the word still carried
some whiff of the sty and some echo of a grunt; far more wounding to
be called a *villain* when this still conjured up an image of the un-
washed, malodorous, ineducable, gross, belching, close-fisted, and surly
boor. Now, who cares? Language meant solely to hurt hurts strangely
little.

This can be seen clearly when we catch a word 'just on the turn'.
Bitch is one. Till recently—and still in the proper contexts—this accused a woman of one particular fault and appealed, with some success, to our contempt by calling up an image of the she-dog's comical
and indecorous behaviour when she is in heat. But it is now increasingly used of any woman whom the speaker, for whatever reason,
is annoyed with—the female driver who is in front of him, or a female

magistrate whom he thinks unjust. Clearly, the word is far more wounding in its narrower usage. If that usage is ever totally lost— as I think it will be—the word will sink to the level of *damn her*. Notice, too, how *cat* (of a woman) is still strong and useful because the image is still alive in it.

An important principle thus emerges. In general, emotional words, to be effective, must not be solely emotional. What expresses or stimulates emotion directly, without the intervention of an image or concept, expresses or stimulates it feebly. And in particular, when words of abuse have hurting the enemy as their direct and only object, they do not hurt him much. In the field of language, however it may be in that of action, hatred cuts its own throat, and those who are too 'willing to wound' become thereby impotent to strike. And all this is only another way of saying that as words become exclusively emotional they cease to be words and therefore of course cease to perform any strictly linguistic function. They operate as growls or barks or tears. 'Exclusively' is an important adverb here. They die as words not because there is too much emotion in them but because there is too little—and finally nothing at all—of anything else.

In this there is not much to be lamented. If a mother with a baby, or lovers in each other's arms, use language so emotional that it is really not language at all, I see no ground for shame or offence; and if men in an orgy of resentment, though (in the physical sense) they articulate, are really no more speaking—are saying no more—than a snarling animal, this is perhaps all for the best. The real corruption comes when men whose purpose in speaking is in fact purely emotional conceal this from others, and perhaps from themselves, by words that seem to be, but are not, charged with a conceptual content.

We have all heard *bolshevist, fascist, Jew,* and *capitalist,* used not to describe but merely to insult. Rose Macaulay noticed a tendency to prefix 'so called' to almost any adjective when it was used of those the speaker hated; the final absurdity being reached when people referred to the Germans as 'these so-called Germans'. *Bourgeois* and *middle class* often suffer the same fate.

A literary man of my acquaintance, on reading an unfavourable reference to his own works, called it *vulgar*. The charge brought against him was one that only highly educated people ever bring; the tone of the passage not otherwise offensive than by being unfavourable; the phrasing perfectly good English. If he had called it false, unintelligent, or malicious, I could have understood, though I might have disagreed. But why *vulgar*? Clearly, this word was selected solely because the speaker thought it was the one that the enemy, if he could hear it, would most dislike. It was the equivalent of an oath or a growl. But that was concealed from the speaker because 'This is vulgar' sounds like a judgement.

When we write criticism we have to be continually on our guard against this sort of thing. If we honestly believe a work to be very bad we cannot help hating it. The function of criticism, however, is 'to get ourselves out of the way and let humanity decide'; not to discharge our hatred but to expose the grounds for it; not to vilify faults but to diagnose and exhibit them. Unfortunately, to express our hatred and to revenge ourselves is easier and more agreeable. Hence there is a tendency to select our pejorative epithets with a view not to their accuracy but to their power of hurting. If writing which was intended to be comic has set our teeth on edge, how easily the adjectives *arch* or *facetious* trickle out of the pen! But if we do not know exactly what we mean by them, if we are not prepared to say how comic work which errs by *archness* and *facetiousness* differs from comic work which errs in any other way, it is to be feared that we are really using them not to inform the reader but to annoy the author—*arch* or *facetious* being among the most effective 'smear-words' of our period. In the same way work which obviously aspires and claims to be mature, if the critic dislikes it, will be called *adolescent*; not because the critic has really seen that its faults are those of adolescence but because he has seen that adolescence is the last thing the author wishes or expects to be accused of.

The best protection against this is to remind ourselves again and again what the proper function of pejorative words is. The ultimate, simplest and most abstract, is *bad* itself. The only good purpose for ever departing from that monosyllable when we condemn anything is to be more specific, to answer the question 'Bad in what way?' Pejorative words are rightly used only when they do this. *Swine*, as a term of abuse is now a bad pejorative word, because it brings no one accusation rather than another against the person it vilifies; *coward* and *liar* are good ones because they charge a man with a particular fault—of which he might be proved guilty or innocent. As applied to literature, *dull, hackneyed, incoherent, monotonous, pornographic, cacophonous,* are good pejoratives; they tell people in what particular way we think a book faulty. *Adolescent* or *provincial* are not so good. For even when they are honestly used, to define, not merely to hurt, they really suggest a cause for the book's badness instead of describing the badness itself. We are saying in effect 'He was led into his faults by being immature' or 'by living in Lancashire'. But would it not be more interesting to indicate the faults themselves and leave out our historical theory about their causes? If we find words like these—and *vulgar*, and others—indispensable to our criticism, if we find ourselves applying them to more and more different kinds of things, there is grave reason to suspect that—whether we know it or not—we are really using them not to diagnose but to hurt. If so, we are assisting in verbicide. For this is the downward path which leads to the graveyard of murdered words. First they are purely descriptive; *adolescent* tells us a man's age, *villain*, his status. Then they are specifically pejorative; *adolescent* tells us that a man's work displays 'mawkishness and all the thousand bitters' confessed by Keats, and *villain* tells that a man has a churl's mind and manners. Then they become *mere* pejoratives, useless synonyms for *bad*, as *villain* did and as *adolescent* may do if we aren't careful. Finally they become terms of abuse and cease to be language in the full sense at all.

LANGUAGE AND THE THEORY OF SIGN
Jacques Maritain

I should like here to take up again some parts of an outline on a general theory of the sign I wrote a number of years ago,[1] and to make use of them to propose some considerations on language. These considerations may be grouped under three headings: language and awareness of the relation of signification; language and the magic sign; language and reverse or inverted signification.

No problems are more complex or more fundamental to the concerns of man and civilization than those pertaining to the sign. The sign is relevant to the whole extent of knowledge and of human life; it is a universal instrument in the world of human beings, like motion in the world of physical nature.

Signum est quod repraesentat aliud a se potentiae cognoscenti. A sign is something that makes something other than itself present to

From *Language: An Enquiry Into Its Meaning and Function*, Harper & Brothers, New York, 1957.

[1] Cf. "Sign and Symbol," in *Journal of the Warburg Institute* (1937–1938), Vol. 1. Also cf., with considerable additions, my book *Ransoming the Time*, Charles Scribner's Sons, New York, 1941.

knowledge. A sign manifests and makes known something for which it stands vicariously and to which it is related as the measured is to the measure.

The ancients drew a distinction between the natural sign (*signum naturale*) and the conventional sign (*signum ad placitum*). In their view, a sign is what it is by virtue of its specific and characteristic function of making known some other thing. The relation of the sign to what it manifests is a real relation, i.e., is founded in reality in the case of a natural sign, since a natural sign is better known than that which it manifests, and since the property of being more knowable, and this in relation to something else that is thereby made knowable, is a real property, not a purely ideal relation (*relatio rationis*) existing as such in thought only. The fact that smoke gives us knowledge of fire rather than of water, and that tracks of oxen give us knowledge of the ox rather than of man, and the concept of a horse of the horse rather than of stone—all this is based on a real intrinsic proportion between these signs and the things they signify. This realistic notion of the natural sign rests, in short, on a metaphysics for which intelligibility and being are consubstantial (*verum et ens convertuntur*).

This real relation is not one of efficient causality. Sign strictly keeps to the order of "objective causality" or of the formal causality of knowledge, not of efficient or productive causality. When a sign produces an effect it is never by virtue of being a sign. The sign is not even the efficient cause of the knowledge of the thing signified; it makes it known only by standing in lieu of the object within the cognitive faculty to which it brings the presence of the object, thus functioning in the same line of causality as the object itself (formal causality).

Not every image is a sign, and not every sign is an image. For the image (which "proceeds from another as from its principle and in the likeness of that other") may be of the same nature and have the same ontological status as that of which it is an image (the son is the image, not the sign, of his father). And many signs are not images (smoke is not the image of fire, nor is a cry the image of pain). We might define a symbol as a *sign-image* (both *Bild* and *Bedeutung*), a sensible thing *signifying* an object by reason of a presupposed relation of *analogy*.

Signs have to do with all types of knowledge. They are of considerable importance in the psychic life of nonrational animals, and here I think we should interpret the data concerning conditioned reflexes from the point of view of psychology, not merely of physiology.

The external senses make use of signs (I see Socrates when I see his statue; my eye sees him in it), for the use of signs does not necessarily imply discourse. Thus the thing signified has a kind of presence —the presence of knowability—in the sign; it is there *in alio esse*.

The birth of ideas and thus of intellectual life in us seems bound up with the discovery of the signifying value of signs. Animals make use of signs without perceiving the relation of signification. To perceive the relation of signification is to have an *idea*, i.e., a spiritual sign. Nothing throws more light on this subject than the miracle of the first dawning of intelligence in people who are deaf and dumb and blind (like Marie Heurtin, Helen Keller, Lydwine Lachance). It depends essentially on the discovery of the relation of signification between a gesture and the object of a desire. The keystone of the life of the mind is the sign.

In the realm of social life, the part played by signs is no less important: they give rise to social as well as to individual consciousness. It is through its symbols that a city, a class, or a nation becomes conscious of what it is.

Only in God does the life of the intellect make no use of signs. He knows Himself and all things by His essence. That is the privilege of the pure Act.

At this point I should like to submit my first remarks about language. I just alluded to the first awakening of intelligence in blind deaf-mutes. Let us look a little more closely into the case.

For the first stirring of the idea as distinct from images, the intervention of a sensible sign is necessary. Normally in the development of a child it is necessary that the idea be "enacted" by the senses and lived through before it is born as an idea; it is necessary that the relationship of signification should first be actively *exercised* in a gesture, a cry, in a sensory sign bound up with the desire that is to be expressed. *Knowing* this relationship of signification will come later, and this will be to have the *idea*, even if it is merely implicit, of that which is signified. Animals and children make use of this signification; they do not perceive it. When the child begins to perceive it (then he exploits it, he toys with it, even in the absence of the real need to which it corresponds)—at that moment the idea has emerged.

But in "imprisoned souls," among blind deaf-mutes, the first stirring of an idea cannot spontaneously arise for lack of natural sensory signs. These require the convergence of all the senses; a cry which is not heard, a gesture which is not seen—how can these poor walled-in souls actively make use of such to express a desire? With them there can be no natural and spontaneous exercise of a relationship of significa- tion, preceding the knowledge thereof, and hence preceding the birth of the idea.

In order to *exert* the first relationship of signification of which they are to make use, they must *know* this relationship; the idea, the very knowledge of signification must needs come to life at the same time as its first practical use! That is why some external help is indispen- sable. The miracle of awakening to the life of thought will come to pass precisely when—owing to the patiently repeated attempts of the teacher, who denies a desire and then suggests a sign, an *artificial, conventional* sign, intended to procure the satisfaction of the desire he has denied—the child suddenly *discovers* by some sort of sudden eruption of the idea the signification of this conventional sign (for ex- ample, of some gesture or other, in the language of the deaf), and from that moment on progresses with astonishing rapidity. A Marie Heurtin, a Helen Keller achieved the higher levels of intellectual life.

Now it seems to me that the way in which ideas are born to blind deaf-mutes can help us to picture how the discovery of language may have taken place.

The discovery of language, then, coincides with the discovery of the relation of signification, and this would explain why, as a matter of fact, the invention of language and the birth of ideas, the first release of the intellect's power, probably took place at the same time.

It is conceivable, I think, that a genuine language of *natural* sen- sory signs may have preceded language strictly so called (made up of conventional sensory signs), and that the latter may have developed out of the former. The "miracle" would have happened at the mo- ment when man, beyond the fact of using natural gestures to express hunger, anger, or fear, would also have grasped the notion that this gesture was possessed of the virtue of signifying. By the same stroke a field of infinite possibilities would have opened. Then, once the relation of signification was discovered, the process of arbitrarily se- lecting or inventing other gestures and of using them as *conventional* signs no doubt developed quite rapidly.

Did a language made up of simple natural signs ever actually exist? Did, on the other hand, a language made up of conventional signs which were only gestures ever actually exist? It is not within my province to discuss such hyotheses. Moreover, my private opinion is rather that things took place according to an altogether different pat- tern. But as a philosopher I wish to point out that such hypotheses are logically conceivable. I do so in order to emphasize that what defines language is not precisely the use of words, or even of conventional signs; it is the use of any sign whatsoever *as involving the knowledge or awareness of the relation of signification,* and therefore a potential infinity; it is the use of signs *in so far as it manifests that the mind has grasped and brought out the relation of signification.*

Granted the imaginary possibility that a language of gestures ever existed, we might also imagine that later some kinds of vocal gestures or wordless singsongs led to articulate language. In any case, the invention of those particular conventional signs which are words, the creation of a system of signs made up of "phonemes" and "morphemes" was in itself a second "miracle," a further discovery of human intelligence, no less characteristic of man, but less essential than, and by nature not prior to, the discovery of the relation of signification.

So far we have spoken of genuine language. Let us point out that the word "language," when referring to animals, is equivocal. Animals possess a variety of means of communication but no genuine language. I have observed that animals use signs. But, as I also pointed out, no animal knows the relation of signification or uses signs as involving and manifesting an awareness of this relation.

The full import of this is best realized in connection with the use of conventional signs by animals. Karl von Frisch's admirable studies [2] have shown that bees use conventional signs: he has observed that a scouting bee performs two types of dance (a round dance and a wagging dance) to indicate to the other members of the hive in what direction and at what distance the source of food it has visited is to be found. Yet, as Professor Benveniste rightly points out, [3] such conventional signs do not truly constitute a language in the genuine sense of this word.

> The bee's message does not call for any reply from those to whom it is addressed, except that it evokes a particular behaviour which is not strictly an answer. This means that the language of the bees lacks the dialogue which is distinctive of human speech. . . . Moreover, the bee's message cannot be reproduced by another bee which has not seen for itself what the first bee has announced. . . . The bee does not construe a message from another message. Each bee, once advised by the scouting bee's dance, flies out and feeds at the spot indicated, repro-

[2] Karl von Frisch, *Bees, Their Vision, Chemical Senses, and Language,* Cornell University Press, Ithaca, N.Y., 1950.

[3] Emile Benveniste, "Animal Communication and Human Language," in *Diogenes* (1952), No. 1.

ducing the same information on its return, not with reference to the first message but with reference to the fact it has just verified itself. Now the characteristic of language is to produce a substitute for experience which can be passed on *ad infinitum* in time and space. This is the nature of our symbolism and the basis of linguistic tradition. If we now consider the content of the message it is easy to see that it always concerns only one fact, viz., food, and that the only variations of this theme concern the question of space. The contrast with the boundless possibilities of human language is obvious. Furthermore, the behaviour which expresses the bee's message is a special form of symbolism. It consists in tracing off an objective situation of fact, the only situation which can be translated into a message, without any possibility of variation or transposition. In human language, on the contrary, the symbol as such does not trace out the facts of experience in the sense that there is no necessary relationship between the objective reference and the linguistic form. . . . The essential difference between the method of communication discovered among bees and our human language . . . can be stated summarily in one phrase which seems to give the most appropriate definition of the manner of communication used by the bees: it is not a language but a signal code. All the characteristics of a code are present: the fixity of the subject matter, the invariability of the message, the relation to a single set of circumstances, the impossibility of separating the components of the message, and its unilateral transmission.[4]

All this means, in the last analysis, that the relation of signification remains unknown to the bees. They use signs—and they do not know that there are signs. By what process the dance of the bees developed as a conventional sign is a great mystery of biology and animal psychology. But in itself it no more implies language, in the genuine sense of the word, than the fact of a dog's barking when he sees a stranger, or of his crouching down or sitting up when his master utters certain words. The whole thing belongs to the realm of conditioned reflexes, whereas language pertains to the realm of the intellect, with its concepts and universal notions.

A particularly important place in a general theory of sign should be given, I think, to the distinction between *logic* and *magic* signs.

By a *logic* sign, I mean a sign operating under certain functional conditions through which it is a sign *for the intellect* (whether speculative or practical), that is, when the predominance of the intellect defines a particular psychological or cultural regime. Under such conditions the sign, be it in itself sensible or intellectual, speaks ultimately

4 *Ibid.*, pp. 5, 6, 7.

to the intellect and refers ultimately to a psychic regime ruled by the intellect.

I call *magic* a sign operating under a different functional regime, where it speaks primarily to the imagination, regarded as the supreme and ruling standard of the psychic or cultural life as a whole. The sign, be it in itself sensible or intellectual, ultimately speaks to the imaginative faculties and refers ultimately to a psychic regime immersed in the vitalizing depths of the imagination.

My working hpothesis is here the new notion of "functional conditions" or "states," [5] and I am pointing to a fundamental distinction between the state of our developed cultures and another state, in which for the psychic and cultural life as a whole the last word rests with the imagination as the supreme and final law. No doubt the intellect is present, but, in a way, it is not free. That is the kind of "state" I am calling the "magic" regime of psychic and cultural life.

May I add that this working hypothesis was lucky enough to reconcile opposed points of view in a particularly controversial field. Some time before his death, Professor Lucien Lévy-Bruhl was so kind as to write me of his agreement on this point. "As you put it quite rightly," he said, " 'primitive' mentality is a *state* of human mentality, and I can accept the characteristics through which you define it." [6]

As we have seen above, animals make use of signs. They live in a kind of magical world; biologically united to nature, they use signs belonging to a psychic regime which is entirely imaginative.

Intellect in primitive man is of the same kind as ours: it may even be more alive in him than in some more civilized people. But the question here is that of its "state" and of the existential conditions under which it operates. The whole mental regime of primitive man is under the authority of the imagination. In him the intellect is in every way involved with and dependent on the imagination and its savage world. This kind of mental regime is one where acquaintance with nature is experienced and lived through with an intensity and to an extent we cannot easily picture.

This is a state of inferiority, but it is by no means despicable. It is a human state, the state of mankind in its infancy, a fertile state through which we have had to pass. Under this regime humanity

---

[5] I am using the word "state" here in a sense similar to that intended by chemists when they speak of the solid, liquid, and gaseous "states" of matter, or by theologians when they speak of the "state of pure nature," the "state of innocence," etc.

[6] From a letter dated May 8, 1938, and published in *Revue Thomiste*, July, 1938.

enriched itself with many vital truths, a number of which were perhaps lost when it passed on to an adult state. These truths were
known by way of dream or instinct and by actual participation in the
thing known—just as if we imagined that in the knowledge a bee has
of the world of flowers a light which the bee does not possess, the light
of reason or of the intellect, were present in a diffused, undifferen-
tiated state, before becoming condensed into stars and solar systems
separating daylight from darkness.

Here we meet with a difficulty analogous to that which we find
when we try to penetrate the mental life of animals. Whatever *we*
picture to ourselves is bathed in intelligence, and in intelligence which
is free. We have great trouble in depicting to ourselves what another
mental regime can be like. (And if we are Cartesians, it is impossible
for us to do so.)

Let me say in brief that in our logical state, sensations, images, and
ideas are *solar*, bound up with the luminous and regular life of the
intellect and its laws of gravitation.

In the magic state they were *nocturnal*, bound up with the fluid
and twilight mental life of the imagination and of an experience which
was astonishingly powerful but entirely lived through and dreamed.

The same is true of the sign, and of the relation of sign to thing
signified.

Since truth is a relation of the cognitive faculty to the thing and
belongs only to the judgment of the intellect which grasps it as such,
it should be said that in primitive man this relation is experienced but
is not winnowed out for its own sake. It is known, of course, because
the intellect is present, but it is known in a nocturnal manner, since
intelligence is in this case immersed in the powers of the imagination.

When we consider primitive man we may say that in him the relation of the mind to the thing is ambivalent: the same relation is "false"
(in the eyes of our evolved consciousness) to the extent that it asserts,
for instance, the existence of composite tribal ancestors (like duck-men
or kangaroo-men). It is "true" to the same extent that it affirms the
vital union of man and nature of which this myth is the symbol. But
for primitive man a distinction of this kind has no meaning. This is
because his very adhesion to truth is not ours, since for him the idea
of truth has not been winnowed out for itself.

He adheres *en bloc*, at the same time and indistinctly, to the symbol
and the symbolized: here is for him, in indivisible fashion, an image
or a likeness of truth, an equivalent, an *als ob* of truth, without his

having winnowed out the idea of truth for its own sake. In similar fashion a child believes in a story, in the adventures of Alice in Wonderland; awaken the child, withdraw him from the world of the imagination and he knows very well that a little girl cannot enter a rabbit hole. But primitive man does not wake up; he is not yet withdrawn from the motherly bosom of the imagination, which makes him familiar with the whole of nature and without which he could not face the relentless severity of his existence as a cave dweller at war with the beasts. He lives in the world of *make-believe*.

Bergson has admirably shown that what is to be found at the source and basis of magic as a primordial element is the relationship of causality.

> . . . [Man] realized at once that the limits of his normal influence over the outside world were soon reached, and he could not resign himself to going no further. So he carried on the movement, and since the movement could not by itself secure the desired result, nature must needs take the task in hand. . . . [Things] will then be more or less charged with submissiveness and potency: they will hold at our disposal a power which yields to the desires of man, and of which man may avail himself. . . . [The workings of Magic] begin the act which men cannot finish. They go through the motions which alone could not produce the desired effect, but which will achieve it if the man concerned knows how to prevail upon the goodwill of things. Magic is then innate in man, being but the outward projection of a desire which fills the heart. [7]

That which I believe to be lacking in Bergson's theory is that it does not take into account the indispensable instrument of magical activity —the *practical sign*. It is surely true that magic implies an appeal to some cosmic power which brings the desire of man to a happy outcome, an appeal which itself presupposes some sympathy, some compliance in things. But it must be added that magic makes use of signs. Here the relationship proper to the sign, and to the practical sign, necessarily intervenes. Man does not merely outline some causal action; he *makes a sign* (to semi-personal cosmic elements). It is needful that we insist upon the mental characteristics of these practical signs, subject as they are to the nocturnal regime of the imagination.

1. First of all, in my opinion, we here find ourselves confronted with a refraction in the world of imagination, or with a nocturnal

[7] H. Bergson, *Les Deux Sources de la Morale et de la Religion*, Alcan, Paris, 1932, pp. 175–177; *The Two Sources of Morality and Religion* (tr. by R. A. Audra and C. Brereton), Henry Holt, New York, 1935, pp. 155–157.

deformation, of the practical sign in its quality as sign, or considered in the order of the *relationship itself of signification*, that is to say, in the order of *formal* causality, wherein the sign is, by its essence, the vicar of the object. Let us not forget that this relationship of sign to signified is, in its own order, singularly close. The motion toward the sign or the image, says St. Thomas after Aristotle, is identical with the motion toward the object itself. *'Sic enim est unus et idem motus in imaginem cum illo qui est in rem."* [8] In the formal-objective order the sign is thus something most astonishing, whereat the routine of culture alone prevents our wonder. And this marvelous function of containing the object—with respect to the mind—of having present in itself the thing itself *in alio esse*, is fully exercised in primitive man. Words are not anemic or colorless, they are overflowing with life—with their life as signs—for primitive man. But that in itself sets a snare for his imagination. Thanks to the condition of experienced and lived participation wherein is established his whole mental life, the presence as to knowledge of the signified in the sign becomes for him a presence as to reality, a physical interchangeability, a physical fusion, and a physical equivalence of the sign and the signified (invocation of mythical names; magic objects, spells, idolatry). Primitive man is intoxicated with the excellence of the sign; yet the sign never altogether loses its genuine relationship of signification (to some *other* thing). The idol is god and yet is never altogether god.

2. Then again a slurring takes place from formal-objective causality to *efficient causality*. The creation of signs is a mark of the preeminence of the mind, and the instinct of the intelligence quickly informed man that symbols make him enter into the heart of things—in order to know them: at once, in a psychic regime wherein the imagination is dominant, this slurring will take place, man will think that symbols make us enter into the heart of things in order to act physically upon them and in order to make them physically subject to us and in order to effect for us a real and physical union with them. Moreover, are not the signs in question first and foremost practical signs? At once the imagination will take a sign directive toward an operation as an operating sign. And why should we be astonished that the imagination of primitive man cannot distinguish between formal causality and efficient causality, when the intelligence of philosophers so often confuses them?

The sign, then, not only makes men know, it makes things be; it is an efficient cause in itself. Hence all the procedures of sympathetic

[8] *Summa Theologica*, III, 25, 3.

magic. In order to make rain, the sorcerer waters the ground. In order to obtain abundant tubers, he buries in the ground at seed time magical stones of the same shape as the desired tubers, which shall "teach" the yams and the taro to grow big, to reach the same size as the stones. The stones make them a sign, they are pattern symbols. The theory of *mana* among the Melanesians (*avenda* among the Iroquois, *wakonda* among the Sioux), the theory of a force spread throughout nature wherein all things participate in various degrees, seems to be the fruit of a later reflection upon this use of the sign. To the extent that reflection will be intensified, the idea of this semi-physical, semi-moral environment will become more materialized.

3. But the sign, in spite of everything, remains a sign. Inevitably there will take place a return of the order of causality to which it belongs, that is, of formal causality and of the relationship of signification—which with primitive man becomes a relationship of fusion and of physical equivalence—upon the relationship of efficient causality and of operation. And the imagination will oscillate from one way of thinking the sign to the other. In the perspective of efficient causality (as well as in the perspective of the relationship of signification understood in accordance with its true nature) there is a *distinction*, a difference, between the cause and the effect (as well as between the sign and the signified). In the perspective of formal causality denatured by the imagination, and of that intoxication with the sign induced in primitive man by the relationship of signification, there is a physical *interpenetration* and fusion of the sign and the signified.

Since we are by hypothesis dealing with the nocturnal regime of the imagination, and since for the imagination as such (as dreams bear witness) the principle of identity does not exist; and then again, since the intelligence is still present, bound up with and clothed in the imagination, it is easy to understand that for primitive man the identity of things is constantly unmade and made again. It is altogether too hasty for us to say that with him there is simply an identity between the sign and the signified. No, there is an oscillation, there is a going and coming from distinction to identification. When children play by building sand castles, these castles are truly castles for them. If you trample them, the children will cry with rage and indignation. But once their play is at an end, what were castles are only sand. Primitive man believes to be identical (through the living power of the imagination) that which he obscurely knows to be different (through his intelligence, bound up in the imagination). It is impossible to understand anything about his thought if it be conceived from the point of view of the logical or daylight state of the intelligence, taken as the rule and measure of all thought. It is the thought of an awakened dreamer, wherein the role of *play* (and the allowance of *play*) is tremendously great.

If the above remarks are true, we may conclude that language began in mankind in the form of "magical" language. To the mind of the primitive man the word does not signify a concept, and, through the concept, a thing; it directly signifies a thing; and the word and the thing it signifies are both distinct and one, for the word, in so far as it remains a sign (formal causality), is not physically the thing, and in so far as it is a magical sign (confusion between formal and efficient causality), is physically the thing or causes it to exist. Nothing is more natural for primitive mentality than to make the name into a real equivalent of the thing named, and to have a patient as confident in swallowing the prescription as in swallowing the medicine itself. Under cover of the deceit and illusion of magical thought, at least the dignity and sacred mystery of the words were felt and recognized (even though overrated).

Once the mind and the society have passed under the solar regime of intelligence, the sense of this dignity and sacred mystery—now purified of its magical connotations—remains essential to human civilization. When civilization decays, the sense in question dissipates itself and is finally lost. Then, in order to recover it, poetry may possibly be tempted to return to magic and to crave for *the power of words*,[9] as can be seen in Mallarmé and many other modern poets. There is a curious—and tragic—phenomenon, where something great and invaluable is looked for, and missed (namely, the genuine dignity of words, which refers to truth, not to power), and where by dint of refinement the civilized mind retrogresses to that magical notion of the sign which was normal in the childlike state of mankind, yet is for mankind in its adult state but a pathological symptom.

As appears with particular clarity in the consideration of works of art, a final distinction must be made, namely, between the *direct* sign (which denotes an object) and what might be called the *reverse* or *inverted* sign (which manifests the subject). All the signs which we have been considering in this study are direct signs. The letter *A* sig-

[9] Cf. Allen Tate, "Poe and the Power of Words," in *Kenyon Review,* Summer, 1952. (Reprinted in *The Forlorn Demon,* Henry Regnery, Chicago, 1953, under the title "The Angelic Imagination: Poe as God.")

nifies the sound A, mourning weeds signify death. But the sign can also act in the inverse way. While manifesting an object it can by a kind of inverted or retroverted signification also denote the subject itself which is using the sign and its states, its dispositions, and its secrets which it does not admit to itself, the subject being in that case taken as object by some observer. This is the sense in which Freud and his disciples understand the word "*symbol*"; they no longer think of its direct but only of its reverse or inverted signification. The Freudian symbol is a conscious content caused by the unconscious states of which it is the symptom. The birth of Minerva from the forehead of Jupiter is no longer the symbol of the divine origin of wisdom; it is the "symbol" of the idea of physiological birth *ex utero* which has been thrust back into the unconscious, and the idea of the divine origin of wisdom becomes itself the "symbol" of this unconscious representation. As has been pointed out by Roland Dalbiez,[10] it would be better in this case to say "psychic expression," a notion that is valid especially for the products of "dereistic" thought (dreams, hallucinations, neurotic symptoms).

But even in normal thought the signs which man uses to signify things (direct signs) signify man himself (reverse signs). Every work of art is a confession, but it is by discovering the secrets of being (guessed at by dint of suffering the things of this world) that it makes confession of the poet's secret.

As far as language is concerned, the part played by the *reverse* or *inverted* sign appears in an arresting way in those kinds of slang which are not simply spontaneous appropriations of speech to a special (and especially trying) human task or a closed (though possibly large) environment, divided from the society, manners, and speech of "cultivated" people, but which are, in actual fact, discriminating languages, typical for groups which segregate themselves from the community, either because they are composed of derelict, potentially delinquent, or criminal people at war with society or because they are composed of highbrow people who consider themselves privileged, as happens with young persons who have been selected to be trained in certain prominent institutions especially devoted to the formation of a vocational or intellectual elite.

The phenomenon is particularly interesting in this latter case, and it seems to be linked, as a rule, with those rites of initiation which are

[10] Cf. Roland Dalbiez, *La méthode psychoanalytique et la doctrine freudienne.*

called *brimades* in French, and which correspond roughly to "hazing."
As an instance among thousands, I would refer to the book in which
Romain Rolland tells us of his recollections as a student in the École
Normale Supérieure of Paris, a highbrow school for future intellectu-
als; he gives us a curious lexicon of the slang that was used there at
that time. For example, with reference to the Director of the School
(Georges Perrot), to some professors (La Coulouche, Chantavoine, and
Fortunat Strowski), and to a general in charge of military instruction
(General Jeanningros), *faire un Perrot* meant to make a blunder; *faire
un Coulouche,* to play the phrasemonger; *faire un Chantavoine,* to
play the euphuist; *faire un Tunat,* to make a bad pun; *faire un Jeanningros,* to utter a stupidity. [11]

Slang, as a rule, not only signifies concepts and things but also, and
first of all, the subjective behavior, the feelings, habits, oddities, jokes,
tricks, collusions, experiences, and resentments which are peculiar to
the group and differentiate it from any other; it alludes to the secret
life of the group and strengthens this collective life. It affords a particular delight because only the man who belongs to the group can
understand it, and because in using it he immerses himself in this
incommunicable hermetic life. Each time he uses the slang of the
group, he affirms and reinforces his communion with the group and,
in one sense, the giving up of his own personality to the group. The
word becomes a kind of magic and operative sign of the unity of the
group, and of its difference from ordinary mankind. Then, indivisibly
from its function as direct sign, the word is essentially a reverse or
inverted sign of the subjectivity, self-love, and pride of the group.

That is why slang cannot really be translated into ordinary language
without losing its meaning and flavor. More than an object of thought,
it means the overtones that accompany this object in terms of human
and social subjectivity. The human despair and abjection with which
certain abject writers have to saturate the world of things could not be
expressed except in their slang.

Now, if it is true that the essence of language is to manifest thought
and objects of thought, it is difficult not to conclude that the various
slangs of which I spoke invoke a kind of perversion of the function
of language.

Finally, the question I would like to raise in this connection no
longer deals with slang. It is whether, since the event of Babel, all

[11] Romain Rolland, *Le Cloître de la rue d'Ulm,* Albin Michel, Paris, 1952, pp.
18–19.

tongues of the earth—though they are in no way slang but genuine types of language—do not run the risk of being tinged with some admixture of a similar impurity. For peoples divided from each other by their languages, and walled up in their own particular means of intelligible communication, there is an inherent temptation to yield to an inner spiritual trend toward cherishing over and above all the closed subjectivity of the group its difference from the rest of mankind.

No doubt an element of reverse or inverted signification is inseparable from the direct signification of the words. But genuine language, while expressive of the group's subjectivity, gives unquestionable prevalence to objectivity, and direct sign, and to the universality of direct, intellectual meaning; and then the secondary function of language, i.e., the intention of expressing subjectivity, remains itself *open*, it is oriented toward a *communication* of the collective self, which tends to make itself sincerely known to others. The risk of impurity of which I am speaking materializes when this intention of expressing subjectivity becomes oriented toward the *self-assertion* of the group in a *closed*, aristocratic, or resentful manner, and as against all other groups.

The primary and the secondary functions of language are both human. Language attains complete freedom, and the excellence of its own nature, when these two functions are perfectly fused. The subjective function, however, is, as I have said, secondary. Furthermore it remains, as a rule, in an inchoate and unsatisfactory condition, because our words are primarily destined to designate material and external things. As a result, in their secondary function itself they signify the subjectivity of the social group rather than that of the individual person, and they do so in a more or less awkward and rough manner, which depends on the particular history and accidental experiences of the group. Let me say, therefore, that if Angels used words, it is only in the language of Angels that the two functions of which I am speaking would be really and perfectly fused. It is only in the tongue of Angels that language could attain complete freedom and the excellence of its own nature.

But Angels use no words.

Poets, in mankind, desperately endeavor to achieve a certain similarity of the language of Angels, or of perfect language, capable of expressing things and the self together in one and the same breath. Thus, what birds realize by music only, man can somewhat realize by poetry, and his music has also an intelligible significance, a spiritual meaning.

LANGUAGE AS IDEA   *Ruth Nanda Anshen*

Language gives evidence of its reality through three categories of human experience. The first may be considered as the meaning of words; the second, as those meanings enshrined in grammatical forms; and the third and, in the view of this author, the most significant, as those meanings which lie beyond grammatical forms, those meanings mysteriously and miraculously revealed to man. It is with the last category that this chapter will endeavor to deal, for its thesis is that thought itself must be accompanied by a critical understanding of the relation of linguistic expression to the deepest and most persistent intuitions of man. An effort will further be made to show that language becomes imperfect and inadequate when it depends exclusively upon mere words and forms and when there is an uncritical trust in the adequacy of these words and forms as constituting the ultimate content and extent of language. For man is that being on earth who does not have language. Man *is* language.

It is by virtue of the procreative power of language, which grasps, shakes, and transforms, that man is man. For nothing really human can be so without this meaning, whether the language be uttered or silent. In this way, language as the power of universals is given to man in order that he may transcend his environment, in order that he may have a world. It is the law of language to create the world, and it is therefore as futile to search for the origin of language as it is to search for the origin of reason. Both are given with man; both are part of his essential, his ontological reality.

Words themselves are ideas—although not all words. This means that man does not create ideas. He assembles them. In this way he is thrust into a state of universal mobility since he attaches the swift and restless force of his individual existence to the retarded and more massive power of his language. And for this there is only one source of help—Spirit. If words issued from an origin other than Spirit, from one's native land, one's country, for example, they would be born and they would die with it. Thus we would be deceived, tricked into an illusion. It is fortunate that the reasons whereby it is generally proved that language cannot have been invented by man are irrefutable. With the infallibility of the intuitive faculty and with the implacability of logic we must concede that if language does not come from empiric

From *Language: An Enquiry Into Its Meaning and Function,* Harper & Brothers, New York, 1957.

man, it must come from Spirit or God. For God created language even as He created man. And it may further be added that man can no more do without language than he can order or direct it. He can only bestow on it his faith, accord it his confidence, endeavoring by all the spiritual and moral means at his disposal and by the depths and seriousness of his individual experience not to violate it. And thus it might be said that in this very law of our thought is contained the proof of the existence of God.

The problem of this wondrous gift which enables man to communicate with his fellows, to reveal to others the hidden secrets of his being, to raise to God his desires in invocations, his sorrows in grief, or his despair in entreaty, this unique instrument which, entrusted to the written or the spoken tradition, defeats the voracity of time, this is the question concerning us, taxing our minds and our hearts. It is language, full-panoplied and alive, issuing hot and pulsating from the human mouth, it is language severed from all practical, all immediate applicability which here demands our investigation.

Many theories concerning language have been advanced. The fact, however, is that this problem resolves itself into another. Words are the ultimate symbols of ideas. They translate images and desires which when thus articulated acquire consciousness and are rendered operative, enabling man to escape from the loneliness of a closed consciousness, to emerge from the isolation in which he is enveloped and to experience a relationship with one other single being, with many others, with himself, or with God. An association with his fellow men is established whether near or far, living or dead. His soul, by an autochthonous impulse, stretches forth and opens to them as theirs do to him since there is present under the substructure of the formal diversity of the symbol a hidden essence which contains an essential and universal identity. If this essential identity were lacking, if words, however different in sound, did not evoke the identical eternal reality, the result would be sounds, not words.

It has been observed, for example, that mentally disturbed individuals possess no linguistic awareness.[1] They have no language. They have only words. Encrusted within themselves, words have been divested of their power to reveal or to communicate. This is because words then have lost their ontological roots. They no longer flow into action. And this inefficacy of mere words without language unmasks them. The word is obeyed but it is not heard; it is not seen; it has

---

[1] Cf. Kurt Goldstein, *Language and Language Disturbances,* Grune and Stratton, New York, 1948.

lost its connotations, its matrix. And when it no longer has weight it exposes itself, it reveals itself as nothing but a word, sterile, uncreative, the idea sacrificed, just as for Bergson it was the indeterminacy in the reaction that isolated the image from the world. This is true not only for the abnormal but for the normal individual as well.

Words in such a configuration must be distrusted for it is absurd to trust them. Such words, on which a man may so lightly traverse the space of a thought, may be compared to a fragile bridge thrown across a chasm. They may permit crossing but no stopping. A person in rapid motion can use them and get away. But if he hesitates even slightly, this infinitesimal fraction of time breaks them down, and all are plunged into the abyss. The one who rushes must be acrobatic; he must not dwell heavily, for if he does, he soon finds that the most lucid speech is nothing more than a tissue of obscure terms.

Language and "word" are not synonymous. Because of this, languages may be differentiated morphologically. There are, however, evolutions and mutations of words, words which are learned. But at the same time they constitute the varying symbols of the same living reality which is synonymous with the infinite capacity of the human mind. The expression of this capacity might be exemplified by invariable symbols. Leibnitz once proposed that the Chinese ideograms should be adopted to convey the fundamental concepts of philosophy, thus rendering the philosophic ideas intelligible to each in his own language. That great philosopher never relinquished his dream of a *pasigraphy* comprehensible to all men.

Words, it can then be said, are the incarnations of ideas, the mysterious and magic nexus between the ideal and the real. And language thus becomes the revelation of being, even as it is the intermediary between man and his work. Because of this the idea of being known must never surrender to the substitute of being loved, though unknown. For he who abandons the idea of making the word an instrument of knowledge is ready to accept, out of the depths of despair, an antirationalistic theory of language. Life is not above and below language, as some, especially empiricistic, deterministic thinkers, have believed. The universal value of reason and language must be recognized. For finally man, uprooted and alone, is able to achieve identity and definition not in relation to the earth but in relation to language. A man must *be*. Being is synonymous with stability and objectivity. The planet *is* because its course is set. This is the explicit lesson of all Kantian philosophy. Language creates the world just as language enriches the world because of its symbolic function.

It was in this way that words were conceived by man as soon as he began to philosophize. In words he found the exquisite instrument, the mysterious, procreative power by which God engendered the world and by which man, in turn, can find the gods. This concept is conspicuously contained in the cosmogony of India, where the ritual formula possessed a thaumaturgic and inexorable quality. For it is to India and China that we may turn in our effort to discover the meaning of language, since in those two lands the problem of the word aroused the deepest interest and was discussed through the centuries in such a way as to reveal that the solutions reached were finally not different from those which Western thought has propounded in the course of its articulate history. There exists a fundamental similarity of speculative inquiry between the East and the West. Both are propelled by the same doubts, both bewildered by the same problems, and all language points to the paradoxical nature of man and life, the inner contradictory character of reality.

In ancient India the Word was considered to be uncreated. It is by means of the Word that the Creator creates. For there is a seminal magic contained in the spoken Word. When God said let this be done or let that be done, lo, the act was accomplished. Thus it is pronounced: "In the beginning was the Word." The primordial mythus avails itself of this intuition and reveals in what way, at the beginning of time, the Creator, God, existed alone and close beside Him was the Word. God embraced the Word and it became pregnant. It emerged from Him and after procreating the creatures returned again within Him. In this manner, and in mythical language, is portrayed the necessity of thought transmuting itself into action through the power of words. This is the essential moment of the actualization, the corporealization, of the idea, whether by this word we wish to convey the pristine manifestation of archetypes in all things or the evidence of the creative power of the imagination in the wavelike movement of poetry. It is the translation of will into command, the clarification and the development of thought in verbal speech.

Language is representation and presentation. It would be impossible for man to know himself without language. The word is not language when it is contained in a merely isolated or sensate continuum. When it is so contained, then the word may lie, whereas language can never lie. The phonic symbol and the idea should never be severed. It was because of this indissoluble union of the idea and the phonic symbol that the ultimate and supreme principle, the *Brahma,* was referred to by some Indian philosophers as the Word-

Brahman. Thus a monism was postulated, a monism of words identical with the more universally accepted monism of the soul. It is an equilibrum, born out of the tension of spirit and nature.

St. Augustine beautifully portrayed the transempirical character of language, the warning not to betray the inner law of equality, when he drew an analogy between the word and spirit as it manifests itself in music. "When in music there appears a rest sign on the score and the sound thereby ceases, why is our sense not offended by an (apparent) deficiency if it is not because there is something due to the law of equality, of equilibrium, not in sound, but in the extension of time?" [2]

The implication of this is significant for here we have the appearance in rhythm of the being of non-being. The rest, the absence of audible motion, is itself the object of the time-count and plays its role on the same level as the audible sound. Its absence is counted by the extension of time (spatium temporis). The essential point in the attack of Plotinus against Aristotle's "time-is-the-number-of-movement" theory is that there is something like the totality of the constantly recurring motions which necessitates an intellectual accompaniment of the motion. For without this there would be no unity of the past and the present, no one magnitude to be numbered. And the continuum of the law of immutability in language itself would be broken.

This law of immutability is reflected in Brahmanic thought. "The word and the world are born from Brahma who has neither beginning nor end. This is the inexhaustible reality of words, a reality which manifests itself in the multiplicity of things." Words therefore become the solidification of ideas in time. They become the corporeality of ideas. If the idea remains mere potentiality, it is nothing. It is emptied of life and substituted for life. It is ineffectual and inoperative because it is unknowable. It must become sound; it must be heard for it possesses an ecumenical quality; it must spread and give rise to action or to communication. It is of no significance that words themselves live and die. Like all things in time and space they become victims of mutation, are subject to the vicissitudes of history and consciousness; but though they may fade and change, or though they may be usurped by new words, new sound complexes, the primordial source, the procreative matrix of language which gave them birth subsists immutably in the richness and plenitude of its implications. If it is true that some words are born into existence before others, and if, in small degrees, consciousness and experience enrich the content of

[2] St. Augustine, De Musica, 10, 27.

the vocabulary, it is because man in his laborious pilgrimage slowly raises other veils and reveals other mysteries. In this way new relations and new laws manifest themselves in the infinite, irrevocable, and irreducible certainty of nature, as well as in the boundless regions of man's mind.

By virtue of language, human energy is in a sense preserved. It is not transmitted in the course of its transformations. Yet man is a creature who acts. The meaning and purpose of language, metaphysics and science, are contained within the orbit of this universe of action. But action demands freedom and freedom in a state of transition becomes amorphous and elusive. Has civilization developed a mistrust of language? Has it impeded its growth? The enlargement of the framework of reference in language may be compared to the enlargement of new areas for the mind's maturity. It is a conquest which requires perpetually renewed effort on the part of man, an effort which marks an ever increasing progress but which at the same time presupposes existence.

The "real" is in no way immediately given to us. What we are given are merely the objects of our consciousness; and among these objects only those constitute the material of knowledge which permit univocal linguistic expression. There is only one way from the objects of consciousness to "reality," namely, the way of conscious or unconscious intellectual construction, which proceeds completely free and arbitrarily. The most elementary concept in everday thought belonging to the sphere of the "real" is the concept of continually existing objects, like the table in one's room. The table as such, however, is not given to us, but is merely a complex of sensations to which we attribute the name and the concept "table." This is a speculative method based on intuition.

It is this consciousness that postulates existence. Unconsciousness in relation to the one who knows is nonexistence. And knowledge is the revelation of the fact of existence in whose relations the creative element is represented by the ceaseless unsatisfaction and activity of man as a being who thinks. Creation lies in effort, in dissatisfaction, in never-ending movement, in the avid curiosity that makes of man a creature of courage, a vigilant explorer wandering over a boundless world impelled toward a goal he does not know and which perhaps does not even exist. Discovery is his destiny and his privilege. Language captures and obediently marks the discoveries. It actualizes them in their symbols. It communicates and transmits them, enabling them to travel through space and through time making known and manifest to all what until then had been secret and hidden.

What we call Truth, those certainties in which we place our trust, is the primordial light, the *lumen supernaturale,* which radiates from an eternal source, the expansion of a pristine force which has taken form. It is the gradual shaping of an idea in diverse symbols expressing in diverse ways its implications and recondite meanings, varying with the maturity and the capacity of the mind which receives them and is rendered conscious by them. And such ideas will appear now as myths, now consummated in an image, or expressed in the abstraction of a scientific hypothesis. And in each case, language, through its phonic conventions, will determine its multilateral nature and value.

Language is not a mere mechanism, although it is also a mechanism and it is the relation of language as mechanism and language as meaning which must be sought. The hypothesis advanced by some modern linguists who are at the same time positivists and who are committed to the mechanistic theory of language, assuming it to be nothing more than a matter of mechanical stimulus and response, is self-refuting. For this would mean that these responses would reveal some characteristic about the linguists but nothing about language. The mechanistic theory of language has as its purpose a rigid, scientific methodology and therefore appears to employ only direct observations of the communicating persons, forgetting that the observer is also within the mechanism. In reality, however, it inevitably depends upon indirect observations through existing records. We must finally concede that the mechanistic theory of language commits the sin of solipsism, since it is the mechanist himself, an organism like any other, who performs the act of observing and it is impossible to interpret an unknown quantity by itself. Thus language cannot be grasped in all its sacredness, meaning, and power.

For the Word is the Law. It is the means by which, through the agency of God, eternal and immutable values are made known to man. It is the means of communication between the human and the divine. Human societies have not ascribed to man, at his discretion or caprice, the basis of the essential relations between man and man, or man and God. On the contrary, they have almost universally postulated a revelation, an announcement. They have invoked the spoken or written word which is the fountainhead of certainty and on that certainty life is erected. The Word delivers and transmits those commandments and those truths which assure the presence of universal principles that are also fixed points in the life of the mind and in history.

This consciousness of the indissoluble relationship between the word and an immutable idea was clearly portrayed in Mahayana Buddhism. Reality has a twofold nature. One side of it is irreducible and the other is revealed. Being, apart from which all is illusion and vanity, is encompassed by both. The Law, or Dharma, is the phonic expression of the supreme Being, of the Absolute. Thus, so we are taught by the Mahayana Buddhists, the Word, the Word of the Law, in so far as it descends, after it has been heard, touching the depths of our being in the subconscious mind from which emanate the universal forces of life, transforms itself into the antithesis of subconsciousness and of those drives that cause suffering and impede knowledge of the self and therefore salvation. This Word, precipitated into the darkness and travail of life, issues like an emanation of the supreme truth and cancels the fatal ignorance that accompanies life, and in this way conditions and prepares that ultimate enlightenment which will enable one to pass into another plane, that of Nirvana, into the body of the Buddha.

It may again be said that language which we mutter through words is not created by man. For man, moved by the desire to *express* his feelings and his thought, using the vocal chords with which he is endowed, evokes through sound the words, each of which has an independent autonomous existence by virtue of its inner life with language, by virtue of its *belonging* to language. Language exists *ab aeterno*, immutable in its transcendent purity and revealing itself from time to time in the historical existence of mankind.

There are, of course, those logicians who concede that the word, whatever may be the origin of its relationship with the object or the reality it designates—either by divine revelation or by ancient convention—does indeed express a universal and a particular thing, and according to circumstances one or the other acquires importance in discourse, depending upon the stress that he who speaks places on one or the other of its aspects. It was one of the greatest logicians (Vatsyayana, in the fourth to the fifth century) in India who affirmed that, when we wish to insist on the difference between one thing and another and when the notion refers to the destructive characteristics of that same thing, then the person is the predominant factor. But if the person and the difference are not brought into relief and if the notion concerns common and general conceptions, then the prevalent fact will be the universal. Above all, the universal is eternally present in the word, and the universal is a reality, and *ens*, contained in the word and bestowing meaning and value on the word.

At the beginning of the nineteenth century Wilhelm von Humboldt laid the foundations for the *science of language*, seeking to understand its nature in the harmony within man of his spiritual and moral being. He closely approximated the Buddhist conception of the Word by emphasizing the organic interaction of the moral and the spiritual elements of being out of which the nature of language is to be understood since it is but a reflection of the eternal idea in the universe of the presence of the Absolute in the relative. This interrelationship manifests itself in the personality of the individual since we might mistrust his speech but we still hold to the expression of the speaker, who to one of insight can never betray the truth contained in language, although his words may do so when they are emptied of the Absolute inherent within them.

If words are not bound to a situation arising from historical cultures but are themselves eternal, or are the expressions of eternal ideas, then language becomes a magic instrument in the hands of man which enables him to maintain himself in harmony with the eternal. The Word is the mysterious bridge between what is beyond time and what is within time. The Word then acquires a much greater value than that generally attributed to it, the value of an instrument of which we often make arbitrary use, often an inappropriate use, so that words are nibbled away; little by little they decay, are emptied of their meaning, acquire erroneous and unprecedented accents by excess or deficiency of content. For if those assumptions to which we have referred are true, the decay, the disintegration, or the darkening of the word's essential meaning, the fact that *it no longer corresponds to the idea which evoked it*, would mean that we have strayed from the world of our *mothers*, who are the fountainhead and reason of our being and our thought. The corruption of language, its confusion, its lack of precision, the amorphousness of expression, verbal equivocations—these are an insult and injury to truth, not a mere insult and injury to words.

"The first step in knowledge for civilized thought is to give a name." Bosanquet, in uttering these words, realized that to adequate the name and the thing is indeed the prerogative of genius. In fact, the number of terms which are inherited from Plato and Aristotle is the most striking evidence of the immense advance which they have achieved for the human intellect. These two seminal minds defined the world of knowledge in its essential features much as this knowledge exists even

in our own time, and bestowed upon its main divisions the names they
still retain. And in the East during the last journey Confucius took in
the State of Wei in the hope that the prince would confer on him the
direction of the State, a scholar enquired of him: "Should the king
entrust you with the task of government, what would be the first thing
you would start by doing?" "I should restore to each thing," the sage
answered, "its true name." "But would that be possible?" the other
incredulously insisted. "You miss the mark; what would be the use
of this rectification of names?" "How crude you are!" replied the
Master. "A wise man takes great care not to say and not to do what
he does not know. If names do not correspond to things, the result is
confusion in the language. If there is confusion in the language, people do not do their duty; if people do not do their duty, moderation
and harmony are neglected: then penalties are no longer proportionate
with the faults. If this occurs, the people no longer know how to act.
The sage therefore gives to things the names proper to them, and he
behaves towards them in conformity with the name given them.
Therefore, in the selection of names he is very attentive."

Still another Chinese thinker, Hsün tzu, wrote: "Names have been
fixed to denote realities, both to make known what is noble and what
is vile, and to distinguish similarities and dissimilarities. Our thought
will not run the risk of being misunderstood and in affairs we shall not
incur the calamity of their being hindered or ruined."

According to this philosopher, words have not a transcendent basis
but an immutable ethical content. They are determined by an identity
of reaction in man (as a sentient and thinking being) to the same things,
to the same stimuli. And this essential identity of human reactions
imparts to them a value: even if the denomination given them is the
work of man, it has an inevitable constancy, the moral law, which lies
at the basis of all human certainties. The word, thus laden with the
experience of ages, becomes an entity which is neither equivocal nor
ambiguous and on which rest social and moral relations between
men. Hence the rectification of names, the vigilant care to see that
each word says neither more nor less than its own implicit meaning,
is the surest guaranty of the stability of the human community.

In the conception both of Confucius and of Hsün tzu, the wise,
those who govern, those who wish to set an example and to be a guide,
must watch to see that words preserve their full and precise meaning.

"When the kings," Hsün tzu further said, "had regulated the names,
settled the words (appropriate to the things) and had thus distinguished
the several realities, and when the principles they laid down had been

applied and their decisions made known, they proposed to unify their subjects (on the basis of the universality of the ethical conscience). Therefore the introduction of inopportune distinctions between words, the creation of new terms, the confusion of the correct expressions for things to arouse doubts in the minds of the subjects and to cause disputes, was considered a very serious iniquity."

This evaluation of language would indeed seem to be necessary in our own epoch since now, as in the time of Confucius, Hsün tzu, or, to mention a Western thinker, Thucydides,[3] words often change their essential meaning and assume that which is arbitrarily imposed; the eternal idea inherent in language is violated, and thus a collapse of the moral conscience takes place. To rectify language, to bestow upon it the full and entire meaning which it is intended to express, would demand a rectification of ideas, a definition of their content in their absolute signification. This would also demand that we must maintain uncorrupted and inviolable all those universals which it is man's very entelechy to make manifest in his speech—and in his deeds—of which he is the depository and the transmitter. Human consciousness and human speech are inseparable since both the conscious human mind and language spring from the common elemental foundation of the universal spirit. Therefore language, properly speaking, cannot be taught, although words may be; it can only be evoked and man can only nourish the conditions and leave it to its own unfolding. To paraphrase Pascal, we could not seek language if we had not already found it. This truth is exquisitely portrayed in children, who may be said never to *learn* a language since we can only learn that which does not belong to us. It can in reality be said that we become acquainted with what we already know, as a kind of spiritual remembering, Plato's *anamnesia*. For how could the learner, merely through the expansion of his own developing consciousness, master the spoken thought if there were not in speaker and hearer the same essence, only differentiated for the sake of individual existence and communion, so that a symbol is refined and yet so personal that the articulate sound is sufficient to relate, as a mediator, both speaker and hearer in a pristine harmony?

Words are the instruments by means of which ideas become acts. Thus it is evident that the responsibility of men in the use they make of words is a heavy one. By means of words man inserts himself in the cosmic order, either as friend or as foe. He may continue the divine

[3] Corcyracean Revolution, Peloponnesian War.

creation. He may interpret it and assist it. He is either the executor of the eternal idea or a demiurge who offends and disturbs the natural order of things. The word is power; "the power of life or death lies in the tongue." And it is power precisely because it awakens to life secret and latent forces. Its work is that of evoking powers hitherto hidden or inert but awaiting only that summons to bring them into the light, to reveal them, to foster their entrance into existence and into time. Such was the power that, from the very inception of civilization, man has attributed to the word, to the Verb, to the *Logos*.

The name is the person, the expression of the mysterious essence of things, revealing or controlling the inner reality. That is why the essential name of the person may not be revealed; why he who knows this essential name has indeed power over that person, because of the absolute and necessary nexus between the thing and the name, between word and idea. Man possesses this precious key which can open the jewel case of immutable and eternal ideas. He must guard the key, see that it is not injured or broken, for should it be, he will lose the means of communicating with the ground and reason of his being, of his thought and of his deed. For language possesses a life both deeper and less conscious than its articulate, logical life. Language is a process of liberation from conceptual, logical, discursive reason. Language not only articulates, connects, and infers; it also *envisages*, as the Platonic *intellectus esse* reveals, and the intuitive grasping of language is the primary act and function of that one and single power which is called reason. Language is not only logical but, first and foremost, ontological.

The universe itself is language, the corporealization of thought that has been born through the medium of *logos*. The word intervenes between the motionless, primordial omnipresence and omnipotence of the idea and its materialization. This idea of *logos* was contained in some of the gnostic thinking in India, placing this conviction at the very beginning of creation, at the very moment in time when the universe was created, when it was determined in all its variety, in its spatial essence and its temporal becoming. The dialogue began, the dialogue between Siva and Parvati, between the universal conscience and the creative, seminal force of the universe. Parvati, by her creative power, by her questions, evokes a timeless plenitude of absolute thought, the cosmic unfolding and ripening. The question asked by the goddess, in its verbal concreteness, causes the birth of the formation of things, a transition process, the transmutation of thought into reality. This is obviously a myth. But it is a myth which claims for the word creative power and which places at the beginning of time the daily occurrence of the miracle, the miracle of the transmutation of thought into act through the medium of speech. Action is the archetype. The word is the phonic sign, expressed or unexpressed, explicit or implicit. It may even be said that each intellectual archetype is mated with its phonic archetype. Time itself is scanned by the rhythm of mental representations and verbal denominations; it consists in a succession of images and sounds; it is a complex series of thoughts possessing corresponding phonic expression in which the universe is actualized in consciousness arising spontaneously from an initial quivering and moving of original, motionless, absolute Idea.

Thus language is not only being. It is also becoming, existing anterior to the split between thinking and thought. But the corporealization of the word presupposes a possible dichotomy in language. For the rise of duality coincides with the formation of words, when, so to say, a "sacrifice" of pure thought sets in. According to some schools of philosophy in India, words move on the plane of *māyā;* they represent and reproduce a scheme of relations whose basis is the exteriorization of the becoming, of the *ens.* Words on this level possess a certain inexactitude. The linguist may then study the "parallelism" of the logical and the grammatical, as if, on the one hand, logic were given in the heaven of ideas and, on the other, grammar were given on earth. Language thus would become expression but not experience; it would become anonymous, or dead.

When the archetypes are formed and defined in the cosmic conscience, they enter inevitably into the temporal process. Exteriorized in words they decline into temporal and spatial limitations. Therefore, reintegration into the *ens,* the passage from the temporal to the eternal, may take place when the word, and thereby discriminated thought, comes to a halt. Pure consciousness will then be recovered in a totality beyond all duality, and in the silence of the *ens* multiplicity will be absorbed into Unity. Then silence becomes not a state of privation but a condition of plenitude. The images and experiences that illuminate and beatify us in moments of contemplation and meditation engender a death and a rebirth. George Bückner pointed to the implacable void, the fear of silence which possesses so many, especially in an age when both solitude and self terrify: "Do you not hear," he asked, "the terrible voice that howls around us on the horizon, the voice that is usually called silence?" This voice would extinguish us all. But then we remember the teaching of the Upanishads; we remember that very silence which implies language, that silence which gathers within itself and pervades all of language because it constitutes the totality of knowledge which is non-knowing, because it manifests itself at that point where knowledge is transcended, where the totality of language is silence, where "the blind man has found the jewel, one who has no fingers has gathered it, one who has no neck has adorned himself with it, one who has no voice has sung its praises." Language with this power is the Word of God; it possesses the sound and voice of the divine mystery. For then one hears oneself speaking out of the depths of one's silence, and language as idea is not betrayed.

FURTHER READING

Two of the most interesting of the general popular books on language are Charlton Laird's *The Miracle of Language* (Cleveland, 1953) and Margaret Schlauch's *The Gift of Language* (New York, 1955). Among the more technically linguistic treatments, the two major American books are Leonard Bloomfield's *Language* (New York, 1933) and Edward Sapir's *Language: An Introduction to the Study of Speech* (New York, 1921). All of Otto Jespersen's books on language are valuable but one is especially relevant here: *Language: Its Nature, Development and Origin* (New York, 1933). Excellent summaries of the various aspects of language study, along with extensive bibliographies, are provided in John B. Carroll's *The Study of Language* (Cambridge, Mass., 1953), and in John B. Hughes's *The Science of Language* (New York, 1962), which also provides a unique listing of language periodicals.

Students interested in the history of the English language are fortunate in that four well-written, scholarly texts are available. In order of their publication they are: Albert H. Marckwardt, *Introduction to the English Language* (New York, 1942); Stuart Robertson and Frederic G. Cassidy, *The Development of Modern English*, Second Edition (Englewood Cliffs, N.J., 1954); Albert C. Baugh, *A History of the English Language*, Second Edition (New York, 1957); Margaret M. Bryant, *Modern English and Its Heritage*, Second Edition (New York, 1962). Two compact histories of American English are Albert H. Marckwardt's *American English* (New York, 1958) and Thomas Pyles's *Words and Ways of American English* (New York, 1952). A lively British history of the language is Simeon Potter's *Our Language* (Harmondsworth, Middlesex, England, 1950), a volume which includes helpful bibliographical essays. Finally an honored place must be given to Otto Jespersen's famous *Growth and Structure of the English Language*, Ninth Edition (New York, 1956).

In the areas of grammar and linguistics, two older treatments of English grammar which retain their value are Otto Jespersen's *Essentials of English Grammar* (New York, 1933) and George O. Curme's *English Grammar* (New York, 1947). More recent treatments which maintain a connection with traditional views are Margaret M. Bryant's *A Functional English Grammar* (Boston, 1959) and Ralph B. Long's *The Sentence and Its Parts: A Grammar of Contemporary English* (Chicago, 1961). A useful bridge between traditional and structural approaches to grammar is provided in James Sledd's *A Short Introduction to English Grammar* (Chicago, 1959). Once thoroughly involved in the newer approaches, students have available four concise, authoritative texts: Charles C. Fries, *The Structure of English* (New York, 1952); Harold Whitehall, *Structural Essentials of English* (New York, 1956); W. Nelson Francis, *The Structure of American English* (New York, 1958); and H. A. Gleason, Jr., *An Introduction to Descriptive Linguistics*, Revised Edition (New York, 1961). Gleason's book is notably rich in bibliographical aids. A convenient summary of both new and old approaches is presented in a triad of sprightly texts written by Paul Roberts: *Understanding Grammar* (New York, 1954), *Patterns of English* (New York, 1956), and *English Sentences* (New York, 1962). One of the newest approaches to problems of grammar and linguistics—the "generative" or "transformational" (cf. the essay "Transformations" in the present volume, p. 144) is presented in Noam Chomsky's influential *Syntactic Structures* (The Hague, Netherlands, 1957), and in Robert B. Lee's *The Grammar of English Nominalization* (Bloomington, Ind., 1960).

The study of usage should begin with a classic in the field that explains the forces behind normative doctrines of usage, Sterling A. Leonard's *The Doctrine of Correctness in English Usage, 1700–1800* (Madison, Wis., 1929). An example of scholarly research on usage problems is the monograph by Albert H. Marckwardt and Fred G. Walcott, *Facts About Current English Usage* (New York, 1938). A newer, comprehensive study is that by Margaret M. Bryant, *Current American Usage* (New York, 1962). A lively, even belligerent defense of the liberal position in matters of usage is given by Robert A. Hall, Jr., in *Linguistics and Your Language* (Garden City, N.Y., 1960). Finally, as an example of sensible, informed attitudes not only upon the question of usage but also upon all matters pertaining to the practical use of language, Porter G. Perrin's *Writer's Guide and Index to English*, Third Edition (Chicago, 1959), is highly recommended.

Among the important periodicals devoted primarily to studies of language are: *Language; Word; General Linguistics; Language Learning; American Speech; Word Study*. The annual bibliography of language studies in *PMLA* is perhaps the most convenient source of further titles.